Bustle Fashions 1885-1887

Scientific Garment Cutting

Bustle Fashions
1885-1887

41 Patterns
With Fashion Plates
And Suggestions for Adaptation

Edited and with Additional Material by
Frances Grimble

Lavolta Press
20 Meadowbrook Drive
San Francisco, CA 94132
www.lavoltapress.com

Bustle Fashions 1885–1887: 41 Patterns with Fashion Plates and Suggestions for Adaptation is a new work first published by Lavolta Press in 2010. All new text and illustrations; the selection and arrangement of period text, illustrations, and patterns; and revised versions of the period materials are protected by copyright. They may not be reproduced or transmitted in any form without prior written permission from Lavolta Press.

First edition

ISBN: 978-0-9636517-8-5

Published by:
Lavolta Press
20 Meadowbrook Drive
San Francisco, CA 94132
www.lavoltapress.com

Book design, cover design, scanning, scan editing, page layout, and production management by Frances Grimble and Allan Terry

Printed and bound in the United States of America

Cataloging-in-Publication Data

Bustle fashions 1885–1887: 41 patterns with fashion plates and suggestions for adaptation / edited and with additional material by Frances Grimble.
    p. cm.
    Includes bibliographical references and index.
    ISBN 978-0-9636517-8-5

1. Dressmaking --United States --Patterns. 2. Dressmaking --United States --History --19th century. 3. Costume --United States --History --19th century. 4. Fashion --United States --History --19th century. 5. Millinery --United States --History --19th century. I. Grimble, Frances. II. Bustle fashions 1885–1887 : forty-one patterns with fashion plates and suggestions for adaptation. III. Title.

TT504.4 .B87 2010
646.4/78–dc22   2010925549

Acknowledgments

My husband, Allan Terry, helped to design the cover and interior. He edited the cover scans and draw the apportioning scales. He also did prepress work, kept my computer running, and performed countless other tasks. Our printer, McNaughton & Gunn, did their usual high-quality job.

To David Eisenmann

Contents

 **Contents**

Contents

Contents

8. Home Dressmaking

Contents

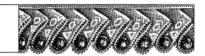

Contents

1. Introduction

This book contains 41 women's garment patterns from 1885 through 1887, the height of what is sometimes called the "second bustle period." During these years, the waist was flattered by a closely fitted bodice, a large tournure (back fullness), and ample skirt draperies. The foundation of this silhouette consisted of a corset and a bustle; a pad and steels in the skirt back sometimes supplemented or substituted for the bustle. Under-garments consisted of a chemise, a corset cover, drawers, and at least a short and a long petticoat. (See Chapter 2.) The bulk was often reduced by wearing "combinations" of chemise and drawers, or corset cover and drawers, or corset cover and short petticoat.

Most dresses worn outside the home consisted either of two main garments, a long polonaise worn over a skirt, or of three, a bodice and over-skirt (or drapery) worn over a skirt. (See Chapters 4–6.) The waist was further emphasized by long bodices, often pointed in front and back; vest and plastron bodice fronts; over-skirts showing much of the skirt front; and skirt fronts with vertical applied panels. Asymmetrical effects were popular.

Two or more materials differing in color and/or texture were commonly used to make and trim an ensemble, and garments were sometimes made (or recycled) to coordinate with several different ensembles. Although some street suits and coats were plainly tailored, many garments were highly decorated. This task was facilitated not only by widespread ownership of sewing machines, but by the availability of commercially made braids and braid appliqués; tucked, plaited, and ruched trimmings; beaded laces, appliqués, and passementeries; and machine-embroidered trimmings, including large ones shaped for specific garment sections. (See Chapter 9.) Outer wear included jackets (which sometimes doubled as street bodices), both short and long coats, dolman wraps of various lengths, and long capes. (See Chapter 7.)

Home wear included simpler dresses, wrappers, and tea gowns. (See Chapter 3.) The two latter were distinguished not by their cut, but by their materials and trimmings. Illustrations showing them with flowing fronts and sashes loosely tied below the abdomen hint at maternity use.

Toilettes were often varied (even from day to evening wear) by the use of accessories. These included home-made jabots, chemisettes, gilets, collars, hats, bonnets, and muffs, as well as purchased fans, parasols, belts, and other articles. (See Chapter 10.)

Using This Book

The patterns in *Bustle Fashions 1885–1887* are designed to be enlarged by drafting with the National Garment Cutter, one of a number of popular Victorian and Edwardian apportioning scale systems. Apportioning scales are special rulers that make it easy to accurately draft the patterns designed for that system to fit an individual's body measures. Each scale has units of a different size. The scales for smaller sizes have smaller units, and the ones for larger sizes have larger units. Therefore, the units printed on the pattern can be used to draft any size. No arithmetic or drafting experience is required; you "draft by the numbers."

Most pattern measures are projected in proportion to one crucial body measure–the bust measure for bodices, and the waist for skirts. That is, these patterns have built-in sizing. However, the system recognizes that height is not necessarily in direct proportion to the bust or waist. The instructions explain how to draft patterns for the taller or shorter person after checking a few important measures with an inch ruler.

The National Garment Cutter System. The National Garment Cutter scales were reconstructed for this book by comparing two sets of wooden originals. The units were mathematically corrected

to account for variations in manufacture (including duplications of the same units on supposedly different scales), and shrinkage in the wood. The scales were also visually redesigned for ease of use. (See Appendix A.)

The set of National Garment Cutter tools included a large combination curve or "scroll." The scroll provides a variety of curves on the different sides and ends, enabling you to turn it to draw the exact shapes of the armholes, bodice center backs, skirt bottoms, etc., used in the National Garment Cutter system patterns. It is provided in Appendix A.

Figure 1 shows the remainder of the tools in the National Garment Cutter set. These are a patent folding L-square to hold the scales during drafting, an inch tape measure, and a tracing wheel. You will need an ordinary modern L-square; an inch ruler (preferably transparent); pattern paper; and, of course, a pencil, eraser, and scissors. If you do not wish to use the scroll, you will need a modern hip/armhole curve. In addition, you may find it handy to have a set of French curves, a flexible or "spline" curve, a yardstick, and a double tracing wheel.

The Patterns and Instructions. These patterns are drawn from *The National Garment Cutter,* which was the instruction book packaged with the drafting tools, and *The Voice of Fashion,* a quarterly magazine that provided customers who had

previously bought the tools with more up-to-date patterns. The publishers (and tool sellers) were Goldsberry, Doran & Nelson. (It may be of interest to know that the man in Figures 2–5 resembles published photographs of William H. Goldsberry.) The original publications used are among the firm's earliest. Goldsberry, Doran, & Nelson appears to have first published *The National Garment Cutter* in 1884, and *The Voice of Fashion* in 1886. This book includes patterns from the 1885, 1886, and 1887 issues of *The National Garment Cutter,* and from the Spring/Summer 1886 and Winter 1886 issues of *The Voice of Fashion.*

All of the patterns that were chosen have been redrawn for greater ease of use. Those too small or crowded with labels to see clearly were enlarged, and those too large to fit on a page were divided. The straight lines and right angles have been trued. More legible labels have been applied, and missing ones have been added. The originals contained some errors in measures and text labels, which have been corrected. All of the edited patterns have been proofread several times.

Some new diagrams have been drawn for pattern pieces that were described but not provided. More commonly, the publication omitted some garment section (typically a sleeve) or an essential entire garment (typically a skirt), and directed

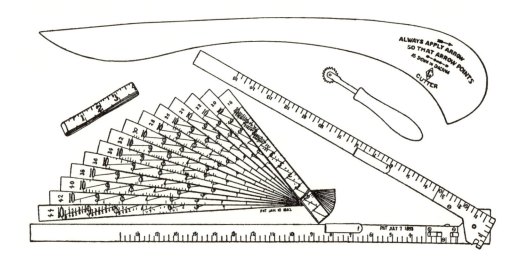

Figure 1. The National Garment Cutter tools

readers to use one from another pattern, or to choose from "any other pattern in this issue." The patterns were reorganized for this book, and numerous cross-referenced parts would have inconvenienced readers. Therefore, suitable ones have been chosen and included with the relevant pattern. The patterns for the main parts of all ensembles are listed separately in the index. You can freely select from and combine the sections that compose a garment, and the garments that compose an ensemble. As the original instructions say, "Often a pleasant result is obtained by using parts of different patterns. That is to say, the back of one and the front of another, etc. Take care to put the different parts together so that the seam lines, waist-lines, etc., come out properly." The pattern pieces are arranged the way they are sewed together, as well as the page size allows.

The patterns in *The National Garment Cutter* and *The Voice of Fashion* are so similar to those published months or even years earlier by Butterick, that it seems likely Goldsberry, Doran & Nelson copied Butterick patterns—whether by legitimate license or otherwise. Many of their illustrations strongly resemble ones in Butterick's *Delineator* magazine, and the pattern pieces correspond to the *Delineator's* descriptions. Many others are patchworks of *Delineator* illustrations—a bodice drawn from one illustration and an over-skirt from another, or the trimmings for one garment transferred to another. Again, the descriptions of the elements correspond.

However, the fashion descriptions and assembly instructions in *The Delineator* are significantly more detailed. Wherever possible, the relevant information from *The Delineator* has been included after each *National Garment Cutter* or *Voice of Fashion* pattern. The text has been edited for clarity and consistency, and the illustrations have been edited to correct deterioration. Also included after each pattern, are illustrations and descriptions sufficiently similar that readers already familiar with modern flat pattern techniques can use the *National Garment Cutter* or *Voice of Fashion* pattern as a base for developing more Butterick styles. Other readers may simply enjoy browsing the extra illustrations, or try their hand at flat patterning with the aid of the books recommended in Appendix D.

Victorian home and professional dressmakers consulted a variety of fashion magazines to garner hints on constructing new styles. In that spirit, each chapter of this book is prefaced with a series of edited quotes from other publications. (See Appendix D.) In addition to *The Delineator*, the main source is *Harper's Bazar*, a magazine that published home-dressmaking patterns, but which was more stylish than *The Delineator*. Chapter 8 consists of a dressmaking manual reworked from a series of articles in *Godey's Lady's Book*–a less stylish magazine than *The Delineator*. Also useful are the patterns and supplementary material in this book's companion volume *Directoire Revival Fashions 1888–1889*, which complements this book rather than overlapping it.

Using Apportioning Scales

Using the National Garment Cutter scales to draft the patterns in *Bustle Fashions 1885–1887* is quite easy. It is a matter of enlarging them to your size, rather than designing styles from scratch. First take your measures over the foundation garments and undergarments you will wear. Choose the correct scales for your measures and the garment section. The scales have size labels that correspond to inch measures. Suppose you wish to draft a three-piece ensemble with a 34-inch bust and a 27-inch waist. You would choose the size 34 scale to draw the bodice, and the size 27 scale to draw the skirt and over-skirt.

Drafting the Pattern. After choosing your scales, lay out a large piece of pattern paper printed with marks at 1-inch intervals. Pencil a vertical baseline, and use your scale to mark off the measures shown on the pattern piece. From these, draw horizontal cross-lines to the measures shown. You then draw the curves. Choose a curve tool that fits to the ends of the lines you drew and looks like the pattern shape. You may need parts of two tools.

The fitted bodice patterns, such as tight linings, were designed with very little ease. It is best to use a scale one to two sizes larger than your bust and leave large seam allowances. The proportionally determined waist size is small for many modern women, but can be enlarged. Check all back waist, sleeve, and skirt lengths until you become familiar

with the system's fitting standards. Remember that skirt length measures must include the hem and the belt (waistband) seam. "Drafting a Ladies' Basque" recommends making most corrections for individual measures during the drafting process. However, the patterns can be drafted as given, then altered by standard modern techniques and/or during fitting.

Finishing the Pattern. Measure edges that will be seamed together. If they are different lengths, check the original measures and redraw as necessary. Add pattern markings such as notches and stars. Sometimes you must true seam lines where material will be folded into darts, plaits, or facings. Fold the pattern like the material and redraw lines that do not match.

The instructions and pattern labels claim that seam allowances are provided, but some are overly narrow by modern standards. It is safest to use 1 to 2 inches on side seams, 1 inch on seams of sections that fit tightly, and 1/2 inch on seams of loose-fitting sections. To add a seam allowance, measure out from the pattern edge with a clear plastic ruler. For straight edges, measure each end and connect the lines. For curved edges, draw short lines at such frequent intervals that they connect. Or use a double tracing wheel to indent the paper, then pencil over the indents.

To finish the pattern piece, draw a grain line following a vertical row of pattern paper dots. Label the piece with the pattern source, garment type, and style date. Indicate how many times each piece will be cut from the outer material, the lining, the underlining, and/or the interfacing. Add any markings or notes you find helpful.

Although the National Garment Cutter system produces a good fit, Victorian patterns assume the dressmaker adjusts a lining or a muslin before cutting garment material. This is strongly recommended.

Chapter 9 gives many suggestions for trimmings. Draft and mark them with an inch ruler after completing the rest of the pattern. You can test size and placement on the muslin.

The step-by-step instructions that appeared in the 1885 *National Garment Cutter* and other publications are given below. They have been rewritten and reorganized to eliminate the confusion and repetition that resulted from Goldsberry, Doran & Nelson having layered new text onto old without integrating it. However, one continually stressed point does bear repetition here. If you are unaccustomed to drafting, you need to not only read the instructions for the Ladies' Basque before drafting the pattern you plan to sew, but use those instructions to practice drafting before moving on to other patterns. Most people cannot fully absorb technical instructions without carrying them out.

Frances Grimble

Drafting a Ladies' Basque

These instructions should be very carefully studied by the beginner before trying to draft this or any other garment. This will save much valuable time and be far more efficient. All garments are drafted on the same general plan of work. The instructions for different garments apply only to their special features.

Taking the Measures. The first step is to carefully take the measures, as no one can get a well-fitting garment with improper measures. Take the bust measure with the tape measure straight around the largest part of the bust, high up under the arms (see Figure 2). Take a snug, close measure, neither too tight nor too loose. Take the measure around the waist as tight as the dress is to be worn (see Figure 3). Take the length of the waist from the large joint, where the neck and body join, down to the waist (see Figure 4). The sleeve measure is taken from the center of the back to the wrist joint, with the arm raised and the elbow bent (see Figure 5).

This basque is in six pieces: Front, back, side back, collar, and two sleeve pieces. In cutting out, place the narrow end of the collar on a crosswise fold of the material to avoid a center seam. Cut all of the other parts lengthwise. The quantity of material required is 4 yards if 22 inches wide, and 2 1/2 yards if 48 inches wide.

Drafting the Bodice. Supposing the bust measure to be 32 inches, use the scale marked 32. Or if the bust measure is 36 inches, take the scale marked 36, etc. Fasten this scale on the square by passing the screw through the scale and both parts of the square.

Drafting the Bodice

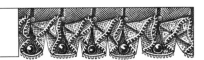

Figure 2. Measuring the bust

Figure 3. Measuring the waist

Draft the back piece first. Square the draft by drawing the first cross-line and the base-line, as shown by Figure 6. The upper-right corner of a draft is the starting point.

Measure all of the numbers on the base-line as given on the diagram. Always keep the angle of the square to your right. Measure down from the upper-right corner to 1 1/4 spaces, and make a dot; 2 1/2 and 6 1/4 the same. At 10 make an X to show it to be the place to commence measuring again. Move the square down and measure 5 more spaces from the X, or 15 from the starting point. At the end of the scale make an X again and move

the square, measuring 2 1/4 more, or 22 1/4, then 28 and 28 1/4.

Now turn the scale without taking it off the square, from the long blade to the short blade of the square. Beginning at the base-line, measure out 2 1/4 on the first cross-line and mark. This is to get the width of the garment. Do not measure from 1 1/4 as it is to cut to. Place the square on the base-line point exactly on the measure. At 2 1/2 measure out 6 1/2 spaces, and draw a cross-line following the diagram. From the third point, 6 1/4 on the base-line, measure 6, drawing a line as before. Draw a line from 10 as before.

5

Correcting the Waist Length. Before measuring the width from the point at 15, take the tape measure and measure down from 1 1/4 along the base-line, the waist length of the person you are cutting for. If this distance is the same as that of the scale measure, which if scale 32 is used will be 16 inches, you make no change. But supposing the person's measure is more or less than the scale measure, change the point and measure from the point given by the tape measure. Say the person's waist length is 15 inches; measure 15 from 1 1/4. Measure from this point 1/2 and 2 3/4 spaces, drawing a cross-line to the base-line. If this line has been raised or lowered, raise or lower the lines at 22 1/4, 28,

and 28 1/4 the same distance; measure and draw a line as before. These are all of the measures.

For the shoulder, draw a diagonal line to connect 2 1/4 on the first cross-line to 6 1/2 on the second cross-line. For the neck, take the scroll and connect the first point on the first cross-line and the first point on the base-line, following the diagram. Draw the curve for the back part of the armhole. (See Figure 7.) Draw a curve from the armhole to the next line, then down to the waist-line. Draw curves on all of the other points as shown by the diagram.

The arrows on the diagrams show which way to turn the scroll, which is always with the largest

Figure 4. Measuring the back waist length

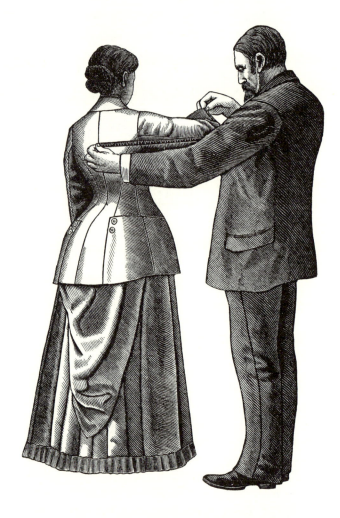

Figure 5. Measuring the sleeve length

First cross-line

Square when moved down to locate points on base-line beyond end of scale

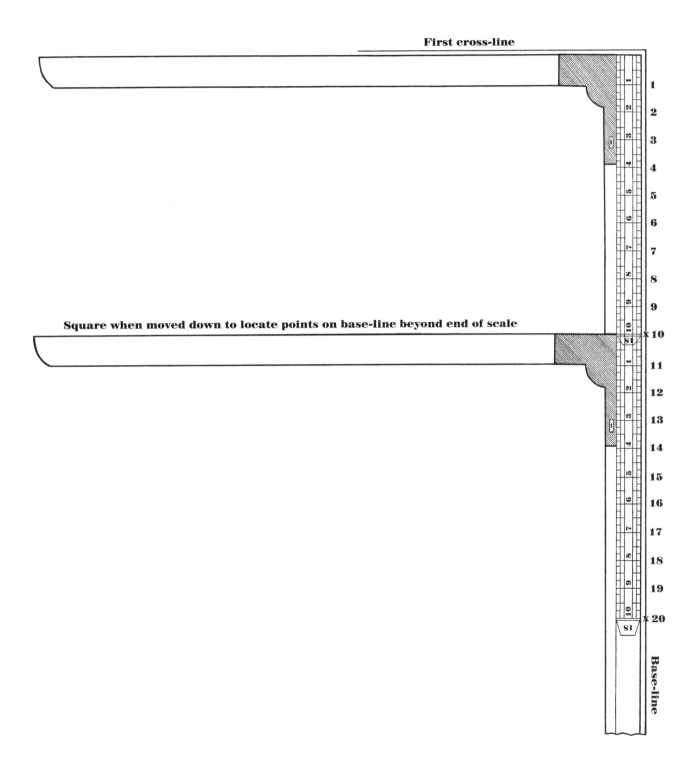

Figure 6. Drawing the first cross-line and the base-line

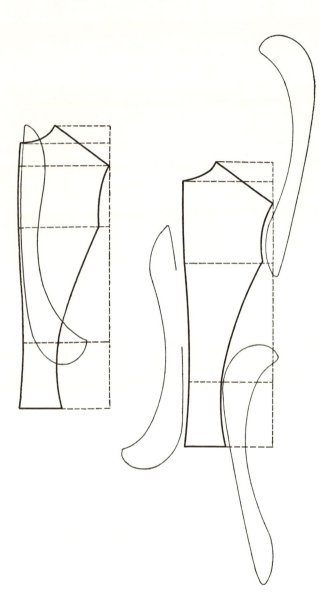

Figure 7. Positions of the scroll for backs

part in the direction in which the arrow points. The arrows are not given on all diagrams, as one diagram mastered is the key to all others. In many cases a slight variation of the exact location of the scroll does not impair the results of the work.

Next draft the side back on the same general plan. If the waist-line on the back has been raised or lowered, raise or lower the waist-line on the side back to correspond.

Draft the front next. If the waist-line has been raised or lowered on the back, raise or lower it the same distance on the front. Raise or lower the top dart line, at 11 3/4, half of the distance. All lines below the waist-line should be changed the same distance as the waist-line. Never change any lines above the dart line. Draw all straight and curved lines except for the under-arm dart lines. Figure 8 shows how to draw the curves.

Correcting the Waist Size. Before drawing the under-arm darts, measure off 1 1/2 spaces on the front for the hem, and 1 1/4 spaces on the side back for the same purpose. For seams, measure off 1/2 space on each side of the back, the side back next to the back, and on each side of the under-arm darts.

Then measure the pattern across at the waist-line, omitting seams already marked off and darts. If the pattern measures the exact size of the waist measure of the person to be fitted, between the seams and hems, the size is correct. If it is not, change the under-arm dart to the correct size, changing a quarter of the amount on each side of the under-arm dart. If the change to be made is greater than 3 inches, change part of it equally at 15 1/2 on the front and on the side back. Because the material is cut double, this will give the correct size. Now draw the dart and seam lines.

Drafting the Sleeve. For the upper sleeve piece, measure from the upper-right corner down to 2, and make a dot. Measure 4 spaces with the scale, then at 10 make an X and move the square down to the X. The next number on the base-line is 11. This is obtained by measuring 1 from 10. The next number is 17 1/2; get this by measuring 7 1/2 from 10. The next is 19 1/2, obtained by measuring 9 1/2 from 10. These are all of the numbers on the base-line.

Draw the cross-lines, to get the width of the sleeve, by measuring from the base-line to 4 on the first cross-line. Next come to the point made at 2; place the square exactly on the base-line. Measure 1 1/4 and dot, then 8 and dot, drawing a cross-line to the base-line, connecting the points 8, 1 1/4, and 2. Omit drawing a line at 4 as that is to cut to. From 11 and 19 1/2 draw a line the same as at 2 using the numbers as shown on those lines;

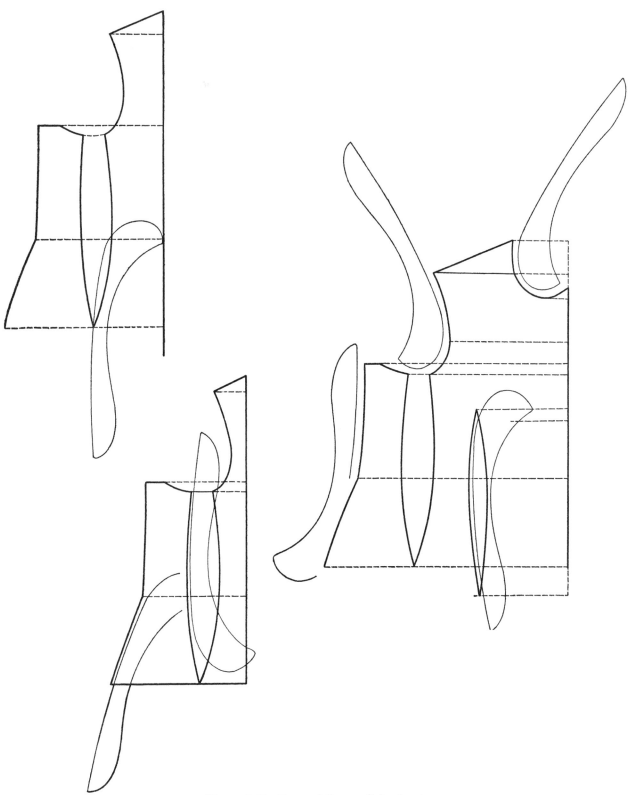

Figure 8. Positions of the scroll for fronts

then draw a diagonal line from 17 1/2 to 4. Draft the under sleeve in the same way. Draw the curves with the scroll as shown by Figure 9.

Correcting the Sleeve Length. Use the person's measure from the center of the back to the wrist. Deduct the width of the back piece minus 1 inch for seams; then you will have the exact length of the sleeve. Measure from the top of the upper sleeve to the point marked 19 1/2 on the base-line. Make this point correspond to the tape measure, by raising or lowering it. Raise or lower the point marked 17 1/2 the same distance. If these points are changed, raise or lower the elbow line. Alter the under sleeve in the same way.

Determining Seam Allowances. Cut your pattern exactly on the lines drawn. All seams are allowed. They are of different sizes and are usually marked. Seams are usually 1/2 space on dresses, except for the shoulder seam, which is 1 1/4 spaces. The extra width for shoulder seams and under-arm parts is allowed so that if the garment is to be made over after wearing, there will be plenty of material to work on. The seams may be made smaller if desired before cutting, which makes no difference to the fit of the garment. Use small seams for sleeves.

1885 *National Garment Cutter*

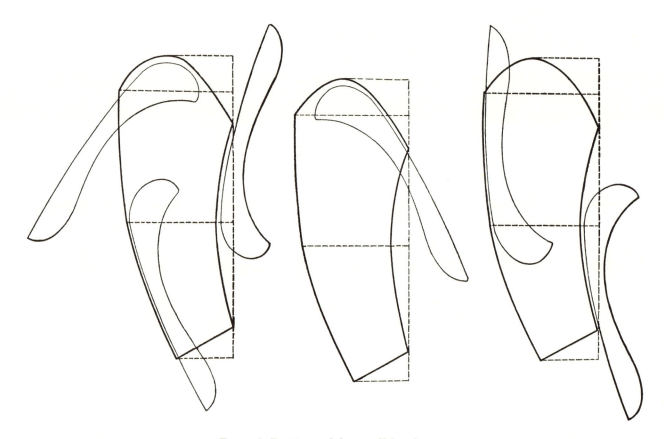

Figure 9. Positions of the scroll for sleeves

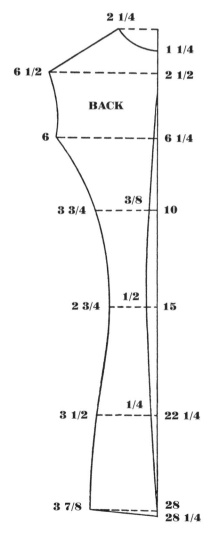

2 1/4

6 1/2 — — — — 1 1/4

2 2/4 2 1/2

BACK

6 — — — — 6 1/4

3 3/4 — — — 3/8 — 10

2 3/4 — — — 1/2 — 15

3 1/2 — — — 1/4 — 22 1/4

3 7/8 — — — — 28
28 1/4

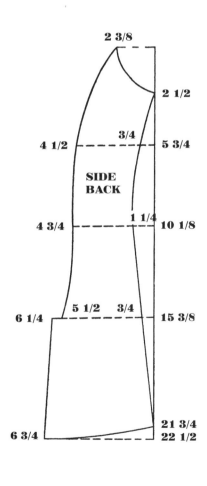

2 3/8

2 1/2

4 1/2 — — — 3/4 — 5 3/4

SIDE
BACK

4 3/4 — — — 1 1/4 — 10 1/8

6 1/4 — 5 1/2 — 3/4 — 15 3/8

6 3/4 — — — 21 3/4
22 1/2

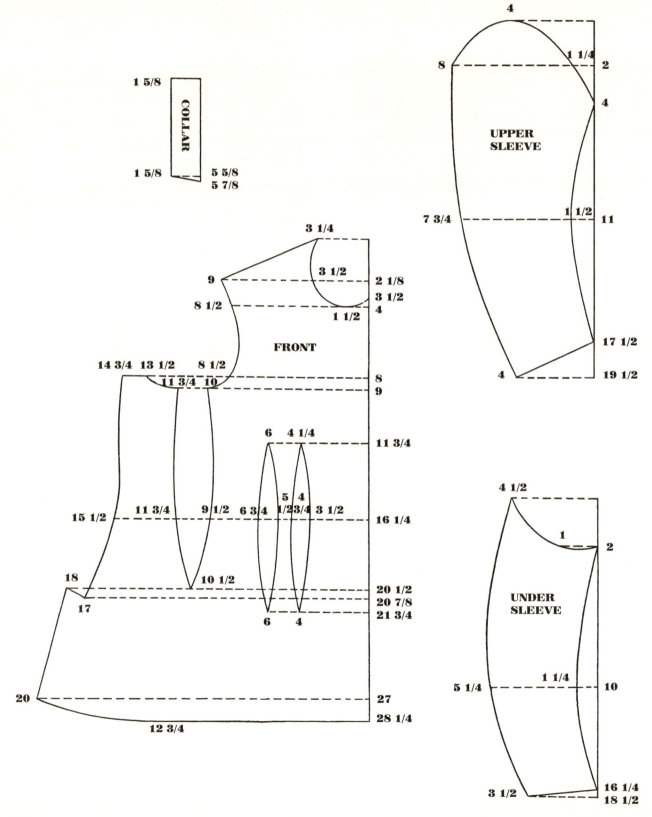

2. Under-Garments and Night-Gowns

Under-vests are made of smooth, all-wool, cotton-and-wool, or silk-and-wool flannel, or of cashmere or wash silk. The colors most favored are white, pink, blue, red, and all shades of écru. The sleeves may be short or long. The fronts turn under in wide, close hems and close their depth with button-holes and small pearl buttons. There is a bust dart and an under-arm dart in each side of the front, and a dart in each side of the back. The long sleeves are in coat shape, with a dart seam extending to the elbow at the outside of the arm. When the sleeves are shortened, there is no outside seam.

The seams may be herring-boned flatly, or they may be first run on the outside and the seam afterward stitched in, so as to form a thin welt on the inside and conceal the raw edges. The neck and sleeves may be cut in small scallops and embroidered with silk floss, a small dot being worked inside each scallop. Or else the edges may be bound with lustring ribbon or flannel binding, or bordered with silk or cotton Hamburg edging. Knitted lace, for which very fine yarn is preferable, is a pretty decoration. A narrow ribbon is run through the open-work of the lace and tied in tiny bows on the shoulders and the outsides of the arms.

October 1882 *Delineator*

Heavy qualities of cotton or linen are chosen for drawers. These are made quite narrow at the knees and short, with a belt that has a draw-string at the top. Close needle-work done on the material is the most substantial trimming. Next to this clusters of tucks with good torchon laces are most used. There are very handsomely trimmed drawers in sets to match the chemise and night-gown, made with fine tucks in blocks alternating with squares of embroidery or Valenciennes insertion, or else with plain cambric blocks that are hem-stitched and have ribbons passed through them.

The chemise is cut in the French sack shape. To take away superfluous width below the bust, two or four darts are introduced there. The top fits smoothly above the armholes, or so nearly smooth that only a draw-string is needed. This may be a narrow tape run in a casing on the wrong side, or else narrow ribbon or a silk lacing string may pass through the eyelets of the embroidery or lace trimming. Ladder-stitching, herring-boning, or feather-stitching are set in the darts of fine chemises, while plainer ones have these seams felled. The new chemises have pointed V-shaped necks. The fancy is to trim these with a bias fold of linen or lawn put on with open ladder-stitching, and a smaller fold edges the armholes and serves as sleeves. The end of the chemise is finished with a hem and ladder-stitching.

Embroidery in small, close designs done on the neck and sleeves is the most useful and durable of all trimmings for chemises. The new fancy is to work eyelets, stars, wheels, and scallops in very pale blue or pink in button-hole stitches. Very fine torchon laces, and the open showy Medici laces, are the most used for all under-garments. Imitation Valenciennes insertions and edgings are used on cambric and percale garments. Many women content themselves with rows of very fine tucks, ruffles of the material scalloped in button-hole stitches, and needle-work done directly on the garment.

For night-gowns, ladies who suffer from cold wear at this season French sack gowns made of fleece-lined piqué. These are trimmed around the neck and wrists, and down the front, with a scant ruffle of the piqué 2 inches wide, with scalloped edges, and dots wrought in the scallops. The shape is a sack front with a pointed yoke at the back; this yoke is doubled for greater warmth. There is a standing band around the neck to hold the ruffle. A strip of feather-stitched cambric is set on this band, on the sleeves, and down the front.

Those who object to thick garments in bed wear cambric night-gowns with tucked yokes, trimmed with embroidered sheer nainsook ruffles, which are considered more becoming than those of thicker cambric embroidery. For serviceable and inexpensive gowns, American muslins without dressing are used, and simply trimmed with Hamburg edging. Very luxurious night-gowns (and also dressing sacks) are made of India silk of the palest blue or rose shades, made in a very loose and ample fashion, with a wide collar and cuffs edged with a plaited frill of the silk.

February 6, 1886 *Harper's Bazar*

Pretty cambric petticoats have their front gores ornamented to the belt, so that the breakfast dress or tea gown may be left open from the waist down whenever desirable.

July 1887 *Delineator*

Drawers with Yoke

This garment is laid off by the waist measure. It is in two pieces, body and yoke. Two yards of material 36 inches wide are required. The seam allowance is 1/4 space.

Close the seam of the leg, leaving the front and back seam of the body open, and in making up neatly face them with the material. The backs of the drawers overlap about 1 inch at the top. Gather the top evenly and attach it to the yoke, fastening the front securely with buttons.

1885 *National Garment Cutter*

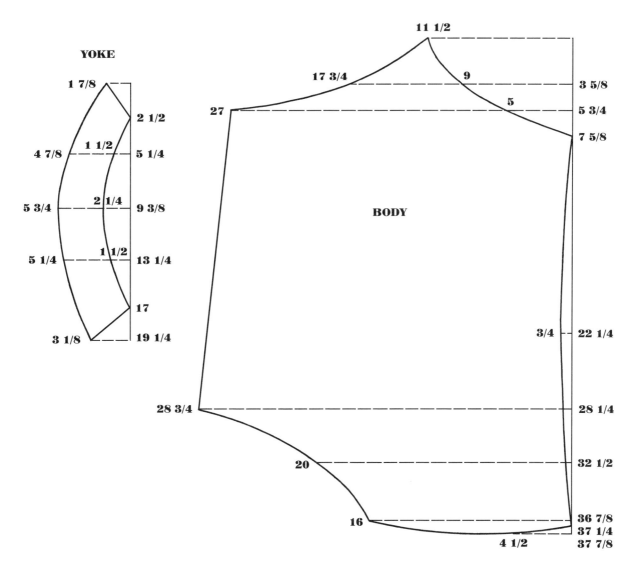

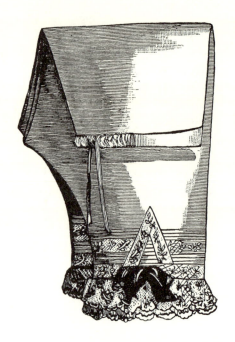

Open Drawers

Only half of the pattern is given. Use the scale corresponding to the waist measure. The length is regulated with the tape measure. Allow for the tucks. The belt can be made any width desired. The drawers require 2 yards of material 36 inches wide.

Winter 1886 *Voice of Fashion*

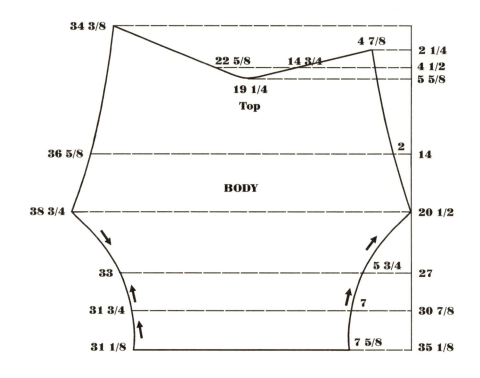

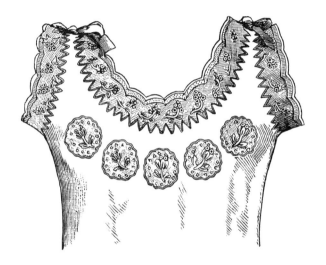

Plain Chemise

This garment is laid off by the bust measure. It consists of three pieces: Front, back, and sleeve. It requires 2 1/2 yards of material 36 inches wide, 2 yards of insertion, and 2 1/4 yards of edging. Cut both the back and the front with their straight edges on a lengthwise fold of the material, to avoid a center seam. Cut the sleeves with the nearest square edge on the same kind of fold for the same purpose. The seam allowance is 1/4 space. In making up, put in the sleeve with its seam at the under-arm seam. Hem the bottom, and finish the neck and sleeves with Hamburg edging and insertion, or lace if preferred.

1885 *National Garment Cutter*

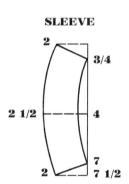

SLEEVE

2

3/4

2 1/2

4

2

7

7 1/2

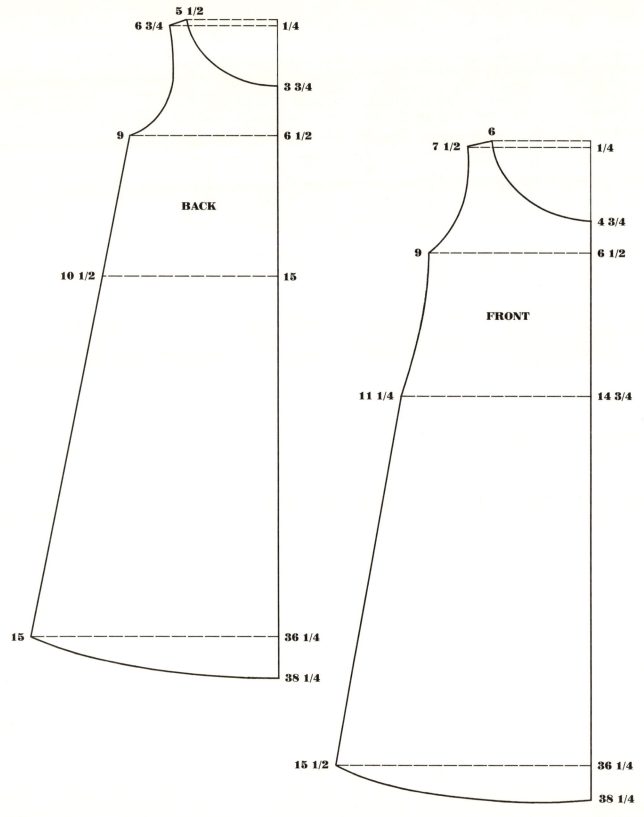

BACK

5 1/2
6 3/4
1/4
3 3/4
6 1/2
9
10 1/2   15
15
36 1/4
38 1/4

FRONT

6
7 1/2
1/4
4 3/4
6 1/2
9
11 1/4   14 3/4
15 1/2   36 1/4
38 1/4

Sack Chemise. This pattern is adaptable to either a round or a square neck. The square neck is shown by the front view, and the round neck by the back view. The chemise has short seams on the shoulders and seams at the sides, the latter springing out to give ample width about the lower edge. The garment is shaped to fit in curves about the arms and does not require sleeves. Cambric was chosen for the making, and the armholes and neck edges are bordered with lace edging set on under lace insertion.

It is a matter of individual taste how the lower edge of a chemise is finished. A plain hem is always neat and appropriate, but many ladies add a deep or narrow ruffle and cut the lower part long enough to permit of a cluster of tucks. The same arrangement of edging and insertion that finishes the neck is preferred by others.

For a lady of medium size, this chemise requires 2 1/2 yards of material 36 inches wide.

July 1887 *Delineator*

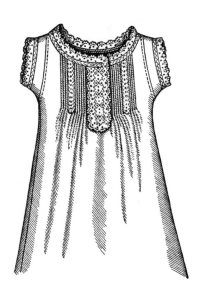

Chemise with Tucks. White cambric was selected for making this chemise. Hamburg edging and insertion, and fancy stitching, provide the trimming. The back and front are each in one piece. They are joined by curved seams under the arms and short seams on the shoulders. The seams may be made in the flat fell or French fell style, both being neat and popular.

The neck edge is rounded, and at the back it is gathered for a short distance on each side of the center. A binding decorated with feather-stitching, and headed by a frill of embroidered edging, completes the neck.

An opening that extends some distance below the top is made at the center of the front for the closing, which is done with button-holes and pearl buttons. An underfacing finishes the right edge, and an underlap is sewed to the left edge. Some distance back of the closing, a cluster of six forward-turning tucks is made in each side. A few inches back of these is a cluster of four similar tucks, which extends the depth of the closing. A band of insertion, shaped to a point at the lower edge, covers the space between the clusters of tucks. Another band that is edged with embroidery, and similarly pointed at the lower edge, is placed over the closing. Feather-stitching decorates the edge of the insertion.

The sleeves are narrow, and each has a seam at the top and bottom. A line of machine-stitching is visible at the armhole edge. A tiny band that is delicately feather-stitched and edged with embroidery completes the outer edge. The lower edge of the chemise may be finished with a hem. Or else it may be trimmed with a ruffle of the material edged with lace or embroidery, or simply stitched.

Muslin, flannel, linen, silk, and other materials appropriate for under-garments are made up in this way. Embroidery, lace, tucking, or cambric ruffles trim all cotton materials. Fancy stitching decorates flannel and silk. Hand embroidery is much used on this style of chemise, and it is frequently applied in the form of button-holed edges and tiny embroidered dots. For a lady of medium size, this garment requires 2 3/4 yards of material 36 inches wide.

July 1888 *Delineator*

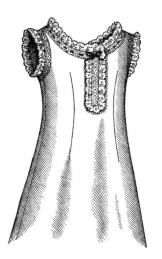 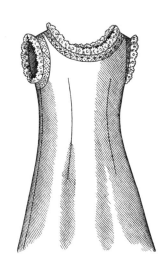

Princess Chemise. Cambric is the material chosen for this example, and a ruffle of the same, lace insertion, and edging constitute the decorations. The back and front are each cut on a fold of the material at the center. They are joined by curved seams on the sides and short seams on the shoulders. The side seams are sprung out toward the bottom to give all of the width necessary there. A narrow, straight cambric ruffle with edging finishes the lower edge. The superfluous width about the bodice part is removed by a dart in each side of the front, and another in each side of the back. These darts extend far enough above and below the waist-line to perfect the adjustment without rendering the garment too close. The neck is cut low and round, and an opening extending some distance below it is made in the center of the front. This opening is narrowly hemmed at its left edge, and to its right side is sewed a lap.

A band of lace insertion surmounted by one of edging passes all around the neck, and the insertion is carried down over the lap, the edging being continued all around the latter. The pattern of the insertion is quite open, and in the interstices is run a narrow ribbon, the ends of which are tied in front. Button-holes and small pearl buttons perform the closing invisibly. There are no sleeves, and the armholes are finished with lace and insertion to accord with the neck.

To make the garment for a lady of medium size, requires 2 1/4 yards of material 36 inches wide. Cambric is liked for summer under-garments, but many ladies prefer fine muslin. Ladies who wear thin flannels all summer, with the chemise outside the corset, will be pleased with this shape because of its method of fitting. Finely figured cotton lawns also have their admirers, and those whose inclination and purse are in friendly alliance often select surah and wash silks. The decorations may be varied to suit the fancy, and may be as elaborate as desired.

June 1885 *Delineator*

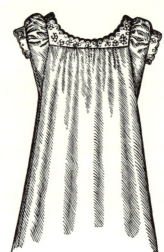

Chemise with Yoke

This garment is drafted with the scale corresponding to the bust measure. The length is regulated with the tape measure. There are six pieces: Front, back, front yoke, back yoke, sleeve band, and sleeve. For material 36 inches wide, 2 3/4 yards are required.

1887 *National Garment Cutter Instruction Book*

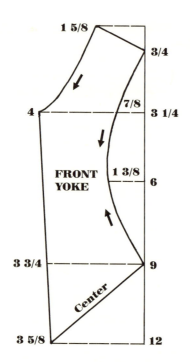

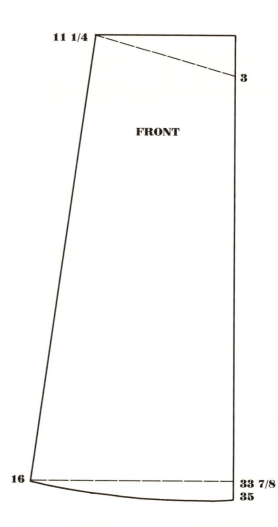

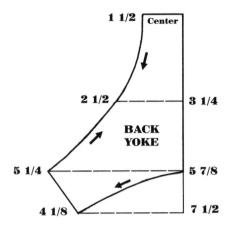

1 1/2   Center

2 1/2   3 1/4

BACK
YOKE

5 1/4   5 7/8

4 1/8   7 1/2

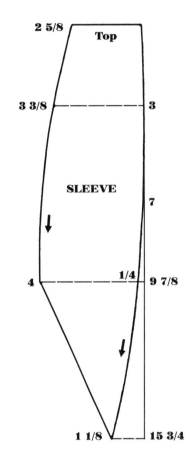

2 5/8   Top

3 3/8   3

SLEEVE

7

4   1/4   9 7/8

1 1/8   15 3/4

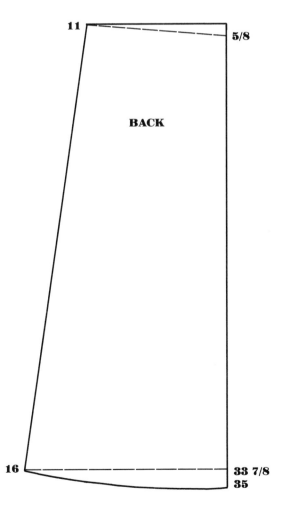

11   5/8

BACK

16   33 7/8
35

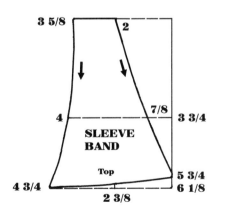

3 5/8   2

4   7/8   3 3/4

SLEEVE
BAND

Top

4 3/4   5 3/4
6 1/8

2 3/8

23

Chemise with Yoke. Bleached muslin was used for this example. Narrow embroidered edging borders the neck, the overlapping front edge of the yoke, and the bands of the sleeves. The deep yoke is pointed at the center of the front and has shorter points in front of the sleeves, the back being cut straight across. There are short seams on the shoulders. To the lower edge of the yoke is sewed the body part, which is cut in the requisite shape and slightly gathered. The under-arm edges are curved to proportion the width properly, and are seamed together to within a short distance from the top.

Each sleeve is composed of a single section, which is cut to a deep curve toward the center at its outer edge and slanted off very narrowly toward the ends. The slanted edges are seamed together. The curved edge is gathered and sewed to a band, which is deepened to a point at its center to accord with the outline of the curve. The inner edges of

the sleeve are joined to the unseamed edges of the front and back as far as the tops of the latter. The remainder is gathered and sewed to the yoke between the two parts of the chemise proper.

A short, lengthwise slash is made at the center of the front below the yoke, and its edges are finished with narrow hems. The front of the yoke is closed with three button-holes and small buttons. The lower edge of the chemise may be finished with a plain hem about 1 inch wide, or with the same trimming used for the neck and the sleeves.

This chemise may be made of muslin, cambric, nainsook, lawn, linen, and all other materials in vogue for such garments. The yoke and sleeve bands may be formed of strips of insertion, cut from embroidered net, or hand embroidered. Yokes and bands of rick-rack or feather-edge braid may be developed in numerous pretty patterns. To make the chemise for a lady of medium size, requires 3 yards of material 36 inches wide.

October 1883 *Delineator*

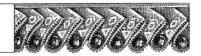

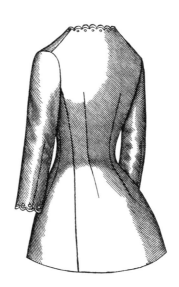

Under-Vest

This pattern is laid off by the bust measure. It is in three pieces: Front, back, and sleeve. It requires 3 1/2 yards of material 27 inches wide, or 3 yards of material 36 inches wide, and 15 buttons. In cutting the material, place the pattern for the back with its back edge on the lengthwise fold of the material to avoid a center seam. Cut the other two parts lengthwise of the material.

In making up, turn under each front at the point marked 1 1/2 for a hem. Close the sleeve seams. Attach the sleeves to the body of the garment with the inside seams at the front of the armhole. Hold the sleeves toward you while sewing them in, and fasten the extra fullness in a forward-turning plait under the arm. Close the front with button-holes and buttons. If the under-vest is made of flannel, cut the neck and lower end of the sleeves in scallops and finish them with button-hole stitching. Also embroider a dot in the center of each scallop. The neck may be cut out and the sleeves cut shorter, and the edges finished as above described, or in any more pleasing manner.

1885 *National Garment Cutter*

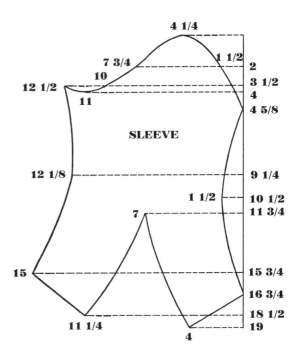

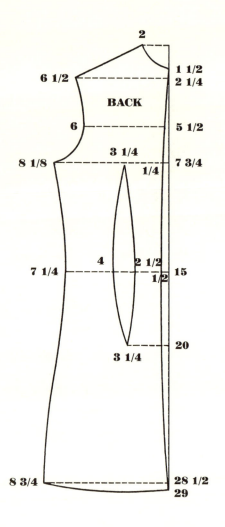

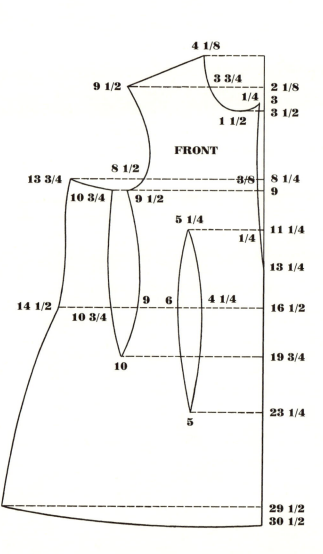

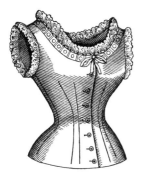 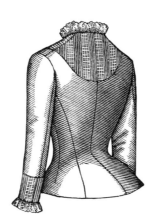

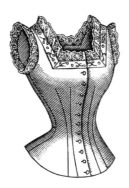 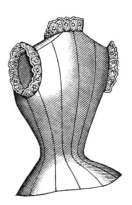

Corset Cover. The back view shows this corset cover cut with a high neck and full-length sleeves, and the front view shows it cut with a low neck and the sleeves omitted. Muslin is the material represented in the engraving. The fronts are turned down for hems, and closed with buttons and button-holes. Two bust darts and an under-arm dart are taken in each side. The back has a curved center seam that fits much like that of a French basque, all of the spring necessitated by the tournure being allowed below the waist-line. A narrow hem, or an underfacing, finishes the lower edge.

In the front view, the neck is finished with a band of insertion headed by one of edging, and a narrow ribbon is run through the openings and knotted in front. The armholes are simply finished with edging. In the back view, the neck is overlaid in round yoke shape with lace tucking, and the neck is simply bordered with lace edging. The full-length coat sleeves have cuff-facings of the tucking bordered at the lower edge with lace edging. The material is usually cut out from beneath lace tucking, lace net, embroidery, or any similar decorative material. Darned net is much admired for trimming corset covers when a diaphanous effect is desired without cutting the garment low. The designs are worked so that the net may be cut into strips for insertion.

Cambric is lighter and consequently cooler than muslin for summer wear, and thin flannel is liked by many ladies for cold weather. For a lady of medium size, this corset cover requires 1 7/8 yards of material 36 inches wide.

February 1885 *Delineator*

Corset Cover. The garment may be cut with a close high round neck or a low square neck. It is composed of side pieces, side backs that reach nearly to the neck on the shoulders, backs joined by a curved seam, and fronts closely fitted by double bust darts. The seams are all curved, and the adjustment is as close and smooth as that of a tight-fitting basque. The fronts are hemmed and closed with button-holes and buttons. The high neck is finished with a standing band of embroidered edging, and the low neck is decorated with a band of insertion and a standing frill of embroidery. The armholes are finished with embroidered edging.

All materials used for under-garments are devoted to corset covers. Cambric and nainsook are liked for fine covers, while muslin is popular for more durable ones. Laces of all washable varieties, and all kinds of pretty edgings, are effective trimmings. For a lady of medium size, this garment requires 1 1/4 yards of material 36 inches wide.

August 1888 *Delineator*

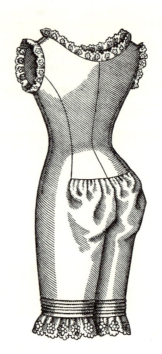

Combination Chemise and Drawers

This garment is drafted with the scale corresponding to the bust measure. Regulate the length with the tape measure. No allowance is made for the tucks. There are three pieces: Front, back, and sleeve. Diagrams are given for both a high and a low neck on the front and back. The engraving shows the high neck on the left and the low neck on the right. The quantity of material 36 inches wide required is 3 3/8 yards.

Winter 1886 *Voice of Fashion*

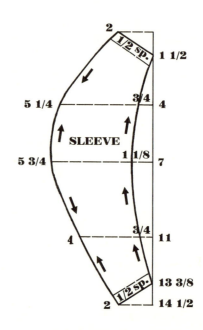

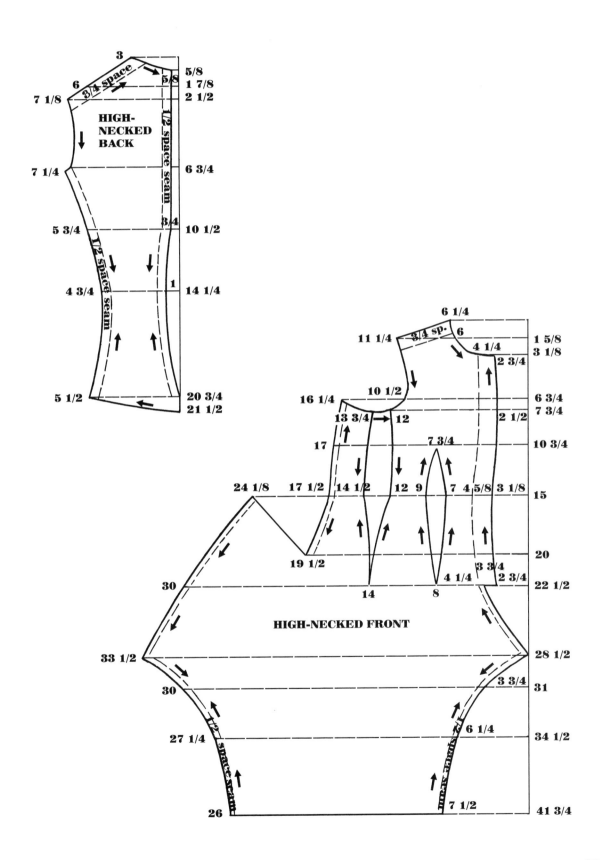

HIGH-NECKED BACK

HIGH-NECKED FRONT

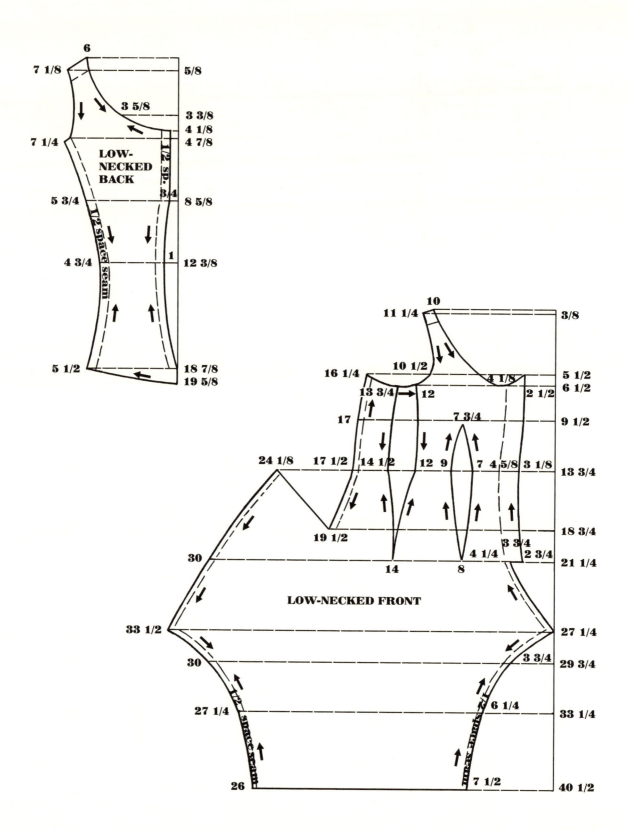

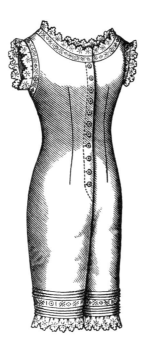 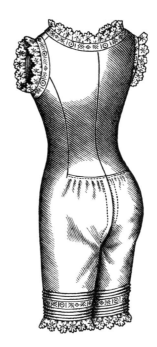

Combination Corset Cover and Drawers.
The bodice part of the back has two sections, which extend a few inches below the waist-line and have a curved center seam. Each side of the front is fitted by a bust dart. The fronts are curved out considerably at the closing edge and widened to form the entire drawers part of the front. After the front and back are joined at the under-arm seams, the extension forming the back of each leg is gathered at the top and sewed to the lower edge of the back. The drawers are partly seamed at the inner edges. The open edges are finished with narrow underfacings, while the back edges are lapped and sewed together for a few inches from the end of the center back seam. The front edges of the bodice part are underfaced and closed to a little below the waist-line with button-holes and flat buttons.

This example is made of bleached muslin. The bottom of each leg is finished with a ruffle of torchon lace, surmounted by two clusters of tucks separated by a band of insertion. Tiny puffs may take the place of the tucks. The low, round neck is edged with a band of lace set on under a band of insertion. A similar finish is added to the armholes, the garment being completed without sleeves. For a lady of medium size, these combinations require 2 3/4 yards of material 36 inches wide.

June 1882 *Delineator*

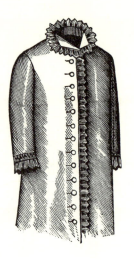

Circular Night-Gown

This night-gown is drafted with the scale corresponding to the bust measure. It may be made any length by taking your measure with the tape measure, laying off the pattern thereby. All seams and hems are allowed for. There are three pieces: Front and back combined into one main piece (parts A and B are to be put together before drafting the pattern), sleeve, and collar.

This night-gown requires 4 1/2 yards of material 36 inches wide, and 19 buttons. Cut the material with the shortest end of the collar pattern on a lengthwise fold of the material. Cut the main piece with the front edge of the pattern on the selvage, and the sleeve laid lengthwise on the material.

In making the garment, turn under the front edge of the main piece at the point marked 1 1/2 for the left side, and about 1/4 space less for the right side. Take up all seams evenly. Attach the collar with its center at the seam at the back. Turn it up, felling the lining over the seam, and turning its corners over at the points marked 1/4, 1, and 1 1/2. Close the seams of the sleeves, and attach them to the garment with the inside seam at the front of the arm-hole. Hold the sleeve toward you while sewing it in, and fasten any extra fullness in a forward-turning plait under the arm. Close the night-gown with buttons and button-holes, making the latter in the wider hem. Trim it with torchon lace, embroidery, braid, or in any other manner desired.

1885 National Garment Cutter

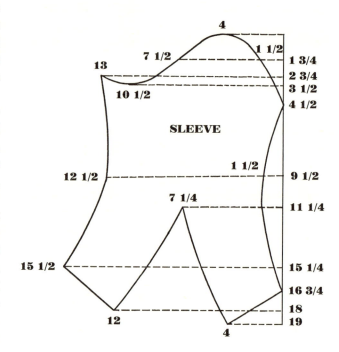

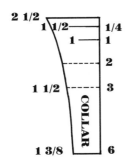

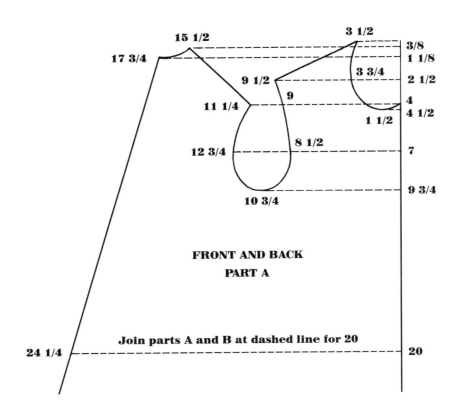

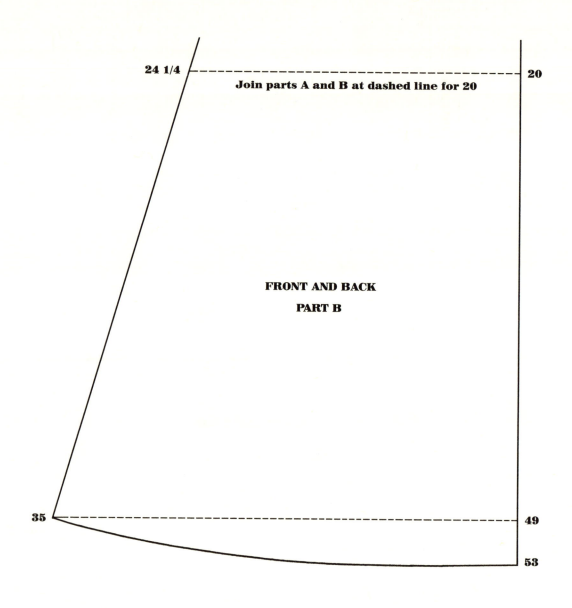

24 1/4 — — — — — — — — — — — — — — — 20

Join parts A and B at dashed line for 20

FRONT AND BACK

PART B

35 — — — — — — — — — — — — — — — — 49

53

Circular Night-Gown. The night-gown represented is made of muslin and trimmed with lace tucking and torchon lace edging. The front edges are folded under for hems, and closed their entire length with button-holes and pearl buttons. The back has a bias seam at the center which, with the shoulder seams, performs the adjustment. The night-gown fits smoothly about the shoulders and widens symmetrically toward the lower edge. The latter is finished with a hem. The sleeves are in coat shape. A narrow band or choker collar, which is cut from a crosswise strip of tucking, finishes the neck.

On each side of the front (beyond the hem) is applied a bias band of lace tucking, which is about 3 inches wide when finished. Bias cuff-facings of lace tucking are about the sleeves. The wrists and neck are finished with frills of narrow torchon lace. The material beneath the lace tucking, or any other kind of open-work that may be used as a decoration, may be cut away or not, as preferred. Hamburg, lace net, or lace tucking may be applied in yoke shape on the upper part in front, and on the back if desired.

Linen, lawn, cambric, percale, wool and cotton flannels, and all other materials in vogue for such garments make up satisfactorily. For a lady of medium size, this night-gown requires 3 7/8 yards of material 36 inches wide.

February 1885 *Delineator*

3. Wrappers and Tea Gowns

Wrappers of linen lawn are among the comforts to be appreciated in midsummer. The yoke wrapper, with straight breadths gathered to the yoke in Mother Hubbard fashion, and loose flowing, is liked. The back may be shirred across the waist-line, and the fronts hang straight; or else hemmed strings of the lawn are set in the side seams to tie in front. The yoke may be tucked in lengthwise 1/2-inch tucks. The skirt may also have a group of tucks above the hem, and the ends of the strings should be tucked also.

June 13, 1885 *Harper's Bazar*

Wrappers for morning wear or the sick room are made in redingote shape, with double-breasted fronts and square sleeves. Or else the front is loose (that is, without darts being taken up) and the back is close fitting, with full straight breadths gathered on below the waist-line. These redingote wrappers are very handsome made of striped velvet and without trimming, having merely a deep rolling collar, broad cuffs, and wide square pockets on the hips. Large button molds covered with plain velvet fasten the front and ornament the pockets. Other velvet wrappers, of red, green, and brown stripes, have a soft vest of salmon surah extending down the entire front, the velvet being scalloped on each side and lapping over the vest. The surah vest is shirred just below the neck, and folded thence in plaits to the waist-line, where it is again shirred in rows.

Simpler wrappers for general use are of cashmere, or of the eider-down flannels, which are thick, soft, and warm, yet very light in weight. Cashmere wrappers in dark red or pale blue shades have a vest of striped velvet down the front from the neck to the bottom. The shape is a loose front without darts, while the back of the waist is adjusted to the figure down to the full gathered skirt breadths. The sides fit smoothly over the hips. They may have sash ends on the left side and a large pocket on the right; but pockets are usually preferred for both sides, and the sash is omitted. All of the fullness of the skirt is massed at the back in a very narrow space, usually being confined to the width below the center backs, while the side pieces extend quite plain from the armholes to the bottom. Sometimes a width of the striped velvet used in the front is placed in the center of the back of the skirt between breadths of cashmere the same width as the velvet.

January 23, 1886 *Harper's Bazar*

Elaborate tea gowns are adjusted to the figure at the back, and straight and flowing in front. They combine plush with lace; surah with lace, rich brocades, or white wools with embroidery; or lace over silk. Some are fitted like a princess dress, opening down the front over light silk folded diagonally, and embroidered across the bottom.

Morning wrappers, whether of silk or of flannel, are smoothly fitted in redingote style. All of the fullness is massed below the two center backs. It is usually attached there in projecting plaits; or else the pieces are pointed, and the skirt fullness is gathered and puffed slightly. For elaborate wrappers, the fronts are turned back in lapels to disclose a finely pressed plaiting, usually of surah, from the neck to the bottom. This has a box-plait like a shirt front in the bodice, with studs and feather-stitching, and fine plaits beside it. Below the waist-line are two breadths of the surah, either gathered or plaited, and feather-stitched above the hem at the bottom.

November 6, 1886 *Harper's Bazar*

Tea gowns made of pretty but inexpensive silk and trimmed with lace and ribbon are very generally worn. Women who find them becoming wear them, when at home on quiet evenings, with skirts that have outlived their bodices.

January 1887 *Delineator*

Ladies' Wrapper

This garment is laid off by the bust measure. It is in eight pieces: Front, back, front yoke, back yoke, sleeve, collar, pocket, and fly—the latter being used for buttons. All seams are allowed for. Figures on the front and back diagrams show where the plaits are to be laid.

This wrapper requires 9 5/8 yards of material 22 inches wide, 5 1/8 yards of material 36 inches wide, or 4 yards of material 40 inches wide. Cut the front with its front edge, the back with its back edge, the back yoke, and the fly with the longest straight edge of their respective patterns on a lengthwise fold of the material; by so doing a center seam will be avoided. Cut the sleeve lengthwise on the material. Cut the collar on the bias.

Turn under each front yoke at the points marked 1 1/2 for a hem. Make three box-plaits in both the back and the front as shown by the cut of the upper ends, and crease them as indicated by the figures on the diagrams. Attach the collar and roll it over as shown by the curved dashed line. Attach the pocket as shown by the diagram, turning the point downward for a lap. Close the seam of the sleeve and attach it to the garment with the inside seam at the front of the armhole. Sew buttons onto the fly, which is to be attached to the undermost box-plait for that purpose. Trim the wrapper with ribbon bows at the neck, the lower closing of the yoke, at the top of the slash in the sleeves, and at the point of each pocket lap.

1885 *National Garment Cutter*

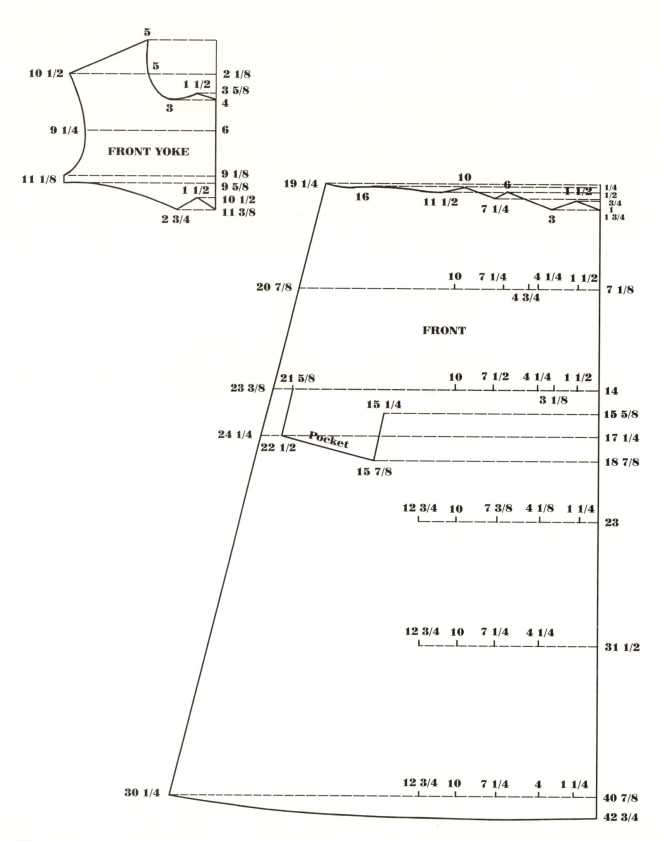

FRONT YOKE

FRONT

Pocket

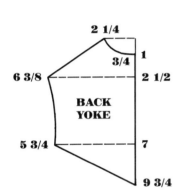

2 1/4

3/4   1

6 3/8   2 1/2

**BACK
YOKE**

5 3/4   7

9 3/4

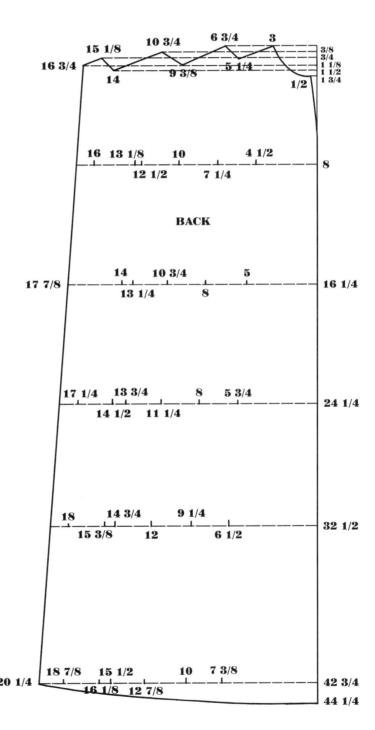

6 3/4   3

15 1/8   10 3/4

3/8
3/4
1 1/8
16 3/4   5 1/4   1 1/2
14   9 3/8   1 3/4
1/2

16   13 1/8   10   4 1/2

12 1/2   7 1/4   8

BACK

14   10 3/4   5

17 7/8   13 1/4   8   16 1/4

17 1/4   13 3/4   8   5 3/4

14 1/2   11 1/4   24 1/4

18   14 3/4   9 1/4

15 3/8   12   6 1/2   32 1/2

18 7/8   15 1/2   10   7 3/8

20 1/4   42 3/4

16 1/8   12 7/8   44 1/4

39

POCKET

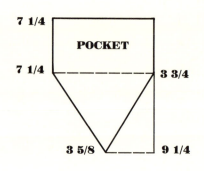

7 1/4

7 1/4   3 3/4

3 5/8   9 1/4

COLLAR

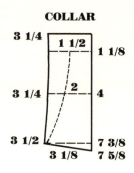

3 1/4   1 1/2   1 1/8

3 1/4   2   4

3 1/2   7 3/8
      3 1/8   7 5/8

FLY

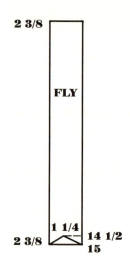

2 3/8

2 3/8   1 1/4   14 1/2
                  15

SLEEVE

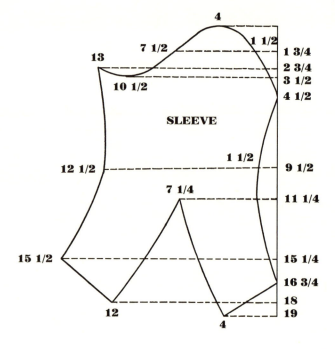

4

7 1/2   1 1/2   1 3/4
13   2 3/4
      10 1/2   3 1/2
                             4 1/2

12 1/2   1 1/2   9 1/2

      7 1/4   11 1/4

15 1/2   15 1/4
                          16 3/4
                          18
      12   4   19

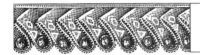 

Mother Hubbard Wrapper. This example is made up in floriated sateen. The upper part of the wrapper is a yoke of becoming depth, fitted by shoulder seams. To this is joined the lower part, consisting of four pieces united by center and under-arm seams, and turned in quite deeply at their tops for a finish. The back, and each side of the front, are each shirred once far enough from the top to leave a heading. The shirrings are drawn up sufficiently to adapt these parts to the size of the yoke, to which they are sewed. The shirrings do not extend quite to the armholes. This provision, in conjunction with the spring of the center and under-arm seams, gives the necessary adjustment without introducing too much fullness. Button-holes and pearl buttons close the front, the right side of both the yoke and the lower potion being hemmed and the left underfaced. A standing collar with curved ends finishes the neck. The fitted coat sleeves are completed at the wrists with a becoming plainness–which may, however, give way to any style of trimming admired.

Cambric, lawn, mull, prints, gingham, and all kinds of cotton materials, as well as nun's veiling, delaine, and other seasonable wools, are made up in wrappers of this style. For a lady of medium size, the material required is 8 3/8 yards if 22 inches wide, 5 3/4 yards if 36 inches wide, or 4 yards if 48 inches wide. Lace, embroidery, rick-rack, braid, narrow ruffles, etc., may be applied as trimming. The yoke may be made of lace or embroidered webbing, lace tucking, and other kinds of open or semi-open meshed decorative material. Ribbons may tie the fronts together, or lace may be arranged in a jabot the entire length of the closing.

May 1884 *Delineator*

Tea Gown

Use the scale corresponding to the bust measure. Regulate the length with the tape measure. This garment is in eight pieces: Front, front lining, front plaiting, side piece, back, two sleeve pieces, and collar. It requires 5 1/2 yards of material 40 inches wide, and 1 5/8 yards of satin. The front plaiting is laid in five forward-turning plaits and fastened to the lining, and the upper front is blind-stitched over it. The velvet lapels may be omitted or made of lace, which gives a very pleasing effect. The back is laid in two double box-plaits. Take care to connect the waist-lines.

Winter 1886 *Voice of Fashion*

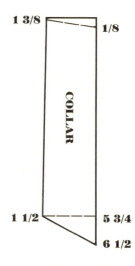

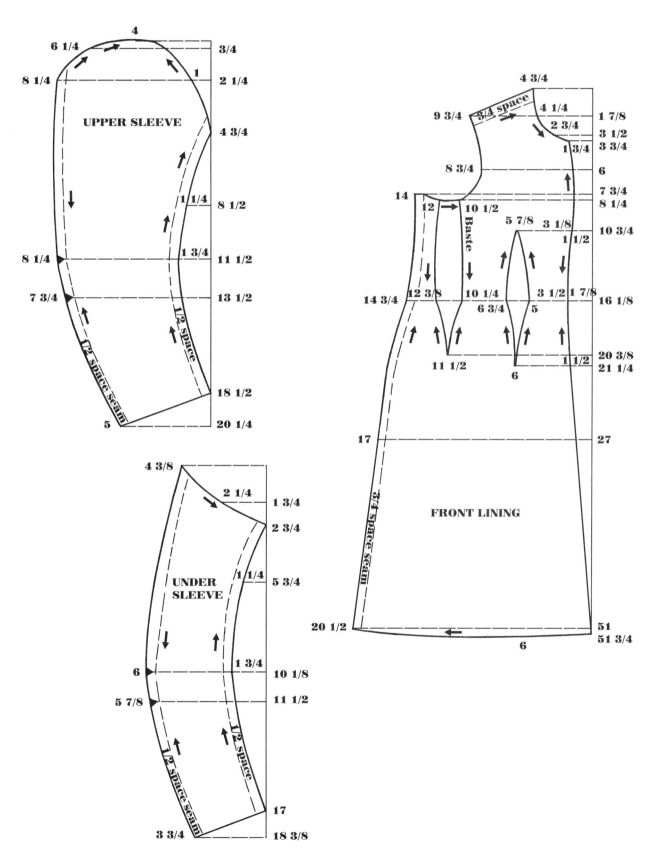

UPPER SLEEVE

4

6 1/4   3/4

8 1/4   2 1/4   1

4 3/4

1 1/4   8 1/2

1 3/4   11 1/2

8 1/4

7 3/4   13 1/2

1/2 space

1/2 space seam

18 1/2

5   20 1/4

UNDER SLEEVE

4 3/8   2 1/4   1 3/4

2 3/4

1 1/4   5 3/4

6   1 3/4   10 1/8

5 7/8   11 1/2

1/2 space

1/2 space seam

17

3 3/4   18 3/8

FRONT LINING

4 3/4

9 3/4   3/4 space   4 1/4   1 7/8

2 3/4   3 1/2

1 3/4   3 3/4

8 3/4   6

7 3/4

14   8 1/4

12   10 1/2   5 7/8   3 1/8   10 3/4

Baste   1 1/2

14 3/4   12 3/8   10 1/4   3 1/2   1 7/8   16 1/8

6 3/4   5

11 1/2   1 1/2   20 3/8

6   21 1/4

17   27

3/4 space seam

20 1/2   51

6   51 3/4

43

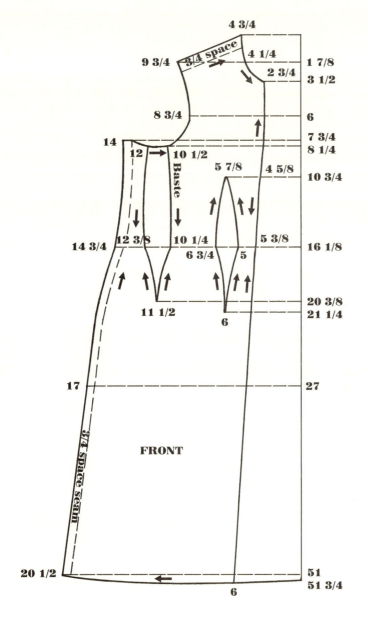

FRONT

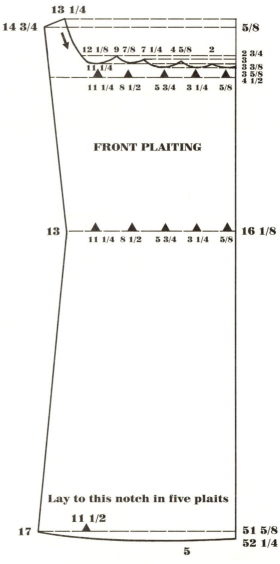

FRONT PLAITING

Lay to this notch in five plaits

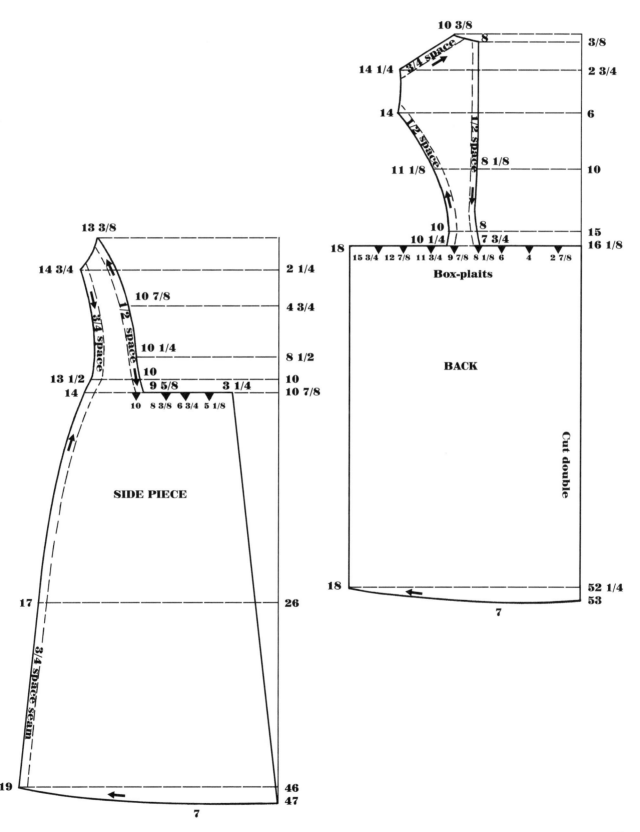

Wrappers and Tea Gowns

Trained Wrapper. For this example plain cashmere and polka-dotted surah are united. Both materials, lace, and ribbon are associated in the trimmings. The center front has a plain foundation, on which the center part is adjusted to form two full puffs above a deep flounce. Of the shirrings that assist in forming the puffs, one line is made at the neck edge, another a little below the waist-line, and the remaining one about a third of the distance from the bottom. None of the shirrings extend quite to the side edges. All of them are sewed through to the foundation, and the lower two are concealed by downward-turning plaits folded in the edges above them. The lower edge is turned under for a hem, and falls even with the bottom of the foundation. The center front is overlapped by the side fronts, and is sewed permanently in place for its entire length on the left side. The right side is closed by buttons and button-holes in a fly from the right shoulder to some distance below the waist-line, the right side edge below the closing being sewed in place.

The side fronts and the back are in the princess shape. They are fitted by single bust and under-arm darts in the front, a curved center back seam, and the shoulder and side seams. The side seams are placed well to the back, and the center back seam is discontinued a little below the waist-line at the top of extra width. This, in conjunction with corresponding extensions on the front edges of the back, is folded under to form two box-plaits, which are double at their inner and single at their outer folds. The back is lengthened to form a long, oval train, for which these plaits supply ample fullness.

On each side of the front rests a pocket, the square outline of which is varied by turning the top over triangularly. Lace is sewed beneath the lower and back edges and turned over flatly on the outside. The reversed part is faced with the material, and on the corner a ribbon bow is fastened.

The overlapping side-front edges, which are curved, are bordered with lace laid on flatly. Inside the high standing collar is sewed a full frill of lace, which falls over and conceals it. Below the collar is a pinked silk ruching laid in triple box-plaits. This ruching is carried down each side front, back of the lace edging. The outside seam of each coat sleeve is discontinued far enough from the wrist to permit of turning the lower part back in cuff fashion. The reversed part is faced with the dress material, and lace is turned flatly from the wrist over the facing.

Wrappers of this kind are made of Madras silk, flannel, surah, and all materials in vogue for handsome négligé house wear. The trimming is varied according to the material selected or the fancy of the wearer. Down in pink, blue, lemon, or white may take the place of ruching. For a lady of medium size, this garment requires 12 3/4 yards of material 22 inches wide, 8 7/8 yards of material 36 inches wide, or 6 1/2 yards of material 48 inches wide. As represented, it needs 6 1/2 yards of material 40 inches wide for the main part, 3 1/4 yards of silk 20 inches wide for the center part, and 1 5/8 yards of silesia for the vest lining.

May 1886 *Delineator*

Morning Dress

This garment is drafted with the scale corresponding to the bust measure. Regulate the length with
the tape measure. It is in seven pieces: Front, side
back, back, skirt back, collar, and two sleeve pieces.
The quantity of material 22 inches wide required is
8 1/2 yards. Sew the back and side back together
first. The skirt back is turned down 2 inches. Gather
it and sew it to the back on the slanted line from
18 1/4 on the base-line, and to the side back on the
slanted line from 12 1/2 on the base-line. The bottom of this garment may be finished with plaited
or gathered ruffles.

   1887 *National Garment Cutter Instruction Book*

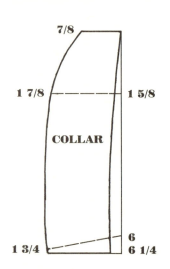

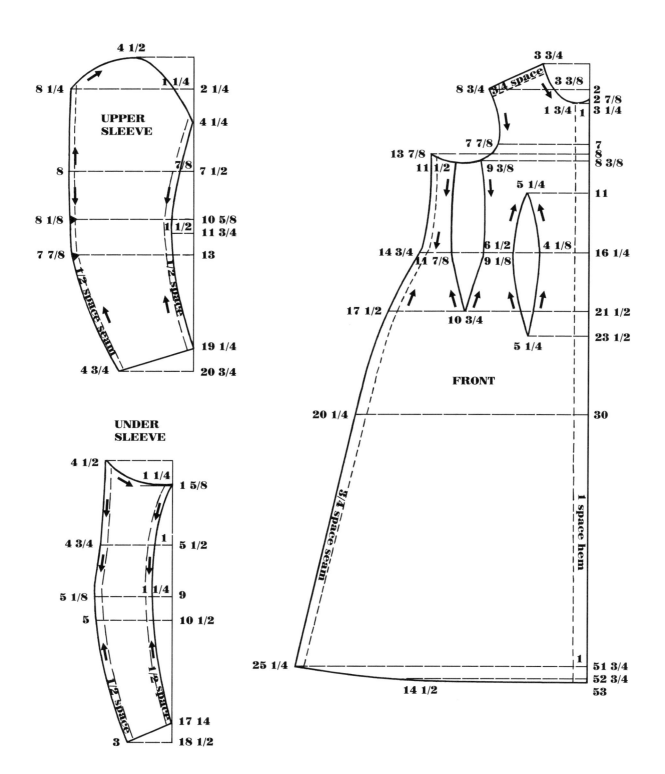

UPPER SLEEVE

4 1/2

8 1/4   1 1/4   2 1/4

4 1/4

8   7/8   7 1/2

8 1/8   10 5/8
         1 1/2   11 3/4

7 7/8   13

1/2 space seam   1/2 space

19 1/4

4 3/4   20 3/4

UNDER SLEEVE

4 1/2   1 1/4
              1 5/8

4 3/4   1   5 1/2

5 1/8   1 1/4   9

5   10 1/2

1/2 space   1/2 space

17 14

3   18 1/2

FRONT

3 3/4

8 3/4   3/4 space   3 3/8   2
                           2 7/8
                           3 1/4
1 3/4   1

7 7/8   7
13 7/8   8 8 3/8
11 1/2   9 3/8

5 1/4   11

14 3/4   6 1/2   4 1/8   16 1/4
11 7/8   9 1/8

17 1/2   10 3/4   21 1/2

5 1/4   23 1/2

20 1/4   30

3/4 space seam

1 space hem

25 1/4   1   51 3/4
              52 3/4
14 1/2   53

49

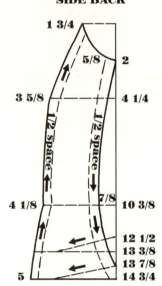

SIDE BACK

1 3/4

5/8　　2

3 5/8　　　　4 1/4

1/2 space　　1/2 space

4 1/8　　7/8　10 3/8

12 1/2
13 3/8
13 7/8
5　　　　　14 3/4

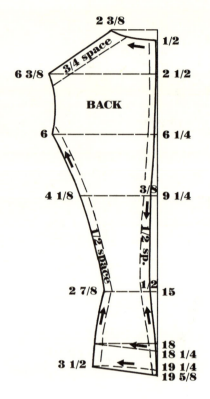

2 3/8

3/4 space　　　1/2

6 3/8　　　　　　2 1/2

BACK

6　　　　　　6 1/4

4 1/8　　　　3/8　9 1/4

1/2 space　　1/2 sp.

2 7/8　　　　1/2　15

18
18 1/4
3 1/2　　　　19 1/4
19 5/8

21 1/2

SKIRT BACK

21 1/2　　　　　37

Ladies' Wrapper. The material represented is striped cambric, and the decoration consists of bias bands of the same. The fronts are in princess shape and close their length with button-holes and buttons, the right side being hemmed and the left underfaced. In each side are double bust darts and an under-arm dart. The rest of the adjustment is accomplished by center back and side-back seams. The bodice part of the back does not extend very far below the waist-line. On its lower part is sewed the skirt, which consists of a full breadth turned in at the top for a finish and shirred three times far enough from the upper edge to leave a heading. It is sewed in place through the shirrings.

On each side of the front rests a pocket, which is folded over at the top in kerchief fashion, its reversed part being faced with the material and its edges bordered by a narrow bias band. The neck is completed by a high standing collar overfaced with a bias band. The sleeves are in coat shape and fit the arms handsomely, but not too closely. Each sleeve is bordered at the wrist with a bias band about 2 inches wide. A band of similar width passes down one side of the front, its direction curving backward from the closing toward the lower edge. The band is carried about the skirt a little above the bottom and up the opposite front.

All kinds of cotton materials are the first choice for wrappers intended for practical use. Pongee, surah, nun's veiling, and fancy cashmeres are made up for garments for which only occasional service is required, and lace, embroidery, and ribbon are added to them. To make the wrapper for a lady of medium size, requires 8 1/8 yards of material 22 inches wide, 5 yards of material 36 inches wide, or 3 5/8 yards of material 48 inches wide.

June 1885 *Delineator*

Ladies' Wrapper. The wrapper is shown made of white lawn. It is trimmed with a ruffle of the material, two widths of embroidered edging, insertion, and ribbon bows. The fronts are fitted by a long under-arm dart in each side. At the front edge of the right front is folded a box-plait, and the left front is completed with a hem. The closing, which extends the full length of the garment, is made with buttons and button-holes. Some distance from each side of the closing, two forward-turning tucks of medium width are made from the shoulder to the lower edge. Extending from beneath the first tuck on each side is a frill of embroidery. From beneath the embroidery on each side start ribbon ties, which are bowed at intervals over the closing. A triangular patch pocket is placed on each front near the end

of the dart, the edges being followed by insertion, and a ribbon bow being placed in the center.

The sides and back are adjusted by side backs and a curved center back seam, the back extending only to basque depth and pointed at the end of the center back seam. Extra width allowed between the side backs supplies the required width of the back, the upper edge being coarsely gauged and joined to the lower edge of the back. A frill of embroidery headed by a band of insertion is placed over the join, and a full ribbon bow is sewed at the end of the left side-back seam.

Narrow insertion edged on each side by a frill of narrow embroidery overlies the high standing collar. The sleeves have but one seam, which is at the inside of the arm. The lower edge is sloped toward the inside, gathered almost to the seam,

and finished with a narrow wristband of insertion. The latter is trimmed with a falling frill of wide embroidery, showing decreased width toward the inside of the arm. A ribbon bow placed at the end of the seam completes the sleeve decorations. A deep ruffle of the material, edged with embroidery and having narrow tucks sewed in above the embroidery, trims the bottom of the garment, back of the tucks in the front.

Nun's veiling, cashmere, challis, gingham, seersucker, chambray, and all seasonable wools, silks, and cottons make up well in this style. Braid, lace, stitched bands, fancy-edged ribbon, embroidery, etc., may serve as trimmings. Colored embroideries may decorate cottons, and velvet may decorate any material. To make the wrapper for a lady of medium size, requires 9 yards of material 22 inches wide, 6 1/2 yards of material 36 inches wide, or 5 3/4 yards of material 44 inches wide, each with 2 1/2 yards of insertion.

July 1888 *Delineator*

4. Bodices

Jerseys have become a staple article, and are brought out with new trimmings each season. At present those of wool are considered more stylish than the elaborate silk and beaded affairs. The newest shapes are shorter at the back than in front. Some are fitted with all the seams of a basque. In others the front darts are omitted, and a vest is inserted in short seams that shape the jersey to the figure. For morning and plain wear, dark jerseys have three lengthwise lines of Hercules braid 2 inches wide, passing over the shoulders and to the end in back and front, to represent box-plaits. A belt of this braid is added, with a buckle to fasten it. More dressy jerseys of poppy red or cardinal have a vest, and a border on the hips, collar, and sleeves made of rows of soutache set on end, with one edge turned in curves while the other is raveled out like fringe. For yachting and other summer pleasures are navy blue jerseys trimmed with white braid, and with lapels on which are embroidered anchors or stars. The only beaded jerseys shown have the beads set in clusters at intervals, or in lines or stripes. A velvet vest is inserted in silk jerseys, and bands of narrow velvet ribbon are placed lengthwise along the edge of the garment.

March 21, 1885 *Harper's Bazar*

Belted bodices are in great favor for summer dresses, especially wash dresses of cambric, gingham, sateen, chambray, batiste, and the most inexpensive prints. There are several ways of making these bodices, but those most easily ironed are plain in the shoulders, and merely gathered to a belt in the center of the front and back. The fronts are buttoned up close to the throat with small pearl buttons, round as a pea, but with eyes sunk in for sewing them on. The back is made all in one piece. It is stayed with a linen facing, which begins on the shoulders, follows the outline of the armhole, and is sewed in with the belt.

Others prefer to keep the bodice separate from the skirt. They extend the whole bodice a finger deep below the waist-line, for this part to pass under the dress skirt. The bodice is drawn into shape by a draw-string, or it is gathered outside to an underbelt.

More fanciful belted bodices are made with a cluster of gathers at the top of the front just below the collar, and also at the waist. The back is in fan shape, with fullness extended to the shoulders from the waist-line. These bodices should be made on a lining, as there are side pieces that require to be fitted smoothly.

The surplice bodice lapped to one side is the most dressy of the belted bodices. It is much used for thin lawns and batistes. The fronts are tucked or edged with lace. Instead of being cut out to fit the neck, the straight front is gathered to the back at the top, thus throwing a pretty fullness over the bust.

The yoke bodice is still used. It is tucked for plain muslins and lawns, and embroidered for dresses that are otherwise trimmed with embroidery. It is in nicer taste to have the yoke of the dress material than to have a colored dress with a white yoke.

Spencer bodices, or round bodices with a basque below the belt, are also worn. They are made of white Swiss muslin, with lengthwise insertions of embroidery or lace, a ribbon belt, and a ruffle of the trimming around the part below the belt. For variety the trimming may be set in to represent a Zouave jacket, or a vest of embroidery may be set in, or else the vest is outlined with a gathered ruffle of embroidery.

High, straight collars, and those turned over in points, are on many of these bodices. The square-cornered Byron collar turned over all around is still used.

 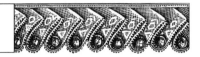

For plain gingham or sateen dresses, basques are made without lining, yet with all the darts and pieces used in richer materials. The seams must not be left raw, or uncovered. They should first be sewed as if the garment were being made wrong side out. Then the right sides should be turned together, and by another seam the edges are covered. These seams are necessary for neatness on thin, sheer materials, but are also comfortable on thicker cottons.

June 13, 1885 *Harper's Bazar*

Cloth postilion basques made double breasted and edged with braid in tailor fashion are used by many instead of a jersey, as an extra bodice to wear with various skirts. A dark blue or wine-colored basque, with an edge of silver or gilt braid, is worn with skirts of black silk or blue satin merveilleux, or with any of the new striped wools or silks. A very light tan postilion, with darker brown or gilt braid on the edges, is quite dressy and contrasts well with many colors. White cloth basques are also very stylish.

The right side of the front laps over to fasten on the left side at the top, about 2 inches down the shoulder seam. It then slopes away diagonally, reaching the center of the front at the waist-line, and below this forms two sharp points. The standing collar is from 1 1/2 to 2 inches high. It is made straight on the front edges, and touching. It is there fastened by a small clasp, or by two button-holes through which linked buttons are passed, or by a small brooch. Instead of fastening the front with the usual metal buttons, sometimes leaf-shaped clasps are used with a hook and eye under each leaf.

September 19, 1885 *Harper's Bazar*

A simple and new way of finishing the back pieces of bodices is to shape them in four scallops, one in each piece, and line them with satin. Below these are two larger scallops gathered at the top and sewed underneath the two center scallops of the four pieces. In other basques, especially those of velvet, only two scallops are seen, one on each of the center back pieces. The short side pieces are then separated about 2 inches from these and pointed below.

November 7, 1885 *Harper's Bazar*

Ladies' Basque

This basque is in six pieces: Front, back, side back, collar, and two sleeve pieces. In cutting out, place the narrow end of the collar on a crosswise fold of the material to avoid a center seam. Cut all of the other parts lengthwise. The quantity of material required is 4 yards if 22 inches wide, and 2 1/2 yards if 48 inches wide.

Supposing the bust measure to be 32 inches, use the scale marked 32. Or if the bust measure is 36 inches, take the scale marked 36, etc. Fasten this scale on the square by passing the screw through the scale and both parts of the square.

Draft the back piece first. Square the draft by drawing the first cross-line and the base-line, as shown by Figure 1. The upper-right corner of a draft is the starting point.

Measure all of the numbers on the base-line as given on the diagram. Always keep the angle of the square to your right. Measure down from the upper-right corner to 1 1/4 spaces, and make a dot; 2 1/2 and 6 1/4 the same. At 10 make an X to show it to be the place to commence measuring again. Move the square down and measure 5 more spaces from the X, or 15 from the starting point. At the end of the scale make an X again and move the square, measuring 2 1/4 more, or 22 1/4, then 28 and 28 1/4.

Now turn the scale without taking it off the square, from the long blade to the short blade of the square. Beginning at the base-line, measure out 2 1/4 on the first cross-line and mark. This is to get the width of the garment. Do not measure from 1 1/4 as it is to cut to. Place the square on the base-line point exactly on the measure. At 2 1/2 measure out 6 1/2 spaces, and draw a cross-line following the diagram. From the third point, 6 1/4 on the base-line, measure 6, drawing a line as before. Draw a line from 10 as before.

To get the length of the waist: Before measuring the width from the point at 15, take the tape measure and measure down from 1 1/4 along the base-line, the waist length of the person you are cutting for. If this distance is the same as that of the scale measure, which if scale 32 is used will be 16 inches, you make no change. But supposing the person's measure is more or less than the scale measure, change the point and measure from the point given by the tape measure. Say the person's waist length is 15 inches; measure 15 from 1 1/4. Measure from this point 1/2 and 2 3/4 spaces, drawing a cross-line to the base-line. If this line has been raised or lowered, raise or lower the lines at 22 1/4, 28, and 28 1/4 the same distance; measure and draw a line as before. These are all of the measures.

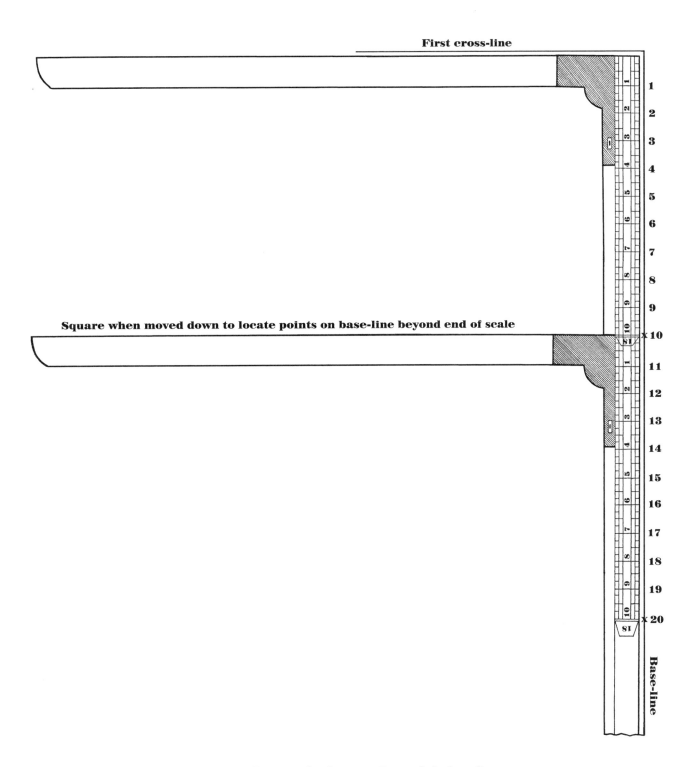

Figure 1. Drawing the first cross-line and the base-line

For the shoulder, draw a diagonal line to connect 2 1/4 on the first cross-line to 6 1/2 on the second cross-line. For the neck, take the scroll and connect the first point on the first cross-line and the first point on the base-line, following the diagram. Draw the curve for the back part of the armhole. (See Figure 2.) Draw a curve from the armhole to the next line, then down to the waist-line. Draw curves on all of the other points as shown by the diagram.

The arrows on the diagrams show which way to turn the scroll, which is always with the largest part in the direction in which the arrow points. The arrows are not given on all diagrams, as one diagram mastered is the key to all others. In many cases a slight variation of the exact location of the scroll does not impair the results of the work.

Next draft the side back on the same general plan. If the waist-line on the back has been raised or lowered, raise or lower the waist-line on the side back to correspond.

Draft the front next. If the waist-line has been raised or lowered on the back, raise or lower it the same distance on the front. Raise or lower the top dart line, at 11 3/4, half of the distance. All lines below the waist-line should be changed the same distance as the waist-line. Never change any lines above the dart line. Draw all straight and curved lines except for the under-arm dart lines. Figure 3 shows how to draw the curves.

To test the size of the waist: Before drawing the under-arm darts, measure off 1 1/2 spaces on the front for the hem, and 1 1/4 spaces on the side back for the same purpose. For seams, measure off 1/2 space on each side of the back, the side back next to the back, and on each side of the under-arm darts.

Then measure the pattern across at the waist-line, omitting seams already marked off and darts. If the pattern measures the exact size of the waist measure of the person to be fitted, between the seams and hems, the size is correct. If it is not, change the under-arm dart to the correct size, changing a quarter of the amount on each side of the under-arm dart. If the change to be made is greater than 3 inches, change part of it equally at 15 1/2 on the

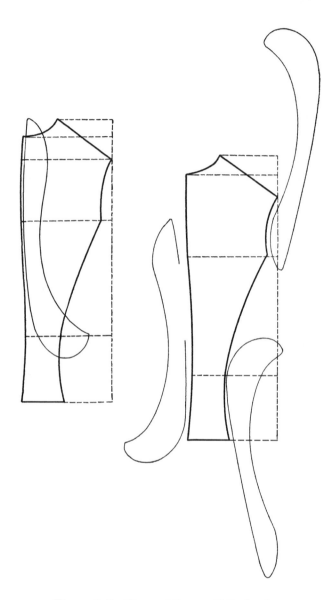

Figure 2. Positions of the scroll for backs

front and on the side back. Because the material is cut double, this will give the correct size. Now draw the dart and seam lines.

For the upper sleeve piece, measure from the upper-right corner down to 2, and make a dot. Measure 4 spaces with the scale, then at 10 make an X and move the square down to the X. The next number on the base-line is 11. This is obtained by measuring 1 from 10. The next number is 17 1/2; get this by measuring 7 1/2 from 10. The next is

58

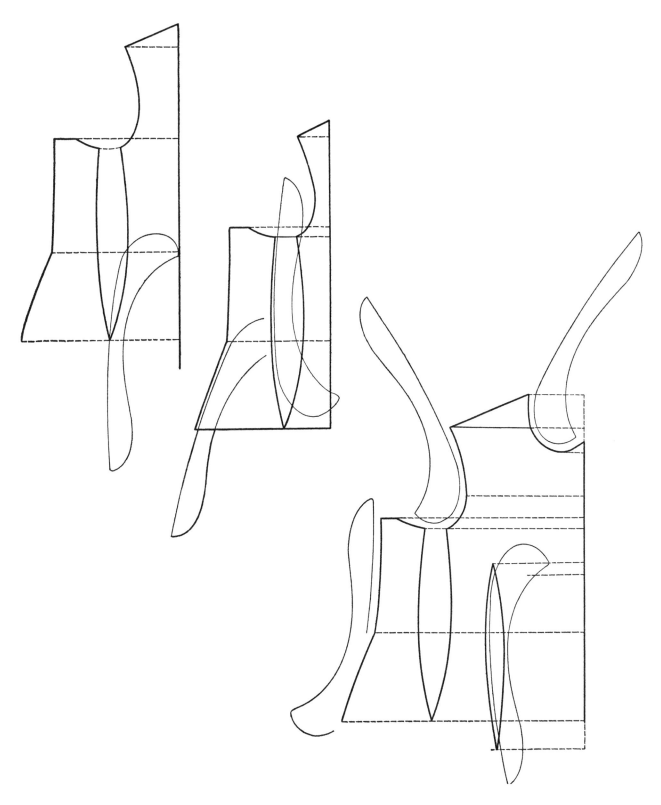

Figure 3. Positions of the scroll for fronts

19 1/2, obtained by measuring 9 1/2 from 10. These are all of the numbers on the base-line.

Draw the cross-lines, to get the width of the sleeve, by measuring from the base-line to 4 on the first cross-line. Next come to the point made at 2; place the square exactly on the base-line. Measure 1 1/4 and dot, then 8 and dot, drawing a cross-line to the base-line, connecting the points 8, 1 1/4, and 2. Omit drawing a line at 4 as that is to cut to. From 11 and 19 1/2 draw a line the same as at 2 using the numbers as shown on those lines; then draw a diagonal line from 17 1/2 to 4. Draft the under sleeve in the same way. Draw the curves with the scroll as shown by Figure 4.

To test the length of the sleeve: Use the person's measure from the center of the back to the wrist. Deduct the width of the back piece minus 1 inch for seams; then you will have the exact length of the sleeve. Measure from the top of the upper sleeve to the point marked 19 1/2 on the base-line. Make this point correspond to the tape measure, by raising or lowering it. Raise or lower the point marked 17 1/2 the same distance. If these points are changed, raise or lower the elbow line. Alter the under sleeve in the same way.

Cut your pattern exactly on the lines drawn. All seams are allowed. They are of different sizes and are usually marked. Seams are usually 1/2 space on dresses, except for the shoulder seam, which is 1 1/4 spaces. The extra width for shoulder seams and under-arm parts is allowed so that if the garment is to be made over after wearing, there will be plenty of material to work on. The seams may be made smaller if desired before cutting, which makes no difference to the fit of the garment. Use small seams for sleeves.

1885 *National Garment Cutter*

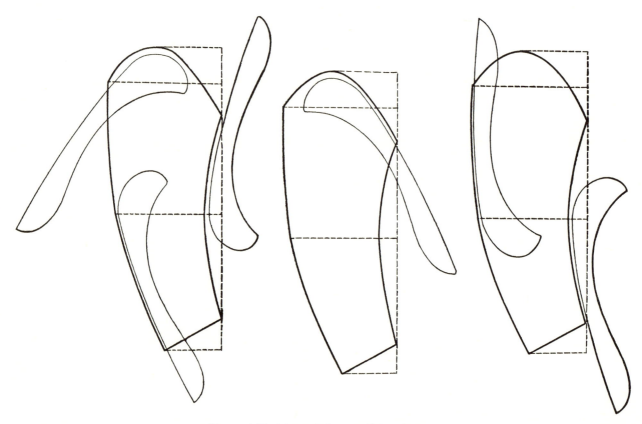

Figure 4. Positions of the scroll for sleeves

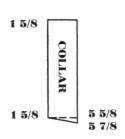

1 5/8

COLLAR

1 5/8

5 5/8
5 7/8

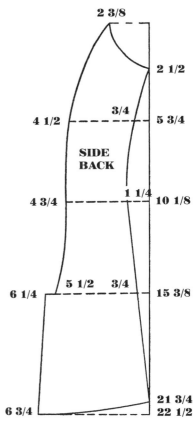

2 3/8

2 1/2

4 1/2   **3/4**   **5 3/4**

SIDE BACK

4 3/4   **1 1/4**   **10 1/8**

6 1/4   **5 1/2**   **3/4**   **15 3/8**

21 3/4
6 3/4   **22 1/2**

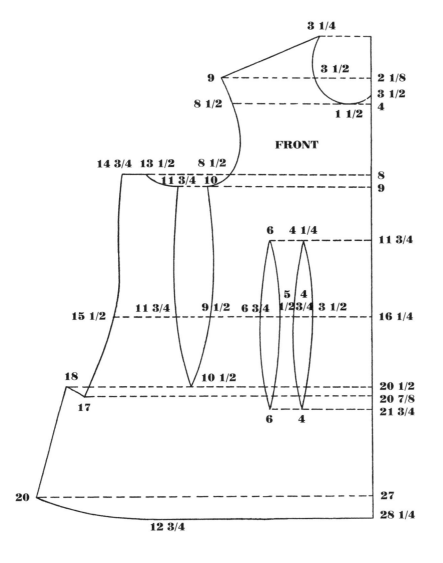

3 1/4

3 1/2

9   **2 1/8**
3 1/2
8 1/2   **4**
1 1/2

FRONT

14 3/4 13 1/2   8 1/2   **8**
11 3/4 10   **9**

6   4 1/4   **11 3/4**

5   4
11 3/4   9 1/2   6 3/4   1/23/4 3 1/2   **16 1/4**
15 1/2

18   10 1/2   **20 1/2**
20 7/8
17   **21 3/4**
6   4

20   **27**
28 1/4
12 3/4

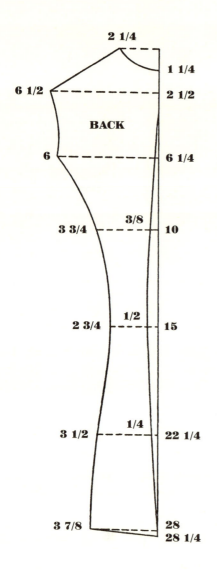

2 1/4

1 1/4

6 1/2   2 1/2

BACK

6   6 1/4

3 3/4   3/8   10

2 3/4   1/2   15

3 1/2   1/4   22 1/4

3 7/8   28
28 1/4

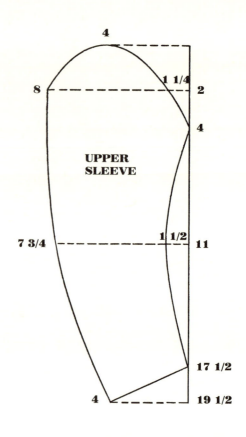

4

1 1/4
8   2

4

UPPER SLEEVE

7 3/4   1 1/2   11

17 1/2
4   19 1/2

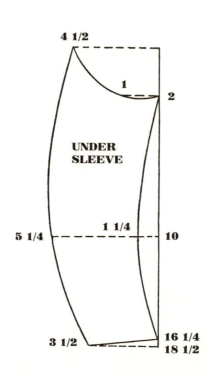

4 1/2

1   2

UNDER SLEEVE

5 1/4   1 1/4   10

16 1/4
3 1/2   18 1/2

62

Ladies' Basque. This example is made up in plain dress material and trimmed with braid. The fronts close with button-holes and buttons, the right side being hemmed and the left underfaced. The lower edge is given a nearly uniform outline all the way around, the depth being increased toward the back just enough to produce a symmetrical effect. Single bust and under-arm darts, side backs, and a center back seam perform the fitting. The center back and side-back seams end a little below the waist-line at the top of extra widths, which are underfolded to form two double box-plaits on the outside. These plaits give a graceful spring over the tournure, which accords well with any style of drapery and does not interfere with the application of trimming. In this instance, the outline is reproduced by a band of wide braid placed just above the margin. Each coat sleeve is encircled by a band of braid at the wrist. The high standing collar is overlaid with braid.

This is an attractive mode for the bodice of a tailor costume, and is much liked for cloths, flannels, and such suit materials as are made up for street wear. Machine-stitching, invisibly applied underfacings, etc., may form the finish. Braid having tinsel interwoven in it is a fashionable trimming for all kinds of plain dress materials, and is attainable in all colors and various widths. To make the garment for a lady of medium size, requires 4 yards of material 22 inches wide, or 1 7/8 yards of material 48 inches wide.

May 1885 *Delineator*

Ladies' Coat. A coat in this style is a jaunty completion for a tailor costume of any material. This example was developed in cloth, with zephyr and soutache braids for trimmings. The coat is fitted by curved closing edges, a bust dart and an underarm dart in each side of the front, and a curved seam at the center of the back. The center back seam is discontinued a little below the waist-line. Below it is allowed extra width, which is folded in a double box-plait on the outside.

A braid passementerie ornament, somewhat resembling a four-leaf clover, is placed over the top of the plait. From beneath the underfold on each side extend three double strips of braid, which are folded to form points where they are turned at their outer extremities. They are enclosed by lines of soutache coiled in a tiny loop at each corner.

Buttons and button-holes close the front. On each side, between every two buttons and button-holes, a strip of wide braid, turned as on the back

and enclosed by lines of soutache, is arranged. These braid decorations graduate shorter in length toward the waist-line, and their inner ends terminate beneath the closing edges. A curved pocket opening is made in each side of the front, and its position is outlined by a strip of soutache.

The sleeves are in coat shape. At their wrists braid of the two widths is arranged in the manner already described, except that its disposal is perpendicular instead of horizontal. The edges of the high standing collar are outlined by a line of soutache.

Cloth in neutral shades is made up into coats of this style to wear as independent garments with costumes of any kind. To make the coat for a lady of medium size, requires 4 1/4 yards of material 22 inches wide, 2 1/8 yards of material 48 inches wide, or 1 3/4 yards of material 54 inches wide. Braid is the decoration usually chosen when plain underfacings or machine-stitching is not preferred. Braid having tinsel interwoven with wool may be obtained in all of the leading cloth shades, with the tinsel in either gold or silver. The width varies from 1/4 inch to 2 or 3 inches; for coats the narrow widths are oftenest chosen.

May 1885 *Delineator*

Double-Breasted Coat. Fancy cloth was chosen for this example, with buttons and machine-stitching for finishings. The fronts lap in regular double-breasted fashion and close with button-holes and buttons, a row of buttons being also added to the overlapping side. There is a single bust dart and an under-arm dart in each side of the front. Each side has a curved pocket opening. Its edges are stitched, and its ends are stayed with crows' feet done with silk twist.

At the back are side backs and a center back seam, all of which end a little below the waist-line. Extra width allowed below the center back seam is underfolded in a box-plait. On the adjoining skirt edges of the back and side-back pieces are cut extensions, which, after having their corresponding edges seamed, are arranged in a side-plait turning backward underneath on each side, their arrangement perfecting the appearance of two box-plaits on the outside. The ends of the center back and side-back seams are stayed with crows' feet done with silk twist.

The coat is of ample length. Its lower edge is finished with double lines of machine-stitching. The sleeves are in coat shape, and an easy fullness is allowed over the top of the arm in sewing them in. Each has double lines of stitching made far enough from the wrist to outline a round cuff. On the upper side, in front of the outside seam, two buttons are placed. Double lines of stitching finish the high, rolling collar.

Plain and brocaded velvets, bengaline, Astrakhan, corduroy, and all kinds of plain and fancy coatings are made up in this way. Fur, feathers, braid, etc., may be added for trimming. For a lady of medium size, this coat requires 4 3/4 yards of material 22 inches wide, 2 1/4 yards of material 48 inches wide, or 2 1/8 yards of material 54 inches wide.

October 1885 *Delineator*

Double-Breasted Coat. Short, double-breasted cloth coats are fashionable as completions to tailor costumes of the same material, and also as independent garments to wear with suits of any material. This example is made in fancy cloth of a deep seal brown shade, the buttons and braid forming the finish. The fronts lap broadly at their upper parts and curve in toward the waist-line, the double-breasted part being joined to each side by a seam curved to assist in the adjustment. A single bust dart and an under-arm dart in each side of the front, side backs, and a curved center back seam perfect the fit. The three back seams end a little below the waist-line. Below the center back seam is allowed extra width, which is underfolded in a double box-plait. Below the side-back seams, shaped extensions are cut on the back edges of the side backs and lapped over the backs; the joins of the corresponding parts being continued flatly beneath the overlapping edges.

These edges, as well as the lower and front edges of the coat, are bound with braid, the braid being continued along the top of the overlapping part of the front. The closing is made with button-holes and buttons, a row of buttons being placed on the overlapping side in a duplicate of the closing outline. A button is also placed on the point of each overlapping side-back edge. A triangle worked with silk twist strengthens and ornaments the end of the center back seam. A strap of the material sewed beneath the side-back seams, halfway between the waist-line and the lower edges, holds the plaits in their folds. About the neck is a high, standing collar, which is bound with braid.

The sleeves are in coat shape, and fitted to slip easily over the dress sleeve and yet sit fashionably close to the arm. Each has a band of braid stitched double far enough from the wrist to outline a round cuff. The collar and wrists are often trimmed with fur or bands of Astrakhan. If the wearer is not inclined to stoutness, the overlap is bordered with fur, faced with or cut from Astrakhan cloth, the less expensive Astrakhan braid, or other decorative material. Marabou feather trimming is fashionable and effective.

To make the coat for a lady of medium size, requires 4 1/4 yards of material 22 inches wide, 2 yards of material 48 inches wide, or 1 3/4 yards of material 54 inches wide.

November 1885 *Delineator*

Dressing Sack. This easy-fitting garment is illustrated in striped flannel, with velvet for decoration. The fronts are hemmed, lapped in double-breasted fashion, and closed with button-holes and fancy buttons; a row of buttons being added to the overlapping side to perfect the double-breasted effect. Below the closing, each side is cut away diagonally to the lower edge, and back of the diagonal parts the outline is about uniform. There is a single bust dart in each side of the front. At the back is a curved center seam, while between the front and back are side pieces. The center back seam terminates some distance from the lower edge, and below it is allowed sufficient extra width for a double box-plait; the plait being formed underneath. Two bands of velvet ribbon border the lower edge and extend along the diagonal edges to the end of the closing. A bow of satin ribbon is fastened at the top of the double box-plait at the back, and two bands of velvet ribbon encircle each coat sleeve at the wrist. The high rolling collar is faced with velvet matching the brighter stripe in the flannel. The ribbon is the same shade as the collar facing.

All kinds of fancy and plain flannels, including the eider-down varieties, are made up in sacks of this style, and cashmere and surah are also liked. When a dressing sack is intended to make its appearance in the breakfast room and perhaps at the informal lunch table, it may be made as fanciful as desired; but when limited to the dressing room it is generally simply completed. To make this garment for a lady of medium size, requires 4 3/8 yards of material 22 inches wide, 2 3/4 yards of material 36 inches wide, or 1 7/8 yards of material 48 inches wide. Also required is 1/8 yard of velvet 20 inches wide for the collar.

October 1885 *Delineator*

Ladies' Basque

This pattern is laid off by the bust measure. It is in six pieces: Front, back, side back, side piece, sleeve, and collar. Allowance is made for seams and hems. If you desire to make the second bust dart higher than the first, draw a cross-line from 11 to 6 1/4 on the front.

For material 22 inches wide, 3 5/8 yards is required; for material 48 inches wide, 1 5/8 yards. Cut the collar with either end on a lengthwise fold of the material to avoid a center seam. Cut the back, side back, and side piece with the waist-line on a crosswise thread of the material. Cut the other parts lengthwise.

After closing the back seam as far down as the extra width, arrange that of the right half over that of the left, basting the top invisibly to the proper position. Close the sleeve seams. Place the inside seam at the front of the armhole, holding the sleeve toward you while sewing it in, and fasten the extra fullness under the arm in a forward-turning plait. The edges may be bound, underfaced, or finished in any preferred manner.

1885 National Garment Cutter

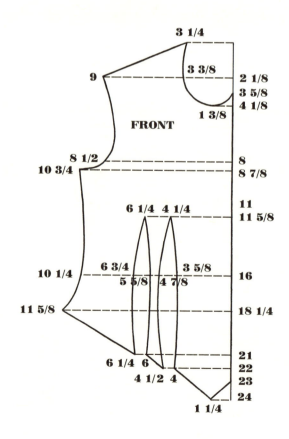

 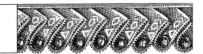

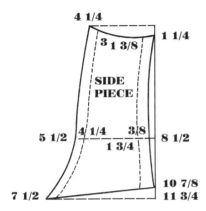

4 1/4

3 1 3/8

1 1/4

SIDE PIECE

5 1/2 **4 1/4** **3/8** **8 1/2**

1 3/4

7 1/2 **10 7/8**

11 3/4

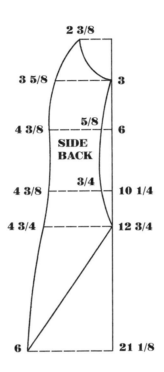

2 3/8

3 5/8 **3**

5/8

4 3/8 **6**

SIDE BACK

3/4

4 3/8 **10 1/4**

4 3/4 **12 3/4**

6 **21 1/8**

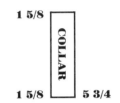

1 5/8

COLLAR

1 5/8 **5 3/4**

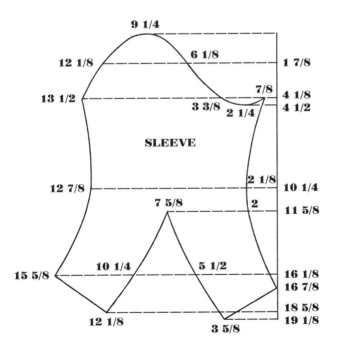

9 1/4

12 1/8 **6 1/8** **1 7/8**

7/8 **4 1/8**

13 1/2 **3 3/8** **2 1/4** **4 1/2**

SLEEVE

2 1/8 **10 1/4**

12 7/8 **7 5/8** **2** **11 5/8**

15 5/8 **10 1/4** **5 1/2** **16 1/8**
16 7/8
18 5/8
12 1/8 **3 5/8** **19 1/8**

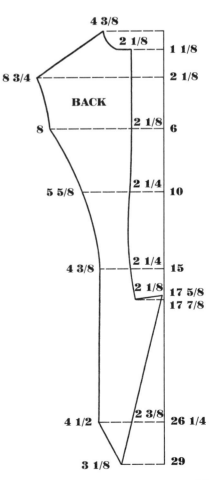

4 3/8

2 1/8 **1 1/8**

8 3/4 **2 1/8**

BACK

8 **2 1/8** **6**

5 5/8 **2 1/4** **10**

4 3/8 **2 1/4** **15**

2 1/8 **17 5/8**
17 7/8

4 1/2 **2 3/8** **26 1/4**

3 1/8 **29**

Ladies' Basque. This basque is adapted to all kinds of dress materials, plain suiting being represented, with embroidery for trimming. The garment is of medium length. It closes with button-holes and buttons from the neck to a little below the waist-line, the right side being hemmed and the left underfaced. Below the closing, each side is cut away with a slight flare to the lower edge. There are two bust darts in each side of the front. At the back are side backs and a center seam, while between the front and back are side pieces. The side-back seams terminate a little below the waist-line, and below the end of each extra width is allowed. This is arranged in a box-plait on the outside, the top of the plait be-ing turned under at the corners to shape to a point. The center back seam extends but a little lower down, and below it a V-shaped space is formed by the slanted edges of the center parts. Embroidery, turned upward flatly, borders all of the lower edges, and extends along the flared edges of the front and back. The sleeves are in coat shape and fit the arms closely. Each is ornamented at the wrist with two bands of embroidery, both turning upward, and the lower slightly overlapping the upper. A frill of embroidery is turned down over the high standing collar. To make the basque for a lady of medium size, requires 4 3/4 yards of material 22 inches wide, or 1 1/2 yards of material 48 inches wide.

July 1884 *Delineator*

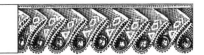

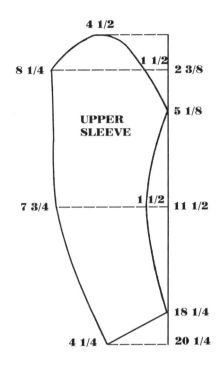

Spencer Bodice

This garment is laid off by the bust measure. There are five pattern pieces: Front, back, two sleeve pieces, and collar. If the shape of the sleeve pattern is not that desired, any other given for ladies' bodices and polonaises may be selected. The sixth piece, the belt, is but a straight piece of the material of sufficient length and 2 3/8 spaces wide.

The bodice requires 2 1/2 yards of material 22 inches wide, or 1 5/8 yards of material 36 inches wide. Cut the back with its back edge, and the collar with the end at the top of the diagram, lengthwise of the material.

Gather the back and each front across the lower edge, the back between the notches marked 3 1/2 on its lowermost line, and the front between the notches marked 3 and 7 1/2 on its lowermost line. Gather both again 2 3/8 spaces above the lower edge and immediately above the other gathers. Close the main seams and attach the belt. Close the seam of each sleeve and turn up the lower end for a cuff. Add button-holes and buttons to the front.

1885 *National Garment Cutter*

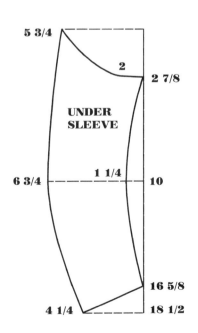

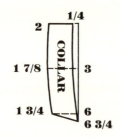

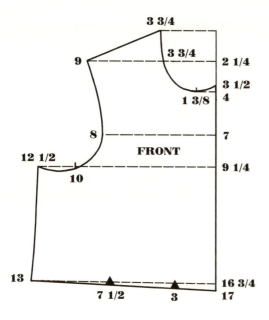

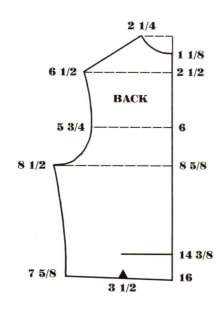

Spencer Bodice. Round bodices are fashionable for house wear. This example is developed in dress material of a plain texture, and has seams on the shoulders and on the sides. The back is cut on a fold of the material. The fronts are closed with buttons and button-holes, the right side being hemmed and the left underfaced. In each side of the front beyond the closing, and also at the center of the back, a short shirring is made in the lower edge, and corresponding lines a little above. A belt is applied, with its top just covering the upper lines of shirring, and the lower edge is finished with an underfacing. A couple of hooks and eyes close the belt. The coat sleeves are finished at the wrists with lace turned back flatly in cuff fashion. There is a high, close collar about the neck, and inside it is fastened a lace frill that falls over and conceals the collar.

All kinds of soft wool materials are made up in this way, the bodice usually matching the skirt. Cuffs and a collar in a high contrasting color are in good taste for house wear and go far toward adapting a neutral or unbecoming color to the wearer. For a lady of medium size, this bodice requires 2 5/8 yards of material 22 inches wide, 1 1/2 yards of material 36 inches wide, or 1 1/8 yards of material 48 inches wide.

September 1884 *Delineator*

Plain Basque

This basque has six pieces: Front, side back, back, collar, and two sleeve pieces. Select the scale that corresponds to the bust measure. Draft the back of the basque first. Find the first number on the base-line, which is 1. Measure 1 with the scale and make a dot. Measure the next point, which is 2 1/2, and dot next 6, then 7 1/2. At the end of the scale make an X even with the figure 10 on the scale. Move the square until the end is just at the X. The next number is 14 3/4, or 4 3/4 spaces from the X measure. Then measure 19 3/4, which is 9 3/4 from the X. Now make another X, move the square as before, and measure 20 3/4, or 1 more.

Now draw the cross-lines, as follows. Measure 2 on the first cross-line, and pass over the next point. At the one below it, place the end of the square exactly at the point, keeping the long arm of the square exactly on the base-line, so the lines will be drawn square across. Measure out 6 1/4 spaces, and draw a line to the base-line. Draw a line 6 spaces long at the next point. On the diagram of the back, you will see two figures on the next line, one at 1/4 and one at 5. Make a dot at each measure and draw a line as before. Skip the X and go to the next point below, then measure 1/2 and 2 3/4, drawing a line; at 19 3/4 draw a line 4 spaces long.

Now proceed to draw the outlines. For the center back, connect 2 1/2 on the base-line with 1/4 (across from 7 1/2). Continue this line on down to 1/2 at the waist. These lines may be curved if desired. Then go to the shoulder and connect 2 on the first cross-line with 6 1/4 on the line below. This line also may be straight or curved as desired. Move to the neck-line and connect 1 on the base-line with 2 on the first cross-line, using the scroll. Draw the back of the armhole with the scroll from 6 1/4 to 6. Draw the line from the bottom of the armhole to the waist, by using the scroll to connect the three points 6, 5, and 2 3/4. The line from the waist to the bottom is drawn from 2 3/4 to 4. The bottom of the basque is drawn from 4 to 20 3/4. Finally, draw the curve in the center of the back below the waist from 1/2 (across from 14 3/4) to 20 3/4.

Draft the side back next, then the front, using the same scale and the same general plan as for the back. If the waist has been raised or lowered on the back, raise or lower the waist on the side back and the front to correspond. Draft the sleeves using the same scale as for the rest of the garment.

Spring and Summer 1886 *Voice of Fashion*

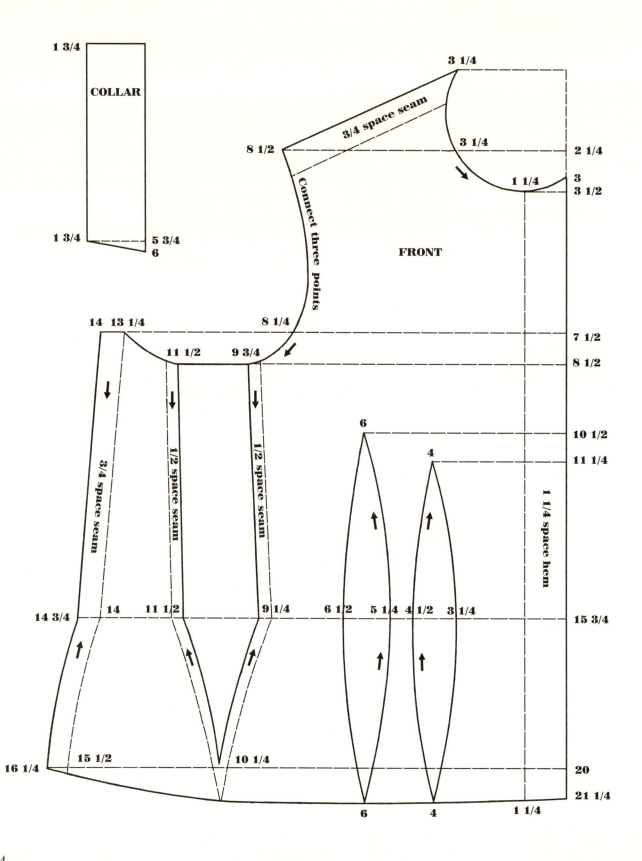

COLLAR

FRONT

1 3/4

1 3/4

5 3/4
6

3 1/4

3/4 space seam

8 1/2

Connect three points

3 1/4

2 1/4

1 1/4

3
3 1/2

14   13 1/4

8 1/4

11 1/2

9 3/4

7 1/2

8 1/2

6

4

10 1/2

11 1/4

3/4 space seam

1/2 space seam

1/2 space seam

1 1/4 space hem

14 3/4   14

11 1/2

9 1/4

6 1/2   5 1/4   4 1/2   3 1/4

15 3/4

16 1/4

15 1/2

10 1/4

20

6

4

1 1/4

21 1/4

74

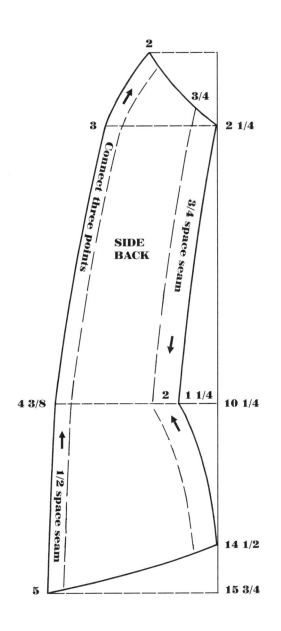

SIDE BACK

2

3/4

3 — 2 1/4

Connect three points

3/4 space seam

4 3/8 — 2 — 1 1/4 — 10 1/4

1/2 space seam

— 14 1/2

5 — 15 3/4

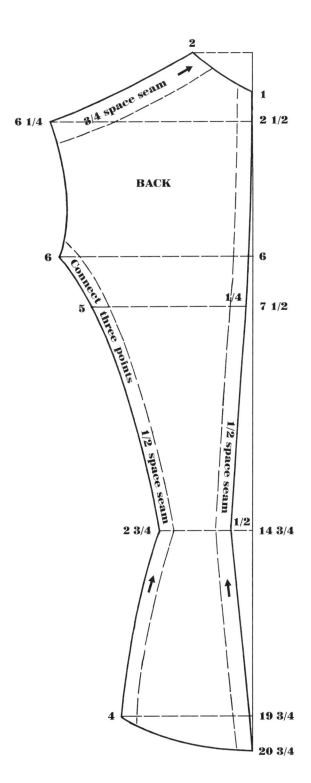

BACK

2

1

3/4 space seam

6 1/4 — 2 1/2

6 — 6

1/4

5 — 7 1/2

Connect three points

1/2 space seam

1/2 space seam

2 3/4 — 1/2 — 14 3/4

4 — 19 3/4

20 3/4

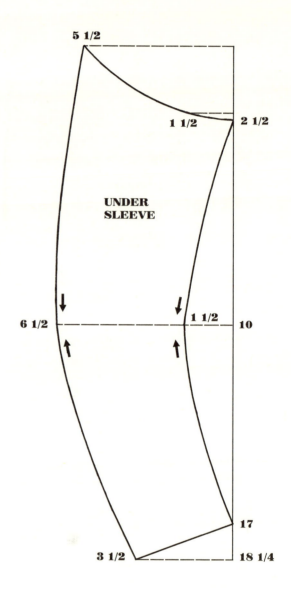

UNDER SLEEVE

5 1/2

1 1/2   2 1/2

6 1/2   1 1/2   10

17

3 1/2   18 1/4

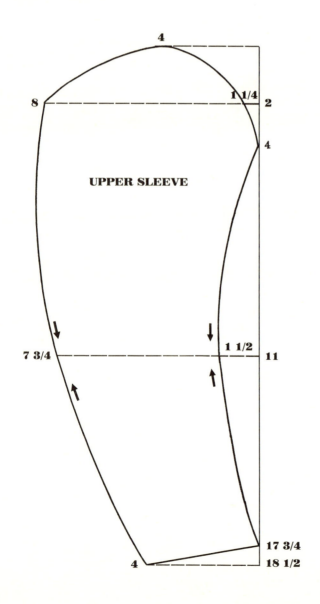

UPPER SLEEVE

4

8   1 1/4   2

4

7 3/4   1 1/2   11

17 3/4

4   18 1/2

 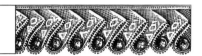

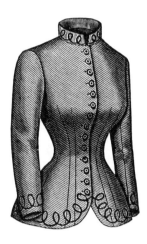 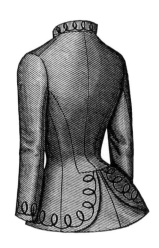

Ladies' Basque. Plain dress material was selected for this example, and soutache braid was chosen as trimming. The fronts close with button-holes and buttons, the right side being hemmed and the left underfaced. Below the closing, both sides are rounded off toward the hips. Double bust darts, under-arm darts, side backs, and a curved center back seam perform the adjustment. The side-back seams end a little below the waist-line. Below their terminations, extensions are allowed on both the backs and the side backs. Those on the backs extend beneath the side backs and are sewed into the under-arm seams. Those on the side backs are rounded upward from their lower edges and lapped on the backs, their tops being invisibly sewed in place.

Soutache braid is arranged in a scroll design on the lower edges of the fronts and about the side-back edges. The coat sleeves are similarly trimmed at the wrists. There is a high standing collar about the neck, which also displays the soutache trimming in reduced size.

When the basque forms a part of a costume in which two or three materials are united, the collar is usually of contrasting material and the sleeves have cuff-facings to match, a vest-facing being often applied on the front. Such basques are very stylish completions to house and street toilettes, and are adapted to any material in vogue. A very pretty basque of this style for house wear is of embroidered velvet, with full jabots of lace on the front. The sleeves are slightly shortened and trimmed with lace.

To make the basque for a lady of medium size, requires 3 1/4 yards of material 22 inches wide, or 1 1/2 yards of material 48 inches wide.

December 1884 *Delineator*

Ladies' Costume. Cloth was chosen for this example, and braid and Astrakhan form the trimming. The skirt is composed of three gores and a back breadth. The gores are fitted smoothly by darts, and the fullness is drawn into the proper space by gathers. Tapes are fastened beneath the side-back seams and tied together, to regulate its closeness to the figure. A broad band of Astrakhan trims the lower part. Surmounting this trimming is braid applied in a simple but fanciful design.

The drapery is permanently adjusted on the skirt. It comprises a full breadth for the back and an oval tablier for the front. The tablier is conformed to the shape of the gores at the top by darts. It is raised on each side by four upward-turning, overlapping plaits folded just below the hip. After these plaits are laid, the side edges are inserted in the side-back seams of the skirt, and the back drapery is arranged.

The latter is gathered three times across the top, there being only about 1/4 inch between the lines of stitches. All of its edges are turned under for hems wide enough to form a handsome finish. No plaits or other means of draping are made in the back drapery. Its side edges are basted over the side-back seams, and both draperies are sewed with the skirt to the belt, the placket opening being finished on the left side. No decoration is added to the drapery.

The basque is quite as well adapted to street as to house wear. It is of medium length and rounded in outline. Its fit is produced by double bust darts, side pieces, side backs, and a center back seam. The three back seams spring out below the waist-line. The front is closed invisibly, the right side being hemmed and the left underfaced. A band of Astrakhan conceals the high standing collar, and passes

down each side of the front and about the bottom of the basque. Below the trimming on the neck, back of it on the front and above it on the lower edge, braid is arranged to accord with that on the skirt. The sleeves fit the arms well, with a high but not exaggerated curve across the shoulder, and are completed with cuff-facings of Astrakhan surmounted by a decoration of braid.

All kinds of cloths and cloth-finished suitings, as well as velvets, silks, etc., are made up in this way, with decorations in keeping with the material. The skirt may be trimmed to any depth desired, or it may be finished with only a foot plaiting. Braid in graduated or uniform widths, applied in parallel lines, is effective and fashionable. Fur in standard and fancy varieties is also much in vogue on all winter materials. To make the suit for a lady of medium size, requires 11 3/4 yards of material 22 inches wide, or 5 5/8 yards of material 48 inches wide.

December 1884 *Delineator*

Misses' Basque

Use the scale that corresponds to the bust measure. This garment has six pieces: Right front, left front, side back, back, and two sleeve pieces. The collar is a straight band of the length and width desired. Instead of being cut diagonal as given, the basque may be drafted full double-breasted. Any style of diagonal or double-breasted basque may be drafted on this plan. Or else the basque may be cut straight by using the piece given for the left front, for both fronts.

Spring/Summer 1886 *Voice of Fashion*

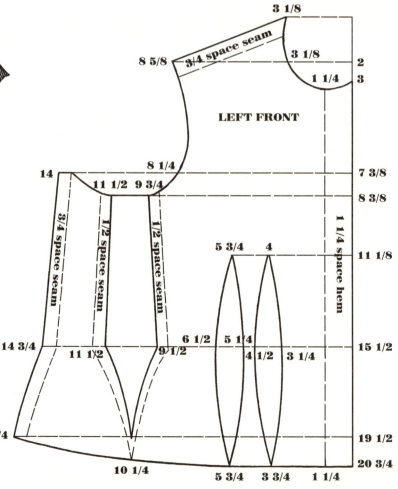

Misses' Basque

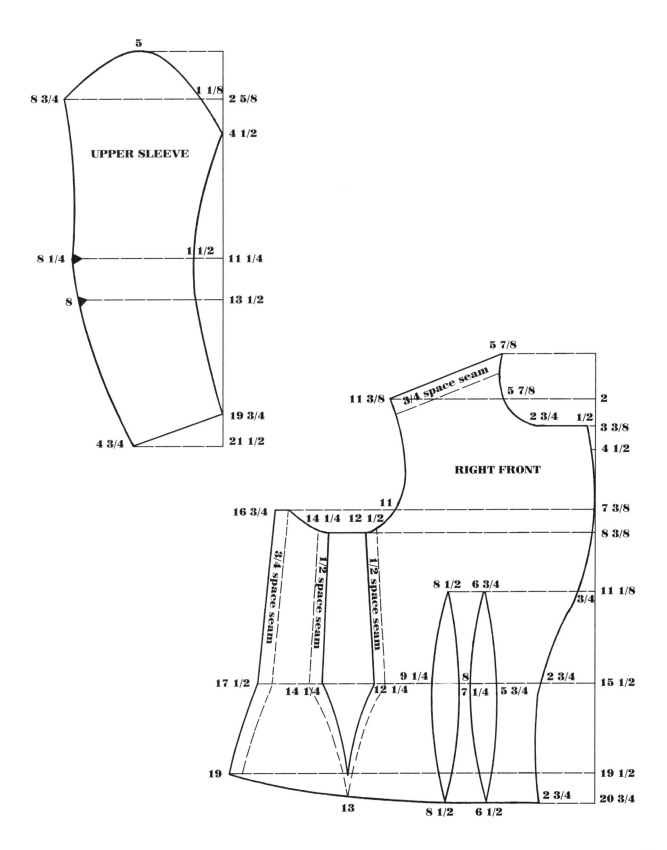

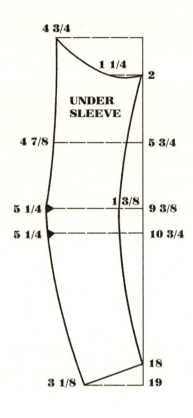

UNDER SLEEVE

4 3/4

1 1/4

2

4 7/8   5 3/4

5 1/4   1 3/8   9 3/8

5 1/4   10 3/4

18

3 1/8   19

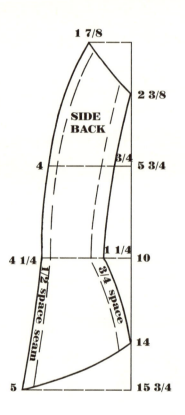

SIDE BACK

1 7/8

2 3/8

4   3/4   5 3/4

4 1/4   1 1/4   10

3/4 space

1/2 space seam

14

5   15 3/4

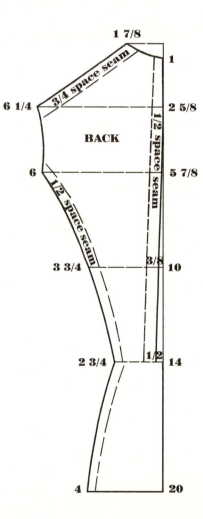

BACK

1 7/8   1

6 1/4   3/4 space seam   2 5/8

1/2 space seam

6   5 7/8

1/2 space seam

3 3/4   3/8   10

2 3/4   1/2   14

4   20

Ladies' Basque. Fancy dress material was selected for this basque, and facings of Astrakhan and metal clasps form the decorations. The fronts lap diagonally in double-breasted fashion, the overlap being faced with Astrakhan. The closing is made with the clasps assisted by hooks and eyes—the latter being, of course, invisible. Double bust darts, side pieces, side backs, and a curved center back seam are used for adjustment.

The depth below the waist-line is quite short. The center and side-back seams end a little below the waist-line. Below their terminations extra widths are allowed, which are underfolded to form two double box-plaits that spring out over the tournure. The suggestion of a postilion thus produced contrasts effectively with the high arch of the sides and the oval outline of the front.

The coat sleeves are faced at the wrists with Astrakhan. Astrakhan is also used for the high standing collar, one end of which is pointed and fastened over the other with a clasp, above the closing.

Velvet, plush, or any contrasting material may be used for facings instead of Astrakhan. Basques of this style are often made up of fancy material to wear with skirts of plain or fancy silk in the house, and of cloth to complete street toilettes. To make the garment for a lady of medium size, requires 3 3/8 yards of material 22 inches wide, or 1 5/8 yards of material 44 inches wide, with 5/8 yard of Astrakhan 27 inches wide.

December 1886 *Delineator*

Ladies' Basque. This style is particularly well adapted to wear with a close-fitting street wrap. While all of the spring necessary to adjustment over any style of drapery is allowed below the waist-line, there are no plaits or fullness that might interfere with the fit of the outer garment. Plain dress material was chosen for this example, and Astrakhan braid and a cord ornament form the trimming.

The fronts close with buttons and button-holes—the right side being hemmed—and are adjusted with double bust darts. The back is fitted by side backs and a center seam, and side pieces contribute to the good effect of both back and front. The lower outline of the front is rounded, and the sides are curved high over the hips, while the back is deepened with a suggestion of the postilion effect.

A band of wide Astrakhan braid borders the lower edge. A braid of the same width extends diagonally from each shoulder seam, over the bust, nearly to the closing. Between the ends of these bust ornaments, triple loops of cord are fastened between medallions. The high standing collar is overlaid with braid. A band of wide braid is applied about the wrist of each sleeve, simulating an ornamental cuff.

Astrakhan braid is made in all of the leading colors and in various widths. It has a rough surface somewhat similar to Astrakhan. However, any other kind of braid, wool lace, or any decoration preferred may take its place. This mode is adapted to all materials, from silks and velvets to serges. To make the basque for a lady of medium size, requires 2 3/4 yards of material 22 inches wide, or 1 1/4 yards of material 48 inches wide.

October 1885 *Delineator*

5. Skirts and Over-Skirts

The apron drapery that finds most favor for simple dresses is made to fall in two or three long straight folds down the left side, and to curve upward very high on the right side, where it joins the back drapery. Its beauty consists of the full long curves that begin on the right side in plaits sewed in with the belt, but disappearing as they fall into the folds on the left side. This leaves a large part of the lower skirt in view on the left side, which may be trimmed across with bands of galloon, or have a lengthwise fan made of bands of braid.

The back fullness is massed in two large plaits, or else it is bouffantly puffed at the top, and hangs straight below. Almost all back draperies now cover the foundation skirt from top to bottom. They are therefore closely sewed down the sides, no matter how much they may be trimmed there. It is, however, more stylish to trim the back fullness across the end only. When the lower skirt covers the foundation skirt all around, and it is not necessary to cover it with drapery, the favorite arrangement of the back of the over-skirt is to plait all the top and the right side of straight breadths into the belt, leaving a pointed drapery that is very full at the top, and which may be allowed to form a single burnous fold at the angle of the breadths.

May 9, 1885 *Harper's Bazar*

The foundation skirts of dresses must be narrow in order to be stylish. The mistake of amateur dressmakers is to make the back of the foundation skirt as wide as the outside, which gives a most ungraceful effect. The greatest width of short walking skirts is 2 1/4 yards. However, the draw-strings must not be too low down, or the back fullness will be tossed from side to side as the wearer walks.

July 18, 1885 *Harper's Bazar*

The narrow foot plaiting that is sewed on the foundation skirt supports the outside skirt and draperies, and makes the skirt look more graceful. It should be placed there even when it is not visible. To prevent the skirt being thrust forward at every step, make three slits upward in the bottom of the front gore of the foundation skirt. Each slit is 2 or 3 inches long, and the braid that binds the skirt extends up the slits also. Of course, these open spaces are hidden entirely by the outside skirt.

March 6, 1886 *Harper's Bazar*

To hold up weighty skirts, modistes sew a strip of silk, in which three lengthwise button-holes are worked, across the back of the basque, attaching it to the inside belt. Three buttons to meet these holes are placed on the belt of the dress skirt.

April 10, 1886 *Harper's Bazar*

Demi-trained dresses to wear in the drawing-room in the afternoon or evening, are made to lie 12 inches on the floor. They have four breadths in the small flowing train, which is entirely untrimmed. It is made bouffant by turning over the tops of the breadths in short pointed wings, or else letting them droop in burnous folds.

November 6, 1886 *Harper's Bazar*

Three breadths of silk are again used for the entire back of the skirt, drapery and lower skirt being thus combined. These breadths are cut 1/2 yard longer than the foundation skirt. They are set in many lapped plaits meeting in the center at the top, and are then turned over in two pointed ends on the tournure. The greatest latitude is allowed in arranging such draperies at the top. The burnous folds dropping down from the belt are still popular. The jabot back drapery, which was formerly made with two stiffly folded narrow jabots—one down each side—is now arranged in a single large jabot of very easy soft folds down the center of the back, dropping from the belt to the floor.

The most popular apron draperies are those plaited to the belt, and thus having their fullness falling in lengthwise folds rather than in the cross-wise wrinkles made by many plaits on each side. To illustrate this, take a breadth of cashmere. Letting one corner form the bottom, plait the top to the belt in six plaits (three on each side, meeting in the center). Then catch up slightly the center plait on each side to break up its stiffness. A hem or facing 3 or 4 inches wide edges the apron, and may be either machine-stitched or done in blind-stitches.

May 7, 1887 *Harper's Bazar*

In the furnishing stores, steels are put in the skirts of all wash dresses. However, ladies who superintend their own wardrobes make petticoats of striped dimity or coarse muslin, with bars of cords that will hold starch well, and arrange this stiff material in flounces across the back. This is worn as a short under-skirt, and when tied back gives the effect of a long bustle. A short bustle of steels or whalebones is sometimes added at the top. Over this is worn a cambric petticoat with an embroidered or tucked flounce, which is pretty enough to be seen through sheer lawn skirts.

When steels are used in wash dresses, the upper steel is placed so near the top that a pad can be dispensed with, as it is too warm for comfort. The upper casing is 5 or 6 inches below the belt. It is slit open by the placket hole, and the steel crosses the slit uncovered. Tapes are attached to the ends, and must be left untied until the wearer puts the skirt on, as otherwise there would not be enough room for her to pass it over her shoulders. The steels lower down are permanently tied when the dress is made.

August 6, 1887 *Harper's Bazar*

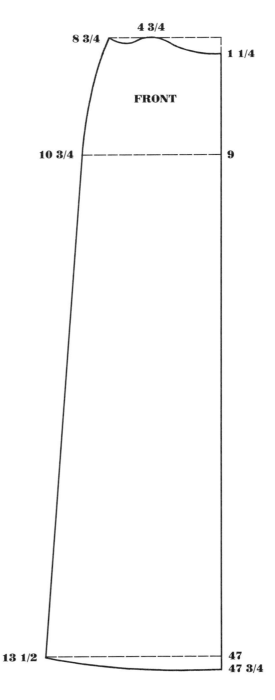

FRONT

8 3/4   4 3/4   1 1/4

10 3/4   9

13 1/2   47
47 3/4

Plain Skirt

This garment is in three pieces: Front, back, and side gore. It is laid off with the scale that corresponds to the waist measure in inches. The back widths are perfectly straight, and their length is regulated with the tape measure. The belt is simply a plain strip long enough to fasten around the waist, and the width to suit.

Cut the front gore and the back with the longest straight edge of each piece on a lengthwise fold of the material, to avoid center seams. Cut the side gores with the straight edge of each lengthwise on the material. Take up a plait in the center of the top of both the front and the side gores, equal to about a third of the width of each at its narrowest point. Fasten only the top of each plait. Join the pieces properly. Gather the back at the top to fit the belt.

1885 *National Garment Cutter*

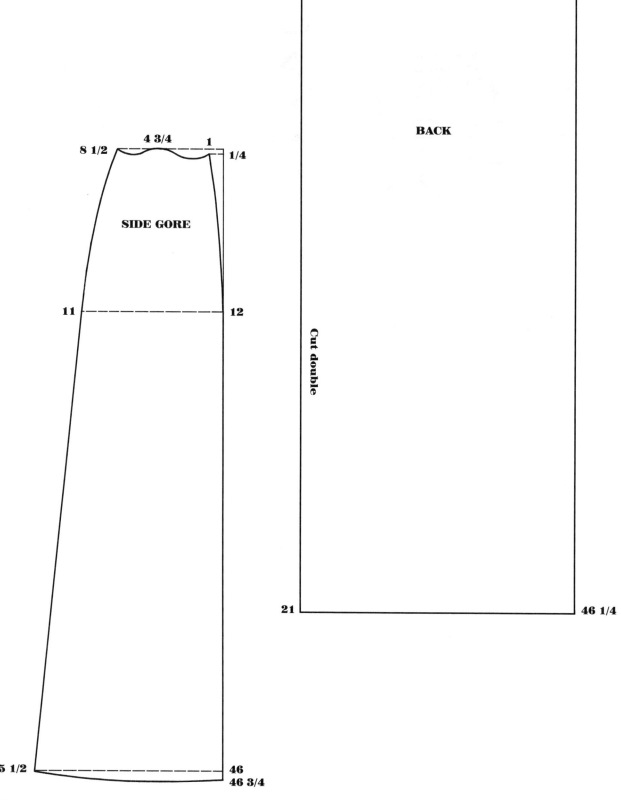

88

Four-Gored Skirt. A variety of materials and trimmings may be used for this skirt. In making it, three gores and a full breadth are united, the gores being fitted smoothly by darts, and the breadth gathered across the top on each side of the placket opening. The breadth is rounded across the top with sufficient curve to permit of the pad, improver, or short bustle being worn without interfering with the uniform roundness of the lower edge, which is an indispensable attribute of a perfectly hanging walking skirt. When this extra length is not required by the bustle, it may be deducted from the length of the skirt at the top without injury to the shape. Tapes, fastened beneath the side-back seams and tied together, regulate the closeness of the skirt to the figure.

The finish for the lower part of the skirt depends on the material and the fancy of the wearer. Cotton skirts may be finished with a hem. For wool and silk skirts, an underfacing and a braid binding are usually added, an interlining of crinoline being added when the material is light-weight. Trimming of any kind may be used.

To make the skirt for a lady of medium size, requires 4 1/2 yards of material 22 inches wide, 3 3/8 yards of material 36 inches wide, 2 3/8 yards of material 48 inches wide, or 2 1/4 yards of material 54 inches wide.

May 1886 *Delineator*

Ladies' Petticoat. Bleached muslin was chosen for this example, with Hamburg embroidery and tucks for trimming. The three gores composing the front and sides are cut the full length of the garment. At the top they are fitted by darts as smoothly as a dress skirt. The back breadth is only about two-thirds of the requisite length and is scantily gathered on each side of the placket opening. The remaining length necessary at the back is secured by an added part, which is really a short breadth much wider than the upper part, to which it is sewed after being gathered for some distance on each side of the center. This arrangement retains the fullness at the back, while giving the front and sides the close adjustment necessary to a fashionable disposal of the dress skirt. A flounce of medium-wide Hamburg embroidery trims the bottom of the petticoat, and above it is a cluster of fine tucks.

The upper edge is sewed to a belt. A little below the top of it, on each side of the placket opening, a stitching is made to form a casing, through which a tape is run. The inserted end is fastened securely in a line with the dart in the side gore. The free ends are tied together, to regulate the final adjustment of the petticoat.

Cambric, gingham, flannel, or plain or fancy skirting of any kind makes up well in this way. To make this garment for a lady of medium size, requires 5 yards of material 22 inches wide, or 3 7/8 yards of material 36 inches wide. White petticoats may be elaborated to any extent desired. If tucks are used for decoration, allowance for them must be made when cutting out the petticoat.

August 1884 *Delineator*

Trained Skirt

Trained Skirt. This skirt may be made with a full-length train as shown on the left, or a demi-length train as shown on the right. It is suitable for a bridal, reception, or full-dress toilette. Brocaded silk was chosen for this example, a light shade being shown by one view and a dark shade by the other.

Three gores for the front and sides, and a full breadth for the back, are united in the formation. The gores are fitted smoothly about the hips, while the back breadth is gathered on each side of the placket opening. The side gores are sprung out toward their back edges to merge into the oval train, which falls elegantly over a long or short bustle. A heavy silk cord trims the lower edge of the skirt, and beneath is set a lace-edged plaiting of Swiss. A belt finishes the top of the skirt. Beneath the side-back seams are sewed tapes, which are tied together to regulate the final adjustment.

Skirts of this style may have any becoming arrangement of trimming, but when they are made up of rich material a simple finish is in the best taste. If the front is of moiré or other material contrasting with the back, the same material is used for trimming, but not for making the entire bodice.

For a lady of medium size, the skirt with a full-length train requires 8 3/8 yards of material 22 inches wide, or 3 3/4 yards of material 48 inches wide. The demi-train length requires 7 1/4 yards of material 22 inches wide, or 3 1/4 yards of material 48 inches wide.

September 1886 *Delineator*

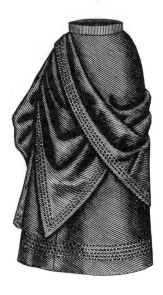 

Misses' Over-Skirt

This over-skirt has two pieces: Front drapery and back drapery. Draft it with the scale corresponding to the waist measure. Regulate the length with the tape measure. The seam allowance is 1/4 space.

In each front drapery, make two plaits turning backward according to the single notches in the top, and three turning upward according to the single notches in the back edge. Also make three downward-turning plaits in each side edge of the back drapery, according to the six notches nearest to the lowest one. Lap the left front drapery over the right so as to bring the corresponding double notches in their upper edges together. Arrange the draperies over their respective skirt parts and close the side-back seams, leaving the back drapery loose below the lowest notch. Gather the back drapery, and sew it onto the belt. Sew tapes underneath to the side-back seams to draw the fullness backward. Bands of velvet, satin, silk, or any contrasting material may border the drapery edges.

1885 *National Garment Cutter*

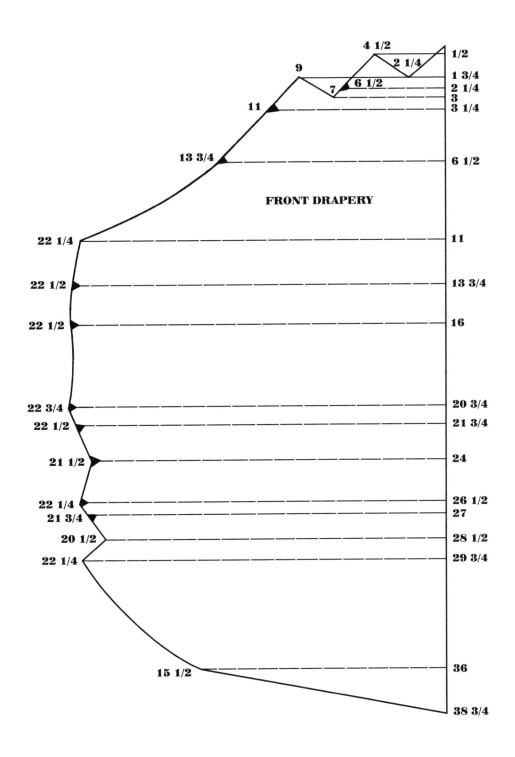

FRONT DRAPERY

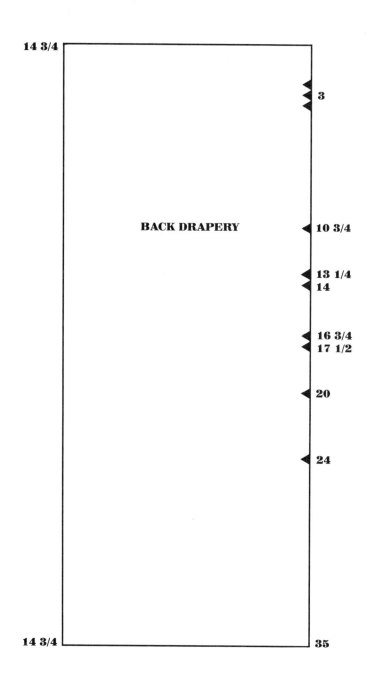

14 3/4

3

BACK DRAPERY

10 3/4

13 1/4
14

16 3/4
17 1/2

20

24

14 3/4   35

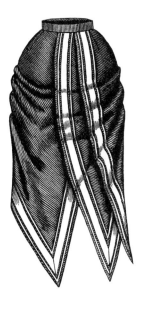
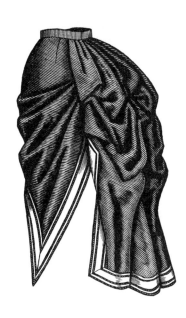

Ladies' Over-Skirt. This example is made up in cotton material with a cloth-like texture, and trimmed with braid. Three sections are united in the front. Of these, two are on the left side, the narrower being laid over the wider and each being separately fitted by three short darts. In the back edge of each section are folded four upward-turning plaits divided into two pairs. Owing to the arrangement of these plaits and the outline of the lower edges, the narrower part falls in a point back of the wider one. Darts also fit the top of the third section, and four plaits, divided into pairs, raise its back edge. Its front edge is overlapped by the adjoining edges of the two sections first described. The underlapping edge is sewed in with the seam of the first dart in the broader section, while the overlapping edge of the latter is likewise included in the seam of the first dart in the underlapping side. Although these seams are short, this arrangement holds the different parts securely in place. The back is a full breadth, with two pairs of downward-turning, overlapping plaits in each side. Its top is gathered to the proper size, the placket opening being made at the center.

A belt finishes the top of the over-skirt. A tape is fastened to one end. To this tape the center of the breadth is basted three times to uphold it in the bouffant position illustrated. All of the edges of the over-skirt are bordered by a band of wide braid between two narrower bands. Tapes or elastics are fastened beneath the side seams to hold the front closely to the figure, and retain the back within a fashionably narrow limit.

This is an especially graceful pattern for lawn, mull, piqué, and all kinds of cotton materials, as well as for nun's veiling, albatross cloth, and seasonable silks. For a lady of medium size, the over-skirt requires 6 5/8 yards of material 22 inches wide, 4 3/8 yards of material 36 inches wide, or 3 1/2 yards of material 48 inches wide. Lace, embroidery, fringe, or any stylish trimming may border the edges, or they may be finished plainly.

July 1884 *Delineator*

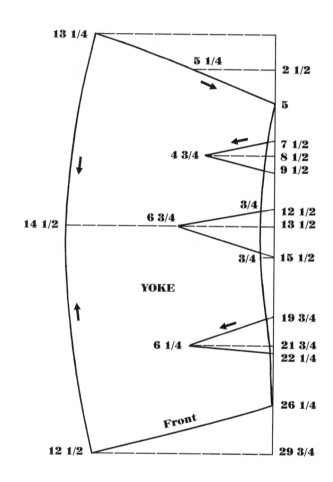

Kilt Skirt

This garment is drafted with the scale corresponding to the waist measure. Regulate the length with the tape measure. It has two pieces: Yoke and skirt plaiting. There are 36 plaits in the skirt, but only 12 1/2 are given here; the rest are drafted accordingly. Press the plaits carefully and sew them to the yoke. The quantity of material 36 inches wide required is 4 1/2 yards.

Winter 1886 *Voice of Fashion*

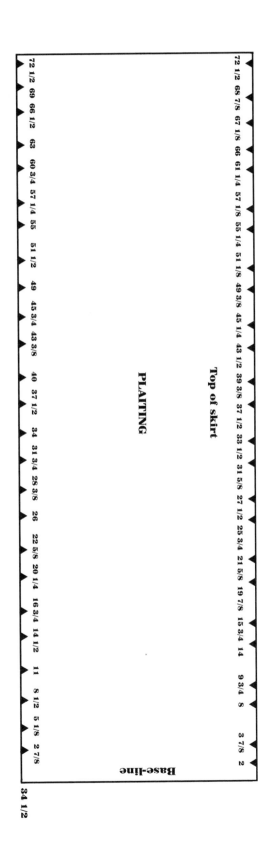

Kilt Skirt. Among the latest fancies of fashion is a preference for kilt skirts in which the plaits are deeply folded. The one illustrated is very popular for all kinds of suit materials. The yoke is in one piece. It is cut on a fold of the material at the center of the front, and folded under for hems at its back edges. To the lower edge is sewed the skirt proper. The skirt is formed of straight breadths joined together, turned under for a wide hem at the lower edge, and laid in wide side-plaits all turning the same way at the top. The plaits are lapped sufficiently at their tops to ensure a close adjustment about the hips. Toward the bottom they flare and give a spring to the edge. A tape is basted to the under sides of the plaits about a third of the distance from the top, to hold them securely in their folds. A belt is sewed to the top of the yoke. Button-holes and buttons close the yoke and belt.

Skirts of this style may be worn with polonaises or deep jersey basques. Or they may have short draperies attached to conceal the yoke, thus permitting them to be worn with any style of bodice. Lace, embroidery, braid, or any flat trimming may be applied before the plaits are laid. Three graduated folds of cashmere on a silk skirt to be worn with a cashmere bodice, are very stylish. Sateen, silk, velvet, cambric, and all seasonable materials, from the cheapest to the most expensive, may be made up in this style. To make the skirt for a lady of medium size, requires 10 yards of material 22 inches wide, 6 1/8 yards of material 36 inches wide, 4 3/8 yards of material 48 inches wide, or 4 yards of material 54 inches wide.

July 1884 *Delineator*

6. Ensembles

Mull, organdy, and French nainsook are the sheer plain muslins used for dresses to be worn for midsummer at the watering places. To these may be added embroidered Swiss muslin in sprigs and dots, with embroidered flounces of various widths finished with scalloped edges. Thick embroidery is preferred this season, but open patterns are still used, especially for heavier muslins.

A combination of plain and embroidered muslin is seen in most of these dresses. The embroidery forms the short basque, and the plain lower part of the front and sides of the skirt. Plain muslin is draped as a short wrinkled apron, with the edges turned under and sewed to the foundation skirt. The back drapery may be long and bouffant, of plain muslin simply hemmed. Or it may be tucked across from the belt to the bottom and hang plainly, or else there may be three, four, or five embroidered flounces gathered across the back. The embroidered basque is not lined, but has two darts and two side pieces, and is edged all around and up the front with narrow gathered scalloped embroidery. In other dresses, the front and sides of the skirt are covered with three or five embroidered flounces, while in still others wide insertion is alternated with lengthwise box-plaits of muslin. All of these skirts are made over a foundation skirt of plain muslin that has a gored front and side breadths, with a straight back breadth tied back by tapes underneath.

One of the best arrangements for the back drapery of these wash dresses, because it is simple and easily ironed, is to make a single very deep puff at the top of the back. To the band where this puff is drawn below, add a gathered breadth or flounce of embroidery. Or else continue the plain muslin to the bottom, trimming it up both sides and across the bottom with embroidered edging, and perhaps a band of insertion. This back fullness has a separate belt of its own, which buttons in front after the belt to which the foundation skirt is attached has been buttoned at the back. The back drapery is basted across the foundation skirt at the end of the puff, and down each side below the puff.

April 11, 1885 *Harper's Bazar*

Tucked skirts of sheer wool dresses are made without any foundation skirt, but merely a deep facing of crinoline and alpaca, and are therefore very light and pleasant for summer wear. The full double width of the material is used for the back breadth. On each side of this is a narrow side gore measuring 3/8 yard at the top, with perhaps 1/16 yard added at its greatest width at the bottom. Between these is the front gore, about 5/8 yard wide at the bottom, and narrowed at the top by two or three darts taken deep enough to make it fit smoothly across the wearer. This is cut long enough to allow for eight or ten tucks, each 2 inches wide. The lowest tuck is not exactly at the bottom, but falls on a fine knife-plaiting that drops as low as the skirt binding, and forms a finish. All of the fullness at the top is gathered or plaited into the back of the belt, extending 1/8 yard on each side of the back placket opening. Two or three sets of tapes sewed to the side gores, tie behind and hold the front and sides in place.

To finish this is a short apron drapery in front sewed in with the belt of the lower skirt. At the back there is a sash drapery made of two uneven loops and ends of the wool material taken lengthwise about 1/2 yard wide, and finished with a hem and tucks.

99

The bodice should be fitted smoothly over a lining; thin silesias in figures and stripes of color with white, or with a whole gray surface, are used for such dresses. The bodice is stitched across the waist-line to dispense with a belt. It should have narrow lengthwise tucks in front and at the back. The fronts between the tucks are each left plain, and are about 3 inches wide. When lapped double they represent a vest, which is completed by a row of small buttons down each side.

July 18, 1885 *Harper's Bazar*

Simple designs that are easily taken apart, yet give an appearance of fullness, are most in favor for the light-colored batistes, embroidered muslins, and ginghams, whose constant freshness is their beauty. A gathered basque and long draperies are liked for such dresses.

If the material is colored and quite transparent, it is the custom to make the basque double. That is, if the dress is of écru batiste or pink mull, the basque is lined throughout with the same batiste or mull. This is done so that the bodice is the same shade as the skirts, which are of course doubled. If the basque is of opaque material such as gingham or cambric, it is made without a lining, and worn over a white corset cover. The same is true of the embroidered materials that come in open designs, in stripes, and in all-over patterns.

The fullness is confined to the front of the basque, and is made in various ways. The simplest plan is to add 2 or 3 inches of extra width to the fronts when cutting them by any basque pattern, and gathering this fullness at the neck, the waist-line, and at the end of the basque. In other basques three plaits or folds, each 1 inch wide, are laid at the neck, pressed flatly down the fronts, and shirred across at the waist-line. Still others have this effect given by straight scarves of the material set on down each side of the buttons and button-holes.

The back of such basques is smoothly fitted with some postilion plaits, or else is bunched up in soft drapery on the tournure. The fronts and back are longer than the sides. The edge is finished with a bias piping fold faced on. A high standing collar of the material is stitched on the edges. The coat sleeves have a gathered scarf near the wrist to match the fronts. Small pea-shaped tinted pearl buttons fasten the basque.

For more elaborate basques, embroidery is added in lapels beside the gathered vest, or it is inserted in V shape down the back and front alike. Insertions with straight edges are used for the V, while an edging that is scalloped on one side is needed for the lapels. White open-work embroidery is used; but there is also a great fancy for embroidery of the dress color, or combining the dress color with several others.

Round bodices gathered to a belt, and yoke bodices that simulate guimpes, are also liked for simple muslin dresses. They are easily fitted, and as they need not be lined they are easily washed. Bands of insertion and lengthwise tucks can make these bodices very dressy. However, they are quite pretty enough for general wear when merely finished with a high collar of the material doubled, or at most an embroidered scalloped band used for the collar and cuffs.

Surplice fronts are also used with these round bodices, leaving the neck open in V shape. These are made by gathering the straight fronts in at the shoulder seams without curving them out for the neck. The V fronts are trimmed with soft frills of lace or embroidered edging. They are sometimes lapped at the waist-line.

Long draperies may be permanently sewed to a foundation skirt. However, the home dressmaker is advised to make separate over-skirts, or at least to use the least intricate patterns, with straight breadths that may be caught up by buttons, tapes, drawstrings, or ribbon bows. Three or four wide plaits down the left side are held in place by cross-tapes basted underneath them. The front breadths sewed

next to these are drawn across to the right side, and caught up in folds by buttons and loops. The back breadths are straight, and are gathered to the belt. Regular apron over-skirts are worn with short or long fronts, as the wearer chooses, and merely hemmed, or else edged with embroidery or lace. One or two narrow ruffles, either gathered or plaited, edge the lower skirt of cotton materials.

April 3, 1886 *Harper's Bazar*

A black lace dress may be mounted without lining, and be worn over different skirts and bodices. For example, of black satin, of white moiré, and of silk of any becoming color–green, blue, lavender, or rose. The deep lace skirting measuring 40 inches or more should be used. The scalloped edge is at the bottom all around. The plain edge is plaited to a belt, one end of the scallops being then carried up the back as a jabot. If this skirt is too long,

after the plaits are laid it should be caught up near the top, allowing the plaits to droop over gracefully in a cluster. Or else the plaits may be spread out like an opened fan, and a bunch of ribbon loops to catch the skirt up may be placed under the fan to drop still lower. A round bodice of silk without other lining is made to match each skirt. The coat sleeves may be put in without a binding, and only basted in the armhole, so that they can be removed and leave the lace sleeves transparent.

July 2, 1887 *Harper's Bazar*

Ladies' Polonaise

This pattern is laid off by the bust measure, the scale selected thereby. It is in eight pieces: Back and back drapery in one (parts A and B are to be put together before drafting), front, side piece, side back, collar, front drapery, and two sleeve pieces. In cutting the material, lay the square end of the collar pattern on a lengthwise fold of the material, to avoid a center seam. Cut the side back and side piece with the waist-line in the pattern of each, on a cross-thread of the material. Cut all of the following laid lengthwise on the material: The longest straight edge of the front drapery, either edge of the back drapery, the front edge of the front, the points of the shortest lengthwise curve of the upper sleeve, and the upper half of the under sleeve. The side of the back drapery at the base-line is the left side.

In making up the material, turn under the right front as far back as the point marked 1 1/2 for a hem, and underface the left front a trifle farther. Close the center back seam, and fasten the extra fullness at its termination in a double box-plait underneath. In the right edge of the back drapery, make two upward-turning plaits, as shown by the extreme ends of the lines drawn at 24 1/2 and 29 1/4 on the base-line. On the left side, make seven plaits as shown by two numbers given above five others below them. Baste the lapped lower edges of the front permanently. Lay three upward-turning plaits in the left end of the front drapery. Lay two similar

plaits in the right end. Join the top of this drapery to the lower edges of the fronts, side pieces, and side backs with its center at that of the front; also join its plaited ends to the corresponding ends of the back drapery. Sew the collar to the neck with its center at the center back seam, then turn it up and fell the lining over the seam. Close the seams in the sleeve, and attach it to the garment with the outside seam at the back of the armhole. Hold the sleeve toward you while sewing it in, and fasten the extra fullness in a forward-turning plait under the arm. Close the front with buttons and button-holes.

Decorate the loose edges of the front drapery with bands of braid, fastening one end of each band under the loose edge, and terminating the others in a loop about 4 inches from the edge. Trim each front with horizontal strips of braid, terminating the ends nearest the center front in loops. Trim the wrists of the sleeves with upright bands of braid, fastening one end of each band under the lower edge, and terminating the other in a loop about 4 inches above; or any preferred decoration may be adopted.

The skirt is drafted with the scale corresponding to the waist measure. The length is regulated with the tape measure. There are three pieces: Front, side gore, and back.

1885 *National Garment Cutter*

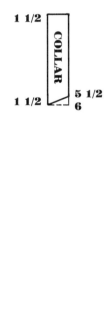

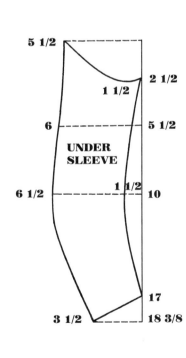

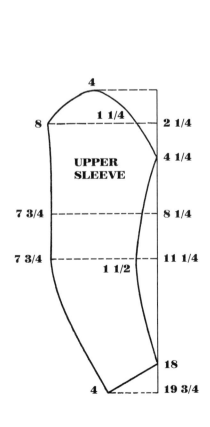

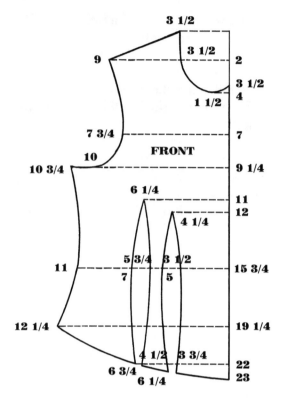

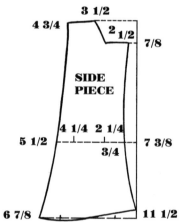

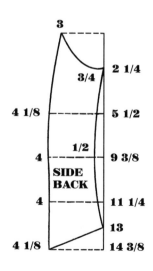

 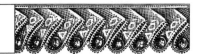
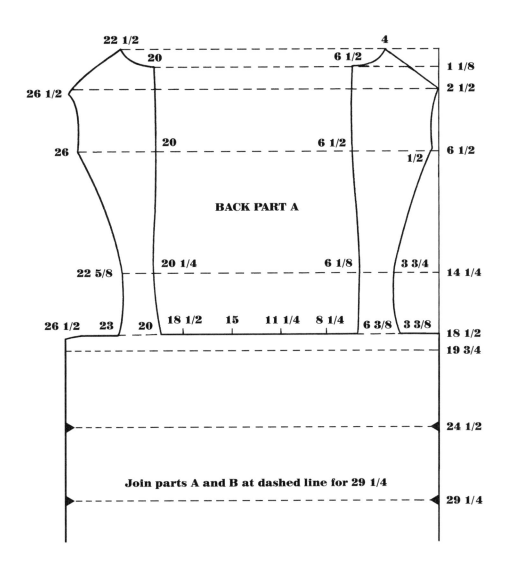

BACK PART A

Join parts A and B at dashed line for 29 1/4

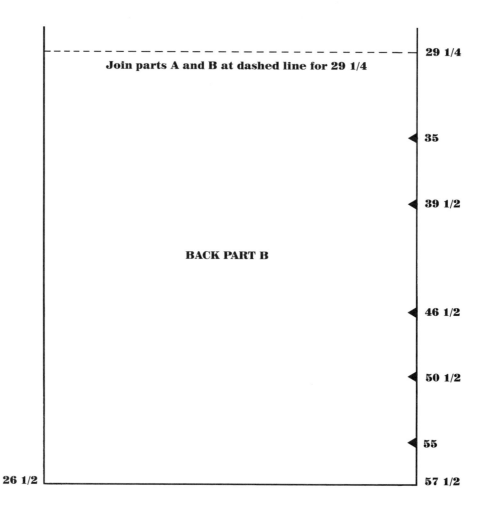

Join parts A and B at dashed line for 29 1/4

29 1/4

35

39 1/2

BACK PART B

46 1/2

50 1/2

55

26 1/2   57 1/2

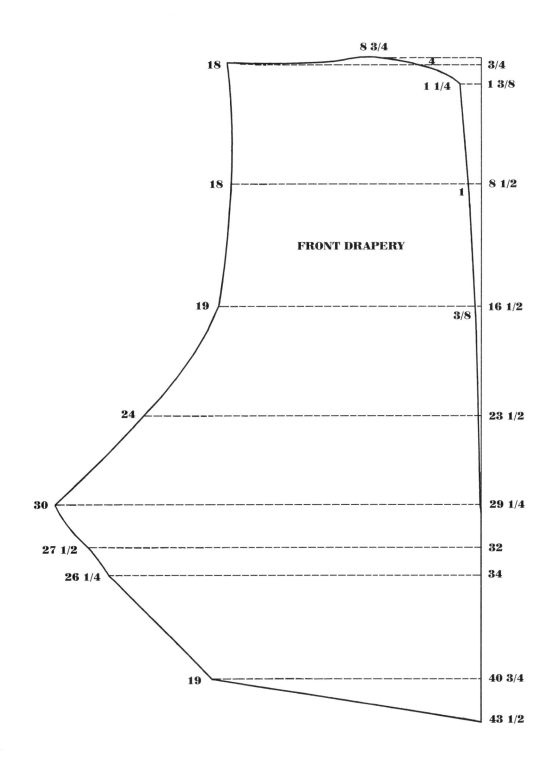

8 3/4

18   4   3/4

1 1/4   1 3/8

18   1   8 1/2

FRONT DRAPERY

19   3/8   16 1/2

24   23 1/2

30   29 1/4

27 1/2   32

26 1/4   34

19   40 3/4

43 1/2

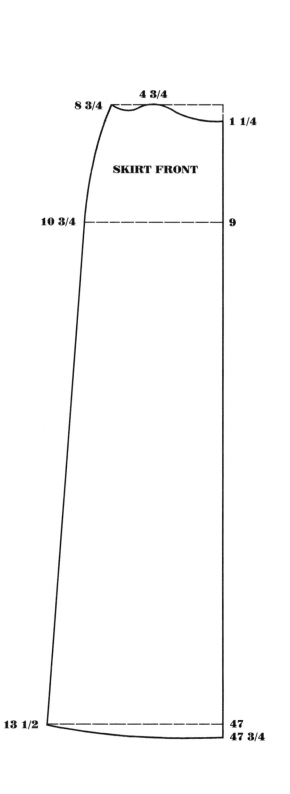

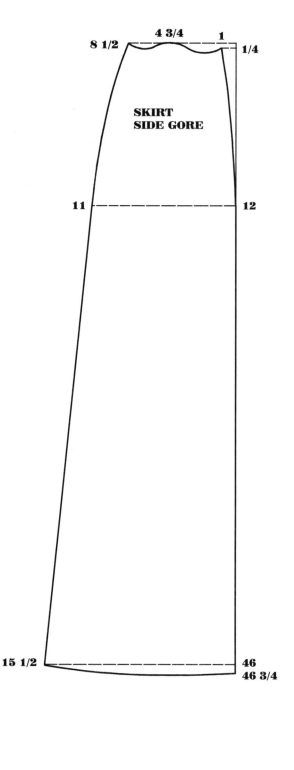

21

SKIRT BACK

Cut double

21 46 1/4

Ladies' Polonaise

This garment is laid off by the bust measure. It is in five pieces: Back and side back in one, front, collar, and two sleeve pieces. Parts A and B of the back, and likewise parts A and B of the front, are to be put together before drafting. All seams are 1/2 space except the shoulder seam.

The quantity of material required is 7 1/4 yards if 22 inches wide, or 3 3/8 yards if 48 inches wide. Cut the back with the back edge of its skirt, and the collar with either end, on a lengthwise fold of the material to avoid a center seam. Cut all of the other pieces lengthwise.

For hems, turn under the front edge of each front skirt to the point marked 1 1/2, and that of the bodice part of the right front to the point marked 1 1/2. In the back edge of each front make four upward-turning plaits, the lower one at the cross-line marked by 29 1/2, and the others between that line and the next one above. Make

four corresponding plaits in each back part where it joins the front. Close the back seam, and fasten the extra fullness at its termination in a box-plait underneath. Also fasten the extra width on each side-back seam in a backward-turning plait underneath. Underface the left edge of the bodice part of the left front. If you wish to bring the center fronts up even with the plaits on the side, make a line of shirring along the center front seam and arrange a stay under it. This polonaise may be trimmed to suit the fancy.

The skirt is drafted with the scale corresponding to the waist measure. The length is regulated with the tape measure. There are three pieces: Front, side gore, and back.

1885 *National Garment Cutter*

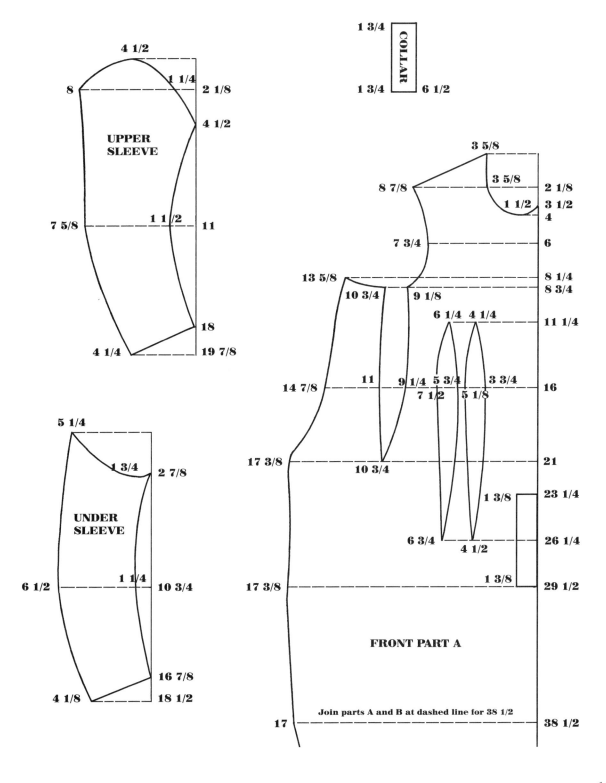

1 3/4

COLLAR

1 3/4   6 1/2

UPPER SLEEVE

4 1/2

1 1/4   2 1/8

8

4 1/2

7 5/8   1 1/2   11

18

4 1/4   19 7/8

3 5/8

3 5/8   2 1/8

8 7/8   1 1/2   3 1/2
            4

7 3/4   6

13 5/8   8 1/4
      8 3/4

10 3/4   9 1/8

6 1/4   4 1/4   11 1/4

14 7/8   11   9 1/4   5 3/4   3 3/4   16
            7 1/2   5 1/8

UNDER SLEEVE

5 1/4

1 3/4   2 7/8

17 3/8   10 3/4   21

1 3/8   23 1/4

6 3/4   4 1/2   26 1/4

6 1/2   1 1/4   10 3/4

1 3/8   29 1/2

17 3/8

FRONT PART A

16 7/8

4 1/8   18 1/2

Join parts A and B at dashed line for 38 1/2

17   38 1/2

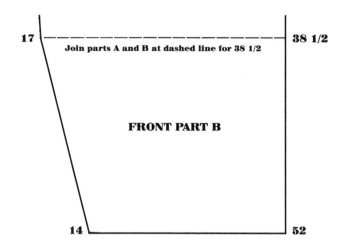

FRONT PART B

17   Join parts A and B at dashed line for 38 1/2   38 1/2

14   52

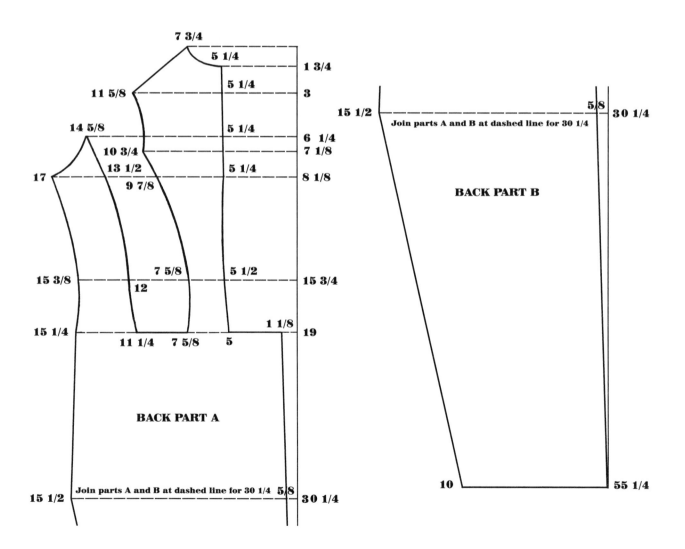

BACK PART A

BACK PART B

7 3/4

5 1/4   1 3/4

11 5/8   5 1/4   3

14 5/8   5 1/4   6 1/4

10 3/4   7 1/8

17   13 1/2   5 1/4   8 1/8

9 7/8

7 5/8   5 1/2   15 3/4

15 3/8   12

15 1/4   1 1/8   19

11 1/4   7 5/8   5

15 1/2   Join parts A and B at dashed line for 30 1/4   5/8   30 1/4

15 1/2   Join parts A and B at dashed line for 30 1/4   5/8   30 1/4

10   55 1/4

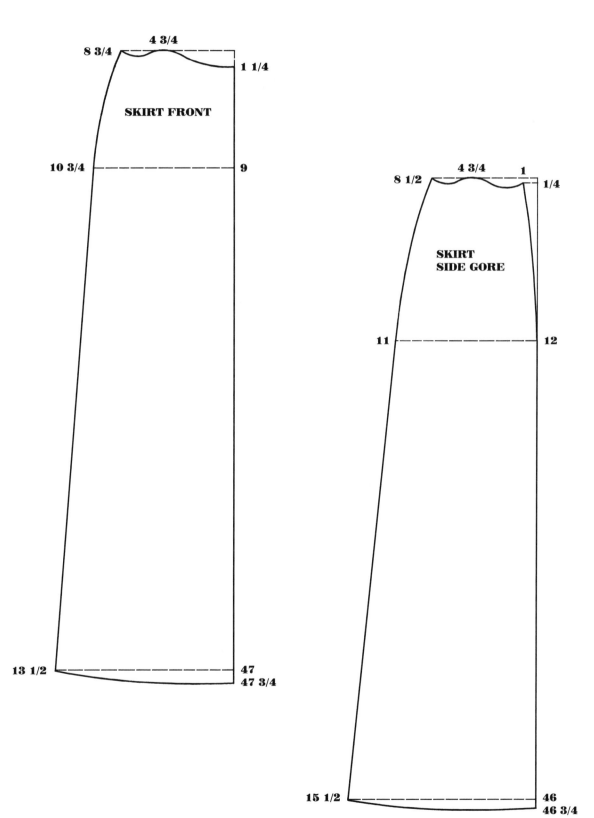

SKIRT FRONT

SKIRT
SIDE GORE

21

SKIRT BACK

Cut double

21

46 1/4

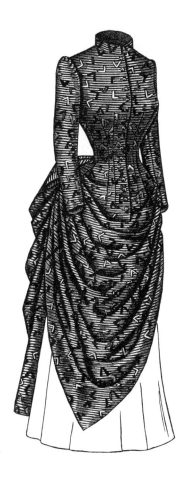

Ladies' Polonaise. Figured cotton material showing an Ottoman weave is represented in this polonaise. Although the finish is entirely plain, the effect is ornamental, the material having a light blue ground on which are strewn small geometric figures showing contrasting colors. The coat sleeves are finely fitted to the arms. Enough fullness is gathered in across the top to give them a graceful curve over the arms. A high standing collar completes the neck.

The front closes from the neck to below the waist-line with buttons and button-holes, the edges being finished with underfacings. Below the closing it is all in one piece, its lower outline being shaped to fall in a deep point on the right of the center. The adjustment of the garment is accomplished by means of double bust darts, single under-arm darts, side backs, and a center back seam.

The center back and side-back seams terminate a little below the waist-line, and at the end of each is allowed extra width, arranged as follows. The width at the end of each side-back seam is underfolded to form a backward-turning plait. That at the end of the center back seam is drawn up with a double-looped bow effect by tapes run through a double casing sewed on the under side. The casing extends perpendicularly for some distance from the top, and the tapes are tied to other tapes sewed below the casing, after having been first drawn up as closely as possible. A hook is sewed beneath the top of the casing, and fastened to a loop that is made a little above the end of the center back seam. This arrangement permits of letting out the back

drapery smoothly whenever pressing or laundering is necessary. It accords with the arrangement of the sides, which are lifted high up on the hips by tapes run through casings arranged in the same manner. The tops of the casings are almost in a line with the draping of the back, and their lower extremities are a little above the ends of the side seams. The side drapings contribute to the bouffant effect of the back and cross-wrinkle the front gracefully. Tapes or elastic straps, sewed beneath the ends of the side casings, regulate the closeness of the polonaise to the figure. The back drapery is deep and square, and its outlines contrast effectively with the contour of the front.

Although the means of draping and the general construction of this polonaise are adapted to wash materials and cottons that need frequent laundering or pressing, this mode is just as well suited to nun's veiling, challis, delaine, mohair, China and Japan silks, canvas-woven materials, bourette, bison cloth, and all kinds of seasonable silks and wools. For a lady of medium size, it needs 8 7/8 yards of material 22 inches wide, 5 5/8 yards of material 36 inches wide, or 4 5/8 yards of material 48 inches wide.

July 1885 *Delineator*

Short Princess Dress

Use the scale for the bust measure to lay off this pattern. It is in four pieces: Back and side back in one, front, and two sleeve pieces. Parts A and B of the back, and likewise of the front, are to be put together before drafting. Draft the back first. On the back, 15 1/4 on the base-line represents the waist-line. Using the tape measure, measure the person's waist length from the point marked 1 1/4. If this measure differs from 15 1/4, raise or lower the waist-line. Raise or lower point 15 1/2 on the base-line of the front the same distance.

The quantity of material required is 7 3/4 yards if 22 inches wide, 5 1/4 yards if 36 inches wide, and 3 5/8 yards if 48 inches wide, plus 32 buttons. In cutting the material, place the pattern for the back with the back edge of its skirt on a lengthwise fold

of the material, to avoid a center seam. Cut the other pieces lengthwise.

In making up the garment, turn under the right front at the point marked 1 1/2, and that of the left front a little less, for hems. Close the center back seam. Fasten the extra fullness at its termination in a double box-plait underneath, with the edges of the plaits together. Also fasten the extra width at the side-back seam in a backward-turning plait underneath. Cut a standing collar or binding for the neck from a straight piece of the material, and attach it to the dress. Close the seams in each sleeve. Sew the sleeves in with the outside seam of each at the back of the armhole, and the extra width in a forward-turning plait under the arm. Hold the

sleeve toward you while sewing it in. Attach a row of three buttons to the wrists in front of the outside seam. Close the front with button-holes and buttons, attaching the buttons to the left front. If desired, the hems may be fastened permanently together from a little below the waist. Plaited lace, ruffles, or flat bands may be used for trimming.

1885 *National Garment Cutter*

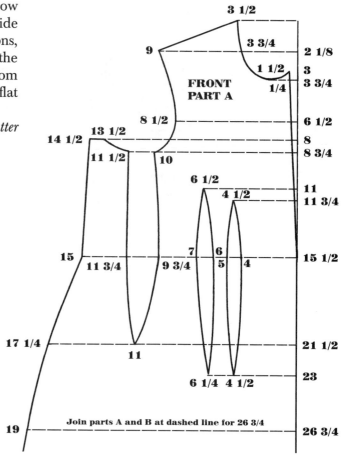

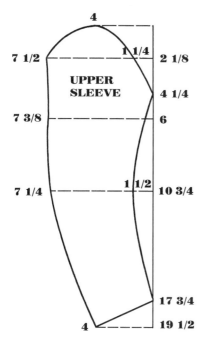

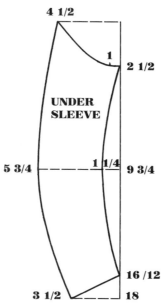

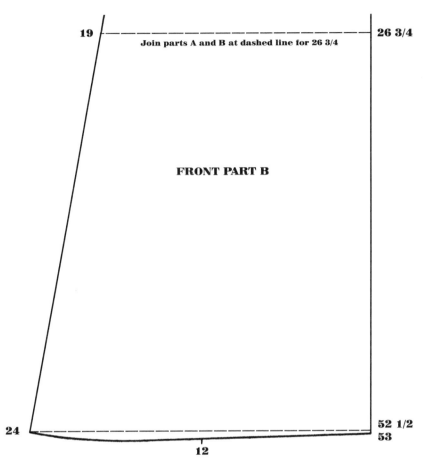

19 — Join parts A and B at dashed line for 26 3/4 — 26 3/4

FRONT PART B

24 — 52 1/2 / 53

12

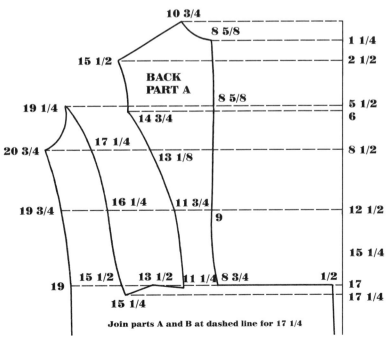

10 3/4

8 5/8 — 1 1/4

15 1/2 — 2 1/2

BACK PART A

8 5/8 — 5 1/2 / 6

19 1/4 — 14 3/4

17 1/4

20 3/4 — 13 1/8 — 8 1/2

16 1/4 — 11 3/4 — 12 1/2

19 3/4 — 9

15 1/4

19 — 15 1/2 — 13 1/2 — 11 1/4 — 8 3/4 — 1/2 — 17 / 17 1/4

15 1/4

Join parts A and B at dashed line for 17 1/4

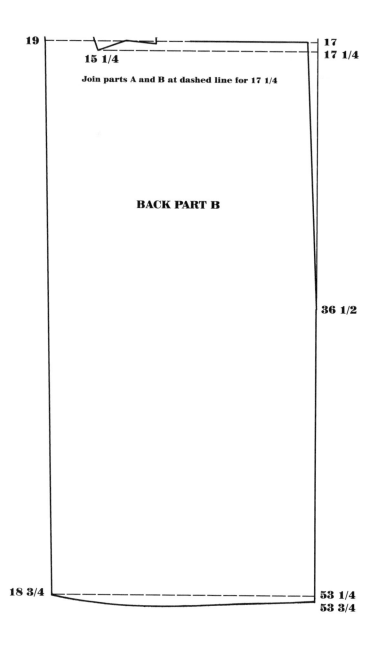

19   17

15 1/4   17 1/4

Join parts A and B at dashed line for 17 1/4

BACK PART B

36 1/2

18 3/4   53 1/4

53 3/4

House Dress. The dress is pictured made of calico having a cream ground and black figures, and decorated with ruffles of the material. The easy adjustment is due to single bust and under-arm darts, together with side backs and a curved center back seam. The latter is discontinued a little below the waist-line at the top of an underfolded box-plait, which falls into the skirt. The front edges are hemmed their entire length, and the closing is made from the neck to a considerable distance below the waist-line with buttons and button-holes. The hems below the closing are lapped and basted down to the lower edge.

A rounded patch pocket is placed on each side of the front, near the end of the under-arm dart. It is trimmed at the upper edge with a downward-turning frill of the material headed by a band of the same. The neck is finished with a standing frill. The sleeves are in the smoothly fitting coat shape, the under sleeve being narrower than the upper sleeve, which is gathered at the elbow to ensure greater comfort. The sleeves are trimmed at the wrist with a band headed by an upward-turning frill of the material. A calico ruffle finished to form a self-heading trims the lower edge of the skirt.

This garment may be made dressy by the choice of trimming, white wash materials being usually decorated with lace or embroidery. Figured or plain cashmere may have lace cascaded down the closing and about the neck and sleeves, and one or two flounces of the same may trim the skirt. Ribbon of any kind may be arranged at the waist and tied in a bow at the front or sides. Figured China and India silks, nun's veiling, challis, and tennis flannel develop well in this style. To make the house dress for a lady of medium size, requires 7 3/4 yards of material 22 inches wide, 4 7/8 yards of material 36 inches wide, or 3 7/8 yards of material 44 inches wide.

June 1888 *Delineator*

Double-Breasted Coat. Fancy cloth of a seasonable quality was chosen for the coat pictured. The three seams that incline the back to the figure are visible for only a short distance below the waistline. The one at the center ends at the top of extra width, which is underfolded to form a box-plait. In a line with the top of this plait, extensions are allowed on the corresponding edges of the center back and side-back pieces. These are joined together and underfolded in a forward-turning plait on each side. The plaits are pressed so thoroughly as to retain their folds for their entire length. A metal button is placed at the top of each forward-turning plait.

The front is cut in shawl shape at the neck. To the right side is sewed a curved overlap. Its top is shaped in a continuation of the neck outline, and the seam joining it to the coat proper is curved to assist in the adjustment. Fitting is completed by a bust dart in each side of the front and an under-arm dart in each side piece. The collar is in shawl shape, and its right end is extended to pass along the overlap to the visible closing. The closing begins at the top of the overlap and ends a little below the waist-line, being performed by button-holes and buttons, and being similarly continued under the collar. The sleeves are in coat shape and entirely plain in finish. For summer wear they often give way to a flowing sleeve.

All kinds of serges, light meltons, and cheviots are made up in this way; and for summer, surahs, pongees, and lady's cloths. Plain or fancy braid is often applied, lace braid being especially favored. To make the coat for a lady of medium size, requires 11 7/8 yards of material 22 inches wide, 4 1/2 yards of material 48 inches wide, or 4 3/8 yards of material 54 inches wide.

March 1886 *Delineator*

 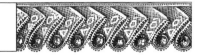

Ladies' Polonaise. The material selected for this example is all-over embroidered cheviot, and the only decorations are the cord ornaments on the front. There are two bust darts and an under-arm dart in each side of the front. The center parts are cut away in a somewhat pointed outline to the first bust dart seams a little below the waist-line. Button-holes and buttons close the upper part of the fronts, the right side being hemmed and the left underfaced. The lower parts fall very low on the figure.

The back has the usual center and side-back seams, all three of which end at the top of broad extra widths allowed below the waist-line. The extra fullness below the center back seam is folded in a double box-plait underneath. The fullness at the end of each side-back seam is cut partly on the front edge of the back, and partly on the back edge of the side back. Its adjoining edges are seamed together and folded in a similar plait underneath, the effect on the outside being that of two double box-plaits between two pairs of overlapping side-plaits. These plaits remain smoothly in their folds for some distance below their tops. Toward the bottom of the polonaise, they spring out enough to accord with the arrangement of the tournure.

The coat sleeves are completed merely by cuff-facings of the material. A high standing collar finishes the neck. Heavy, graduated cord chains, suspended between medallion ornaments, cross the front from the neck to a little below the pointed outline, at intervals of a few inches. Brandenburg ornaments of jetted or plain cord are fashionable. When embroidered material such as this is selected, more elaborate trimmings are undesirable, although fur, bands of plush or Astrakhan cloth, etc., are acceptable. Ladies in mourning trim such polonaises with broad bands of crape, and face the front in vest outline with crape. For light mourning, black braid is not inappropriate. To make the polonaise for a lady of medium size, requires 8 3/4 yards of material 22 inches wide, or 4 1/4 yards of material 48 inches wide.

December 1884 *Delineator*

The front is curved quite high over the hips and deeply pointed at the closing. This is performed with button-holes and buttons, the right side being hemmed and the left underfaced. There is a high standing collar about the neck. The coat sleeves, which are sewed into the armholes with a high epaulet curve over the shoulders, are plainly finished.

The vest is suggestive of the Molière style, being arranged to give a puffed effect. It is curved to fit the neck at the top, and shirred once at its top and twice at its lower edge. A stay is sewed beneath the upper edge, and a binding is added to the lower edge. Hooks are sewed to the ends of the stay. Loops are worked at corresponding points on the fronts of the basque, the vest by these means being attached to droop in a puff from the neck to the waist-line. As the vest is attached only by hooks and loops, it may be removed whenever it is not desired; and the loops, being worked with silk the color of the material, will not be noticeable. Sometimes the vest is in very decided contrast with the basque, and sometimes it is of the same material.

Such basques are constructed of brocaded or fancy material to wear over plain skirts, and they are also made of material matching the skirts with which they are to be worn. Yellow laces, as fine as may be procurable, are worn at the neck and wrists. To make the basque for a lady of medium size, requires 6 5/8 yards of material 22 inches wide, or 3 1/4 yards of material 48 inches wide, together with 5/8 yard of silk 20 inches wide for the puff.

January 1884 *Delineator*

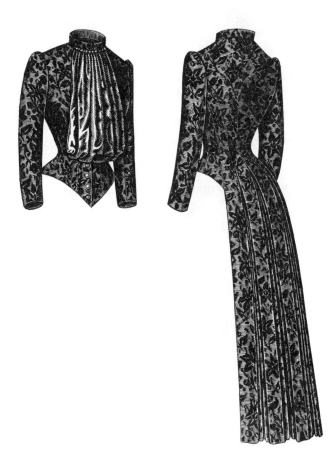

Basque with Waterfall Back Drapery. This basque has an ample back drapery, which falls in long, unbroken lines. Brocaded material is employed in the construction of the basque proper, and plain silk is used in the puffed vest. There are two bust darts in each half of the front, and a side piece on each side, which contributes alike to the adjustment of the back and front. Side-back seams and a center seam divide the back. The center back seam terminates a little below the waist-line in extra widths. These unite in a seam that appears to be a continuation of the center back seam, and are folded in a double box-plait underneath. The side-back seams likewise end in a line with the center back seam, and on the edges below them are allowed extensions, which are also underfolded in a double box-plait on each side. The back drapery should be faced all around or lined throughout, according to the texture of the material.

Trained House Dress. This example is developed in a combination of black satin and light brocaded material. The brocade is used in the petticoat part, as the three gores comprising the front and sides are called. These gores are fitted smoothly about the hips by darts. Those at the sides are widened to spring into the adjoining part of the train, which is cut in one length with the back of the bodice, extra width being allowed below the center back seam and also below each side-back seam. The extra width at the end of the center back seam, and the greater part of that below the side-back seams, is underfolded to form two double box-plaits on the outside. The remainder is sewed

to the side gores and joined with them to the belt, which passes around the figure and fastens at the back under the princess part. This arrangement requires making a placket opening on each side, along the underfold of one of the plaits; when the dress is adjusted on the figure these openings are entirely concealed. The train is of moderate length, and falls into an oval outline.

The rest of the bodice is in basque style. The side backs fall with a pointed effect back of the hips, and curve upward toward their front edges to an even length with the side pieces. The fronts proper are about uniform in length across their lower edges. They are curved at their closing edges, the rest of their adjustment being performed by single bust darts. They are closed by button-holes and

buttons, both sides being underfaced. On each side of the front is applied a narrow vest-facing, which broadens on the bust to describe a becoming shape when the edges are buttoned. The facing is carried in the shape of fitted bands about the lower edges of the basque parts, as far as the front edges of the side backs. The high rolling collar is overlaid with lace. Lace is arranged along the back edge of the vest-facing from the neck to the bust, producing a suggestion of the Zouave.

The sleeves are in coat shape and, like the bodice and train, are of black satin. Their outside seams are discontinued far enough from the wrist to permit of turning the lower part back in cuff fashion. The reversed part is overfaced with brocade, and lace ruffles are sewed inside. Jabots of wide lace overlie the seams joining the side gores to the back. The lower edges of the skirt front and side gores are cut into square tabs of medium length and underlaid with a lace ruffle. Tapes, sewed beneath the side-back seams and tied together, regulate the final adjustment of the skirt.

To make the house dress for a lady of medium size, requires 8 1/4 yards of satin and 3 1/4 yards of brocade 22 inches wide; or 3 3/4 yards of satin and 3/8 yard of brocade 48 inches wide.

July 1885 *Delineator*

Basque with Vest Front and Walking Skirt

This basque has six pieces: Vest front, front, side back, back, and two sleeve pieces. To draft it, use the scale corresponding to the bust measure. The sleeves are drafted with the scroll turned differently than for other sleeves. Connect the points 4, 2 5/8, and 1 1/2 at the same time for the top of the upper sleeve. Connect 4 1/4 on the base-line and 1 1/2 on the line above 4 1/4, with the large part of the scroll turned toward 4 1/4. Connect 8 and 6 1/2 (the third and second cross-lines), with the large part of the scroll toward 8. At the bottom, the line 18 1/2 out to 1/2, then to 4, is the one to cut by. This is to prevent the sleeve from drawing.

In making the basque, if the lining is all that is cut as far back as the under-arm dart, the vest proper will have to be stitched firmly onto the lining. The vest may be of any material desired. The back of the basque is cut plain and no trimming is used. The sleeve may have a cuff put on it of the same material as the vest, and the trimming of the side drapery on the skirt. The collar is a straight band of the width desired.

The skirt drapery is drafted with the scale corresponding to the waist measure. It is cut in two pieces: Back drapery and front drapery. The two parts of the front drapery diagram are to be put together before drafting. Turn the four plaits in the front drapery as shown by the figures.

Turn eight plaits toward the center in the back drapery, as shown by the numbers on the first crossline. Only half of the drapery is given, and four plaits are shown on that part. Turn the first plait on the right side by laying the notch at 20 3/4 onto the center. Make the following three plaits by placing 14 1/4 on 19 3/4, 7 3/4 on 13 1/4, and 1 on 6 1/2. Then lay the plaits on the left side in the same manner. Fasten the plaits securely to the belt. Lay the four plaits on the side, following the figures.

The trimming on the side drapery is a straight strip 4 to 6 inches wide. Fasten the right sides of the drapery with ornaments, leaving it open below the last ornament. The left side is fastened all the way down.

The foundation skirt has three pieces: Front, side gore, and back. It is trimmed with a narrow foot plaiting.

Spring and Summer 1886 *Voice of Fashion*

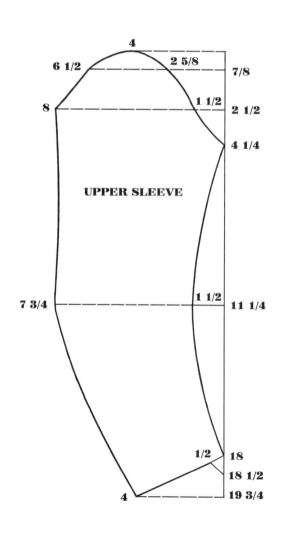

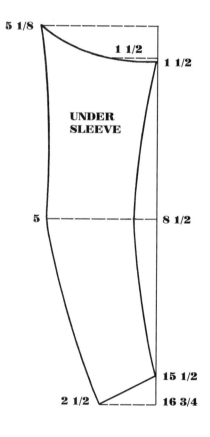

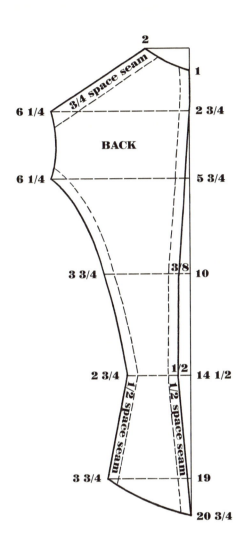

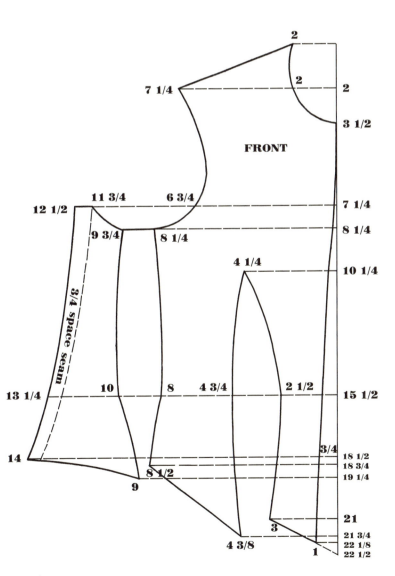

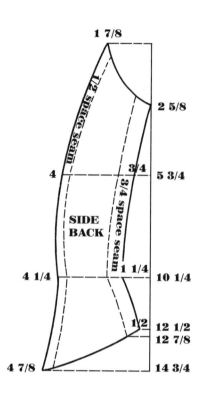

SIDE
BACK

1 7/8

2 5/8

3/4

4   5 3/4

3/4 space seam

1/2 space seam

4 1/4   1 1/4   10 1/4

1/2   12 1/2
              12 7/8

4 7/8   14 3/4

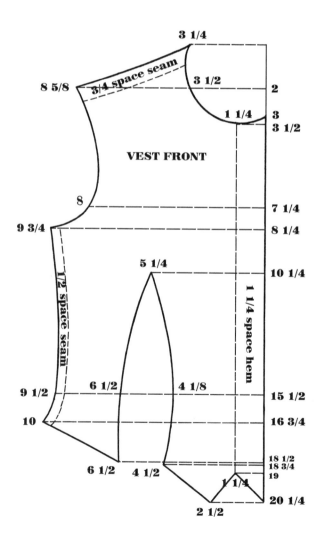

VEST FRONT

3 1/4

8 5/8   3/4 space seam   3 1/2   2

1 1/4   3
              3 1/2

8   7 1/4

9 3/4   8 1/4

5 1/4   10 1/4

1/2 space seam   1 1/4 space hem

9 1/2   6 1/2   4 1/8   15 1/2

10   16 3/4

6 1/2   4 1/2   18 1/2
                            18 3/4
                            19
1 1/4   20 1/4

2 1/2

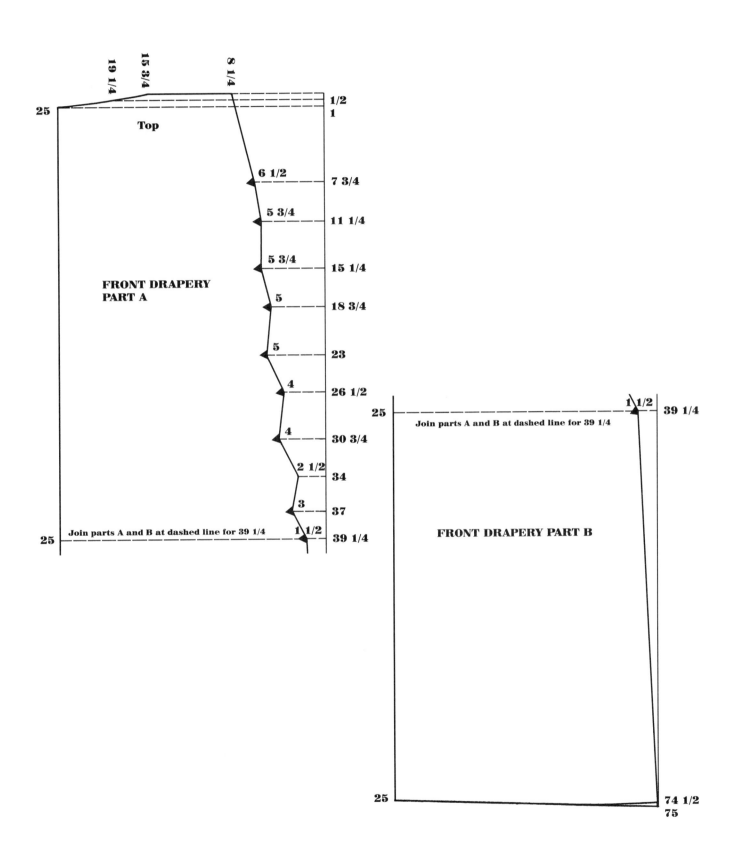

19 1/4

15 3/4

8 1/4

25

Top

**FRONT DRAPERY
PART A**

1/2

1

6 1/2 — 7 3/4

5 3/4 — 11 1/4

5 3/4 — 15 1/4

5 — 18 3/4

5 — 23

4 — 26 1/2

4 — 30 3/4

2 1/2 — 34

3 — 37

25   Join parts A and B at dashed line for 39 1/4   1 1/2 — 39 1/4

25   Join parts A and B at dashed line for 39 1/4   1 1/2   39 1/4

FRONT DRAPERY PART B

25

25   74 1/2

75

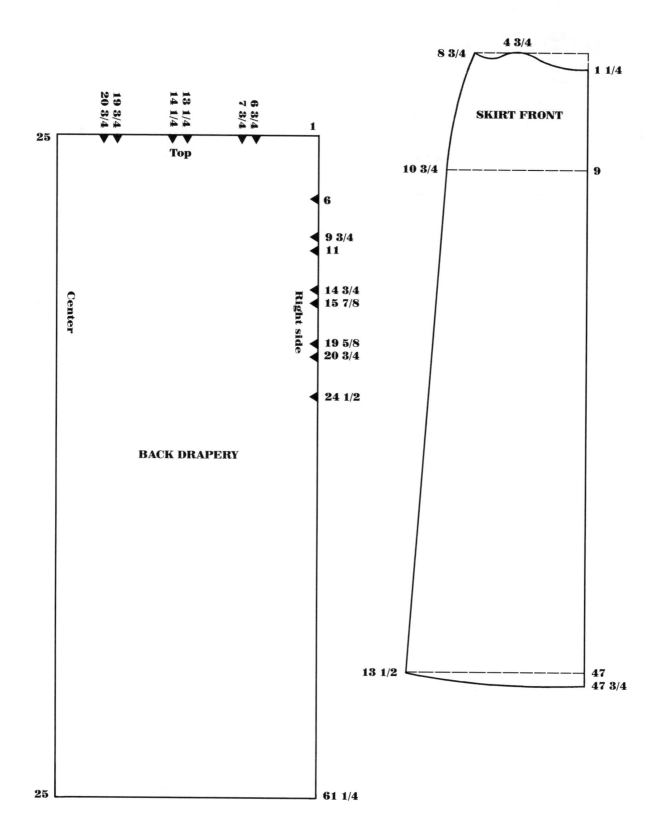

25 **1**

19 3/4
20 3/4
13 1/4
14 1/4
6 3/4
7 3/4

Top

6

9 3/4
11

14 3/4
15 7/8

19 5/8
20 3/4

24 1/2

Center

Right side

BACK DRAPERY

25 **61 1/4**

4 3/4

8 3/4

1 1/4

SKIRT FRONT

10 3/4 9

13 1/2 47

47 3/4

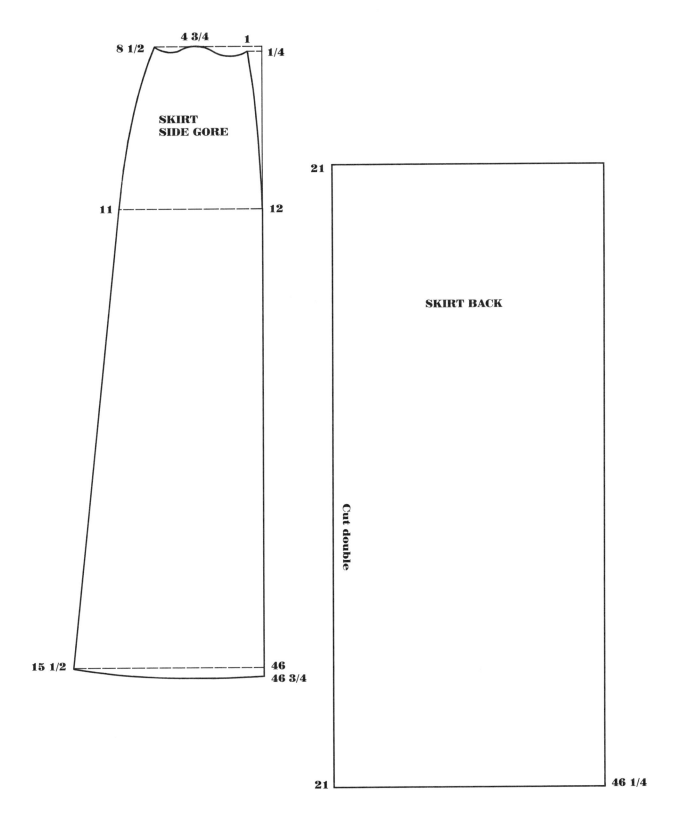

SKIRT SIDE GORE

4 3/4   1

8 1/2   1/4

11   12

15 1/2   46
46 3/4

SKIRT BACK

21

Cut double

21   46 1/4

133

Jacket Basque. Plain dress material was chosen for this example, and ornaments formed of silk and tinsel braid constitute the decorations. The fronts open over a short, slightly pointed vest. The vest is fitted by double bust darts and closes with button-holes and buttons, the right side being hemmed. The fronts have no darts, but are shaped to present a clinging effect, the vest parts being sewed with them at their back edges to the side pieces, and to the back at the shoulder seams. Side-back seams and a curved center seam fit the back, all three of them being carried to the lower edge. This is curved upward over the hips, and deepened to a point at the end of the center back seam. On the overlapping and lower edges of the basque, braid ornaments are placed in a continuous row. They are also arranged on the high standing collar, which is fitted to sit comfortably about the neck. The sleeves are in coat shape, and are close but not too tight to the arms. Each is trimmed at the wrist with a row of braid ornaments.

The ornaments described are purchased in the same manner as passementerie of any kind, but they may be constructed at home if preferred. Sometimes the vest is of contrasting material, or it is elaborately trimmed and the jacket proper finished plainly. Fashion places no limit on the richness of the trimmings that may be applied to the vest, if they are in keeping with the material. For a lady of medium size, the amount of material required for the jacket and vest is 3 1/2 yards if 22 inches wide, or 1 5/8 yards if 48 inches wide.

September 1885 *Delineator*

Ladies' Costume

Ladies' Costume

This costume is cut with a polonaise back and a basque front, with a long drapery in front. It is drafted with the scale corresponding to the bust measure. It is in seven pieces: Front, back, front drapery, rolling collar, standing collar, and two sleeve pieces. The polonaise requires 6 yards of material 44 inches wide.

To make the front of the basque as illustrated, draft it like any other front. Trace on the dashed line running diagonally from 3 1/8 on the cross-line to 10 1/4 on the base-line. Turn the material away, join on the rolling collar, and let it extend to the center of the back. The V in the front may be made of plaited or plain velvet, which combines with any material and gives the costume a very rich and stylish finish.

The skirt is made plain, with a narrow foot plaiting. Draft it with the scale corresponding to the waist measure, and regulate the length with the tape measure. There are three pieces: Front, side gore, and back. The pattern has a point at the top of the back breadth, and four lines running to the opposite side, two of them curved and two straight. These are for steels, which obviate the need for a bustle and give a pleasing effect to the drapery. Stitch a strip of silesia 1 inch wide on each line. Run the steels in, and tie back until the skirt is plain in front.

Winter 1886 *Voice of Fashion*

135

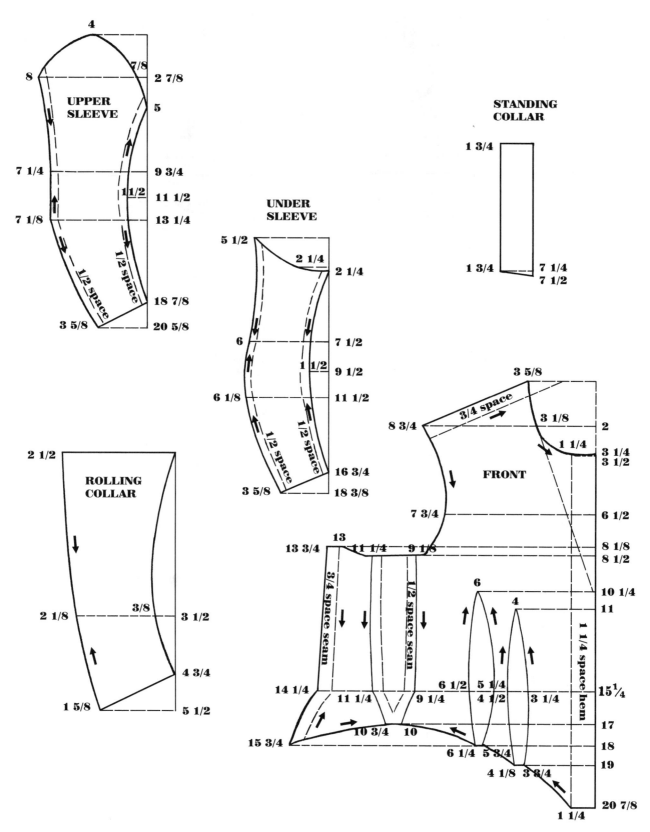

136

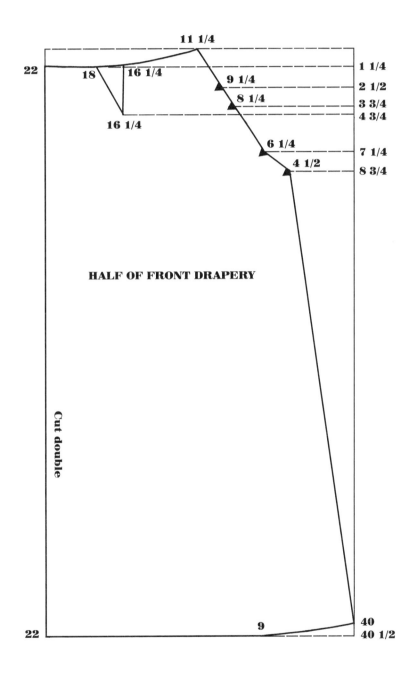

HALF OF FRONT DRAPERY

Cut double

22   11 1/4

18   16 1/4   9 1/4   1 1/4

16 1/4   8 1/4   2 1/2

3 3/4

4 3/4

6 1/4   7 1/4

4 1/2   8 3/4

22   9   40

40 1/2

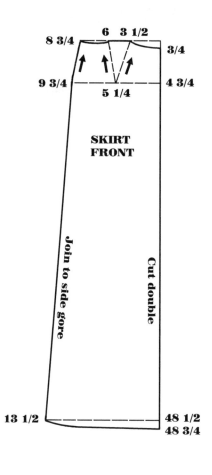

8 3/4   6   3 1/2   3/4

9 3/4   5 1/4   4 3/4

SKIRT FRONT

Join to side gore

Cut double

13 1/2   48 1/2
48 3/4

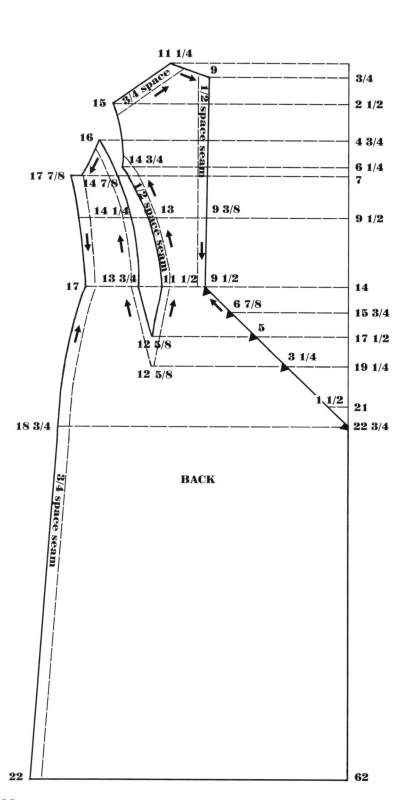

11 1/4   9   3/4

15   3/4 space   2 1/2

16   4 3/4

14 3/4   6 1/4
7

17 7/8   14 7/8

1/2 space seam

14 1/4   13   9 3/8   9 1/2

17   13 3/4   11 1/2   9 1/2   14

6 7/8   15 3/4

12 5/8   5   17 1/2

12 5/8   3 1/4   19 1/4

1 1/2   21

18 3/4   22 3/4

3/4 space seam

BACK

22   62

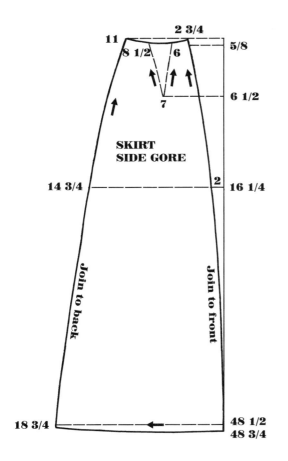

2 3/4

11
8 1/2   6
5/8

7

6 1/2

**SKIRT
SIDE GORE**

14 3/4   2   16 1/4

Join to back   *Join to front*

18 3/4   48 1/2
                        48 3/4

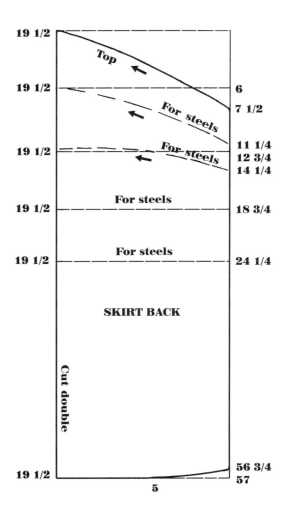

19 1/2

Top

19 1/2   6

For steels   7 1/2

For steels   11 1/4

19 1/2   12 3/4
                        14 1/4

For steels

19 1/2   18 3/4

For steels

19 1/2   24 1/4

SKIRT BACK

Cut double

19 1/2   56 3/4
       5   57

Street Costume

Draft the basque with the scale corresponding to the bust measure. It is in six pieces: Front, back, side back, collar, and two sleeve pieces. Care should be taken to connect the waist-lines.

Draft the skirt with the scale corresponding to the waist measure. Regulate the length with the tape measure. The pattern has a point at the top of the back breadth, and four lines running to the opposite side, two of them curved and two straight. These are for steels, which obviate the need for a bustle and

give a pleasing effect to the drapery. Stitch a strip of silesia 1 inch wide on each line. Run the steels in, and tie back until the skirt is plain in front.

The drapery is in two pieces: Front and back. The right side of the front drapery is laid in four upward-turning plaits, while the left side is laid in four backward-turning plaits. The left side of the back drapery is laid in a double box-plait. The right

side is laid in seven backward-turning plaits, which are all marked on the diagram. The space between 37 3/4 and 51 1/2 on the base-line is a loop that falls underneath the drapery. Bring 1 1/4 on the cross-line running from 37 3/4 on the base-line, and 12 3/4 on the cross-line running from 51 1/2 on the base-line, together at the center of the back.

This pattern also forms a lovely drapery without any looping whatever.

Winter 1886 *Voice of Fashion*

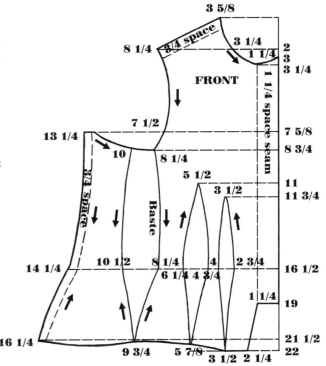

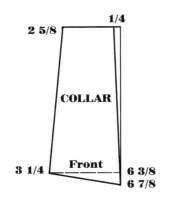

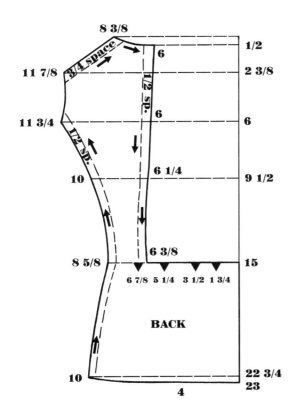

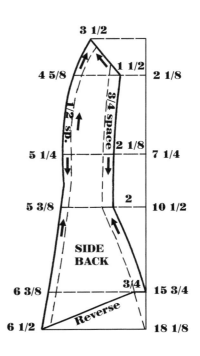

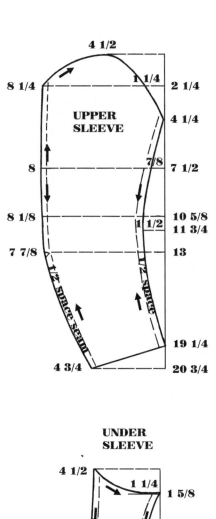

UPPER SLEEVE

4 1/2

8 1/4 | 1 1/4 | 2 1/4

4 1/4

8 | 7/8 | 7 1/2

8 1/8 | 1 1/2 | 10 5/8 / 11 3/4

7 7/8 | 13

1/2 space seam | 1/2 space

19 1/4

4 3/4 | 20 3/4

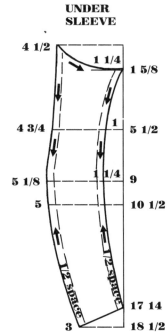

UNDER SLEEVE

4 1/2 | 1 1/4 | 1 5/8

4 3/4 | 1 | 5 1/2

5 1/8 | 1 1/4 | 9

5 | 10 1/2

1/2 space | 1/2 space

17 14

3 | 18 1/2

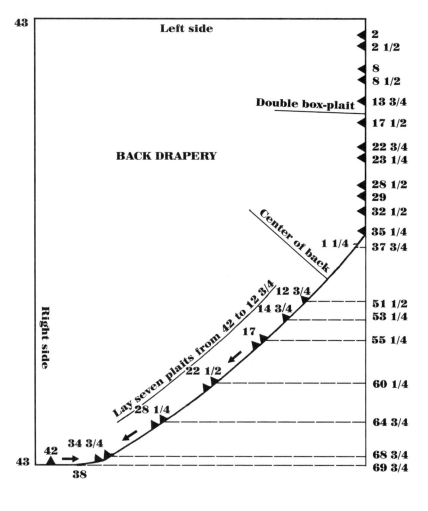

43

Left side

2
2 1/2

8
8 1/2

Double box-plait | 13 3/4

17 1/2

BACK DRAPERY | 22 3/4
23 1/4

28 1/2
29

32 1/2

35 1/4

Center of back | 1 1/4 | 37 3/4

Right side

Lay seven plaits from 42 to 12 3/4 | 12 3/4
14 3/4 | 51 1/2
53 1/4

17 | 55 1/4

22 1/2 | 60 1/4

28 1/4 | 64 3/4

42 | 34 3/4 | 68 3/4
43 | 38 | 69 3/4

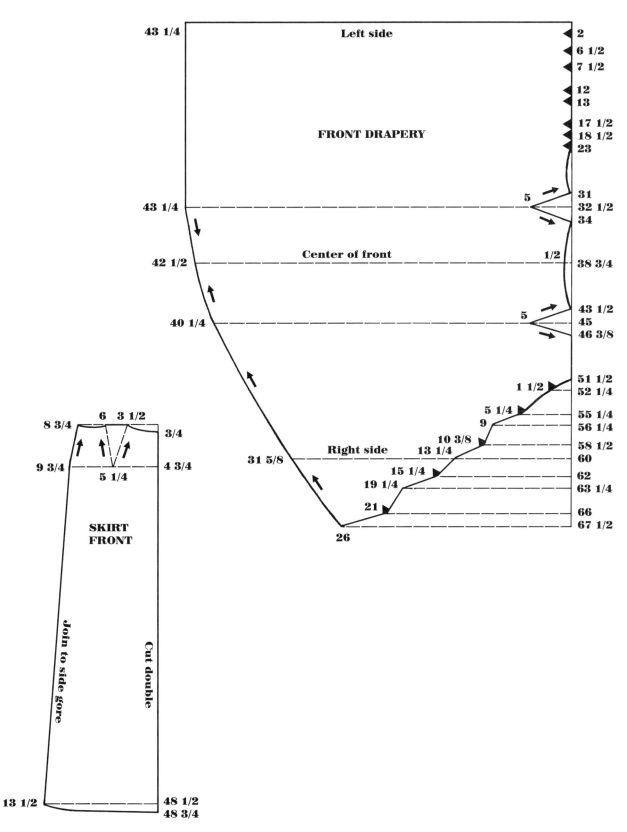

Left side

43 1/4

2
6 1/2
7 1/2

12
13

17 1/2
18 1/2
23

FRONT DRAPERY

43 1/4   5 →   31
32 1/2
→   34

42 1/2   Center of front   1/2   38 3/4

5 →   43 1/2
40 1/4   45
→   46 3/8

51 1/2
1 1/2   52 1/4

5 1/4   55 1/4
9   56 1/4

10 3/8   58 1/2
Right side   13 1/4   60

31 5/8

15 1/4   62
19 1/4   63 1/4

21   66
67 1/2

26

SKIRT FRONT

8 3/4   6   3 1/2   3/4

9 3/4   5 1/4   4 3/4

Join to side gore   Cut double

13 1/2   48 1/2
48 3/4

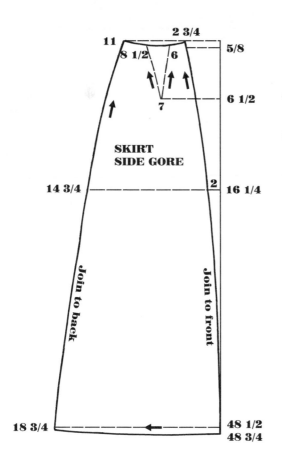

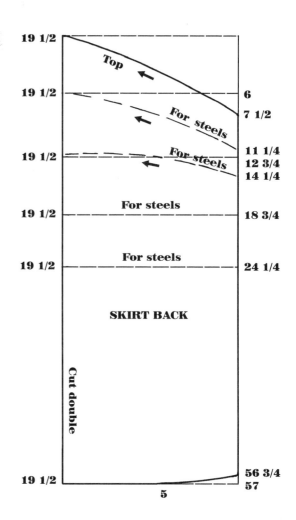

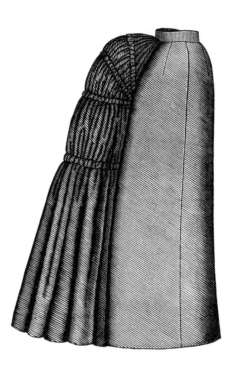

Four-Gored Skirt with Steels. A new arrangement of steels, which obviates the need for a bustle, is the characteristic of this skirt. Dress material was chosen for its development, and the finish is plain. The skirt hangs evenly. The gores are shaped like the former standard style and are fitted by darts. The back breadth is gathered at the top, and across it are arranged four casings for the steels. Three of the casings almost meet at the side-back seams several inches below the top, and spread apart toward the center. The third casing is arranged much lower down. The two lower casings slant toward the bottom, and the two upper toward the top. The steels are firmly adjusted in the casings, securely fastened at their ends, and drawn into curves by tapes or elastic straps. A belt finishes the top of the skirt, and the placket opening is made in the side-back seam.

This skirt may be made up in either light or heavy material. For a lady of medium size, it requires 5 yards of material 22 inches wide, 4 5/8 yards of material 27 inches wide, 3 5/8 yards of material 36 inches wide, 3 yards of material 44 inches wide, or 2 1/2 yards of material 54 inches wide. Any style of drapery may be arranged on it, the materials particularly liked being lace flouncings, nets, tissues, etc. The lower edge may be trimmed or not, as desired. Flounces of the material pinked at the edges are liked on skirts to be worn with house jackets or dressing sacks.

The casings are made either of webbing or of the lining material, and are stitched on at both edges. If webbing is used, the casings are cut 1/2 inch wider than the steels; but if lining material is used they are cut 1 inch wider, to allow for turning in the edges. The casings are sewed across the back breadth underneath so as to droop over the stitching that confines the lower edges; in this way the steels do not shorten the skirt undesirably and it hangs perfectly even. A deep facing of soft canvas is generally added to the bottom of the skirt, and over it a narrower facing of alpaca is arranged before the belt is added.

June 1888 *Delineator*

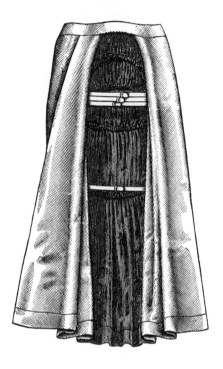

Petticoat with Steels. This petticoat is especially desirable to wear under skirts of lawn and other sheer materials. It is shown made of white cambric. The three gores are fitted by darts, and the back breadth is gathered at the top. This is finished with a belt, the placket opening being made on the left side-front seam. Four casings are formed across the back breadth, two flaring toward the belt at the center and the other two slanting toward the bottom. The upper three casings almost meet at the side-back seams a little below the belt, while the other one comes much lower down. This arrangement ensures a sufficiently bouffant effect without the use of an adjustable tournure. The casings are made either of webbing or of strips of the material. When made of webbing, the casings should be 1/2 inch wider than the steels. When the material is used for them they should be 1 inch wider, to allow for turning in the edges.

The casings are arranged to droop over the sewing of their lower edges, so that the petticoat is not shortened ungracefully. The steels are securely basted at their ends, and drawn into curves by tapes or elastic straps. The arrangement of the straps is clearly illustrated in the view showing the petticoat severed at the center.

A hem finishes the bottom of the petticoat, and in this example a flounce of embroidery headed by a band of insertion trims it. The bottom may be trimmed to suit the fancy, with ruffles, plaitings, tucks, flounces, etc. Every kind of material in use for petticoats is made up in this way—surah, pongee, mohair, satin, silk, muslin, cambric, etc. To make the garment for a lady of medium size, requires 4 5/8 yards of material 27 inches wide, or 3 5/8 yards of material 36 inches wide.

June 1888 *Delineator*

Ladies' Costume

Ladies' Costume

This costume has eight pieces: Basque front, basque back, basque side back, two sleeve pieces, collar, back skirt drapery, and front skirt drapery. The basque is drafted with the scale corresponding to the bust measure. It is perfectly plain, with velvet cuffs and collar to correspond to the skirt, which is made of velvet.

The skirt drapery has two pieces: Front and back. It is drafted with the scale corresponding to the waist measure. Regulate the length with the tape measure. The right side of the front drapery is laid in three upward-turning plaits, while the left side is laid in four backward-turning plaits; press the plaits on the left side, but do not baste them. Lay six backward-turning plaits on the left side of the back drapery, and also six backward-turning plaits on the right side. Bring the two together in the center of the back, forming a loop there, which gives a very graceful drapery.

The skirt is drafted with the scale corresponding to the waist measure. The length is regulated with the tape measure. It is in three pieces: Front, side gore, and back.

1887 *National Garment Cutter Instruction Book*

147

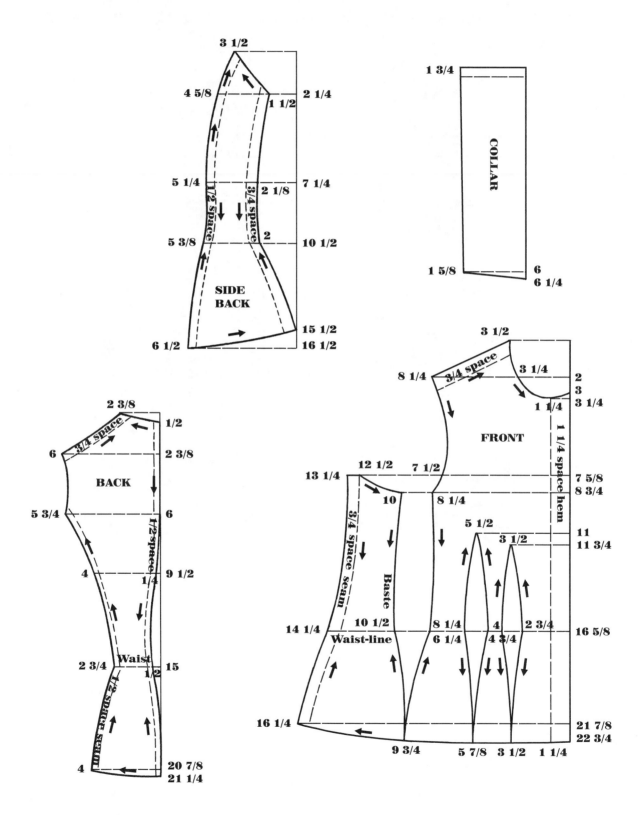

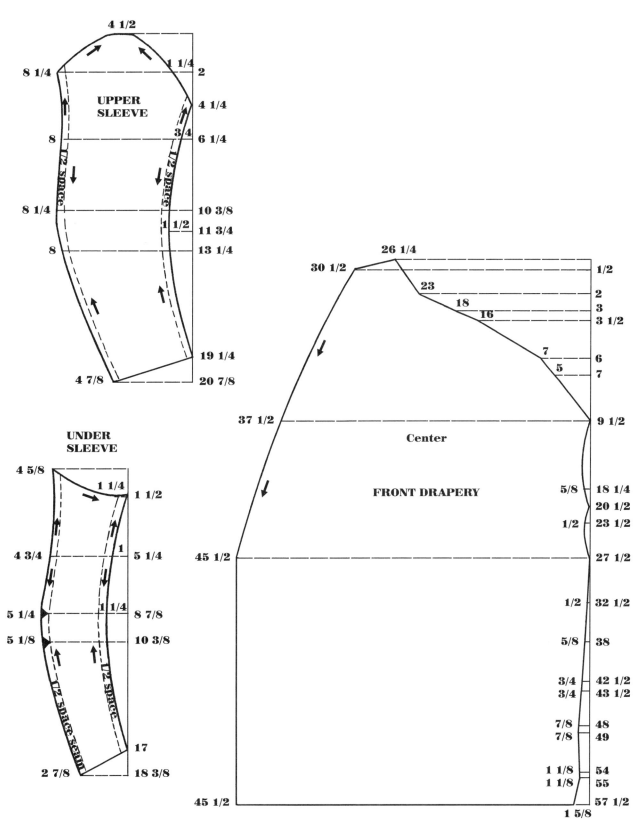

UPPER SLEEVE

4 1/2

1 1/4

8 1/4   2

4 1/4

8   3/4   6 1/4

1/2 space   1/2 space

8 1/4   10 3/8

1 1/2   11 3/4

8   13 1/4

19 1/4

4 7/8   20 7/8

UNDER SLEEVE

4 5/8

1 1/4   1 1/2

4 3/4   1   5 1/4

5 1/4   1 1/4   8 7/8

5 1/8   10 3/8

1/2 space   1/2 space seam

17

2 7/8   18 3/8

26 1/4

30 1/2   1/2

23   2

18   3

16   3 1/2

7   6

5   7

37 1/2   9 1/2

Center

FRONT DRAPERY

5/8   18 1/4
20 1/2

1/2   23 1/2

45 1/2   27 1/2

1/2   32 1/2

5/8   38

3/4   42 1/2
3/4   43 1/2

7/8   48
7/8   49

1 1/8   54
1 1/8   55

45 1/2   57 1/2

1 5/8

149

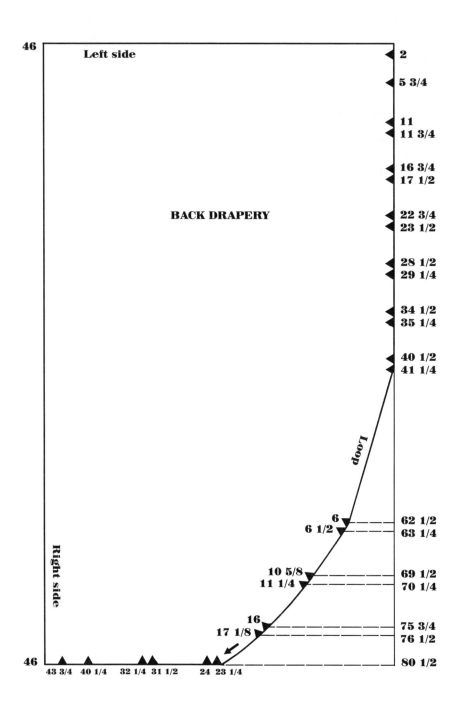

46   Left side   2

5 3/4

11
11 3/4

16 3/4
17 1/2

BACK DRAPERY   22 3/4
23 1/2

28 1/2
29 1/4

34 1/2
35 1/4

40 1/2
41 1/4

Loop

Right side

6   62 1/2
6 1/2   63 1/4

10 5/8   69 1/2
11 1/4   70 1/4

16   75 3/4
17 1/8   76 1/2

46   80 1/2

43 3/4   40 1/4   32 1/4   31 1/2   24   23 1/4

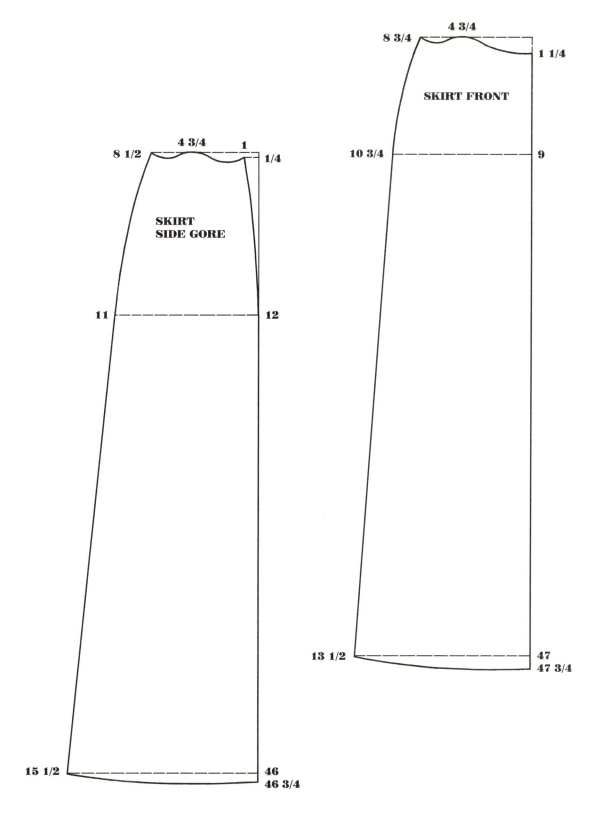

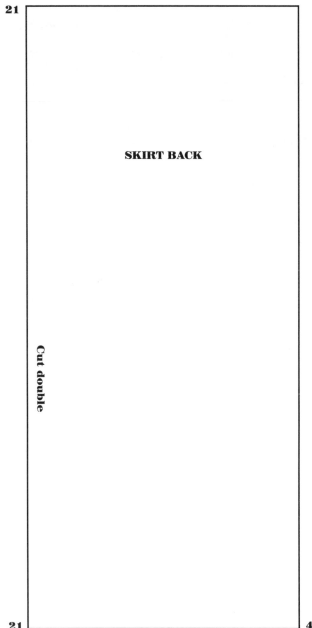

21

SKIRT BACK

Cut double

21   46 1/4

Costume with Walking Skirt. Plain and striped dress materials are associated in this example. The skirt proper is composed of the striped material. It consists of three gores and a full back breadth, the gores being fitted smoothly by darts and the breadth gathered across the top. The skirt is short enough to permit of the addition of a narrow knife-plaiting of the plain material, which is set on underneath. Both skirt and drapery are sewed to the same belt.

Plain material is used for the drapery. The dimensions are obtained by joining straight breadths. The edges are turned under for hems on the left side. The drapery is arranged on the skirt, with the corners of the hemmed edges meeting on the left hip, and flaring toward the lower edge to display the skirt for its full depth on this side. Three overlapping plaits turn toward the hem on the front edge of the drapery. These plaits flare toward the bottom, but are held in their folds by a tape basted to them underneath more than halfway from the top. The hem is also basted to the skirt.

In the drapery, back of the other hem, are five overlapping, backward-turning plaits. These plaits have a tape basted to their underfolds near the top. The tape is likewise basted at its front end to the hem, and the hem is basted to the skirt, so that there is no danger of the drapery spreading too broadly.

153

Just back of the last cluster of plaits described, the top of the drapery is folded and sewed together to form a burnous loop. This loop is allowed to fall inside, the fullness it produces falling into the folds of the plaits. The rest of the fullness at the back is laid in a cluster of six plaits turning forward from the burnous loop. The top of the front is conformed to the shape of the gores by a few shallow plaits that take the place of darts. On the right side the drapery is lifted high by five upward-turning plaits, and basted through these plaits to the skirt over the right side-back seam. The lower edge of the drapery is finished with a hem of medium width. The final adjustment to the figure is regulated by tapes sewed beneath the side-back seams of the skirt and tied together under the back.

Any other preferred combination of materials may be similarly developed. The front drapery may be of lace or embroidered flouncing. Plain and embroidered wools are stylish and dressy.

June 1886 *Delineator*

Over-Skirt

Over-Skirt for Walking Costume. This over-skirt may be made up with a skirt of the same material, and worn with a bodice of plain material. The dress material here chosen is a plaid with a large pattern. The front drapery is a long, pointed tablier. It falls free and straight to the edge of the skirt on the left side, and is lifted with a sweeping curve on the right hip by seven deep plaits arranged to turn forward at the top. Eight forward-turning plaits are also laid in the top near the left edge, and the result of the plaits is evident in the folds of the tablier.

The back drapery presents like effects at the sides, where it falls much shorter than at the center, which descends to the edge. Over the tournure it is very bouffant, the draping being made mostly at the top, where its fullness is simply disposed in two long burnous loops and four backward-turning plaits. Two of the plaits come directly under the burnous loops and the other two directly above them, the folds of all of the plaits meeting at the center. A little below the top, the drapery is caught together at the center to form an inward-falling loop, and in each side a deep, downward-turning plait is laid.

The side edges of the back drapery are included in the side-back seams of the foundation skirt to within a short distance of the lower edge. The placket opening is finished on the left side, a belt completing the top of the foundation skirt and drapery. Two bastings made to the skirt, quite low down on each side, complete the arrangement of the back drapery.

Plaids of any size, striped materials, and plain ones are suited to this mode. Heavy winter cloths and suitings in rough or smooth weaves are liked, and so are velvets and heavy silks. The finish may be plain, or a flat trimming of braid, passementerie, ribbon, or bands of material may be applied.

October 1887 *Delineator*

Ladies' Basque. This basque is illustrated made up in dress material showing a brocaded figure, and small buttons are the only trimmings. The fronts close with button-holes and buttons, the right side being hemmed and the left underfaced. Below the closing, each side is cut off in a short oval. Back of this, the basque is deepened to describe a much longer shape in the same general outline. There are two bust darts and an under-arm dart in each side of the front. At the back are side-back seams and a center back seam. All of the back seams are discontinued a little below the waist-line, and each section of the back is cut to form a little oval tab. The coat sleeves are rounded upward from the wrists toward the outside seams. Each is ornamented on its upper side by five little buttons placed in a row. A standing collar with rounded ends finishes the neck. For a lady of medium size, this basque requires 2 3/4 yards of material 22 inches wide, or 1 1/4 yards of material 48 inches wide.

May 1884 *Delineator*

Ladies' Basque. Sateen is the material illustrated, and lace and ribbon constitute the trimmings. The fronts of the basque close with button-holes and buttons, the right side being hemmed and the left underfaced. There are two bust darts in each side of the front, there is a side piece on each side, and at the back are side-back seams and a center back seam. The side-back seams terminate in dart fashion some distance from the lower edge, and this arrangement aids in adapting the pattern to wash materials.

The lower edge of the basque curves upward slightly from the end of the closing to the back edges of the side pieces. The back, which is considerably deeper, forms two decided points. An ornamental section is arranged flatly beneath the points of the back and falls in a correspondingly shaped point between them. The lower edges of the basque, including all of the edges of the points, are bordered with lace.

The sleeves are in coat shape. Part of their length is turned back in cuff fashion at the wrists, the outside seams being discontinued a little above the lower edges to permit of this process. The reversed parts are faced with the material and bordered with lace. There is a high standing collar about the neck. Over it falls a lace frill. A similar frill sewed below it passes without fullness down the fronts to the bust, and ends at the closing under a ribbon bow.

Any kind of dress material may be made up in this way, the mode being as well adapted to silks and wools as to cottons. For a lady of medium size, this basque requires 3 1/4 yards of material 22 inches wide, 1 7/8 yards of material 36 inches wide, or 1 1/2 yards of material 48 inches wide.

May 1884 *Delineator*

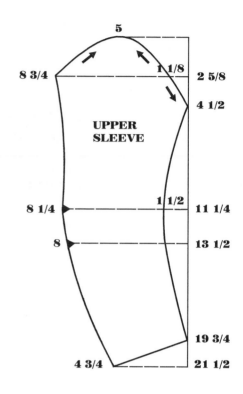

Ladies' Polonaise

This polonaise consists of six pieces: Back, side back, left front, right front, and two sleeve pieces.

In making up this costume, lay two double box-plaits in the back as shown by the diagrams. Join the front and the side back, pressing the seams carefully. Lay four side-plaits on each front as shown by the points; cut in on the space between 17 1/8 and 18 1/8. Sew in the four plaits and press carefully. Set the buttons on the left front.

Loop up the back with one or two loops as desired. Drape the back and the front so that the lower drapery is even.

Bring the drapery on the side back up in five plaits, as shown by the lines between 12 5/8 and 35 1/2. The distance from 12 5/8 to 19 (on the baseline) forms one plait, the center being at 16 1/2, and 19 to 24 forms another. However, it is easier to plait up from the bottom, beginning with 33 to 28 and ending with 19 to 12 5/8.

The skirt is plain, with a foot plaiting. It is drafted with the scale corresponding to the waist measure. The length is regulated with the tape measure. There are three pieces: Front, side gore, and back. Use any kind of buttons and ornaments desired.

1887 *National Garment Cutter Instruction Book*

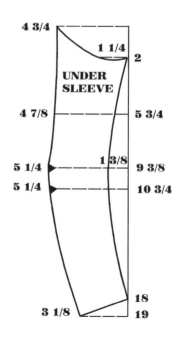

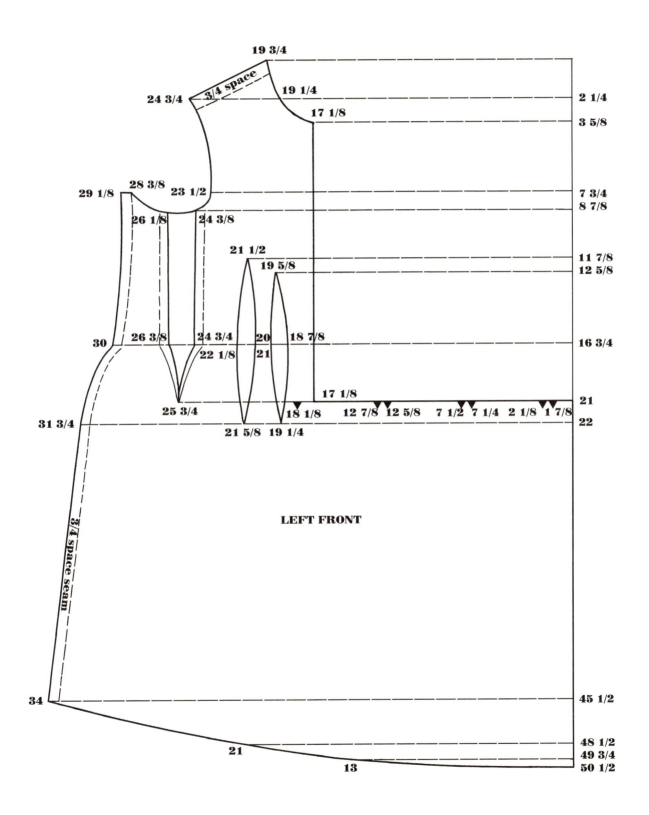

19 3/4

24 3/4   3/4 space   19 1/4

17 1/8

2 1/4

3 5/8

28 3/8   23 1/2

29 1/8

7 3/4

8 7/8

26 1/8   24 3/8

21 1/2

19 5/8

11 7/8

12 5/8

30   26 3/8   24 3/4   20   18 7/8

22 1/8   21

16 3/4

17 1/8

25 3/4   18 1/8   12 7/8   12 5/8   7 1/2   7 1/4   2 1/8   1 7/8

21

31 3/4

21 5/8   19 1/4

22

LEFT FRONT

3/4 space seam

34

45 1/2

21

48 1/2

49 3/4

13

50 1/2

159

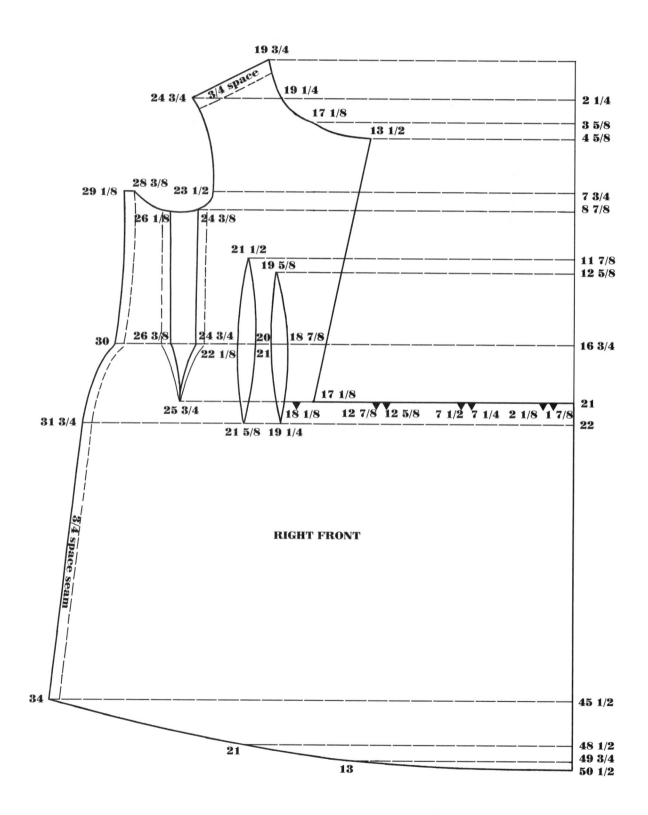

RIGHT FRONT

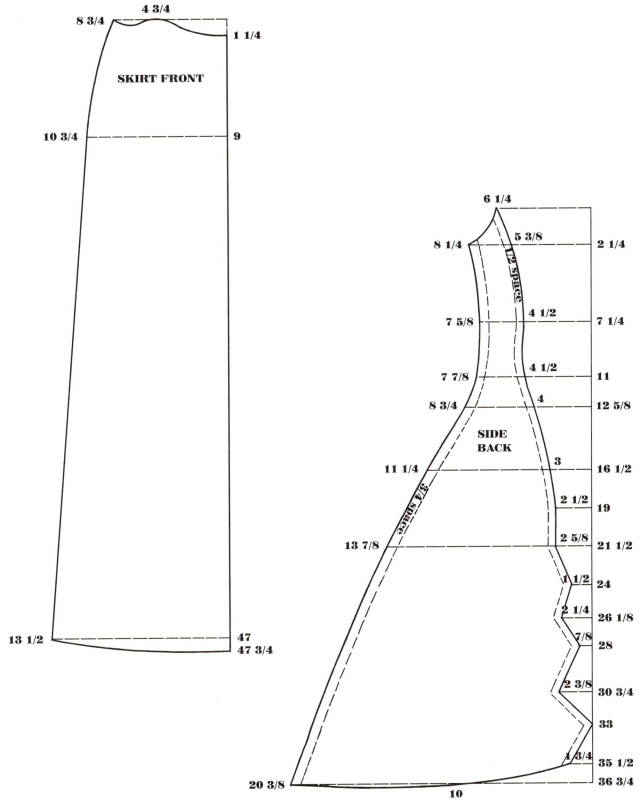

SKIRT FRONT

4 3/4

8 3/4

1 1/4

10 3/4

9

13 1/2

47
47 3/4

6 1/4

8 1/4

5 3/8

2 1/4

1/2 Space

7 5/8

4 1/2

7 1/4

7 7/8

4 1/2

11

8 3/4

4

12 5/8

SIDE BACK

3

16 1/2

11 1/4

2 1/2

19

3/4 space

2 5/8

21 1/2

13 7/8

1 1/2

24

2 1/4

26 1/8

7/8

28

2 3/8

30 3/4

33

1 3/4

35 1/2

20 3/8

10

36 3/4

161

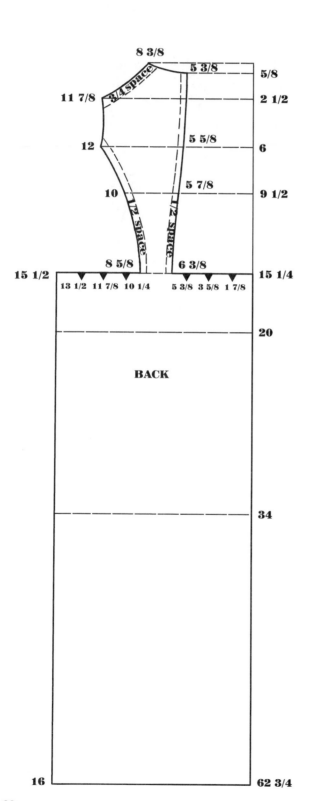

8 3/8

5 3/8   5/8

3/4 space

11 7/8   2 1/2

12   5 5/8   6

10   5 7/8   9 1/2

1/2 space   1/2 space

8 5/8   6 3/8

15 1/2   15 1/4

13 1/2 11 7/8 10 1/4   5 3/8 3 5/8 1 7/8

20

BACK

34

16   62 3/4

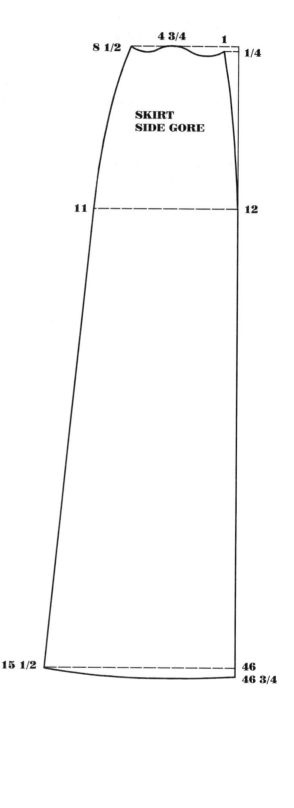

8 1/2   4 3/4   1

1/4

**SKIRT
SIDE GORE**

11   12

15 1/2   46

46 3/4

162

21

SKIRT BACK

Cut double

21   46 1/4

Ladies' Polonaise. This example was developed in broken-plaid dress material, handsome buttons forming its only decorations. It is fitted by double bust darts, single under-arm darts, side backs, and a curved center back seam. The front is closed in double-breasted fashion with buttonholes and buttons. The right side overlaps the left and has a row of buttons added to it to perfect the double-breasted effect. The closing extends to a little below the waist-line, the front edges below it flaring to disclose the skirt. The flare is emphasized by four upward-turning plaits in the back edge of each front.

The back drapery, which is quite bouffant, is arranged by means of an underfolded double box-plait formed from extra width allowed at the end of the center back seam, just below the waist-line. Extra width is also allowed below each side-back seam. This is brought to the outside in a loop, which falls in front of the seam. Two upward-turning plaits are folded in the drapery and basted at the end of the seam. Three upward-turning plaits are folded and basted in regular succession at the center of the back drapery, and bastings are made near the sides lower down to hold the folds in place as illustrated. The entire arrangement is perfected by tapes or elastic straps fastened beneath the side-back seams.

The coat sleeves have three buttons placed in a row on the upper side of each, in front of the outside seam. A high standing collar finishes the neck.

This polonaise may be worn with skirts of the same or contrasting material, and may be trimmed if desired. It may be made of all kinds of standard and fancy dress materials, and of cloths and flannels. To make the garment for a lady of medium size, requires 9 3/8 yards of material 22 inches wide, or 4 yards of material 48 inches wide.

November 1885 *Delineator*

164

 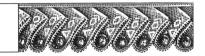

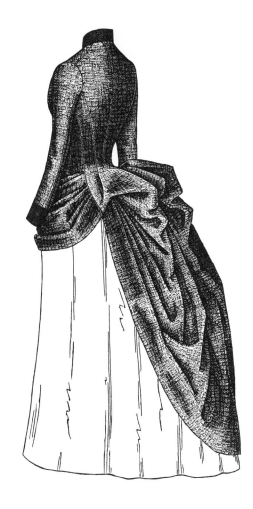

Ladies' Polonaise. This example is developed in fancy dress material, and velvet is introduced effectively. The left side of the front is turned under for a hem at its closing edge. It is then draped high with a pannier effect by six overlapping, upward-turning plaits below the closing, and six other plaits at its back edge, which also turn upward and overlap each other in pairs. The right side is shaped to overlap the left broadly, and its upper part is turned back in a lapel faced with velvet. The closing is invisibly made along the center of the figure with hooks and eyes. The edge below the lapel is also held in place by button-holes and small crocheted buttons, as far as the plaits in the front edge of the pannier. There is a dart near the closing edge of the right side, and two

bust darts are at the opposite side of its center. There is also an under-arm dart in this side. In the left side are two bust darts and an under-arm dart.

The right side falls in a point low on the figure. It is draped by five overlapping, upward-turning plaits laid in its back edge just below the waist-line. Side-back seams and a curved center seam shape the back. All three of them end a little below the waist-line, at the top of extra widths. The latter are arranged to form two box-plaits, which are triple at their inner and single at their outer folds. At the end of the center back seam, seven shallow upward-turning plaits are folded one on the other in the length of the drapery. Their arrangement, together with a single downward-turning plait in each front edge of the back, produces a bouffant effect. The square outline of the back is transformed into a

pointed effect by five upward-turning plaits laid in the left side edge and turned to come crosswise of the drapery under the single downward-turning plait in this side.

Three tapes or elastic straps fastened beneath the side seams hold the fronts closely to the figure, and prevent the back drapery from spreading too broadly. The coat sleeves are finished at the wrists with round cuff-facings of velvet. The neck is completed with a velvet standing collar.

All kinds of plain and fancy materials are chosen for polonaises, and the edge finish is usually plain. When a polonaise to wear with a special skirt is being constructed, its facings, etc., may be chosen with reference to the skirt, but otherwise they had better be of a neutral color. Polonaises of very soft, clinging wools in black, dull red, sapphire, terra-cotta, and warm brown are fashionable with velvet skirts of the same colors. For a lady of medium size, this polonaise requires 7 3/4 yards of material 22 inches wide, or 4 yards of material 44 inches wide. Each requires 1/2 yard of velvet 20 inches wide for the collar, etc.

February 1887 *Delineator*

Ladies' Costume

The quantity of material required for the basque and the skirt is 7 5/8 yards of material 48 inches wide, and 1 1/4 yards of velvet for the vest and the skirt front.

The basque is drafted with the scale corresponding to the bust measure. It is in eight pieces: Vest, front, side piece, side back, back, collar, and two sleeve pieces. The vest may be made of velvet or any material in a contrasting color. It is sewed into the first dart and into the shoulder seam. The sleeves may be finished at the wrist with a small round cuff of the same material as the vest.

The over-skirt is drafted with the waist measure. It is in four pieces: Front, right drapery, left drapery, and back drapery. The front is made of the same material as the basque vest and cuffs. The right side has five side-plaits turning toward the front, as shown on the diagram. The left side consists of two double box-plaits. The back drapery is laid in five plaits turning toward the center of the back. It is draped up to make the bottom even.

The straps across the front are 3 1/2 inches wide. The lower one is 7 inches long, and the upper one is 5 1/2 inches long. Cut the remaining four to correspond, and fasten on the front of the skirt, as shown by the engraving.

The foundation skirt is in three pieces: Front, side gore, and back. It is drafted with the waist measure. The length is regulated with the tape measure. Assemble the foundation skirt and finish the bottom with knife-plaiting 3 inches wide. Press the plaits of the drapery carefully, and baste with tape underneath, to stay the plaits. Fasten the drapery to the foundation skirt at the waist with a belt.

1887 *National Garment Cutter Instruction Book*

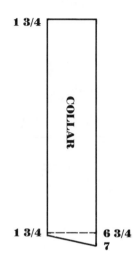

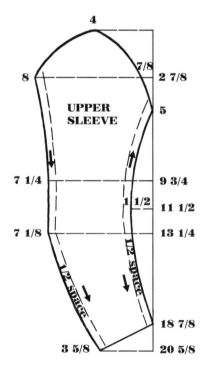

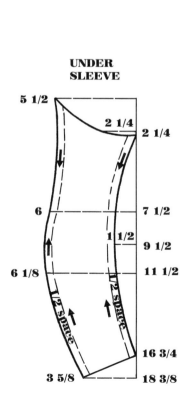

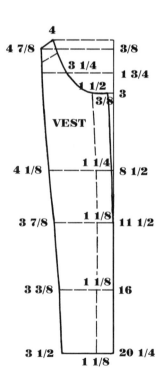

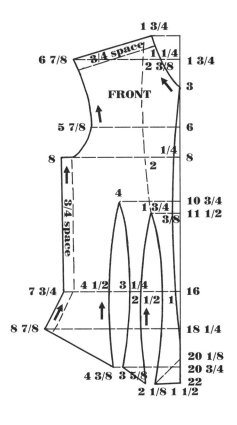

FRONT

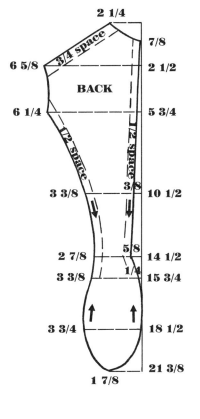

BACK

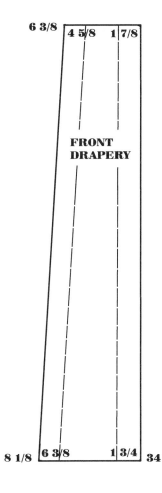

FRONT DRAPERY

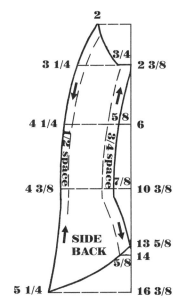

SIDE BACK

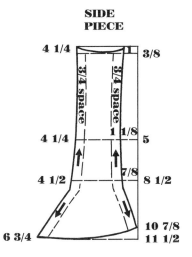

SIDE PIECE

169

Ensembles

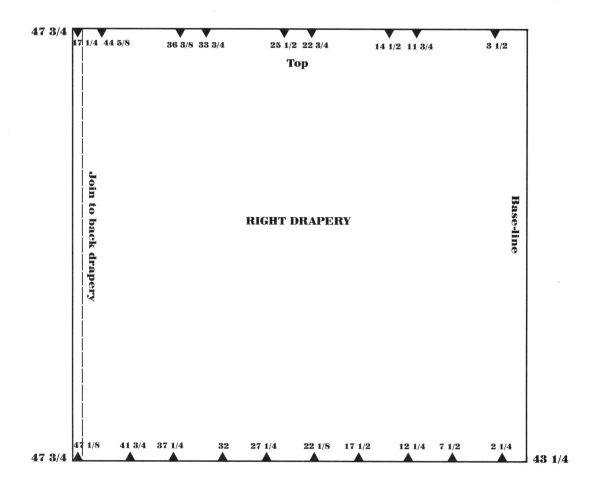

47 3/4

47 1/4 44 5/8   36 3/8 33 3/4   25 1/2 22 3/4   14 1/2 11 3/4   3 1/2

Top

Join to back drapery

RIGHT DRAPERY

Base-line

47 1/8   41 3/4 37 1/4   32   27 1/4   22 1/8   17 1/2   12 1/4 7 1/2   2 1/4

47 3/4   43 1/4

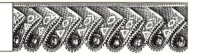

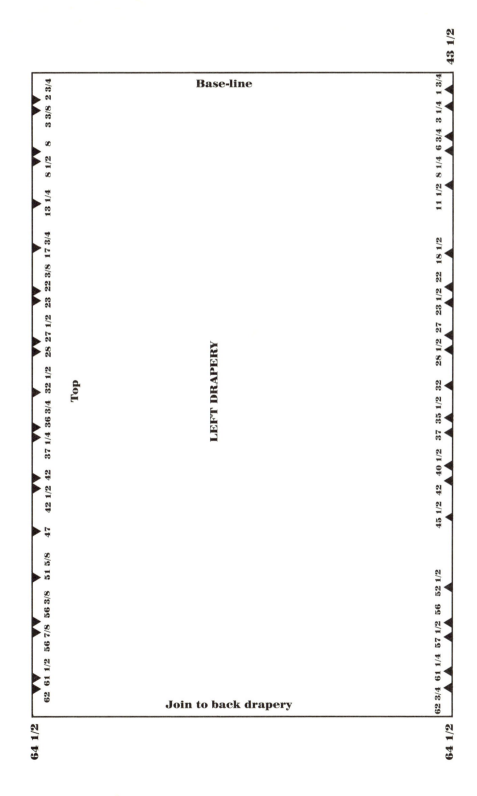

Base-line

Top

LEFT DRAPERY

Join to back drapery

64 1/2

62 61 1/2 56 7/8 56 3/8 51 5/8 47 42 1/2 42 37 1/4 36 3/4 32 1/2 28 27 1/2 23 22 3/8 17 3/4 13 1/4 8 1/2 8 3 3/8 2 3/4

43 1/2

64 1/2

62 3/4 61 1/4 57 1/2 56 52 1/2 45 1/2 42 40 1/2 37 35 1/2 32 28 1/2 27 23 1/2 22 18 1/2 11 1/2 8 1/4 6 3/4 3 1/4 1 3/4

171

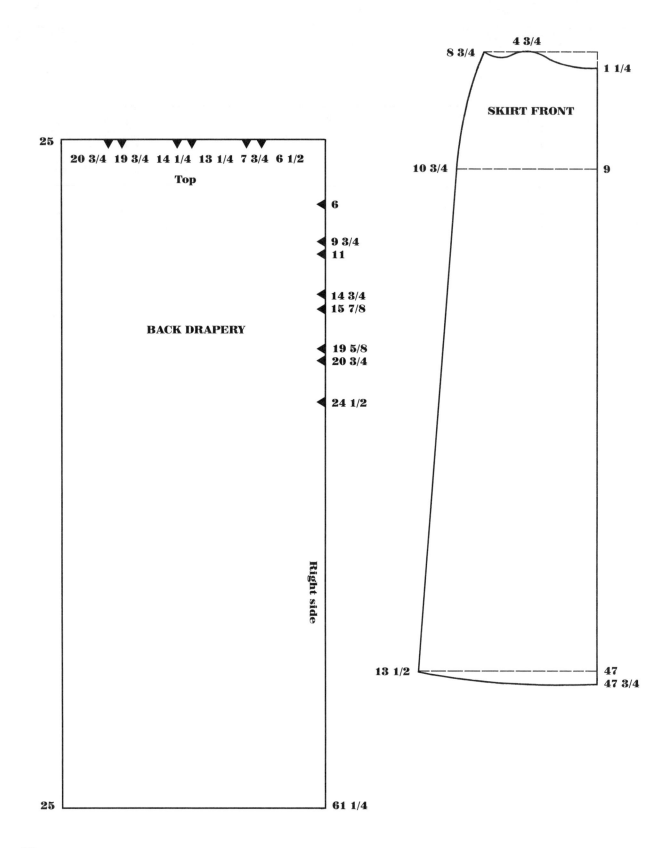

25

20 3/4 19 3/4 14 1/4 13 1/4 7 3/4 6 1/2

Top

6

9 3/4
11

14 3/4
15 7/8

19 5/8
20 3/4

24 1/2

BACK DRAPERY

Right side

25   61 1/4

4 3/4

8 3/4   1 1/4

SKIRT FRONT

10 3/4   9

13 1/2   47
                                                 47 3/4

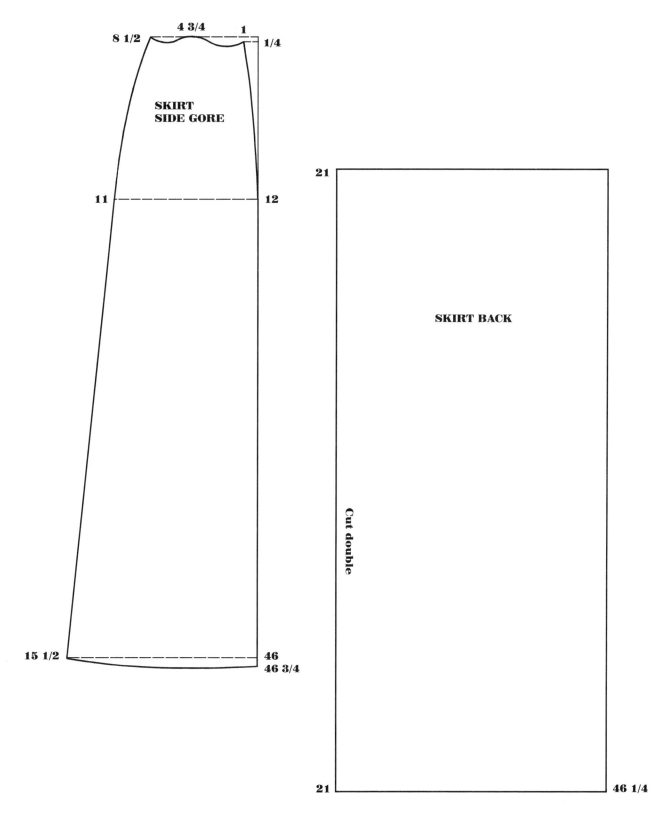

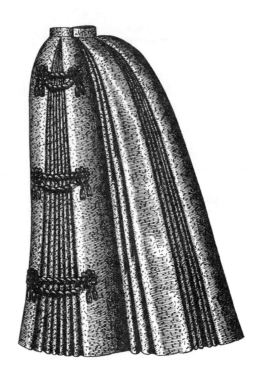

Walking Skirt. This skirt is shown made of fancy cloth, and trimmed with braid ornaments. The gores of the foundation skirt are fitted by darts. The back breadth is gathered across the top and made bouffant by two steels run in casings across it. Tapes are sewed to the side-back seams at the ends of the casings and tied together, to regulate the closeness of the skirt. If a bustle is not to be worn, the extra allowance at the top of the back breadth pattern may be cut off; and if a still less bouffant effect is desired, the steels may be omitted. The drapery falls even with the bottom of the foundation skirt. Both skirt and drapery are sewed to the same belt; the placket opening is on the left side.

The drapery over the front and side gores consists of a single section formed by joining straight breadths. On the left side, it is arranged in a fan of eight plaits, which turn toward each other and flare toward the bottom. Three frog ornaments of cord are arranged across this fan of plaits. The rest of the fullness is taken up by wide side-plaits turning from the right side toward the left. The top is scantily shirred to adapt it to the shape of the gores. All of the plaits are stayed by tapes basted to their underfolds. The side edges are included in the side-back seams of the skirt, as are the side edges of the back drapery. The latter is a wide breadth that is laid in two triple box-plaits. These plaits swing loosely but do not lose their folds.

This mode makes up well in both silks and wools, and is especially admired for rich materials and cloths. The edges of the plaits in the fan may be bordered with beads or drop ornaments. The fan may be made of silk, and the overlapping side edges of the fan may be faced with velvet or other contrasting material. To make the skirt for a lady of medium size, requires 15 1/2 yards of material 22 inches wide, or 8 3/8 yards of material 44 inches wide.

September 1887 *Delineator*

174

Costume with Walking Skirt

Costume with Walking Skirt. This example is shown in heavy dress material, with braid passementerie for trimming. The foundation skirt is covered from the belt to the bottom by the draperies. It is usually made of inexpensive silk or lining material and faced for a desirable distance at the bottom. The three gores are fitted by darts. The back breadth is gathered across the top and made bouffant by two steels run in casings across it. Tapes are sewed to the side-back seams at the ends of the casings and tied together, to regulate the adjustment. A belt finishes the top.

The flat drapery covering the front and side gores has three broad kilt-plaits laid in it on each side. These plaits turn forward, and are stayed underneath to preserve their folds all the way down. The plaits nearest the center of the front are wide apart, so that a panel effect is achieved. Back of the plaits, the drapery also presents a panel effect on each side. A dart under each plait removes all unnecessary fullness at the top. A panel of braid passementerie is applied to the center of the front drapery, and four braid passementerie ornaments are arranged on the plait nearest the back, on each side.

A wide breadth forms the back drapery. Four deep, overlapping, backward-turning plaits are laid in the top, on each side of the center. Just in front of each group, a long burnous loop is formed. The under sides of these loops are basted to the drapery. Three backward-turning plaits are laid in front of each burnous loop. Two upward-turning plaits are laid in each side edge near the belt. About halfway down each side, the drapery is basted to the skirt three times. The draperies are included in the side-back seams of the skirt. The placket opening is on the left side.

Velvet, silk, broadcloth, and all kinds of cloths and suitings may be made up in this way. The center of the front drapery may be faced with velvet, plush, or other contrasting material. The folds of the plaits may be bound or piped.

October 1887 *Delineator*

Ladies' Basque. Vests of heavy white Marseilles and repped piqué are fashionable features of cotton dress bodices for summer. This basque is illustrated in figured wash material with a white vest. The vest is overlapped by the fronts proper in Breton fashion, being sewed into the darts nearest the front edges and joined flatly above them. The vest is closed with button-holes and small ball-shaped pearl buttons. The lower edge of the vest is pointed, as are the fronts proper, which are somewhat deeper than the vest. The lower edges of the fronts curve up quite high back of the points.

In addition to the darts, the basque is fitted by side pieces, side backs, and a center back seam. The center back and side-back seams end a little below the waist-line. The center backs fall in tab fashion, deepening back of the hips with a pointed inclination toward the side backs.

The finish of the coat sleeves is severely plain; they may be worn with narrow linen cuffs. About the neck is a standing collar, which is divided into three sections. One is of the basque material and overlaps the other two, which are of the vest material and sewed to the corresponding sections of the vest.

To make the basque for a lady of medium size, requires 3 1/4 yards of material 22 inches wide, or 1 5/8 yards of material 44 inches wide. In the combination pictured, it needs 1 5/8 yards of figured material and 5/8 yard of plain material 36 inches wide.

April 1887 *Delineator*

 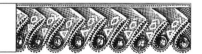

Ladies' Basque. Plain and brocaded dress materials are united in the construction of this basque. The fronts are curved at their closing edges, and the closing is made with button-holes and buttons. In each side is a curved bust dart, and side pieces and side-back seams complete the adjustment. The back, however, is in one piece and tapers off to a point at its lower extremity. The side-back seams, instead of curving into the armholes, are carried to the shoulder seams. The back is cut from brocaded material. A vest-facing of the same is applied on the front, its outline being graduated so that it is of even breadth with the backs at the shoulder seams. A graceful curve is maintained over the bust, while toward the lower edge the width is decreased to a point at the end of the closing. The lower outline of the basque is curved upward slightly over the hips. Beneath the lower edges of the side backs are placed medium-long loops and ends of ribbon, which fall on each side of the center back point.

The sleeves are in coat shape. The outside seam of each is left open for some distance from the wrist, while the length below it is turned back in cuff fashion, and faced with brocade. A full frill of lace sewed inside falls over the wrist. A high standing collar of brocade, over which falls a lace frill, completes the neck.

Plain and plaid materials are often associated in this fashion, as well as plain and figured materials of all kinds. One material may be used throughout, if preferred, and the back and front may be trimmed with braid or any other flat trimming. To make the basque for a lady of medium size, requires 2 5/8 yards of plain material and 1 yard of brocade 22 inches wide, or 1 1/4 yards of plain material and 3/4 yard of brocade 48 inches wide.

May 1885 *Delineator*

Ladies' Polonaise

This garment is drafted with the scale corresponding to the bust measure. It is in six pieces: Right front, left front, back (drafted together with the side back), collar, and two sleeve pieces. It may be made of any material, the quantity of material 48 inches wide required being 4 1/2 yards. The side of the left front is sewed together with the back drapery. Lay four upward-turning plaits on the side of the right front, and fasten them to the back, as shown. The ribbon bow may be omitted if preferred.

On the back, the line running diagonally from 24 3/4 on the base-line to 6 1/2 on the waist-line, extending to 9 5/8 on the waist-line, is laid in five side-plaits, turning toward the center of the back, and fastened firmly to the center of the back. Lay six side-plaits on each side, on the cross-line that runs

from 32 3/4 to 19 3/4. Then press them carefully, and baste to tape to stay the plaits. Omit the basting at the bottom. Lay two loops on each side of the back drapery, as shown by the engraving.

This polonaise may be worn with a kilt-plaited skirt. Or with a skirt plaited in front and on the right side, with a straight back breadth, and narrow knife-plaiting at the bottom, as the drapery falls nearly to the bottom of the skirt at the back.

1887 *National Garment Cutter Instruction Book*

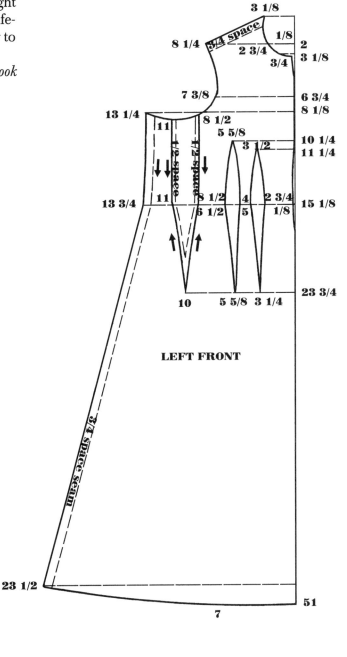

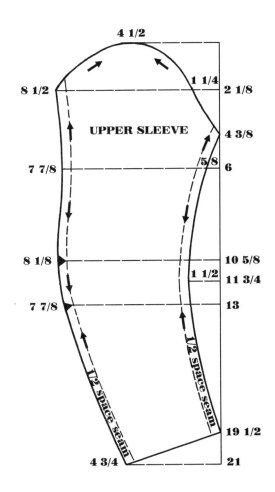

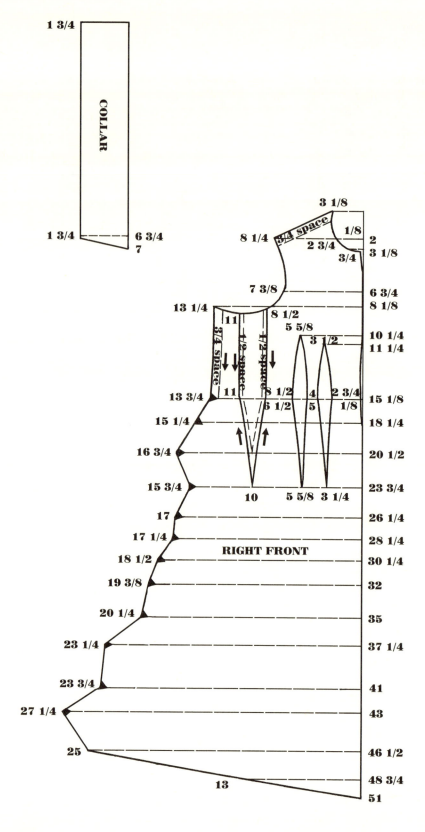

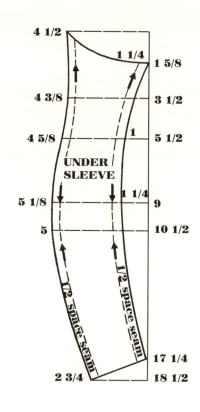

COLLAR

1 3/4

1 3/4   6 3/4
         7

UNDER
SLEEVE

4 1/2   1 1/4   1 5/8
4 3/8   3 1/2
4 5/8   1   5 1/2
5 1/8   1 1/4   9
5   10 1/2
1/2 space seam   1/2 space seam
2 3/4   17 1/4
         18 1/2

3 1/8
8 1/4   3/4 space   1/8   2
         2 3/4   3/4   3 1/8
7 3/8   6 3/4
13 1/4   8 1/2   8 1/8
11   5 5/8   3 1/2   10 1/4
3/4 space 1/2 space 1/2 space   11 1/4
13 3/4   11   8 1/2   4   2 3/4   15 1/8
              6 1/2   5   1/8
15 1/4   18 1/4
16 3/4   20 1/2
15 3/4   23 3/4
         10   5 5/8   3 1/4
17   26 1/4
17 1/4   28 1/4
18 1/2   RIGHT FRONT   30 1/4
19 3/8   32
20 1/4   35
23 1/4   37 1/4
23 3/4   41
27 1/4   43
25   46 1/2
         13   48 3/4
                               51

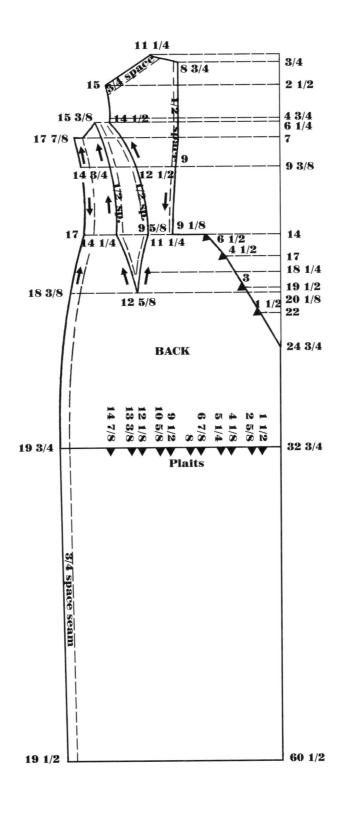

Street Costume

The polonaise is drafted with the scale corresponding to the bust measure. It is in six pieces: Right front, left front, back, collar, and two sleeve pieces. Each plait is marked. The left front has seven upward-turning plaits. The right front has three upward-turning plaits. The two fronts are drafted separately, but the material of which the polonaise is made should be cut double to avoid a seam down the front. However, it is left open from the top to point 25 on the base-lines of the right and left fronts. The back and side back are drafted together. The extra fullness at the back is laid in plaits. There are two loops, one on each side. The back is draped up until it becomes even at the bottom of the skirt.

A plain skirt is worn with this polonaise. There are three pieces: Front, side gore, and back. It is drafted with the scale corresponding to the waist measure. The length is regulated with the tape measure. Any style of trimming may be used.

1887 *National Garment Cutter Instruction Book*

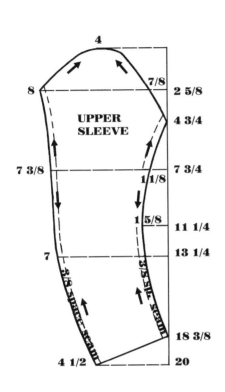

UPPER SLEEVE

4

8   7/8   2 5/8

4 3/4

7 3/8   1 1/8   7 3/4

1 5/8   11 1/4

7   13 1/4

3/8 space seam

18 3/8

4 1/2   20

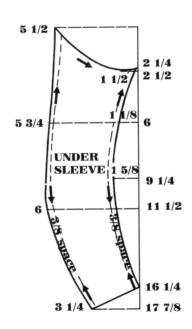

UNDER SLEEVE

5 1/2

2 1/4
1 1/2   2 1/2
1 1/8   6

5 3/4

1 5/8   9 1/4

6   11 1/2

3/8 space

16 1/4

3 1/4   17 7/8

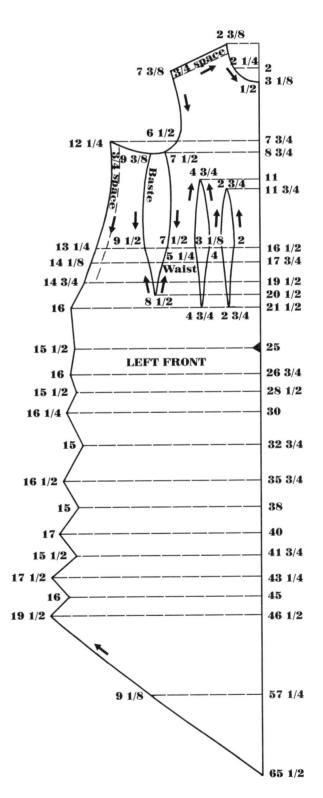

LEFT FRONT

2 3/8

7 3/8   3/4 space   2 1/4   2
   1/2   3 1/8

6 1/2   7 3/4

12 1/4   8 3/4

3/4 space   9 3/8   7 1/2   4 3/4   11
Baste   2 3/4   11 3/4

13 1/4   9 1/2   7 1/2   3 1/8   2   16 1/2
14 1/8   5 1/4   4   17 3/4
Waist
14 3/4   19 1/2
   20 1/2
16   8 1/2   4 3/4   2 3/4   21 1/2

15 1/2   25

16   26 3/4

15 1/2   28 1/2

16 1/4   30

15   32 3/4

16 1/2   35 3/4

15   38

17   40

15 1/2   41 3/4

17 1/2   43 1/4

16   45

19 1/2   46 1/2

9 1/8   57 1/4

65 1/2

183

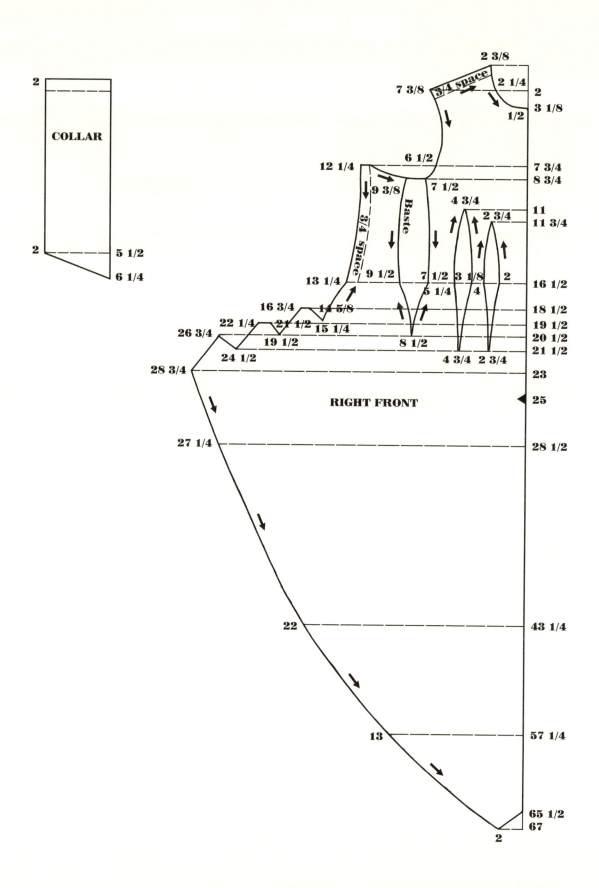

COLLAR

2

2

5 1/2

6 1/4

2 3/8

7 3/8   3/4 space   2 1/4   2

1/2   3 1/8

6 1/2   7 3/4

12 1/4   8 3/4

9 3/8   7 1/2   4 3/4

Baste   2 3/4   11

3/4 space   11 3/4

13 1/4   9 1/2   7 1/2   3 1/8   2   16 1/2

5 1/4   4

16 3/4   14 5/8   18 1/2

22 1/4   21 1/2   15 1/4   19 1/2

26 3/4   19 1/2   20 1/2

24 1/2   8 1/2   21 1/2

4 3/4   2 3/4

28 3/4   23

RIGHT FRONT   25

27 1/4   28 1/2

22   43 1/4

13   57 1/4

65 1/2

67

2

184

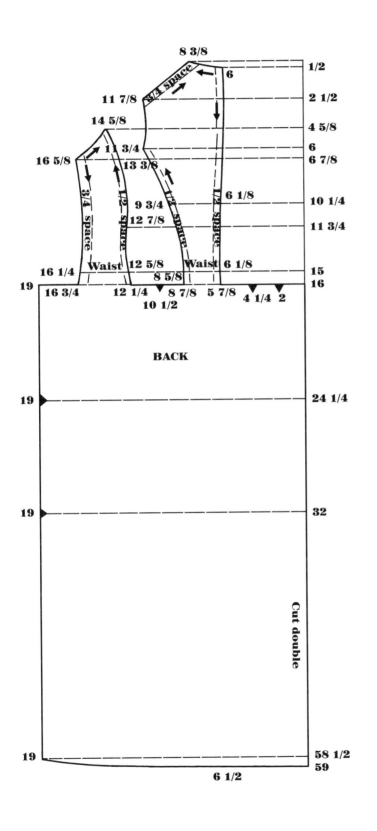

8 3/8

1/2

6

11 7/8

2 1/2

3/4 space

14 5/8

4 5/8

11 3/4

6

16 5/8

13 3/8

6 7/8

3/4 space

1/2 space

1/2 space

9 3/4

6 1/8

1/2 space

10 1/4

12 7/8

11 3/4

16 1/4

Waist

12 5/8

Waist

6 1/8

15

8 5/8

16

19

16 3/4

12 1/4

8 7/8

5 7/8

10 1/2

4 1/4

2

BACK

19

24 1/4

19

32

Cut double

19

58 1/2

59

6 1/2

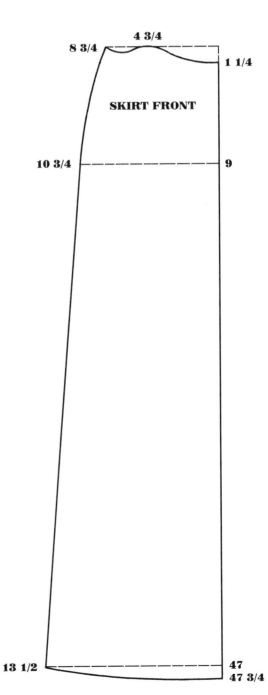

4 3/4

8 3/4

1 1/4

SKIRT FRONT

10 3/4

9

13 1/2

47

47 3/4

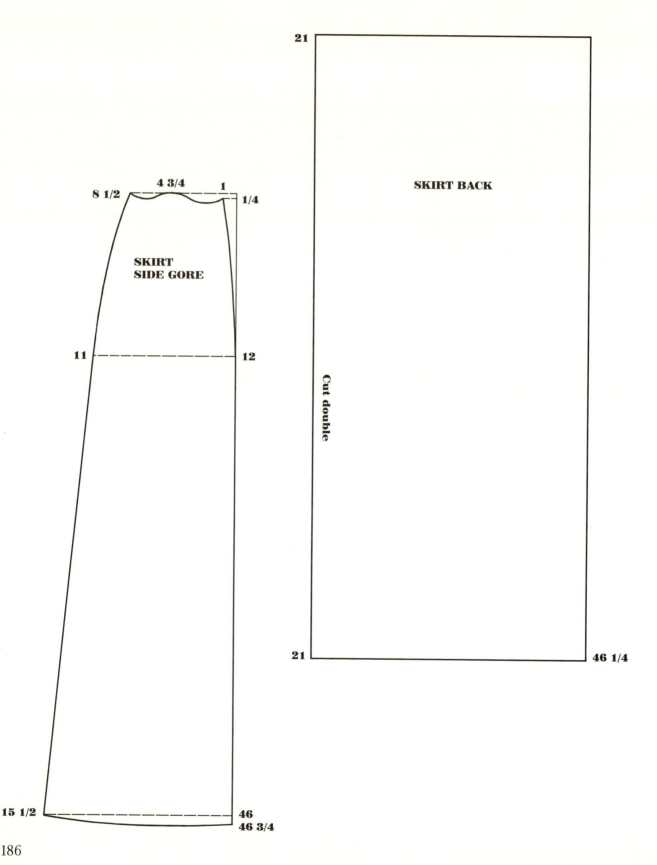

8 1/2 **4 3/4** **1** **1/4**

**SKIRT
SIDE GORE**

11 **12**

15 1/2 **46**
46 3/4

21 **SKIRT BACK**

Cut double

21 **46 1/4**

186

 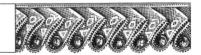

Ladies' Polonaise. Figured foulard is the material pictured, and velvet facings and velvet ribbon bows constitute the trimmings. The closing is made from the throat to below the waist with button-holes and buttons, the right edge being underfaced and the left furnished with a button stand. In each side are two bust darts and an under-arm dart, and at the back are side-back seams and a curved center seam.

The bottom of the front drapery is rounded upward toward the right side. In this side are laid six upward-turning plaits, their folds giving the edge a jabot effect, which is enhanced by a velvet underfacing. Seven upward-turning plaits, folded one upon the other, are laid quite high up in the left side of the front. Below these plaits a narrow extra width is allowed.

The center back and side-back seams end a little below the waist, and extra widths are allowed at their terminations. These widths are folded underneath to form box-plaits, which are double at their inner and single at their outer folds. On the right side edge, a little below the tops of these plaits, is also allowed extra width. This width is underfolded in three backward-turning plaits and a hem. The hem overlaps the folds of the plaits in the corresponding side of the front and is sewed flatly over them. The hemmed edge falls much below the front on this side, and the plaits back of it spread out slightly toward the lower edge.

The left side of the back is also hemmed for a part of its depth below the side seam. Three loops are made in the hemmed part. The upper loop is basted to the lower end of the side seam, and the next loop over the left side of the front. The bottom loop is carried underneath the back drapery and basted a little back of the hem, so as to fall over a group of plaits that take up the remaining length of the back drapery on this side. These plaits are basted to the drapery at the top of the extra width cut upon the front, a basting being made through the loop to render the arrangement permanent. This process brings the bottom of the back drapery partway up the side. The part thus drawn up is turned under for a hem, the hem being invisibly sewed over the extended edge of the front.

The back drapery is raised by a single inward-falling loop basted at the end of the center seam, and by two tapes of unequal lengths basted to the center seam. The opposite end of the shorter tape is basted at the inner folds of the plaits on the left side, and the opposite end of the other tape is basted to the center of the drapery lower down. A strap of wide elastic sewed to the side seams, a little below the waist, confines the back drapery within a becoming space.

The outside seam of each coat sleeve is discontinued far enough from the hand to permit of turning the sleeve back in cuff fashion. The reversed part is faced with velvet. The high standing collar is made of velvet, and a velvet ribbon bow is fastened to it at the left shoulder seam. A long-looped, velvet ribbon bow is fastened over the draping on the right side.

The polonaise may be of the same material as the skirt, or an entirely different material. Étamine, serge, summer flannels and cloths, surah, pongee, foulard silks and cottons, canvas materials, sateens, chambrays, and materials with fancy borders are suitable. The polonaise may be trimmed with embroidery, lace, appliqués, bands, etc. Lace or embroidery may border the lower edges, simulate a vest, and trim the neck and wrists. However, striped materials look best with a plain finish. To make the polonaise for a lady of medium size, requires 10 3/8 yards of material 22 inches wide, 6 1/4 yards of material 36 inches wide, or 4 7/8 yards of material 48 inches wide. Each requires 1 1/8 yards of velvet 20 inches wide for facings.

June 1886 *Delineator*

Ladies' Polonaise. This polonaise is pictured made of plain dress material, and trimmed with velvet cuff-facings, collar, and an ornamental pocket lap that has fancy buttons and simulated button-holes. The garment is closed from the throat to the bottom with button-holes and small buttons, the right side edge being hemmed. It is fitted by double bust darts, single under-arm darts, side-back seams, and a curved center back seam. The center back and side-back seams end at the top of extra widths. These widths are underfolded to form two box-plaits, which are double at their inner and single at their outer folds. A single loose, inward-falling plait is basted at the center of the back, not far below the end of the seam. A little below the waist-line, four upward-turning plaits are folded in regular succession in each side seam. By these means the front is cross-wrinkled and the back rendered bouffant. The drapery is confined to a narrow space at the back with an elastic strap, which is fastened below the plaits in the sides and a little back of the side seams.

Upon each side rests a broad, ornamental lap made of velvet. The lap is sewed in place at the top and turned down over its own seam. Along the top of each lap, three large fancy buttons are placed, and from beneath the buttons extend long, simulated button-holes formed of silk cord. The laps are basted in place at their lower back corners. The coat sleeves are completed with velvet cuff-facings. A velvet collar is sewed to the neck.

Plain, plaid, checked, and striped dress materials are made up in this style to wear with skirts of the same or of different material. The collar, cuff-facings, and ornamental laps may be of the dress material, or of a contrasting material. For a lady of medium size, this polonaise requires 9 1/8 yards of material 22 inches wide, 6 1/4 yards of material 36 inches wide, or 4 1/2 yards of material 44 inches wide. Each requires 3/8 yard of velvet 20 inches wide for the collar, etc.

June 1887 *Delineator*

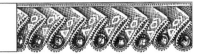

Princess Dress. For dressy house wear, break-fast, five-o-clock teas, and informal receptions, this dress is a charming and simple fashion. It may be handsomely made up even in the least expensive materials. Cashmere is the material pictured, with cashmere, velvet, and ribbon trimmings. The fronts close to the top of the trimming with button-holes and buttons, and along the trimming with hooks and eyes, the right side being hemmed. In each side are two bust darts and an under-arm dart.

At the back are side-back seams and a curved center seam. The center and side-back seams end a little below the waist-line at the top of extra widths. These are underfolded to form two box-plaits, which are single at their outer and double at their inner folds. The back is cut sufficiently long at its front edges to permit of folding three downward-turning plaits in each side a little below the waist-line. Below the end of the center back seam, two upward-turning plaits are folded. These plaits produce a bouffant drapery, which is held in place by two tapes. Each tape is basted at the end of its respective side-back seam and its opposite end to the skirt back considerably lower down, a third basting being made to the skirt a little above the lower end. Tapes are also sewed beneath the side seams and tied together, to regulate the close-ness of the skirt to the figure. The draping leaves the bottom of the skirt uniformly rounded and of walking length.

A double box-plaiting of cashmere, surmounted by a velvet band, trims the bottom of the skirt, the plaiting being about 5 inches deep and the band a little narrower. The outside seam of each coat sleeve is discontinued far enough from the lower edge to permit of turning it back in cuff fashion, the reversed part being faced with velvet. The high standing collar is also of velvet. Velvet lapel ornaments extend from the tops of the shoulder seams to below the waist-line, gradually tapering to a point at the closing. These ornaments turn back over their own seams. A long-looped ribbon bow is fastened over their lower ends.

Cotton materials are much favored for such dresses during the summer. Batiste; chambray; sateen; percale; piqué; lawn; nainsook; and plain, figured, and embroidered novelty materials are especially desirable. Soft wools and silks of all kinds are also suitable. Lace, embroidery, braid, or contrasting bands may be added. The bottom of the dress may be trimmed all around with plaitings, ruffles, bands, etc. To make it for a lady of medium size, requires 8 yards of material 22 inches wide, 5 1/8 yards of material 36 inches wide, or 3 7/8 yards of material 48 inches wide.

May 1886 *Delineator*

7. Jackets and Outer Wear

Dressy mantles for spring are small, and are more often colored than black. For the last cool days they are made of frisé velvet, sicilienne, or figured camel's hair. For summer weather they are of beaded grenadine, velvet-figured grenadine, or lace. They are now lined with glacé silk instead of surah, and this is in changeable colors, checks, or fine stripes. The trimmings are beaded passementeries and gathered frills of lace, which may be imitation thread lace, or the wool lace indiscriminately called yak or angora. Chenille fringes are again used, with jet drops amid their headings, or with tinsel combined with the chenille strands. Galloons, with beads and with tinsel, trim colored mantles.

These mantles are quite short at the back, reaching only a short distance below the waist-line. They have three seams, giving two center back pieces that fit almost as closely as a dress. The sides are shoulder pieces all in one, and may form a small sleeve, or merely lap forward on the arm. The fronts may be very long, or only extend halfway to the knees. A ribbon attached to the back seam inside ties around the waist, and there are other bands of elastic ribbon to hold the sides in place, or to adjust the fullness on the tournure. These mantles are usually very high in the neck, and are trimmed there with a full frill of lace.

All laces are gathered instead of being plaited. A single frill 3 inches wide, set just under the edge of the wrap, is sufficient trimming for plain mantles. This frill extends up each side of the front, and passes around the neck. If there must be more elaborate trimming, the edge of the garment is cut in points. It is finished with jetted pendants that fall on the lace; or else there is a jetted network, or passementerie of jet plaques, stars, leaves, or flowers, with drooping fringe set on above the gathered edge of the lace. There may also be two lace frills, one narrower than the other, and both sewed under the jet trimming. Wide satin ribbon bows, or sash loops and ends, are added on the tournure of some mantles.

Long newmarket coats are made with loose-fitting fronts and close-fitting backs. They have a pointed hood lined with changeable silk, and are without trimming other than the stitching on their edges. They are made of serge, cheviot, diagonal cloths, or the oatmeal or momie cloths with tiny specks raised on the surface. They are closed with large buttons of metal cut in fancy figures. Olive, brown, garnet, and bronze newmarkets are shown in cheviot and other cloths. For midsummer travel similar garments are made of gray, écru, or brown mohair, and also of pongee.

March 21, 1885 *Harper's Bazar*

Plush is the fashionable material for the long evening cloaks that cover the wearer from head to foot. Fawn and pale gray plush cloaks are new, while those of cream or ruby are still popular. Gilt passementerie ornaments, light fur, and feather borders are the trimmings. Rich, large-figured brocades are also used for these long cloaks and for shorter mantles. White or pink basket cloths with feather borders and gay satin linings are for less expensive wraps.

December 19, 1885 *Harper's Bazar*

Cloaks and plaids of English cloth are most used for ulsters that may be worn over any dress, and thus transform it into a traveling toilette. These ulsters are very close-fitting and single breasted, and have the fullness plaited in at the waist-line at the back. They are long enough to conceal the entire dress. This useful wrap is completed with a shoulder cape reaching nearly to the elbows, or with a silk-lined hood.

Coaching ulsters, to be worn when riding on a coach or when driving in gentlemen's open English carts, are of light tan livery cloth of the smooth thick kind called box cloth. These are close fitting and double breasted. They have strapped seams; that is, a band of the cloth with raw edges is stitched on outside the seams, one line of stitching being near each edge. This band is 3/4 inch wide. The velvet collar, which is the same shade as the cloth, is a square-cornered rolling collar attached to a high standing cloth collar. It is bordered all around with a stitched strap of the cloth, and is called a Russian collar. The very large buttons are of white pearl, with etched designs.

An extra jacket worn here as a driving or walking coat is really the "covert coat," which English-women wear over their riding habits on cold days. The seams are lapped to show a raw edge and a single line of stitching, in what are called welted seams. This jacket has the velvet Russian collar and pearl buttons used for ulsters.

Shoulder capes made of beads strung in open meshes, and finished with fringe, are in great favor to wear with summer dresses of lace or silk. Beaded grenadine capes are also made with a fringe of beads. The most stylish mantles are pointed pelerines of grenadine or lace made in V shape from neck to waist in front and back, and finished by a short basque below the waist-line. A gathered frill of lace or of beaded net covers the arms nearly to the elbows.

June 19, 1886 *Harper's Bazar*

When a wrap is fastened with hooks, they are arranged on alternate sides. Otherwise the wrap will continually fly apart.

July 1887 *Delineator*

Small lace hoods are liked on long black wraps. Black fichus of Spanish guipure, chantilly, or any preferred kind of lace may be used for these hoods.

December 1887 *Delineator*

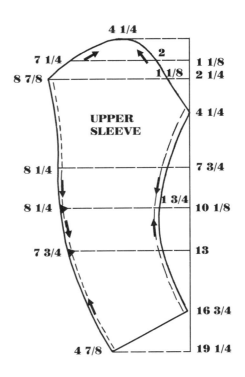

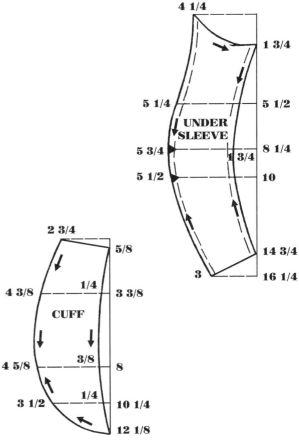

Street Jacket

This garment is drafted with the scale corresponding to the bust measure. It is in ten pieces: Jacket front, lapel, vest front, side piece, side back, back, collar, two sleeve pieces, and cuff. The jacket may be made of any material; if 36 inches wide, 1 7/8 yards are required. The vest is of velvet, and 3/4 yard is required. Lay two double box-plaits in the back. The vest front and the jacket front are joined together with the side piece.

1887 *National Garment Cutter Instruction Book*

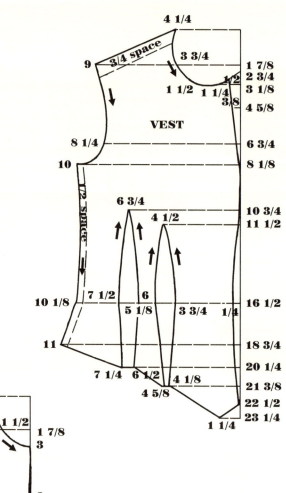

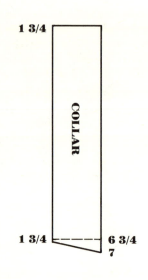

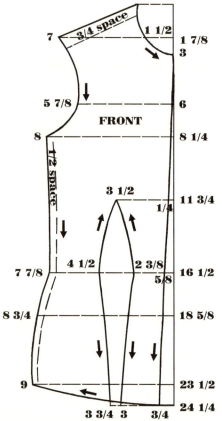

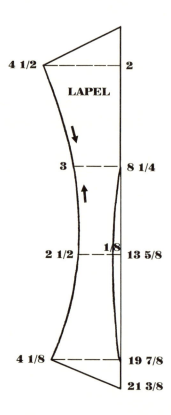

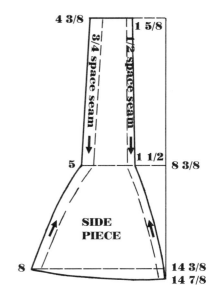

SIDE PIECE

4 3/8 1 5/8
3/4 space seam
1/2 space seam
5 1 1/2 8 3/8
8
14 3/8
14 7/8

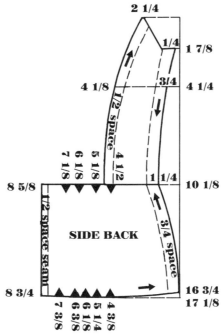

SIDE BACK

2 1/4
1/4 1 7/8
4 1/8 3/4 4 1/4
1/2 space
4 1/2
7 1/8 6 1/8 5 1/8
8 5/8 1 1/4 10 1/8
1/2 space seam
3/4 space
8 3/4 16 3/4 17 1/8
7 3/8 6 3/8 5 1/4 4 3/8
6 1/8

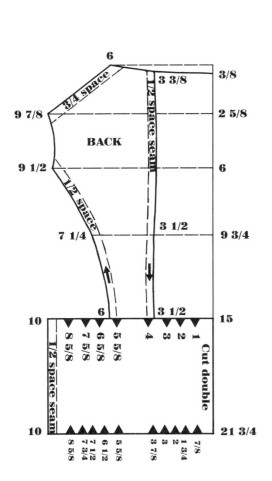

BACK

6 3 3/8 3/8
3/4 space
1/2 space seam
9 7/8 2 5/8
9 1/2 6
1/2 space
7 1/4 3 1/2 9 3/4
6 3 1/2 15
8 5/8 7 5/8 6 5/8 5 5/8 4 3 2 1 Cut double
1/2 space seam
10 21 3/4
8 5/8 7 3/4 7 1/2 6 1/2 5 5/8 3 7/8 3 2 1 3/4 7/8

197

Ladies' Jacket. Small checked cheviot was chosen for this jacket, and plain velvet, fancy buttons, and a clasp constitute the decorations. The fronts of the jacket turn back in tapering lapels from the neck to below the waist-line. Below the lapels they are cut away, disclosing the vest, which comprises two sections. One section is sewed flatly beneath each side of the front, and the width is decreased toward the neck in proportion to the broadening of the lapels. The right side of the vest is turned under for a hem. The closing is made with button-holes and medium-sized buttons. The lapels are faced with velvet, and near the upper corner of each is placed a large button, the lapel being basted beneath it in place. The vest is a little shorter than the fronts proper, and below its closing, the edges are cut away with a notched effect.

Side pieces, side-back seams, and a curved center back seam aid in the adjustment. The center back seam ends a little below the waist-line, extra width allowed below its termination being underfolded to form a double box-plait that springs out over the tournure.

The coat sleeve is closely fitted, but wide enough to slip easily over the dress sleeve. The outside seam is discontinued a little above the wrist, and on the under side is cut a lap, which passes under the upper part and is attached with button-holes and large buttons. The high standing collar is fastened with a clasp at the neck.

Jackets of this style are made of all kinds of cloths, coatings, and fancy jacket materials. They are worn with all kinds of street costumes. They are also made up as parts of special toilettes. They are never elaborately trimmed. To make the jacket for a lady of medium size, requires 3 3/4 yards of material 22 inches wide, 1 3/4 yards of material 48 inches wide, or 1 5/8 yards of material 54 inches wide. Also required is 1/2 yard of velvet 22 inches wide for the facings.

September 1886 *Delineator*

Ladies' Coat. A very effective contrast is shown by the association of black cloth for the coat, cream cloth for the vest, and gold braid for the trimming. The fronts proper are fitted by single bust and under-arm darts. Their edges overlap the vest, which is sewed into the bust dart seams as far as the latter extend and above them are joined flatly. The vest is curved at the closing edges, finished with underfacings, and closed with button-holes and small gilt buttons. Its lower edge is cut to form a point at the end of the closing. Back of the vest, the coat fronts are cut away diagonally and deepened considerably. The back is fitted by side backs and a curved center back seam. The side-back seams end a little below the waist-line. Below their terminations there are extra widths on the side backs, which overlap the back and are sewed flatly in continuation of the side-back seams.

A scroll design is wrought with braid on the lower part of each side back. Another, beginning on the front near its back edge, is carried about the bottom and up each side of the neck, the design being enlarged in the front corners and on the bust. The upper side of each coat sleeve is ornamented with a scroll. A similar scroll decorates the high standing collar.

The vest may be of the coat material or of any material preferred, but there is a strong preference for material that is in very marked contrast to the coat proper. Sometimes the vest is overlaid with appliquéd designs in the same color as the coat, and sometimes with braid arranged with the utmost regularity in crosswise or lengthwise lines. Such trimmings are usually limited to the vest when it is of a contrasting color; when it is of the coat material, they may also be used on the collar and wrists. To make the coat for a lady of medium size, requires 3 3/8 yards of material 22 inches wide, 1 1/2 yards of material 48 inches wide, or 1 3/8 yards of material 54 inches wide. Also required is 3/4 yard of material 22 inches wide for the vest.

September 1885 *Delineator*

Ladies' Basque. The illustration shows the basque made up in dress material of two kinds showing a marked contrast in shade, and trimmed with lace. The vest is of the lighter material and closes with button-holes and buttons, the right side being hemmed and the left underfaced. Below the closing, each side is cut away to a point. Back of the point it is shortened toward the back edge, which is included in the under-arm seam of the corresponding outside front. There is a single bust dart in each outside front, and double bust darts in the vest. The outside fronts do not meet at the neck. Their front edges curve away, while below the vest they are deepened in a long point over each hip.

Side-back seams and a curved center seam fit the back. In closing the shoulder seams, the edges of both the vest and the outside fronts are included. The backs form a short point below the waist-line. On them is draped extra width, which is cut on a fold of the material between the side backs and shaped to form double points. Three lines of shirring are made perpendicularly through its center. These are drawn up and sewed on the backs, producing a double-looped bow effect. Lace is arranged as a ruffle about the points of the back, and is turned flatly from the lower and front edges

of the fronts proper. The coat sleeves may be cut long enough to extend to the wrists, or shortened somewhat and finished with lace ruffles as shown. A high standing collar completes the neck.

Basques of this style are chosen to complete dresses of pongee, nun's veiling, summer silks, and all kinds of dress materials that look best when an elaborate effect is produced. The vest is often of bayadère-striped material or canvas material having tapestry figures. Foulards are often made up in this way, and the vest is overlaid with embroidery in a contrasting color, red and écru being fashionable on dark blue and brown. To make the basque for a lady of medium size, requires 3 1/4 yards of plain material and 1 3/8 yards of contrasting material 22 inches wide, or 1 5/8 yards of plain material and 3/4 yard of contrasting material 48 inches wide.

June 1885 *Delineator*

Cutaway Jacket

Use the scale corresponding to the bust measure. The jacket is in six pieces: Front, back, side back, collar, and two sleeve pieces. It can be made of any material, and worn with any costume. It requires 1 3/4 yards of material 36 inches wide. Interline the collar with canvas. Connect the waist-lines.

1887 *National Garment Cutter Instruction Book*

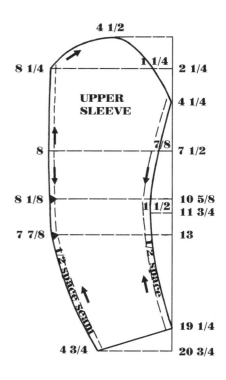

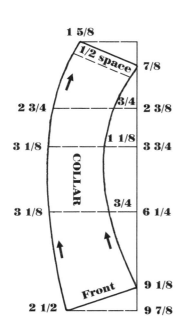

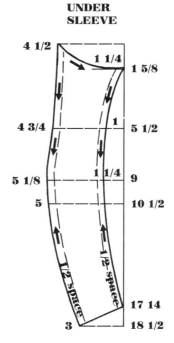

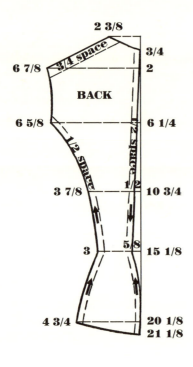

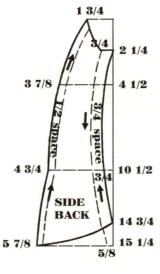

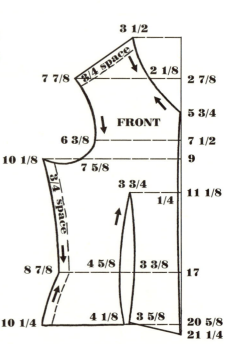

Cutaway Jacket. The jacket is to be worn over a vest of contrasting material. It is represented in washable figured cotton foulard, with bands of plain foulard for trimming. Its fronts are cut away in front of the shoulder seams, flaring quite broadly below the bust. Single bust darts, side pieces, side backs, and a curved center back seam fit the jacket stylishly but not too closely. The three back seams are sprung out below the waist-line, and the length is slightly increased toward the end of the center back seam. All of the edges are plainly finished. A flat collar that broadens slightly toward its ends in lapel fashion finishes the neck, and a fancy metal clasp holds the fronts in place below it. The sleeves are in coat shape.

This mode is adaptable to all kinds of cotton materials, although it is not limited to them. To make the jacket for a lady of medium size, requires 2 3/4 yards of material 22 inches wide, 1 5/8 yards of material 36 inches wide, 1 3/8 yards of material 48 inches wide, or 1 1/4 yards of material 54 inches wide.

May 1886 *Delineator*

Cutaway Coat

This pattern is laid off by the bust measure, and is in eight pieces: Front, back, side back, collar, two pocket laps, and two sleeve pieces. This coat requires 3 7/8 yards of material 22 inches wide, 1 5/8 yards of material 48 inches wide, or 1 1/2 yards of material 54 inches wide. Also required are 14 buttons. The seam allowance is 1/4 space. Cut the side back with its waist-line on a cross-thread of the material. Cut the collar bias. Cut the back with the back edge of its skirt, and the other parts, with the pieces laid lengthwise on the material.

Take up the darts exactly as located. Close the seams of the two back pieces and that of their extra width, turning the latter to the left in a plait underneath. Also fasten the extra width at the side-back seams in a forward-turning plait underneath. Join the widest ends of the collar and sew it to the neck according to the notches. Roll it and the front over at the line of crosses in the pattern.

Cut the upper pocket in the left front only, and attach the small pocket lap. The larger lap is for the lower pocket, which may not be cut or inserted if not desired. Make up and attach the sleeves. If the coat is made of cheviot, face the collar and lapel with the material, continuing the facing down the front edges of the front underneath. Finish with machine-stitching. Outline a cuff with two lines of stitching above the buttons on the upper side, in front of the under seam. Place two buttons near the top of each side-back extra width. If preferred the edges may be bound, piped, or underfaced.

1885 *National Garment Cutter*

 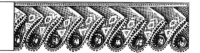

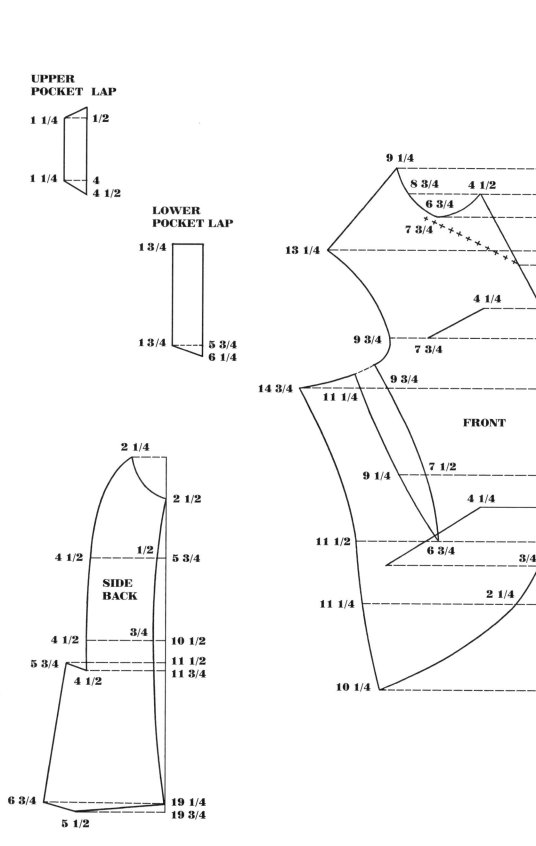

UPPER
POCKET LAP

1 1/4   1/2

1 1/4   4
         4 1/2

LOWER
POCKET LAP

1 3/4

1 3/4   5 3/4
         6 1/4

9 1/4

8 3/4   4 1/2   1 1/2
6 3/4   2 3/4
7 3/4

13 1/4   4 1/2
          5 1/4

4 1/4   7 3/4
9 3/4   7 3/4   9 1/2

14 3/4   9 3/4   12 1/4
11 1/4

FRONT

2 1/4

2 1/2

9 1/4   7 1/2   17

4 1/2   1/2   5 3/4   4 1/4   18 3/4

SIDE
BACK

11 1/2   6 3/4   20 1/2
                   3/4   21 3/4

4 1/2   3/4   10 1/2
5 3/4   11 1/2
4 1/2   11 3/4

11 1/4   2 1/4   24 1/2

10 1/4   29

6 3/4   19 1/4
         19 3/4
5 1/2

205

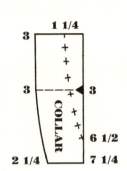

COLLAR

1 1/4
3
3   3
2 1/4   6 1/2
         7 1/4

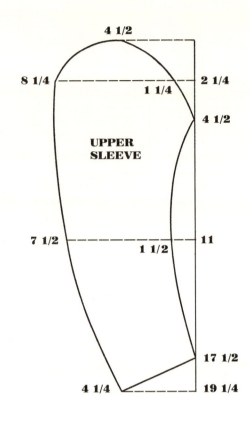

UPPER SLEEVE

4 1/2
8 1/4   2 1/4
     1 1/4
             4 1/2
7 1/2   11
     1 1/2
             17 1/2
4 1/4   19 1/4

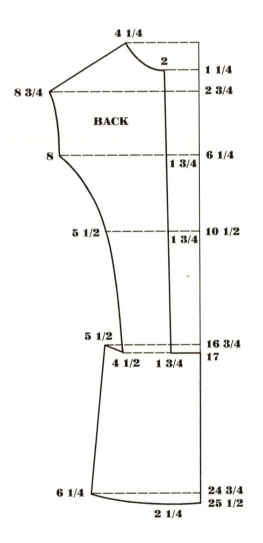

BACK

4 1/4
     2
          1 1/4
8 3/4   2 3/4

8   6 1/4
     1 3/4
5 1/2   10 1/2
     1 3/4
5 1/2   16 3/4
             17
4 1/2 1 3/4
6 1/4   24 3/4
             25 1/2
     2 1/4

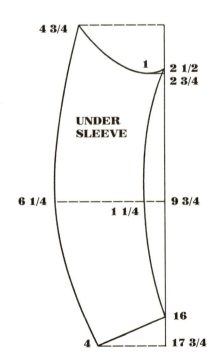

UNDER SLEEVE

4 3/4
          1   2 1/2
               2 3/4
6 1/4   9 3/4
     1 1/4
               16
4   17 3/4

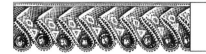 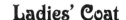 

Ladies' Coat. Velvet and cloth are associated in the construction of this coat. The vest is of velvet, and is closed with button-holes and buttons, the right side being hemmed. Below the closing, each side is cut away diagonally for a short distance. In each side of the vest, as well as in each side of the front, is a single bust dart. Fitting is accomplished by means of side pieces, side backs, and a curved center back seam.

The vest and front are sewed together to the shoulder edges of the back and the front edges of the side pieces. The fronts are cut away from the tops of the shoulder seams nearly to the bust, where they meet, and are closed for a short distance with button-holes and buttons. The edges below the closing are rounded off in cutaway fashion. The center seam ends at the top of narrow extensions arranged in regular coat-lap fashion, each lap being hemmed. Extensions are also allowed on the adjoining edges of the back and side-back pieces, and arranged in a coat-plait turning forward underneath on each side. A triangular ornament is worked in silk twist at the end of each side-back seam.

There is a high standing collar of velvet about the neck. Below it at the back is sewed a notched, rolling collar of the cloth, which extends in lapel fashion along the cutaway edges of the fronts. The sleeves are in coat shape, shortened slightly with a curve toward the outside seams, to permit of adding a round under-cuff of velvet, which is invisibly sewed in place well up beneath the sleeve.

When dress material is chosen for the coat, the vest, standing collar, and cuffs may be of surah, Oriental material, or fancy suiting. Or these parts may be like the rest of the coat and have elaborate decorations of fancy braids. Or else the coat itself may be of velvet, and the rest of fancy material. For a lady of medium size, this coat requires 4 yards of material 22 inches wide, 1 7/8 yards of material 48 inches wide, or 1 1/2 yards of material 54 inches wide. Each requires 1 1/2 yards of material 20 inches wide for the vest, etc.

October 1885 *Delineator*

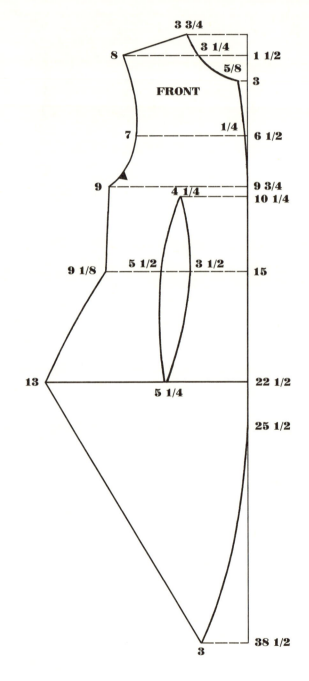

Ladies' Visite

This garment has five pieces: Front, side back, back, sleeve, and collar. Use the scale that corresponds to the bust measure. The seam allowance is 1/2 space. Sew the sleeve in the seam between the back and side back. Put the parts together to correspond to the notches on the diagrams. Trim to suit.

Spring and Summer 1886 *Voice of Fashion*

COLLAR

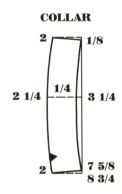

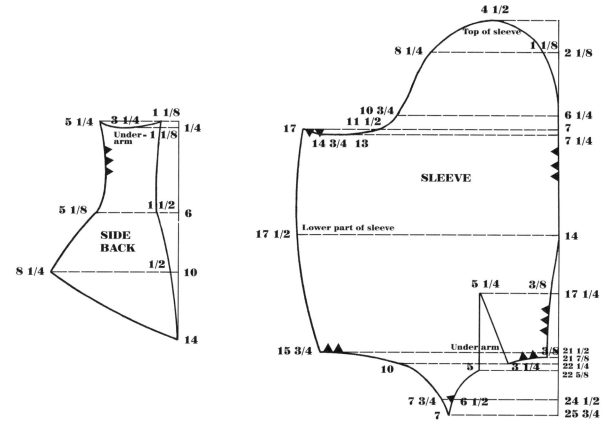

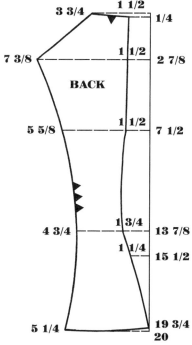

Ladies' Wrap. Close-fitting wraps are dressy accompaniments to costumes of both silk and wool materials. Figured canvas cloth is the material pictured, and wool lace and wooden beads constitute the trimmings. The fronts extend some distance below the waist-line and fall in slender tabs that decrease in curves to meet the short side pieces. The latter are assisted by single bust darts in perfecting the adjustment. The back has a curved center seam and extends but a little below the waist-line, being of even depth with the side pieces at its corresponding edges. The curved outline of the wrap is thus preserved unbroken from one tab to the other.

The sleeves are in the mandarin fashion. Each is composed of two sections, which are united so as to cover the arm without adding uncomfortably to the warmth of the garment, or interfering with the free movement of the wearer. The upper part extends in a curve over the top of the arm, and is held slightly full across the top while being sewed in. It is joined to the under part along the inside of the arm. The two sections are also sewed together along their under sides from their front edges as far as the under part extends, the lower edge of the upper part having a short gathering made in it a little in front of the end of the seam. The join of the two parts is concealed by the overhanging fold of the upper part, which is turned up underneath;

and the back edge of the latter is sewed with the side piece to the front below the armhole. The sleeve is turned back at the wrist, giving a cuff effect. The reversed part is trimmed with a forward-turning band of lace laid on flatly edge-to-edge with it, with a row of beads concealing the edges.

There is a high standing collar about the neck, with curved and underfaced front edges; the closing is made with hooks and eyes. A band of lace turns flatly over the collar and is carried down each side of the front. A row of beads is arranged along the top of the collar, the front edge of the overlapping front, the front edge of the underlapping front below the closing, and along the lower edge of each front. Lace is also arranged to turn toward the lower edges of the wrap, and beads are arranged along its selvage where it is applied, in the same manner as on the sleeves.

This wrap is ornamented to match the rest of the costume when it is made up *en suite*. Beaded trimmings may be obtained in all of the fashionable hues. To make the garment for a lady of medium size, requires 3 5/8 yards of material 22 inches wide, 1 5/8 yards of material 48 inches wide, or 1 1/2 yards of material 54 inches wide.

June 1886 *Delineator*

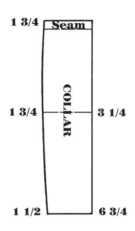

Short Dolman

This garment is drafted with the scale corresponding to the bust measure. It is in five pieces: Front, back, side piece, sleeve, and collar. Gather the sleeve between the notches near the top. Connect the waist-lines when joining the front, side piece, and back. Close the wrap in front with hooks and eyes. Any style of trimming may be used.

1887 *National Garment Cutter Instruction Book*

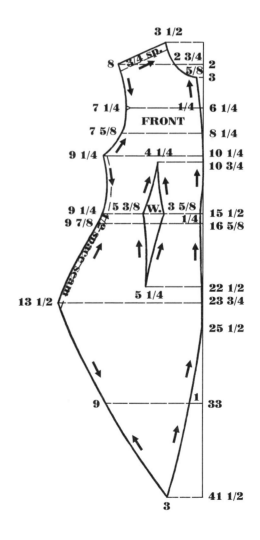

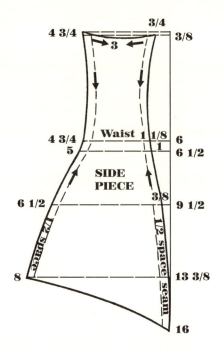

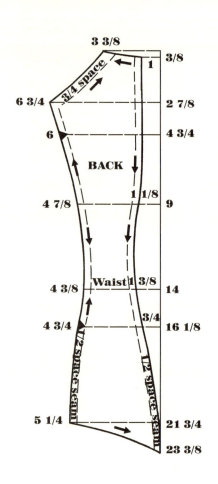

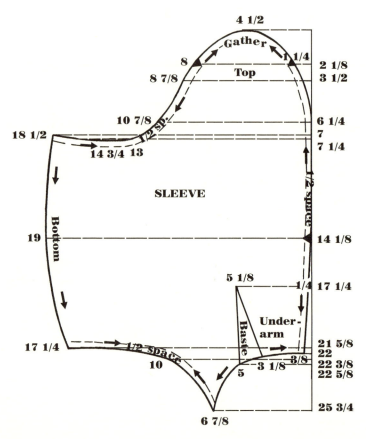

Ladies' Dolman. There is no material more favored than plush for both promenade and evening wraps, and the dolman illustrated is developed in this rich material, with fur for trimming. The fronts are of medium length and in pointed tab shape. They are closed with hooks and eyes. They are extended beneath the armholes to meet the back, which falls only a little below the waist-line and has a curved center seam that extends unbrokenly to the lower edge. The sleeves are each formed of two sections, which are joined along the inside and outside of the arm. The upper part presents a dolman arch over the shoulder, and the wrist opening,

although not exaggerated, is wide enough to present a dressy effect. Below the armhole, the sleeve edges are sewed with the front to the back. There is a high standing collar about the neck. Outside it is a band of fur that passes down each side of the front, and about the tabs and lower edges. Fur also borders the sleeve openings.

Plain and brocaded velvets, all kinds of silks, as well as all kinds of wools and cloths in vogue for wraps, make up handsomely in this way. For a lady of medium size, this dolman requires 3 7/8 yards of material 22 inches wide, 2 yards of material 44 inches wide, or 1 5/8 yards of material 54 inches wide.

December 1886 *Delineator*

Ladies' Wrap. One of the most *recherché* modes in wraps is pictured made of seal plush with fur trimming. It has a short back, and narrow tab fronts that descend to the edge of the costume. The back lies flat on the tournure and is closely fitted by a curved center seam. The fronts are joined to the back on the shoulders and at the back edges, where they are of even length with the back, and then gradually lengthen to form the square tabs. A long under-arm dart in each front achieves a smooth adjustment over the hips.

The armholes are not much larger than is required for a coat sleeve, and when the sleeves are sewed in the garment affords complete protection, being close at the sides. The sleeves have a high dolman arch over the shoulders and are in Chinese style at the wrists, where they are not much wider than a coat sleeve. Each sleeve comprises an outer and an inner part. These are joined by well-shaped seams, the lower edge of the outer part folding up underneath so that the lower seam is not visible when the garment is on the wearer. Below the armholes, the outer part of the sleeves is inserted in the side-back seams.

A high standing collar completes the neck. It is covered by a band of fur. This band is continued down the front edges of both fronts, about the lower and back edges of the fronts, and across the lower edge of the back. A band of similar fur trims the sleeves at the wrist. Hooks and eyes close the fronts to below the waist-line, both edges being underfaced. Below the closing the tabs flare slightly.

These wraps are usually reserved for dressy wear, and consequently are made up in all kinds of silks, velvets, and plushes. Very often the handsomest material is reserved for the lining, which is a necessity in wraps of these materials and of light-weight wools. When the lining is silk, surah, or satin, it may be quilted or not as preferred, but it is usually wadded. Plush-lined silk wraps may be interlined with cotton batting, lamb's wool, etc., to ensure the needful warmth. All kinds of cloakings, cloths, and dress materials may be made up in this mode. Fur, Astrakhan, down bands, beaded or braided passementerie, or any stylish trimming may be added. Such wraps frequently complete special suits, and combinations of two materials are in order. To make this wrap for a lady of medium size, requires 5 1/4 yards of material 22 inches wide, 2 5/8 yards of material 44 inches wide, or 2 1/4 yards of material 54 inches wide.

November 1887 *Delineator*

Ladies' Wrap

This garment is drafted with the scale correspond-ing to the bust measure. It is in five pieces: Front, side piece, back, sleeve, and collar. The quantity of material 36 inches wide required is 5 3/8 yards. There is one double box-plait in the center of the back. Connect the waist-lines in putting the gar-ment together. Gather between the two stars at the top of the sleeve on the cross-line running from 1 1/2 on the base-line to 7 3/4. Fold the sleeve at 13 3/4 on the base-line, where there is a star, after which join it to the back. Any style of ornament may be used.

Winter 1886 *Voice of Fashion*

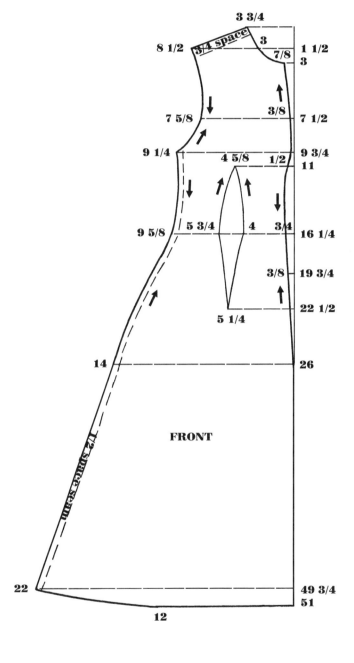

3 3/4

8 1/2   3/4 space   3   1 1/2
7/8   3

7 5/8   3/8   7 1/2

9 1/4   4 5/8   1/2   9 3/4
11

9 5/8   5 3/4   4   3/4   16 1/4

3/8   19 3/4

5 1/4   22 1/2

14   26

FRONT

22   49 3/4
51

12

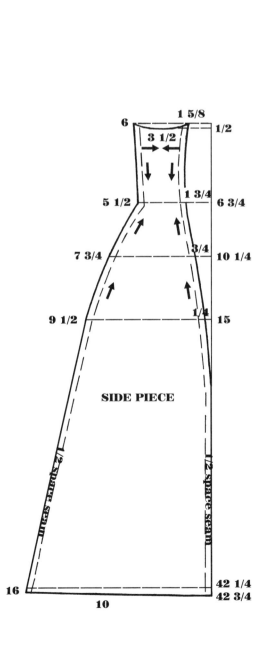

1 5/8
6   1/2
3 1/2

5 1/2   1 3/4   6 3/4

7 3/4   3/4   10 1/4

9 1/2   1/4   15

SIDE PIECE

16   42 1/4
42 3/4
10

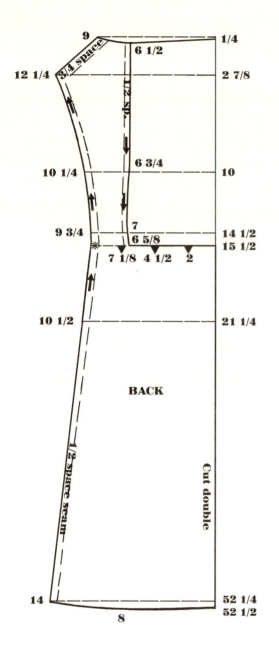

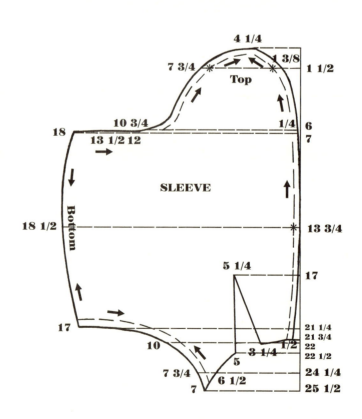

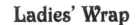 

Ladies' Wrap. Brocaded velvet was employed for this garment, and light fur forms the trimming. The fronts close with hooks and eyes, the right side being hemmed. They are rendered stylishly close without the aid of darts, their back edges being curved out below the shoulders to assist in forming the large armholes requisite for this style of sleeve. The sleeves are really parts of the side backs. They are extended over the tops of the arms in the arch of the dolman shape, and folded up about the wrist in mandarin fashion, the top of the underfolded part being curved out and joined to the corresponding inner edge along the inner side of the arm. The seam joining the sleeve to the front of the armhole, is continuous with the one joining the lower part of the front.

The center back seam and side-back seams terminate at the tops of extensions allowed below them. The extra width below the center back seam is underfolded in a box-plait. That at the end of each side-back seam is joined to a corresponding extension cut on the back edge of the side back, the two being folded in a side-plait turning forward underneath. This arrangement perfects the effect of two box-plaits on the outside. These plaits are retained in their folds by two elastic straps sewed beneath them to the side-back seams. The upper strap is some distance from the top of the seam, and the lower strap quite a distance farther down. The straps yield to the motions of the wearer and take the strain that would otherwise come on the plaits and draw them out of shape.

The wrap has a high standing collar. It is encircled by a band of fur, which is carried down each side of the front to the lower edge. The sleeves are also bordered with fur. All kinds of cloakings, from the plainest and most practical to the richest and most dressy, are made up by this pattern. Braid, chenille, gimp, fringe, and all kinds of fur are added as decoration. Astrakhan is applied in wide bands, and frequently chosen in black to trim colored wraps. For a lady of medium size, this garment requires 8 3/4 yards of material 22 inches wide, or 4 yards of material either 48 or 54 inches wide.

September 1885 *Delineator*

Ladies' Wrap. This model is made of cloth and trimmed with plush. The fronts are hollowed out to assist in forming large, dolman-like armholes. The back has a curved center seam and side-back seams. The center back seam ends a little below the waist-line, and on the edges below it are cut narrow extensions. These are partly underfolded for hems, the left hem being lapped over the right back and basted in place at its top. The side-back parts are widened and shaped appropriately to form the sleeves, which fold up in mandarin shape about the wrists and curve high over the shoulders in dolman fashion. A little fullness is gathered in over the top of the shoulder, and the edges of the sleeve are joined in a curved seam along the inside of the arm. Below the sleeve, the corresponding edges of the wrap are seamed together.

A very broad band of plush trims the bottom of the wrap, and narrower bands border the sleeves.

The high rolling collar is also of plush. Fancy frog or Brandenburg ornaments close the front, which is first turned under for hems on both sides. Similar ornaments are disposed between the waist-line of the side-back seams and the lower back corners of the sleeves.

Wraps of this style, made entirely of plain or fancy plush, or of plain or brocaded velvet, are very elegant. Cloths and cloakings are, however, just as well adapted to the mode, and fur, braid, machine-stitching, etc., may form the decoration. If preferred, the fronts may be closed in the usual manner with button-holes and buttons, or the overlapping side may be trimmed and the closing invisibly performed with the aid of a fly. For a lady of medium size, this wrap requires 6 7/8 yards of material 22 inches wide, 3 3/8 yards of material 48 inches wide, or 3 yards of material 54 inches wide.

December 1884 *Delineator*

221

Short Wrap. Plush is the material employed for this example, and fur and passementerie ornaments form the trimming. The front is closed with hooks and eyes after the right side has been hemmed. Below the shoulder, each side is curved out to assist in forming the large dolman-like arm-hole. The back is narrow. It has a curved center seam that is carried to the lower edge, being sprung out below the waist-line. Each sleeve is composed of a single section, which is folded in mandarin shape about the wrist and curved over the top of the arm in regular dolman fashion. The curve is emphasized by a becoming fullness, which is gathered in before being sewed in place. Below its underfolded part, the sleeve is extended to an even depth with the front and back, and the length of the garment is thus rendered uniform all around.

A broad band of fur borders the lower edge. A narrower band passes up the overlapping side of the closing and about the high, standing collar. A passementerie frog ornament is fastened across the front at the neck, one end being permanently fastened in place and the other attached with a hook and eye. Fur of the narrower width borders the sleeves. A passementerie ornament harmonizing with that at the neck is arranged below the waist-line of the back, its ends being fastened a short distance in front of the side-back seams.

Plain and brocaded velvets, silks, bengalines, and all materials in vogue for wraps make up charmingly in this way. Fur, lace, braid, chenille, marabou, and passementerie ornaments of all kinds are selected for trimming. For a lady of medium size, this wrap requires 4 3/8 yards of material 22 inches wide, 1 7/8 yards of material 48 inches wide, or 1 3/4 yards of material 54 inches wide.

November 1885 *Delineator*

Double-Breasted Coat

Double-Breasted Coat

This pattern is in nine pieces: Front, front piece, front skirt, back, side back, collar, pocket lap, and two sleeve pieces. It is laid off by the bust measure. All seams and hems are allowed for.

The quantity of material required is 6 3/4 yards if 22 inches wide, 3 1/8 yards if 40 inches wide, and 3 1/8 yards if 54 inches wide. Also required are 20 buttons. In cutting the material, cut the collar on the bias. Cut the back with the back edge of its skirt, the front skirt with its longest straight edge, and all of the other pieces laid lengthwise on the material. Also required are three small straps about 2 spaces long and 1 1/2 spaces wide, with one end pointed by cutting off the corners.

In making up the coat, turn under each front skirt at the point marked 1 1/2 for a hem. Take up the darts in the front and close the seams, leaving the center back seam until last. In closing that, commence at the top and close it to the extra fullness. Turn under all of the extra width, and 1/4 space more on the left side for a hem. Lay the extra width of the right side under the hems just formed, and baste its top. Arrange a pocket lap on each front skirt. Underface the front edges of the front pieces. Join the top of the front skirt to the lower edge of the front, front piece, and side back on each side, with the front edge of the skirt as hemmed even with the faced edge of the front piece.

Fasten the extra width on each side-back seam in a forward-turning plait underneath. Make a button-hole in the pointed end of each strap, and sew the square end of the straps underneath to the hem of the left back at an equal distance apart. Sew corresponding buttons to the extra width of the right back, and fasten these extra widths together with straps and buttons.

Join the width of the collar, attach it to the neck, and roll it and the fronts over in their proper position. Close the seams of the sleeves. Sew them in with the outside seam at the back of the armhole. Hold the sleeve toward you while you sew it in, and fasten the extra fullness in a forward-turning plait under the arm. Close the fronts in double-breasted style with buttons and button-holes, making an extra button-hole in each lapel. Attach a round cuff to each sleeve with two lines of machine-stitching. Also machine-stitch the front edge of each side-back plait in place. Place a button at the top of each side-back plait, and two on the upper side of the wrist of the sleeve in front of the outside seam. Any desired decoration may be adopted.

1885 *National Garment Cutter*

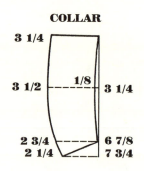

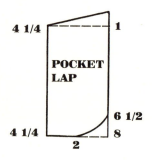

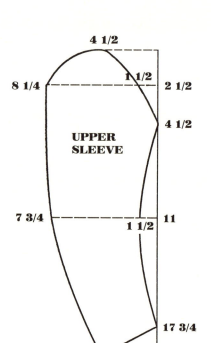

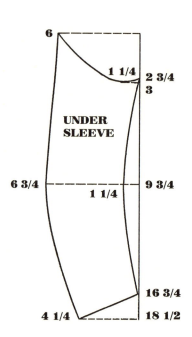

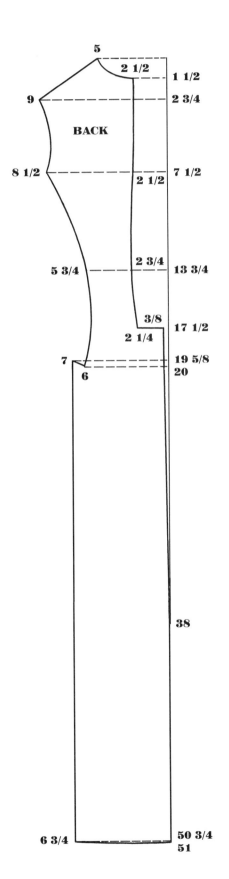

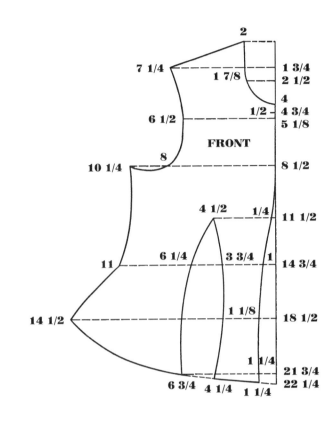

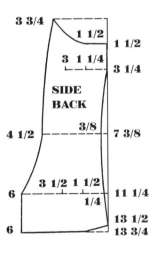

FRONT PIECE

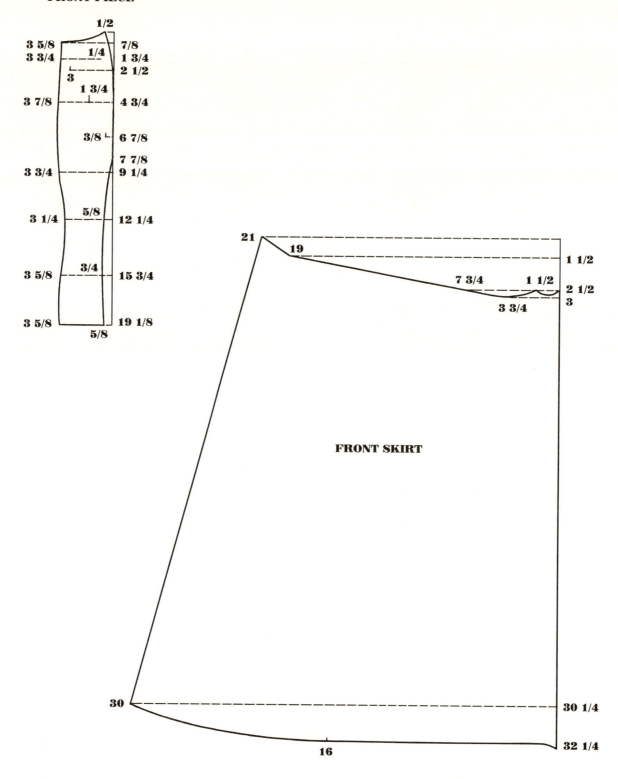

FRONT SKIRT

Ladies' Newmarket

This garment is drafted with the scale corresponding to the bust measure. It is in six pieces: Front, side back, back, collar, and two sleeve pieces. The quantity of material 48 inches wide required is 4 3/8 yards. Lay six plaits in the center of the back, and finish with an arrow-head made of silk twist, or any kind of ornament desired. Use large buttons to fasten the front and finish the sleeves.

1887 *National Garment Cutter Instruction Book*

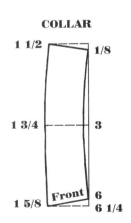

COLLAR

1 1/2   1/8

1 3/4   3

1 5/8 Front 6
              6 1/4

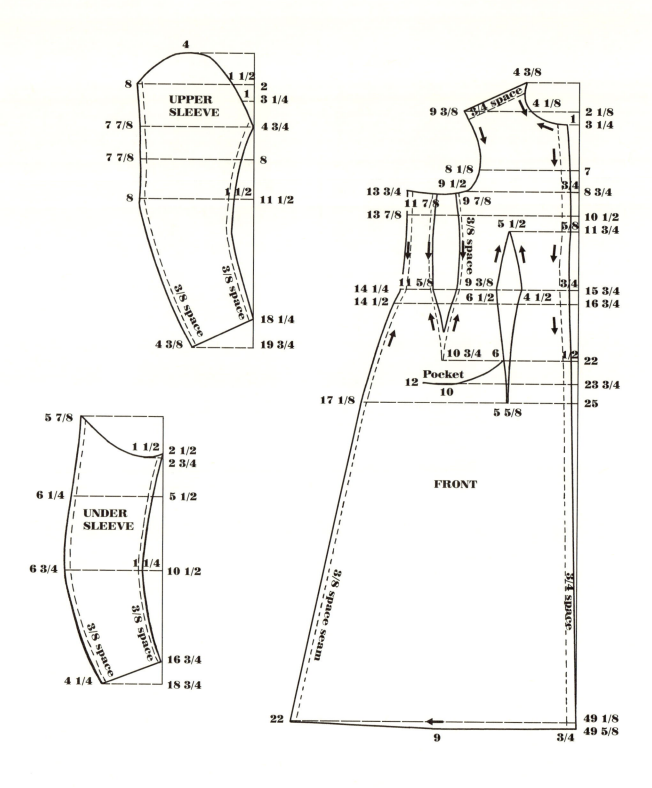

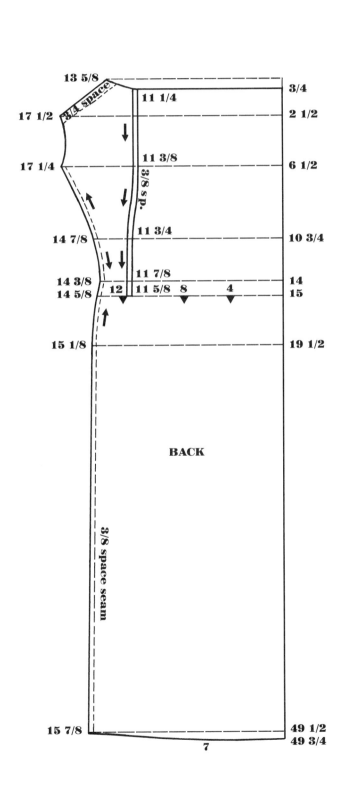

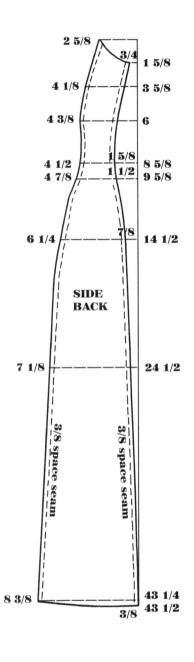

Long Coat. Coats of this style, made up in light-weight materials, are popular during summer for traveling wraps and for general wear. Cheviot of a seasonable quality is the material represented, and machine-stitching and buttons constitute the finishings. The fronts are curved at their closing edges, finished with underfacings, and closed their entire length with button-holes and buttons. In each side is a curved bust dart and an under-arm dart, and at the back are side backs and a curved center back seam. The latter ends a little below the waist-line at the top of underfolded extra width, which forms a triple box-plait. This retains its folds, yet springs out sufficiently toward the bottom of the coat to produce a graceful effect and afford all of the width necessary.

The lower edge is finished with double lines of machine-stitching made far enough from the margin to uphold an underfacing, or a hem if one is allowed for. Single lines of stitching also finish the curved pocket openings made in the fronts below the hips. A single line of stitching completes the high standing collar, while double lines outline cuffs at the wrists of the coat sleeves. Three buttons, placed in a row on the upper side of each sleeve in front of the outside seam and below the stitching, complete the cuff effect. A triangular ornament is worked with silk at the end of the center back seam.

Surah, pongee, mohair, flannel, and all kinds of plain and mixed light-weight cloths are made up in this fashion. Braid may be applied as a binding or as a decoration. To make the coat for a lady of medium size, requires 8 3/8 yards of material 22 inches wide, 4 1/4 yards of material 48 inches wide, or 3 1/8 yards of material 54 inches wide.

June 1885 *Delineator*

 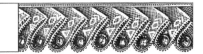

Long Coat. This long, close-fitting coat is developed in plush, and trimmed with otter fur and a fancy clasp. The fronts are curved at their closing edges, and finished with underfacings. They are closed with button-holes and buttons, from the neck to quite a distance below the waist-line. The garment is fitted with a bust dart and an under-arm dart in each side, aided by side backs and a center back seam. Provision for any style of drapery is made by discontinuing the center back seam a little below the waist-line, allowing sufficient extra width for hems and a lap on the edges below it. After the hems are made, the right back is lapped over the left and stitched in place at the top. Fur of medium width borders the overlapping edge, and a much broader band is carried about the lower edges. The narrow width is arranged on each side of the closing and

about the high standing collar. The coat sleeves are sewed into the armholes with only enough fullness to give them an easy adjustment. They are finished with narrow bands of fur at the wrists.

Plush, bengaline, and brocaded velvets are favorite selections for coats not intended for general wear, but cloths woven plainly or in indistinct figures are preferred for more practical coats. Braid; galloon; and bands of Astrakhan, velvet, and other decorative material are often selected for trimming. To make the coat for a lady of medium size, requires 7 yards of material 22 inches wide, 3 3/8 yards of material 48 inches wide, or 2 7/8 yards of material 54 inches wide.

September 1885 *Delineator*

Coat with Bell Sleeves. The coat is shown made of dark red cloth and trimmed with black fur. The back skirt is open at the center, and hemmed coat laps are arranged below the center back seam. This seam, together with the side backs and the single bust and under-arm darts, renders the garment close fitting. Buttons and button-holes may close the fronts all or part of the way down. On each side of the closing is a band of fur, which extends to the lower edge and also passes about the neck, concealing the standing collar. The sleeves fit closely at the top and widen with a pronounced bell effect below the elbow. They have but one seam, which comes at the inside of the arm, and are trimmed at the edges with a band of fur.

Smooth cloths, of both light and dark colors, are particularly admired for this coat. Armure, and brocaded, changeable, striped, and fancy silk and wool cloakings make up richly, a lining generally being added. Plush and velvet are especially handsome. Fur, Astrakhan, braid, and heavy passementerie are fashionable trimmings, and any becoming arrangement may be followed. Tall ladies arrange deep trimmings along the bottom of the coat and on the coat lap. For a lady of medium size, this garment requires 7 1/2 yards of material 22 inches wide, 3 3/4 yards of material 44 inches wide, or 3 1/2 yards of material 54 inches wide.

November 1888 *Delineator*

232

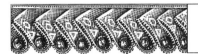 

Ladies' Coat. This coat is very popular as a completion to street suits of all materials. In this instance it is developed in velvet, with fancy buttons for trimmings. The fronts are curved at their closing edges, finished with underfacings, and closed with button-holes and buttons. They form a medium-deep point at the end of the closing. Back of the single bust darts, they are deepened over the hips in the outline peculiar to a gentleman's dress coat. The front is fitted with a bust dart and an under-arm dart in each side, and the back is fitted with side backs and a center back seam. The center backs extend but a little below the waist-line, and are straight across their lower edges.

On the deeper part on each side is sewed a long, ornamental pocket lap, which is turned down over its own seam and curved at its lower edge. Three buttons add to the decorative effect of the lap. The coat sleeves are fitted with a high curve across the top of the arm, which is held in place by a scanty gathering made before the sleeve is sewed into the armhole. A high standing collar finishes the neck.

To make the coat for a lady of medium size, requires 4 3/8 yards of material 22 inches wide, 2 yards of material 48 inches wide, or 1 3/4 yards of material 54 inches wide.

September 1885 *Delineator*

Ulster with Cape

This ulster is drafted with the scale corresponding to the bust measure. The length is regulated with the tape measure. The ulster is in six pieces: Front, back, side back, standing collar, and two sleeve pieces. It may be made of any material. The cape is in two pieces: Main cape piece and rolling collar. The quantity required for the ulster is 4 1/2 yards of material 48 inches wide, and the quantity for the cape is 3/8 yard. Instead of being made of the same material as the ulster, the cape may be made of fur or of Astrakhan cloth. Lay six plaits in the center of the back of the ulster. Use buttons to fasten the front and finish the sleeves.

Winter 1886 *Voice of Fashion*

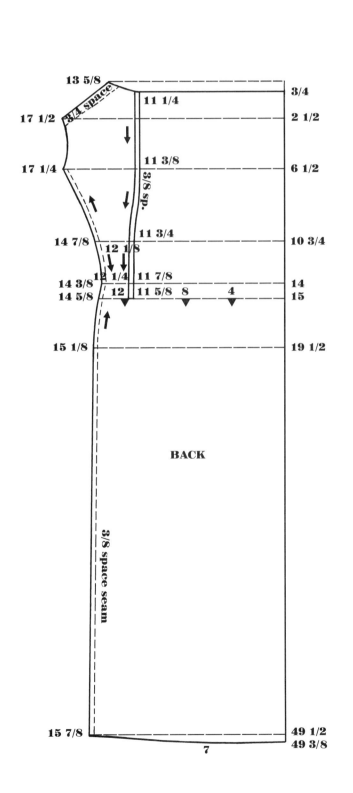

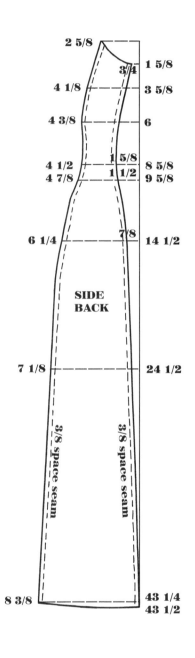

BACK

SIDE BACK

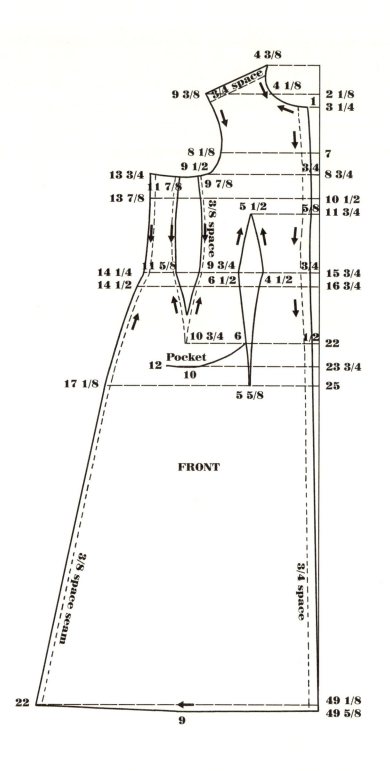

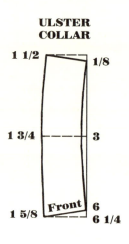

ULSTER
COLLAR

FRONT

Pocket

3/8 space seam

3/4 space

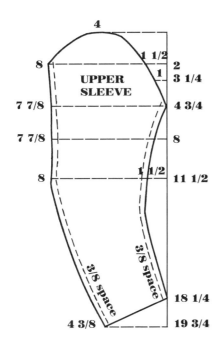

UPPER SLEEVE

4

1 1/2
8
2
1
3 1/4
7 7/8
4 3/4
7 7/8
8
8
1 1/2
11 1/2

3/8 space
3/8 space

18 1/4
4 3/8
19 3/4

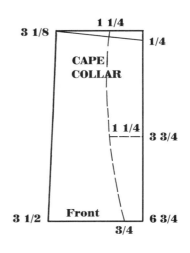

CAPE COLLAR

3 1/8
1 1/4
1/4

1 1/4
3 3/4

Front

3 1/2
3/4
6 3/4

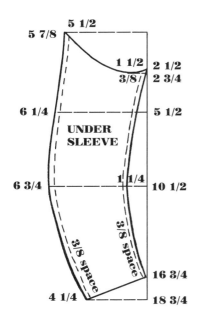

UNDER SLEEVE

5 1/2
5 7/8

1 1/2
2 1/2
3/8
2 3/4
6 1/4
5 1/2

6 3/4
1 1/4
10 1/2

3/8 space
3/8 space

16 3/4
4 1/4
18 3/4

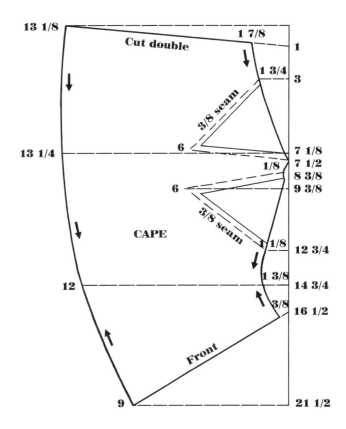

CAPE

13 1/8
Cut double
1 7/8
1
1 3/4
3

3/8 seam

13 1/4
6
7 1/8
1/8
7 1/2
8 3/8
6
9 3/8

3/8 seam

1 1/8
12 3/4
1 3/8
14 3/4

12
3/8
16 1/2

Front

9
21 1/2

Coat with Removable Cape. Coats of this style are fashionable for traveling and general street wear. The mode develops elegantly in all materials, from surah and pongee to flannel and cheviot. This example was developed in fancy cheviot, with machine-stitching, buttons, and a fancy clasp for finishing. The coat is long, and fitted by curved closing edges, single bust and under-arm darts, side backs, and a center back seam. The center back and side-back seams end a little below the waist-line. Below their terminations extra width is allowed, which is underfolded to form two box-plaits on the outside. The plaits give all of the spring necessary to the back; and, while they are kept within their folds for their entire depth, they are allowed to flare

sufficiently toward the lower edge to prevent a stiff effect. The fronts are underfaced, and are closed their entire length with button-holes and buttons. On each side rests a wide pocket lap, which is turned down over its own seam and finished with two lines of machine-stitching along its ends and lower edge.

The sleeves are in coat shape, and are curved across their tops and sewed in with sufficient fullness to give a high arch. Two lines of stitching are made in each far enough from the wrist to simulate a deep, round cuff. A standing collar, cut bias or straight as desired, is sewed to the neck.

The cape is short and jaunty in effect. It is cut on a fold of the material at the center of the back, and is extended in sleeve fashion over the arms. The seams joining the sleeve extensions to the fronts

are continued in dart fashion some distance back of the shoulder seams. Enough fullness is allowed across the top of each arm to give a high epaulet effect. The front edges have wide hems. These are held in place by double lines of stitching, which are continued about the lower part of the cape at a proportionate distance from the lower edge. A high standing collar, with double lines of stitching about its edges, completes the neck, which is closed with a fancy metal clasp.

Frequently bright linings are added to the cape and pocket laps. A lining may be added to the entire coat, if desired. Cloths of light weight, with a pressed or rough surface, are much liked for traveling wraps. These usually include two or more colors in their composition, and are woven in checks, hair-lines, plaids, and mixtures that appear like a plain surface at a little distance. Pongee is admired for its lightness and dust-repelling properties, and so is twilled surah. To make the coat for a lady of medium size, requires 9 yards of material 22 inches wide, 4 1/4 yards of material 48 inches wide, or 4 yards of material 54 inches wide.

July 1884 *Delineator*

Coat with Removable Hood. Long, close-fitting coats of this style are worn as traveling wraps during the summer; their general use is resumed in early autumn. Fancy ulster cloth was used for this example. The fronts are curved at their closing edges and closed with button-holes and buttons, the edges being underfaced. The buttons, although of good size, are not so large as to interfere with the inclination of the garment to the figure. There are two darts in each side, one curving over the bust and the other arching over the hip. At the back are side-back seams and a curved center seam. All three end a little below the waist-line, at the tops of extra widths underfolded to form two box-plaits on the outside. These plaits are held in their folds by an elastic strap basted to them on the under side,

some distance below their tops, and by bastings made lower down. A pocket opening is made in each side of the front, its edges being finished with piping. Its ends, and also the lower end of the center back seam, are stayed by arrow-heads worked with silk. The sleeves are in coat shape, and the collar is in the high rolling fashion, the edges of both being severely plain in their completion.

The hood is adjusted beneath the collar. It is in capuchin shape, being formed of a single section, the ends of which are joined in a seam to perfect the shape. The outer edges are rolled over on the outside, and the top is hollowed out to fit easily about the neck. The hood is lined throughout with silk. The neck edge is finished with a narrow silk binding, the ends being fastened with a hook and eye. The hood is removable and may be omitted when not desired.

Mohair, camel's hair, pongee, flannel, and all kinds of plain and fancy materials are chosen for such coats. Sometimes plain or fancy braids are applied as trimming. To make the garment for a lady of medium size, requires 8 1/4 yards of material 22 inches wide, 3 7/8 yards of material 48 inches wide, or 3 3/4 yards of material 54 inches wide. Also required is 1 yard of silk 20 inches wide to line the hood.

May 1886 *Delineator*

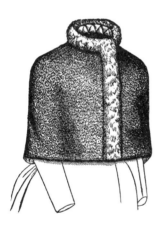

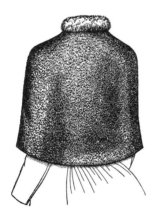

Shoulder Cape. Deep shoulder capes of this kind are fashionable wraps, and are also worn over plain ulsters and coats for extra protection. Seal plush was chosen for this example, with beaver fur for trimming. The back is cut on the fold of the material, and the front edges are consequently bias. When narrow material is selected, a seam is made at the center of the back, or the pattern is laid crosswide on the material when cutting. The latter plan is usually followed for striped material, as the effect is more becoming. Three darts fit the cape over each shoulder. A narrow choker collar finishes the neck, and serves as a support for the band of fur that entirely conceals it and passes down each side of the front. The cape is deep enough to protect the body above the hips, and its warmth is increased by a quilted satin lining.

Plain or figured velvets, frisé materials, Astrakhan cloth, plush, Astrakhan, fur of almost every kind, etc., are made up in this way. The trimming varies with the material, but the principal choice is fur, nice taste being exhibited in making a selection that contrasts or harmonizes prettily with the material. Linings of quilted silk or satin, or plain linings of plush in colors contrasting with the material, are handsome. To make the cape for a lady of medium size, requires 1 1/8 yards of material 27 inches wide, or 5/8 yard of material either 48 or 54 inches wide. Each requires 1 1/2 yards of quilted satin 20 inches wide for the lining.

December 1884 *Delineator*

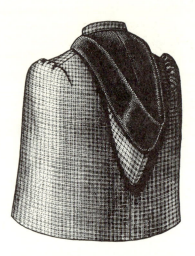

Shoulder Cape and Hood. Both cape and hood may be worn over any style of costume, jacket, or coat. They may be worn together as illustrated, or either may be worn alone. Olive and brown checked cloth were here chosen for both the cape and the hood, and the hood is richly lined with golden brown plush.

The cape has a seam at the center of the back and one on each shoulder. It also shows a curved seam across the top of the arm, a slight fullness being gathered in the lower edge of the seam to make the curve pronounced. There is a standing collar, and a hook and eye close the cape at the neck. The hood is in the capuchin style, and its edges are rolled over to show the lining as a facing. It has two seams. The neck is finished with an underfacing, a clasp fastening it at the neck.

All kinds of cloths and coatings may be used for both cape and hood, with a handsome lining added to each. Sometimes the cape is of Astrakhan, plush, or fur, and the hood is of the coat, jacket, or costume material and lined with the cape material. A plain or machine-stitched finish is often preferred for the cape edges, but sometimes braid, flat bands, passementerie, pipings, etc., are used for trimming. Bands of velvet, plush, down, or fur are much liked as decorations. For a lady of medium size, the cape needs 1 5/8 yards of material 22 inches wide, 1 1/8 yards of material 44 inches wide, or 5/8 yard of material 54 inches wide. The hood requires 5/8 yard of material in any of the above widths, together with 5/8 yard of material 20 inches wide for lining.

February 1887 *Delineator*

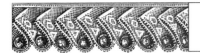 

Circular Cloak

This cloak is laid off by the bust measure. It consists of three pieces: Main or wrap piece, cape collar, and standing collar. The length may be regulated to suit the fancy. The seam allowance is 1/4 space.

Any material suitable for cloaks may be used. The quantity required is 5 yards if 27 inches wide, 2 5/8 yards if 48 inches wide, and 2 1/2 yards if 54 inches wide. If it is fancy material, the cloak should be finished with machine-stitching only. If it is other material, and if so desired, the cloak may be finished with broad bands of plush or fur, and a lining of durola on any prepared material may be added. Close the cloak at the top with a single clasp.

Cut the standing collar with its widest end on a lengthwise fold of the material. Cut the cape crosswise on the material. Cut the wrap piece with its front edge lengthwise on the material. Cut two pockets to cover the places for them marked on the diagram, and attach them on the under side of the cloak.

1885 *National Garment Cutter*

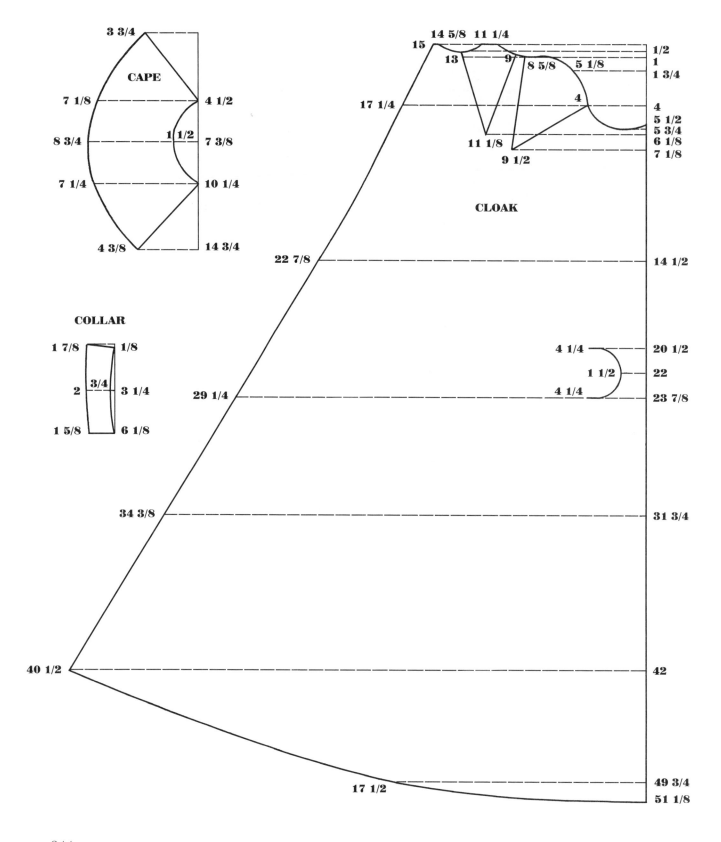

CAPE

3 3/4

7 1/8   4 1/2

1 1/2

8 3/4   7 3/8

7 1/4   10 1/4

4 3/8   14 3/4

COLLAR

1 7/8   1/8

3/4

2   3 1/4

1 5/8   6 1/8

CLOAK

14 5/8   11 1/4

15

13   9   8 5/8   5 1/8   1/2
                                            1
                                            1 3/4

17 1/4   4   4
                                            5 1/2
                                            5 3/4
11 1/8   6 1/8
         9 1/2   7 1/8

22 7/8   14 1/2

4 1/4   20 1/2

1 1/2   22

29 1/4   4 1/4   23 7/8

34 3/8   31 3/4

40 1/2   42

17 1/2   49 3/4
                                            51 1/8

244

  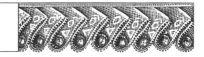

Cloak with Hood. This cloak is pictured made of olive checked cloth, with bronze surah for the hood lining. The shape is circular, but is varied by a line of gathers at the neck, the fullness contributing to the bouffant effect and permitting the cloak to hang well over the drapery. The backs are bias and joined in a seam. The front edges are turned under for wide hems. The cloak is closed only at the neck with a hook and eye, although its edges lap their entire length.

The pointed hood is made of a single section of the material, with a center seam from the neck to the point. Its edges are rolled over in capuchin fashion. The hood is gathered at the neck. It is joined with a high standing collar to the neck of the cloak.

For traveling wear camel's hair, serge, flannel, cloth, mohair, pongee, etc., are much liked. Plain or fancy silk or surah is used for the hood lining,

and it may be of any admired color. For heavier cloaks frisé, cheviot, tricot, and many kinds of seasonable cloakings are used. These may be finished plainly, or with braid along the edges. For evening wear faille Française, satin rhadames, siclienne, grosgrain silk, and handsomely embroidered or decorated wools in black and in colors are suitable. They may be trimmed with down, feathers, raveled ruches of silk, etc. For a plain finish, a thick cord may be used at the edges and to tie the cloak at the throat. The hood lining may be like the cloak lining or a richer material of the same shade. For a lady of medium size, this cloak requires 6 3/8 yards of material 22 inches wide, 3 3/8 yards of material 44 inches wide, or 3 1/4 yards of material 54 inches wide. Each requires 1 yard of silk 20 inches wide for the hood lining.

July 1887 *Delineator*

 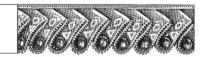

Cloak with Yoke. This cloak is suitable for traveling and for occasions when a wrap that will not crush the toilette is needed. It is almost long enough to cover the costume. Mixed, light-weight cloth was used for this example.

The upper part is a yoke and is composed of two sections that are joined by a seam in the center of the back. To the yoke is joined the deeper part, which is likewise composed of two sections joined by a center back seam. Before being joined to the yoke, the top is drawn into the requisite space by three lines of shirring made a little less than 1 inch apart. The front edges are turned under for hems, which are machine-stitched, and closed with hooks and eyes. A standing collar finishes the neck.

In each side of the front is made an opening for the hand to pass through. Around the opening is arranged a pointed lap, which has two lines of stitching along its ends and back edge. A single line of stitching is made along the lower edge of the yoke, and about the top and ends of the collar. These parts, as well as the laps, are lined with bright surah. Ribbons matching the most prominent shade in the material are fastened at their plaited ends at the neck, their free ends being tied in a bow. Machine-stitching finishes the lower and front edges of the cloak.

Flannel, tricot, plaids, and invisible stripes develop well in this way. A lining may be added throughout. A handsome clasp may replace the ribbon ties at the neck. To make the cloak for a lady of medium size, requires 6 1/2 yards of material 22 inches wide, 3 1/4 yards of material 44 inches wide, or 3 yards of material 54 inches wide.

June 1887 *Delineator*

8. Home Dressmaking

With the help of paper patterns, and fashion illustrations and descriptions, by the use of a little care and patience anyone may become her own dressmaker, and thereby save much of the allowance appropriated for dressing.

Making the Foundation Skirt
Or Under-Skirt

We will commence with the skirt of our dress, and see how we can best arrange to cut it out of the material. (See Figure 1.) If this is very handsome it is not used, but a foundation skirt of cheap silk, alpaca, or cambric is substituted. This foundation skirt does not show at all, being covered by the trimming and drapery. (See Figure 2.)

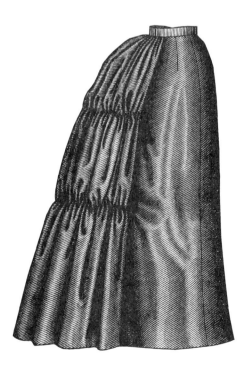

Figure 1. Foundation skirt or under-skirt, 1887

Figure 2. Foundation skirt covered by trimming and polonaise, 1886

Cutting Out and Sewing the Skirt. The skirt is usually from 2, to 2 1/4 yards in width. The front is gored at the top on each side; the gores cut off here are sewed on the lower sides of the breadth if the material is narrow. The two side gores are cut out of one breadth of single-width material, provided there is no figure or nap to interfere. The wide part of one, and the narrow part of the other, come out of the width; one side of these gores is cut straight, the other bias. Two breadths of plain single-width material are sewed together for the back. Then the bias edge of the side gore is sewed on the straight edge of the back breadth; the front gore is then sewed on; next the other side gore is attached to the back breadths. Particular attention should be paid in sewing up a skirt that two bias seams are never sewed together. This makes a skirt hang very badly, and no amount of after fixing can ever make it satisfactory.

Facing the Hem. The skirt should be shaped around the edge to form a graceful curve, sloping toward the back. If the skirt is made of cambric or alpaca, a facing of the dress material, 3 or 4 inches deep, should be put around the outside. Then a facing 9 inches deep or deeper must be put on the under side, and a skirt braid put on, as a binding neatly hemmed down, first on one side, then turned

over and hemmed on the other. Always shrink the braid in warm water and iron it before putting it on the skirt. Many modistes put in a deep facing of haircloth. This keeps the skirt out at the lower edge, and makes it unnecessary to always wear a long bustle. (See Figure 3.)

Putting in Steels. These must be put very high up, so that they will adjust themselves to the wearer's changes of position. (See Figure 4.) They are usually made of whalebone. They should be inserted in casings made of tape, sewed on at intervals of 5 inches apart, five steels being usually put in a dress. The casings commence at the side gores, and are only put across the back breadths. The length of the steels must be regulated by the taste of the wearer, as some persons like the drapery to be more bouffant than others.

Adding Strings. Another mode of arranging the foundation skirt is fastening five sets of strings or elastic bands to the center of the side gores. Two pairs of ribbon strings or tapes are at the top, the upper pair being only 5 inches below the belt. The next two pairs are short elastic bands with ribbons at their ends to tie them together. The fifth is a single elastic band fastened permanently only 10 inches above the bottom of the skirt. This band is about 1/2 yard long, and is basted in two or three

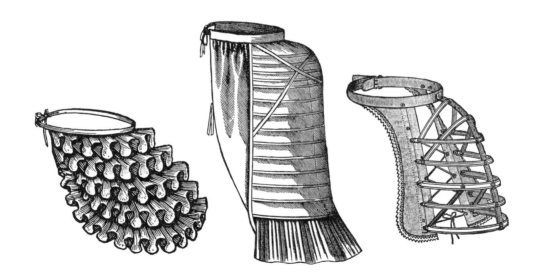

Figure 3. Three bustles, 1888

248

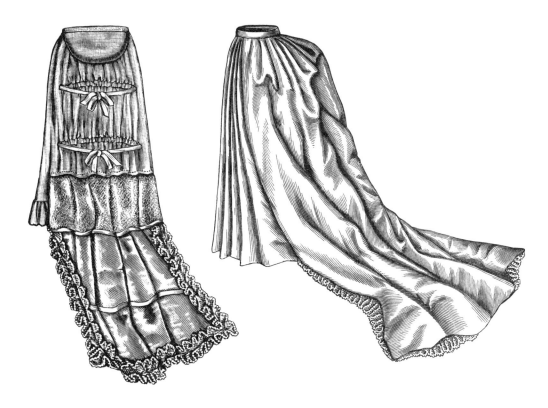

Figure 4. Skirt with steels, pad, and train, 1889

places to the lower skirt. This arrangement is used with fully draped over-skirts when the pad and steels are omitted.

Mounting the Skirt. The back opening should nearly reach the upper steel, and must be neatly hemmed. Mounting a skirt at the waist is done in many ways. Sometimes the upper edge is hemmed with a false hem, through which a tape or ribbon is passed. Or else the front and side gores are eased into a ribbon belt, the back being gauged into the rest of the belt. At the back opening, the belt should lap over itself 3 inches to prevent the pad from escaping. A double set of hooks and eyes must be placed on the belt. One set first hooks the left edge of the opening to the belt on the right, 3 inches from the right edge, this being the waist measure. The right edge laps over and hooks onto the left of the belt, this 3 inches being beyond the waist measure.

Covering the Foundation Skirt With Straight Material

If there is a skirt of the dress material, it is very full and straight. Sometimes it is gathered all around at the top, and sewed to the foundation skirt. But in most cases it is partly plain and partly gathered, or else plaited in wide, loose-looking plaits in the sides or at the back, or wherever it is not covered by drapery. (See Figure 5.)

A simple plan for making a wool skirt is to use double-width material. This is passed around the figure and has but one seam, that at the back instead of the usual gored breadths. All of the fullness is massed in layers of plaits that fall in with the placket opening at the back. Darts are taken in the top of the front and sides to make the skirt fit smoothly over the gored foundation skirt. The lower part may be finished as desired.

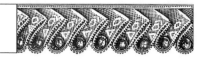

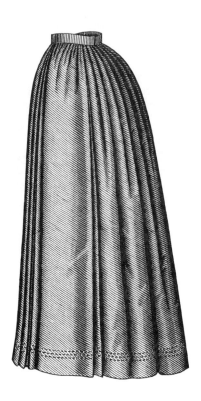

Figure 5. Skirt combining plaits and gathers, 1889

If the wearer is inclined to be stout, a deep yoke is made to fit neatly (see Figure 6). The skirt is hung on the yoke plain in front and on the sides, and full at the back. If the person is slight the skirt is fastened on a belt; the fullness is arranged in the same manner.

Covering the Foundation Skirt With Kilting

If a kilt skirt is desired, the material should be measured off to the depth required and cut straight. (See Figure 7.) A calculation is made as to the number of breadths needed; three times the width of the skirt is required for kilting.

Assembling the Pieces. Sew all of the breadths together. If the material has not a self-colored selvage, the selvage must be cut off and the edges must be over-sewed when joined. Turn up and hem the lower edge by machine; or if by hand, the stitches must be almost invisible on the right side. Press each seam on the wrong side, leaving the last one open so that it will be in a straight piece.

Figure 6. Skirt yoke in two depths, 1886

Then proceed to line the skirt with silk muslin. Cut it the same depth and width as the material. Sew the two together, turn over, and baste carefully along the edge; baste together farther up.

Laying the Plaits. Lay the plaits over so that each one just touches the other, basting them down as you make them, and making sure that all are equal in size. After you have finished your plaiting, lay it down on a lapboard or table. Take cotton the color of the material, and baste the plaits along the top edge.

Figure 7. Kilt skirt with yoke, 1884

Press the plaits with a hot iron on the wrong side; if the material is thick and stubborn, dampen it before ironing it. Turn down the top edge about 1/2 inch, and baste it along with cotton of its color. Press the turn-down quite flat with a hot iron.

Sewing the Plaits to the Foundation. Put tapes across the back at intervals of 4 inches. Baste each plait slightly on the tapes, and proceed to arrange them on the foundation skirt. The hemmed edge should be 1/8 inch above the bottom of the skirt. Stitch the plaits on by machine or by hand, and finish with a narrow belt. Never remove the basting threads from the kilting until the whole dress is finished. Kilting is always covered over with the drapery so that it never shows where it is sewed on. If a whole kilt skirt is desired without drapery, it goes up beneath the basque.

Covering the Foundation Skirt with Box-Plaiting

Box-plaited ruffles, double box-plaitings, and triple box-plaitings are all fashionable. (See Figure 8.) The Greek plait resembles the box-plait, and the fold may be either medium or large. Box-plaited skirts with tucks at the edge are very popular.

Tucking the Skirt. To make a box-plaited skirt with three tucks, cut five breadths 45 inches long, and five breadths 27 inches long. Join all of the long lengths together, then all of the short ones, and join the short to the long. Now turn up the hem all around 3 inches deep. If for machining, it must be basted; if for hemming, pinning will be sufficient. Take a piece of card 5 inches in depth, and make a mark on it 3 1/4 inches from the bottom. Put the bottom of the card to the bottom of the hem, and turn the material to the exact depth of the card. Baste your tuck to the 3 1/4-inch mark on the card. Fix the second and third tucks by leaving 1 1/2 inches between each tuck, as only the stitches of the top tuck are usually shown. You will easily keep your tucks even by cutting the card 3 inches deep, and marking it at 1 1/2 inches. Place one edge of the card at the basting of the tuck below the one you are fixing; turn the tuck to the other edge of the card. The tucks must now be stitched and pressed.

Plaiting the Skirt. Double the five front breadths, putting in a pin to mark the center of the front. The center front plait is 12 inches in width; it takes rather more than one breadth for this plait, as the folds must wrap over under the center of the plait at the back. Leave spaces of 2 inches on each side of this plait. The two plaits at the side measure 10 inches each when finished; they must be made in the same manner as the front plait. The five back breadths must be plaited into three 10-inch plaits, with space as before.

Baste all of these plaits, beginning at the hem. Baste the front breadths six times at regular intervals; for the back breadths four times will be sufficient. Press with a hot iron on the wrong side. After pressing, keep the wrong side to you, and sew two tapes across the plaits at the front breadths.

One tape is to go across the center of the plaits, and one between this and the top of the breadths. You must not tighten the tapes, nor must you take the stitches to the front of the plaits. The back plaitings will not need tapes.

Putting the Plaiting on the Foundation. The foundation skirt should be edged with a foot plaiting 4 inches deep, this plaiting being kilted as described above. It is made of the same material as the skirt, or of a brighter color if desired to correspond with the trimmings. The depth of this kilting may be arranged to suit individual fancy; it is intended to take away the plain look from the edge of the skirt. The bottom of the hem falls over it.

To put on the plaited over-skirt, take the center of the front gore of the foundation and the center of the center front box-plait; pin the plaiting to the foundation center to center. Place the foundation skirt and box-plaiting on a table, and pin closely. Hold the skirt up, shake it, and see that it is even before stitching it to the foundation. When you are satisfied that it hangs evenly, sew it securely.

Finishing a Skirt

A pad is added to every dress (see Figure 4). This is made of satin, silk, or silesia. It should be large enough to keep the skirt from falling inward before the first steel, as often happens if it is too narrow and thick, but it must be proportionate to the figure.

Making a Pad. For this model, cut two pieces of the material 3/8 yard by 1/4 yard. The pad is always wider than long. Many make the lower edge with sharp corners like the upper edge, but it is better to cut it curved. Sew the pieces together, except for the top. Fill the pad with horsehair. Take a needle and thread and knot it at intervals quite through, as a mattress is knotted. The pad should be trimmed all around with lace; if only made of silesia, a common white lace is used.

The pad is sewed to the eye side of the skirt belt, putting the center to the center of the belt. Put a hook on the loose side of the pad, and an eye on the belt to fasten it to; or let it be worn with any dress.

Adding Crinoline. Crinoline is a great improvement plaited in the hack of a skirt, even when steels and a pad are worn. Take three breadths of

Figure 8. Costume with box-plaited skirt of two materials, 1889

crinoline, and join them together. Turn up a hem so that they will be 14 inches deep. Plait in three double box-plaits, leaving the center plait a little larger than those at the sides. Bind it along the top with a piece of tape. Sew it to the inside of the foundation skirt just on the lowest steel casing, and sew it down the sides to the seam of the skirt.

Adding a Pocket. For the pocket, take a piece of the bodice lining 15 inches long and 14 inches wide. Double this lengthwise, turn over two corners together to form a triangle of 6 inches, and cut them off. Face up the slanted top of the pocket with a piece of the dress material, turn the faced side out, and stitch down the short side and along the bottom. Turn the pocket and stitch again about 1/4 inch from the last stitching. Commencing 10 inches below the waist, unpick the side seam of the skirt, and pick out 7 1/2 inches of the seam. Turn the skirt inside out, and sew in the pocket so that the facing shows on the right side of the skirt. At the top of the pocket a piece of tape 10 inches long must be sewed to it, and afterward fastened to the belt.

Making Skirts of Heavy Material

There are several different modes of making the plain skirts used for many styles of costumes, which are especially adapted to heavy materials. By plain skirts we mean those that are untrimmed or that have flat trimmings, such as bands of embroidery, braid, velvet, etc. These skirts require to be rather more full than those trimmed with ruffles, plaitings, or ruchings, but less so than full skirts of plain, thin material, gathered or plaited at the waist. For heavy or figured materials, the front gore of the skirt should be 21 inches wide at the edge, and 13 inches wide at the top. The side gores, one on each side, are 20 inches wide at the edge, and 10 inches at the top. The back breadth is of the same width, 40 inches throughout, giving a total width at the edge of, as nearly as possible, 2 3/4 yards. This requires five breadths of material 20 or 21 inches wide. The tunic and drapery are arranged over this in any manner that may be preferred.

Making a Drapery for a Plain Heavy Skirt. When the upper part of the back breadth is covered by the drapery, it is often arranged as follows. A small breadth 20 inches square forms the top part. The lower part, which is the full width of 40 inches, is gathered or plaited, and joined to one end of this small breadth, as if it were a deep flounce completing the skirt. The breadth thus made is joined to the side gores, and has the advantage of being more economical and less voluminous at the waist; the fullness is also well thrown to the back. The back breadth, whether it is made in one or in two pieces, occupies 6 inches of the belt, the front gore 6 inches, and the side gores 6 inches each, making a total of 24 inches, plaits being made in the front and side gores to reduce them to the proper size. Skirts of this description do not require lining, unless the material is too thin to bear the trimming to be used, or unless it is of a very good quality that needs to be protected from dust, etc., in view of future making over and turning. Hems must be so arranged that the stitches come under the trimmings, or are made invisible in some manner.

Trimming a Plain Heavy Skirt. The trimmings for such skirts are so infinitely varied as to make it impossible to do more than make a few suggestions. Embroidery (in any degree of richness), either worked on the material or applied on it, silk, beads, and chenille are combined in the most exquisite patterns. (See Figure 9.) Nothing, in fact, in the way of embroidery or passementerie ornaments is too costly or handsome for the plain skirts of dresses made of rich, plain materials. All kinds of braids are used for plainer materials, while velvet makes a trimming suitable for almost any material of good quality. Figured materials are less trimmed, but plaitings of plain material are admissable, and wool laces are used with wool, and in some cases with silk materials.

Making a Drapery To Go Over a Box-Plaiting

A suitable design is illustrated by Figure 10. For the front drapery, cut one breadth of the material 22 inches long, and two breadths each 16 inches long. Join these three breadths together straight at the top, the long breadth in the center. Slope the center breadth at the bottom so that it graduates to the side breadths. To put this drapery exactly in

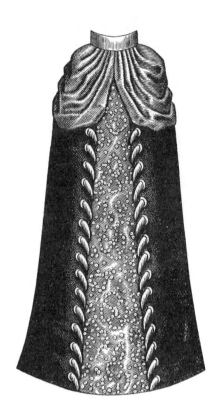

**Figure 9. Plain skirt with beaded panel
and silk cord lacing, 1886**

When the left side is plaited, fasten it just below the belt to the foundation; there will be a straight unplaited piece from these plaits to the seam of the back breadth of the foundation. Now take the end of the drapery and plait it up toward the waist. The drapery must fall quite loosely over the line it was basted on at the bottom. Sew the drapery securely to the foundation just below the belt, where it has been pinned, and neaten it by hemming a piece of ribbon or binding over it.

The sides will be made neat when placing the back drapery over them. Take 3 yards of the material cut in half, join them together, and press

**Figure 10. Costume with drapery
over box-plaited skirt, 1885**

the proper curve, run a basting thread on the skirt, beginning at the side seams 9 inches below the waist, and 20 inches below the waist in the center of the front. Put the basting line in the slope shown by Figure 10; both sides are alike at the bottom of the front drapery.

You will now find it necessary, for arranging the front and back drapery properly, to put the skirt either on a dress stand or on a person. (See Figure 11.) Fold the drapery exactly in half, then pin it to the center basting line and run it to the skirt, taking care not to tighten the drapery. Sew both sides on and begin the plaiting at the waist, first putting a mark in the center of the drapery. Plait the whole of the right side of the drapery into a number of small deep plaits, and pin it to the foundation from the front to the seam of the back breadth. Now arrange the left side of the drapery; at about 2 inches from the front make five plaits close together about 2 inches deep.

Figure 11. Advertisement for dress stand, 1889

the seam; turn under on each side at least 3 inches. Plait the drapery into a large triple box-plait wide enough to cover the back as far as the joins of the side drapery. The center of this box-plait must go exactly to the center of the back; pin it there firmly. On the left side, sew the turn-down piece over the ends of the front drapery. Carry the plait down 17 inches, and turn under 8 inches, so that it forms a deep puff. Sew this plait under the puff to the skirt, and slip-stitch the outer plait 1 inch from the edge, down to the skirt. The rest of this side of the drapery must be turned under to form a second deep puff, which should terminate 9 inches above the bottom

of the skirt. Now go to the right side and loop it up in the same way; this will leave the center hanging loose, which must be looped up and sewed to the skirt about 24 inches below the waist. Plait the lower end of the drapery, and turn it under, allowing it to fall 3 inches lower in the center than at the sides. Sew it firmly to the skirt.

Arranging Various Back Draperies

We will describe four methods of arranging the back draperies of dresses, none of them being very complicated or beyond the powers of the average amateur dressmaker. These draperies may

255

be longer or shorter, draped high on one side and falling straight on the other, or equally on both sides. With them the skirt may be plaited in front, or have a short or long apron, or a shawl front as fancy dictates.

Making a Plaited Back Drapery. A drapery much in vogue is that arranged in vertical plaits of different kinds and dimensions. One of the prettiest modes is a large box-plait in the center, with plain plaits on the right or left; or plain plaits alone are used, ironed quite flat or rounded like organ-pipe plaits. Two breadths, 27 inches wide, are sufficient, and they should be long enough to reach within 6 inches of the skirt's edge. When organ-pipe plaits are employed they are generally three in number, and unless the material is very stiff and rich it is indispensable to line them with a light but stiff muslin.

All plaits, no matter of what kind, must be secured by a tape sewed horizontally across them. These tape bands must be placed at intervals, and the lower they descend the longer each must be, for the drapery should swell out and become wider and wider as it descends the skirt. A well-shaped, strong pad is imperative with this kind of drapery. To complete the work, the plaits must be secured here and there to the skirt, so that they cannot be blown aside by the wind or otherwise disarranged.

Making a Simple Back Drapery. This drapery falls in even plaits on the left side, and is caught up on the right side. It is made of a breadth of material measuring 40 inches in length and 60 inches in width. If the material is narrow, a sufficient number of breadths must be joined together to achieve the width. A square piece, measuring 10 inches each way, is cut out of the top corner on the right-hand side. Two plaits are made at the lower corner on the same side, taking up about 13 inches. The part above this, about 16 inches deep, is lined with silk, and is arranged to fall in a loop on the outside of the drapery. The plaits at the edge are brought up to the waist, the two sides of the small cut-out square at the top are joined together, and this completes the draping on the right side.

The top of the drapery is formed into six flat plaits all folded toward the right, and measuring about 2 1/2 inches in depth. The plait at the extreme left is 4 inches wide to permit of the edge being turned under the revers way, forming a box-plait the same width as the flat plaits.

Making a Pointed Back Drapery. A third style falls in a long point on each side of the short center. This is made of two breadths of material, each measuring from 26 to 28 inches in width, or from 52 to 56 inches in all, and about 48 inches long. The two breadths are joined by a seam, which serves to mark the center of the drapery. Four plaits are made on each side along the top, all folded toward the center, leaving a plain space of 8 inches in the center; when the plaits are brought up close together this center part forms a loop. At the lower edge of this drapery a piece 13 inches high in the center, and sloping down on each side toward the corner, is cut away to form the two points. The piece cut away is the shape of a triangle. Above this the drapery is plain for a space of 13 inches, and the top part is plaited and brought up to the waist, the lined loop being arranged to fall over and conceal the plaits. The coquille drapery at the side is formed by plaiting up the material in one or two folds, and basting these lightly onto the foundation skirt.

Making a Back Drapery with a Dog's-Ear Point. A fourth popular drapery has on the left side an *oreille de chien* or dog's-ear point. This drapery is formed of a square breadth of material measuring 48 inches each way. The left side is left the full length of the material, but sloped off gradually in a rounded shape toward the right, leaving this only 44 inches long. At the top on the right side, 28 inches are measured off and folded into five flat plaits, all of them turned toward the center, and then joined to the belt. The dog's ear is made by plaiting up the left-hand corner of the material. The piece left for the dog's-ear point is 19 inches along the top, and 18 inches down the side. The plaits are small, and closely drawn up and joined to the belt, the point being turned over and arranged to fall in its destined position. The left side below the dog's ear is arranged by joining the lower edge up to the waist under the point. The end left is folded in unstudied coquille plaits going off gradually toward the long center of the drapery. The right side falls in straight plaits.

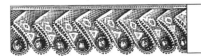 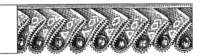

Making Tunics

Tunics gathered in at the top are very fashionable. These are really skirts a little shorter than the foundation skirt, but open in front to show the front panel of the foundation skirt, or on one side over a plaited panel, or some other mode of ornamenting the skirt. In this case the tunic is flat in front, and gathered or plaited at the back. The bodice worn with these full tunics is either quite short waisted, or very nearly so, having only slight points in front, and very short, curved basques on the sides. Gathered or puffed tunics lend themselves well to economical renovations of half-worn toilettes; the best parts of two old dresses will often suffice for making one new dress. The foundation skirt is made of the figured or heavier material of the two, and the plain or lighter material is reserved for the bodice and full tunic.

Trimming Draperies and Tunics. The edges of tunics and draperies may be simply finished with a hem about 1 inch wide, which must be hemmed with fine silk in invisible stitches. Lace flounces may trim the edge, either reversed or loosely floating; coquilles, bows, ruches, or little flounces may replace them; or revers may be added, lined with a different material contrasting in shade. (See Figure 12.)

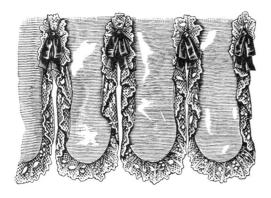

Figure 12. Drapery edge cut into tabs, which are then lined and trimmed, 1884

Making a Basque Bodice

Dress bodices are worn in such a variety of styles that it is impossible to describe all or half that are used. (See Figure 13.) First decide on the style, next procure the pattern. Measure all of the parts with a tape measure to see if the size is correct. If it is too large, it is very easy to turn down the extra material; if too small, 1 inch or whatever is required can readily be added.

Using an Old Lining as a Pattern. Very frequently an old lining, if well fitting, can serve as a pattern for the new one. However, the process of ripping up an old bodice will probably stretch the seams somewhat, and due allowance must be made for this fact. The seams in the old lining are plainly indicated by the stitch marks, and the new lining can be marked by them to show just how deep to take the seams. The darts can also be exactly marked from the old pattern. A tracing wheel saves much time and work; but if one is not at hand, the seams and darts can be marked with a colored lead pencil. It is very important that the darts be in exactly the right place. If a tracing wheel is not used, so that the old stitching can be followed exactly, it is well to snip holes along the stitching, and mark through these holes with a lead pencil onto the new lining. It is seldom possible to get the darts correct by creasing and folding along the former seams.

Choosing the Lining Material. It is generally the best plan to use new lining material; although an old lining, if little worn, may be made to do service again. Double-faced silesia, gray on one side and black on the other, or black-and-white striped or checked on the other, is preferable for black and dark-colored materials. A bodice of light-colored material should be lined with light gray or cream silesia. The silk-finished silesia, which is both fine and firm, as well as soft, is the kind to choose. The cheaper kinds, which pull and stretch out of shape after a few weeks' wear, should never be bought for bodice linings. Drilling should never be used even in common dresses; it is too stiff and heavy. It is very bad economy to use a poor quality of lining.

Cutting Out the Lining. Bodice linings must always be cut across, not lengthwise of the silesia;

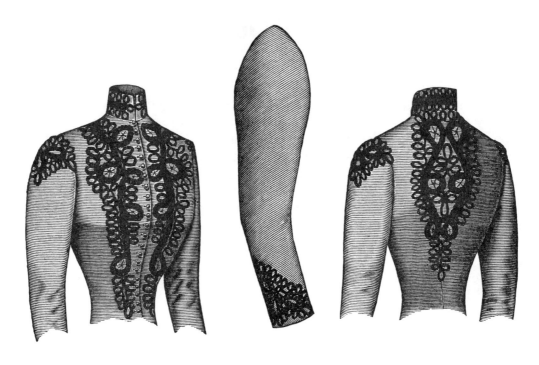

Figure 13. Plain basque with braid appliqués, 1887

that is, the silesia should be unfolded, and the lining laid on so the neck or the bottom of the bodice is on the selvage. When cut in this way, the bodice will keep in shape perfectly, for silesia will not give at all lengthwise, while even the best quality will stretch a trifle crosswise.

Put the pattern down on the silesia and mark the extra size with a piece of French chalk on it before cutting. It is a good rule always to allow large seams on the lining. They can be cut off after the first fitting if not needed, and frequently save a great deal of trouble, where the pattern has been so closely followed. If an old lining is used for a pattern, after it is pinned onto the new material, it must be stretched smoothly up and down and crosswise. Any fullness that then shows itself along the seams must be evenly smoothed down, and the edge drawn into the proper shape.

Basting the Lining. The lining must be carefully basted before it is tried on. Commence with the front dart seam, basting from the point downward. Then baste the second, and follow by basting the front side piece to the front. Baste the back to the side back; it is necessary to proceed differently

for different figures. For an ordinary figure, both pieces should be held evenly from the armhole downward. For one with slightly rounded shoulders, the back should be fulled in a little from 1 inch below the armhole, to about 7 inches downward. For a hollow back, the back part must be held a little tighter than the side piece, at that distance. Then join the back to the front at the side seams. After the other side is similarly treated, join both halves of the bodice in the center of the back. This finished, the shoulder seams should be basted. They will be found shorter in front than at the back. The front part should be gently and uniformly stretched until both parts are even at the neck and armholes.

Fitting the Lining. Put on the basted bodice for fitting wrong side out, with the seams on the outside. You will fit only the right half. Take hold of the two fronts with your left hand at the hollow of the neck, securing both fronts evenly in height and width. With your right hand insert a pin perpendicularly, to secure both guide-lines at that point. Proceed in like manner by taking hold of the two front edges, evening them in width and length until you have secured the desired fit across

the bust. Insert a pin perpendicularly at that point. Now, commencing at the pin already inserted at the neck, pin the fronts together by inserting pins perpendicularly, about 1/2 inch apart, all the way down. Then smooth the back and front of the bodice downward, according to the requirements of the figure. If any fullness appears upward, both parts should be smoothed up to the shoulder seam.

Remove the bodice by taking out the pins from the shoulder and side piece of the left half. By this method the pins are left down the front, and if any alteration has been made you can baste a line down to the pins before removing them. If any changes have been made on the right half of the bodice during fitting, separate the left half therefrom by ripping the seam at the center of the back. Now separate the different parts of the left half of the bodice, and place each smoothly on a table, the outside material upward. Before separating the parts of the right half of the bodice, the horizontal pin line as placed at the waist in fitting should be indicated by a distinct marking line, indicating also the pin lines as they were placed lengthwise in fitting at the seams for either letting out or taking in. After these marks have been made, remove the pins. Then separate the different parts of the right half of the bodice, placing them smoothly on the corresponding parts of the left half. Make all alterations on the left half that were made on the right.

In fitting a bodice, particular attention should be paid to the armholes, where the front sleeve seam is generally placed. It is here where in fitting a close-fitting bodice, a break is quite apt to occur; and it is to one of the following causes that these breaks are due. First, from the armholes being too small in width. Second, from the armholes being too small in length.

There are two ways of remedying the first defect. One is to cut a little toward the front, under the arm, and to let out at the seams. An armhole should never be cut as required, until the last seam is first ripped a little at the upper part, to be cut out if need be. The second defect generally occurs through sloping shoulders, or short waists where the side seams are in too high a position under the arms. Slash or cut into the surplus, commencing from the

front of the armhole, and deepening the slashes as you proceed under the arm. Then rip open the right shoulder seam, and by gently smoothing the front up at that point with your right hand, and the back with your left hand from beneath the arm to the shoulder, that fault will be revealed. The upper part of the shoulder will adjust itself to the shape of the figure, thus altering the previous shape of the neck as required. If the neck of the person is long, however, it will be necessary to let out from the shoulder seam at the neck, and take in the seam proportionately toward the tip of the shoulder. Now, the right arm of the person being fitted should be raised, so the fitter can work the scissors comfortably in shaping the armhole underneath as close to the arm as seems requisite—being careful in so doing that the armhole is not cut too low under the arm nor too high on the shoulder.

Cutting Out the Material. Carefully unpick the lining, crease all of the seams down, then proceed to cut out the material. For silk, wool, or cotton, the material should always be double, so that you cut the corresponding parts together. The lining must now be pinned closely onto the material. If you are using a figured material, with an up-and-down pattern, take care that the pattern is right before cutting, or you may waste a good deal of it. If it is striped, carefully cut it so that the stripes meet where the seams join in the center of the back, and at the side back.

Basting the Bodice onto the Lining. Unpin the bodice fronts, and place the material on the lining, back to back. Pin the material to the lining at the shoulder and neck, material toward you, and smooth with your hand from the shoulder downward, pinning as you smooth, to slightly stretch the material on the lining. Then stretch and pin the material across in the same manner, smoothing it with your hand.

After having pinned each piece of the bodice, commence the basting. You must now have the lining toward you. Baste with white cotton, or any odd lengths of colored cotton that will show on the material. Be particular to follow all of the creases made in the lining from the first fitting. It is also often necessary to take small plaits in the lining to

make it fit properly, which are not put in the outside material; these should be sewed before the material is basted on. In basting the material onto the lining, use short stitches.

Basting the Bodice Together. Proceed to baste the bodice together, following the rules given above. The rounded part of the side back, if long seams are not used, should be shorter than the corresponding part of the back; the object of this is to make the back set perfectly. Be very careful that the little fullness is equally divided, so that when basted and stitched, it is imperceptible. The corresponding side piece must be treated in the same manner. Notch the seams at the waist three times at intervals of about 1 inch. Cut open the darts to within 1 inch of the tops, and notch in the same manner.

Fitting the Bodice. However well your pattern may be cut, and however carefully you may have basted it, the difference in the elasticity of the material may slightly affect the fit, and some alterations may be needed. For this final fitting it is much better to have your material right side out, as it will be worn, as it allows for the size taken up by the seams when next to you. Put your bodice on gently, so that you remove no pins, and break no bastings. Have a large supply of good pins at hand.

Begin your fitting by pinning down the front of the bodice, putting the first pin at the neck. Pin to the basting threads down the front of the bodice, making no alterations at present, unless the bodice is too tight, when of course you let it out so as to meet comfortably down the front. Pass your hand from the front toward the side piece under the arm, and smooth the bodice to see if it fits sufficiently close to the figure; do not make it extremely tight, as the stitched seams will not give as much as the basted ones. Take care to let out both seams of the sides you are fitting to the same extent. If the bodice appears to be very tight, let out a little from the front, because if too much increase is made at the side-piece seams, the armhole will be too large. Now pass your hand from the bust to the shoulder upward and remove the pins, if there is need of alteration. Look well to the darts, and alter, should they be too high or too low. Sometimes

it is necessary to take in a little at the center back seam. Place a pin exactly at the curve of the waist, back and front; that is, if the basting thread is not already at the right place. If the basting thread at the neck is too high or too low, mark the correct line with a few pins, and notch within 1/4 inch of the fitting line. The armholes should not be shaped until the last, as they so easily stretch. Notch them all around, and raise the arm of the person being fitted, to cut away all of the surplus, to conform to the proper shape and size of the arm.

Baste closely to the line of pins before removing them. Now correct the left half by the right half. Pin all of the original bastings of the two sides to correspond exactly with each other around the armholes, the neck, and the under-arm seams. If the darts have been altered, pin the seams very carefully together, and pin around the corrected basting; turn the left front toward you, and baste to the pins.

Sewing the Bodice. Begin by stitching the front darts, and be very careful to do this with precision, observing the bastings. The fronts are to remain detached from the side pieces and shoulders until the back and side-piece seams are stitched, the button-holes made, and the buttons sewed on. Next take the button-hole front, that is the right front. Turn the front down 1/4 inch outside the original front basting thread, and with a needle and thread baste as you turn. According to the dress material, take a piece of satin, silk, or silesia for facing. Turn the inside of the bodice front toward you, and hem your facing just a shade nearer the edge of the front than the basting thread; be most careful not to take a stitch through to the right side. When you come to the curve of the waist, full the facing slightly to give the proper spring when this is hemmed down to the bottom of the bodice. If the bodice material is thick, turn up the facing and cut away the material and lining to within 1/8 inch of the facing hem. If the bodice material is thin, cut only the lining in the same way. Now cut the material so that when the facing is hemmed down the second time, it covers the edge, and makes the front neat inside. With the second hem of the facing, as with the first, be careful not to take any of your stitches through.

If the bodice gapes enough in front to show the white garments at the sides of the button-holes, run a strip of ribbon or a fold of material along the under front, to make a narrow lap.

Adding Button-Holes. Turn the outside of the bodice uppermost, the neck toward your right hand. Take a tape measure, and according to the size of the buttons, measure for the hole. The small buttons used at present will take a 1/2-inch button-hole. To be sure of the button-hole being the correct size, however, it is safer to slip the button through the hole after it is cut. To ensure the button-holes being correctly cut to one size, place a pin in the tape to the required measure. Lay the pin onto the front edge basting thread, and baste a line down to the end of the measure, until you get to the bottom of the bodice. You will find that a pair of button-hole scissors cuts much better button-holes than ordinary scissors. When you have cut a button-hole to the measure, turn the bodice around, with the front edge opposite to you, and cut a tiny triangular piece out of the top of the button-hole by making two slanted cuts of about 1/8 inch, and then a straight cut crosswise. For small buttons, the button-holes should be about 1/2 inch apart. In this you must, of course, be ruled by the size of the button.

To work a button-hole properly, take the front edge of the bodice toward you; have a needle threaded with the twist with which you intend working the button-holes. Begin on the left side close end of the button-hole (not the end from which the triangle is cut), and sew over all around, taking care not to stretch the edge of the button-hole. Now bar the button-hole all around by taking a stitch from the narrow end to the broad end. Put your needle back above the opening of the triangle, and work a bar above it just the width of the cut. Work to the close end of the other side, and repeat, so that you have a double bar of twist to work over, which raises and strengthens the button-hole. Begin to work the button-hole from the same end as you began to over-sew it; let your left thumb-nail rest just below the bar of twist, and work closely and evenly all around.

Adding Buttons. Furnish the button side of the front with the same kind of facing used for the

button-hole side. Take the neck of the front in your right hand, the outer side toward you, hemming the facing 1 1/2 inches from the basting line. Hem to the waist, where full in the same way as you did the facing of the first side; then continue plain to the bottom of the bodice. Turn the inside of the front toward you, and cut off the surplus part of the front to within 1/4 inch of the stitches of the facing. Turn the right side of the bodice toward you, and turn down the edge of the front, so that the facing is just edge-to-edge with the material. Baste the facing down through from the outside just at the basting of the button line. Hem the facing from the bottom to the top of the bodice, taking care that no stitches show through.

To mark for the buttons, take the two fronts, neck toward your left hand. On the button-hole side, put a pin through the top stitch of the basting thread at the neck. Put the pin through to the corresponding basting of the button side of the front; pin the fronts firmly together. Now get someone to hold the bodice just where you have pinned it, or pin it to something firm. Put a pin into the center of the triangle at the top of the button-hole, and through to the basting line for the button exactly opposite to it. Continue to place the pins through all of the button-holes for the entire length of the bodice, holding the button-hole side rather tightly.

Buttons without shanks must be sewed on loosely. About 1/8 inch of the cotton should be allowed as a substitute for a shank. After sewing the button securely, twist the cotton several times around the threads that form the substitute for the shank. A button with a shank can be sewed on tightly. Or it can have small eyelet holes worked in the bodice, the shank passed through, a cord run through them on the wrong side, and each one fastens. This is convenient for persons who desire to use different sets of buttons for one dress.

Basting the Bodice. The bodice must be pinned carefully and then basted. First, pin the fronts to the side pieces, stretching the fronts to the side pieces. Next, measure the waist from the inside of the bodice, holding the tape tightly immediately above the basting line of the waist, with the end of the tape exactly to the edge of the waist button-hole and to

the corresponding button, holding the bottom of the bodice toward you. If the size of the waist needs alteration, enlarge or decrease equally on the side piece and the front. Begin by pinning from the waist-line upward, gradually and carefully, so that the line remains quite even. After this, pin from the waist-line to the bottom of the bodice; baste it carefully. Now pin the shoulders, beginning at the points of the neck on each side, stretching the fronts of the shoulders when putting in each pin, so that the points at the armhole end of the shoulders meet.

Sewing Up the Bodice. When the seams have been closely basted, stitch them. Silk should be used instead of cotton for sewing the bodice seams, and in all places where the stitching shows. Remove all basting threads, except those around the neck and armhole. Cut the edges of the turnings, so that they are even; next, cut them in notches. The curving is to make them look neat; the notching is to make them lie flat, and to prevent the bodice from creasing when put on. Over-sew the turnings, material side toward you; this makes the work neater. If the material is of a very frail description, bind with narrow ribbon instead of over-sewing.

Pressing the Seams. Open the seams, lay them quite flat, and press them on a board covered with a blanket. If the bodice is of silk or velvet, a second person must assist in holding it while the other passes the iron over it. The person holding the bodice should have the top of the seam in her hand. When the darts are pressed, she should hold the seam under the arm and the front of the bodice in a line with the top of the darts.

Adding the Casings. If you use whalebone, you must next run on the casings, which should be of linen tape, or a piece of the bodice lining with the edges turned in on each side. The casings should be under the buttons to the same height as the front dart, on all of the darts, and on all other seams except the curved seams of the side back. The back casing should be about 6 inches long—5 inches above the waist and 1 inch below it. Turn down a loop of the casing about 3/4 inch in length. Begin by sewing at the bottom of the loop, to make it strong. Run on the casing, easing it with your thumb, to make it sufficiently loose for the curve of the bone.

If you use the new bodice steels, you will not need casings, as these steels are already covered. Sew them through the hole at the top, and at distances of about 2 inches, stretching the seam after each sewing. Steels do not, however, require your attention until after you have turned up the bottom of the bodice; but unlike bones, they must be secured before you sew on the bottom facing.

Facing the Bodice. Turn up the bottom of the bodice, beginning at the button side, fixing it with pins. See that you have it turned to a nice shape; when satisfactory, baste it up if you intend to have it simply faced. If you desire to have it corded, run a basting line to where the edge turns; remove the pins. To make the second side exactly like the first, put a pin through the point of the first dart and through the top of the corresponding dart of the other front; repeat this with the second darts. Put a pin through the waist button-hole to the waist button. Then pin to the top of the side piece at the point, passing through the corresponding point of the other side piece. You have your bodice right side out. Pin closely the two basting lines around the under part of the armhole from the point already indicated, to the second seam of the side back. This done, see that the side pieces of the bodice are quite flat at the seams, and along the line of the side turned up and basted. Put pins through to the second side, and before removing them, run a line of basting on the second side in the same place as the pins, after which remove the pins from the first side. You will have the bottom of the bodice perfectly even, when turn and baste it up. Cut off all surplus material, and face.

Cording the Bodice. Some persons like the edge of a basque corded. To do this, cut a piece of material on the cross 3 inches wide. Take a cord and place it on the wrong side of the material, 1/4 inch from the edge. Turn the material down over the cord and baste it with a needle and cotton, quite close to the cord, for the required length. Put a second cord 1/2 inch from the first. Fold the material back with the cord in it so that this second cord lies immediately above the first. Run on the basting line with silk or cotton the color of the material. Baste through the material under both the lines of cord,

 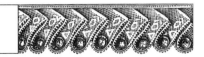

so that they are firmly held together. Pull out the basting, and stitch onto the edge of the basque following the directions already given.

Making the Collar. Measure the neck of the bodice. Place the pattern on a double piece of stiff muslin on the cross. Cut the muslin out allowing 1/2-inch turnings all around. Cut the collar and facing also on the cross. Pin the four thicknesses together, the wrong side of the material next to the muslin; then the facing on the material; pin smoothly and baste all together. Next take the muslin and material at the bottom of the collar, and baste it together, leaving the silk free. This basting is to mark the depth of the collar as to where it should be stitched to the bodice. Stitch the ends and top. Remove the basting except at the bottom. Turn the collar right side out, and baste around about 1/4 inch from the edge to hold the facing in place.

Put the lower basting line of the collar to the basting line of the neck of the bodice. Hold the collar toward you, and take great care not to stretch the neck of the bodice. Stitch through the material and muslin, leaving the facing free to be hemmed down on the inside.

Binding the Armholes. Take a piece of tape or binding about 1/2 inch wide. Baste it around the armhole inside the bodice, beginning at the seam of the side piece. Baste it about 1/8 inch from the lower edge, and continue all around the armhole; be sure not to stretch the armhole nor full it. The tape or binding must be basted exactly to the armhole basting. Cut off the end and turn it down.

Preparing the Sleeves. Pin the pattern carefully on the lining and cut out; do the same with your material. Baste the two together and then pin and baste the front seam, beginning at the top of the sleeve. Begin the back seam at the top. Pin straight until you reach the elbow, which you must gather and pin flatly to its place, and baste the seam down. Notch the seam of the front of the sleeve, turn the sleeve right side out, and it is ready for fitting.

Fitting the Sleeves. Take the sleeve and slip it over the arm. Put the elbow fullness to the elbow, and see if it is in the right place. Carry your eye along the back seam of the sleeve to the shoulder, and see if it is long enough. If not, pull it up to the requisite height, so that you can pin it to the armhole. If the elbow fulling is too high, bend the arm and put in a pin to mark the point of the elbow.

Now we come to the first seam of the sleeve. Turn it under to the basting thread, put a pin into the sleeve through the basting line, and then pass it through the basting at the armhole of the bodice. The front seam of the sleeve should be about 1 1/2 inches to the front of the side-piece seam. Go on turning down to the basting thread, and pinning the sleeve to the bodice until within 2 inches from the shoulder seam.

Look to the back of the sleeve, and see that the under part from the front seam to the back fits properly. Pin it so that it fits. What little fullness remains must be equally distributed at the top of the shoulder. Turn the sleeve up to the proper length and pin it.

Sewing the Sleeves. Stitch the seams exactly to your basting, being quite sure that you have the fullness at the elbow in its right place. Open the seams, and over-sew if the sleeve is of wool material. Pass a roller covered with flannel down the sleeve, and press the seams flat; of course, the sleeve must be inside out. Now turn up the bottom of the sleeve to the required length, and face it with a piece of silk. Take care that not a stitch of the hem goes through to the right side of the sleeve. Turn the sleeve right side out and put on the trimming, supposing it is considered necessary. (See Figure 14.)

Figure 14. Sleeve trimmed with cuff-facing, buttons, and simulated button-holes, 1884

Putting in the Sleeves. Take the front seam of the sleeve and put it exactly to the basting that marks its position. Have the inside of the sleeve and bodice toward you; pin the sleeve and bodice basting lines exactly to each other until within 2 inches of the shoulder seam. Go back to the under seam from which you started, and pin in the second time. When you come toward the top, distribute the fullness equally along about 3 inches at the top. After pinning in, baste closely. Stitch the sleeve in securely. Cut the turnings off within about 1/2 inch of the stitching, and over-sew the edge of the armhole, sleeve, and binding together neatly.

Boning the Bodice. If you use bones, cut them to the length of the casings. Scrape them until they are quite thin at both ends; if this is not done they will soon wear through the bodice. Put each bone in its casing through the loop left at the top; then run the loop to secure the bone in its place at the top. Push the bone close to the bottom of the casing, and sew through the bone. Take the top of the turning and bone casing together and push the bone down as tightly as you can. Hold it in place and sew it securely at the top, just below the loop.

Finishing the Bodice. Sew a broad tape, 1/4 inch smaller than the size of the bodice, to the bone casing and the turning of the back seam immediately above the waist-line. Fasten at the ends with two small hooks and eyes. This serves to keep the bodice in place at the back.

Both the bodice and the skirt should be provided with loops for hanging up.

Making a Round Bodice

There are many who desire to make the old-fashioned, full, round, belted bodice, always more or less worn for ordinary wash dresses. (See Figure 15.)

Making the Lining. Cut and piece the lining as directed for a basque bodice, with the exception that you cut it only 2 inches below the waist all around. Baste the darts, which have to be stitched in the lining only; put the side backs onto the back. Next put the two side pieces onto the side backs. Stitch all of the seams and press them. The seams of the lining for a full bodice, after being

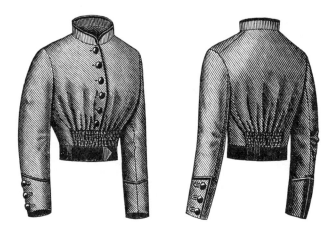

Figure 15. Gathered round bodice, 1880

snipped, are turned toward the material; this makes over-sewing unnecessary.

Making the Front. Put the lining on the material, allowing 15 inches from the edge of the material to the edge of the front lining; this is for the fullness. If you wish more fullness, you must allow it here. Cut the material away to the lining at the armholes, the shoulders, and the sides. Baste across the shoulder, around the armhole, and down the side seam, being sure to place a pin here and there between the under-arm seam and the first dart. Now, go to the neck. If you wish to have a plaited bodice (see Figure 16), commence about 2 inches from the shoulder, and plait up all of the material in small single or box-plaits, as preferred. When this is done, plait at the waist, arranging the plaits to cover the two dart seams on each side. If you wish the fullness gathered, fit the bodice plainly around the neck, and gather it three or four times at the waist, commencing from the second dart.

Making the Back. Cut a piece of material 24 inches wide, and the length for the back. Fold it in half, and pin the lining of the back onto it, with the armhole side next to the selvage of the material. Cut around as described for the fronts; open out the lining and material. Plait or gather the material to the size of the back of the neck and also at the waist. Then lay the lining on the material, and baste down the shoulder, around the armhole, and down the side.

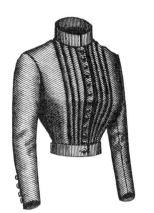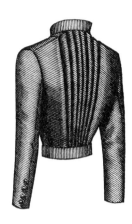

Figure 16. Plaited round bodice, 1885

Assembling the Bodice. Now pin and baste the shoulder and side piece together as directed for the basque bodice. Put it on to see that it fits properly; correct the two sides as before described. Then stitch the backs to the front. When stitching, do not join the side seams next to the front below the waist.

Finishing the Bodice. The fronts are turned down, as described for the basque bodice, and a belt is stitched on over the gathering, to which the over-skirt is sewed. Or the edge can be hemmed or bound with tape, and the over-skirt belt worn over it, a ribbon belt covering the one of the material. When the belt is sewed onto the bodice, the lower edge should be trimmed off to the proper depth, after the belt is basted on where the gathering ends. The sleeves and collar are made and put on as directed for the basque bodice.

Making a Polonaise

It is usual in making a polonaise to baste the lining and material together, and to stitch the seams as when making a bodice; but for the model we are first going to describe a different system is adopted.

Assembling the Lining. The lining is cut out alone, like that of a bodice, the different parts are basted together, and the lining is fitted on the figure. The fronts can now be finished off with buttons or hooks and eyes, and the darts are stitched. The center back seam, and the seams joining the side backs to the backs, are also stitched and finished off.

The shoulder seams are basted only. The front side pieces are covered with the polonaise material, and then basted in place, to be stitched afterward, when the front and back have been fitted on the lining. The short side piece (the depth of an ordinary basque) is alone on the side, no drapery coming there, and is covered with the material.

Draping the Polonaise. This polonaise consists of two breadths of material, each about 1 3/4 yards long, and 48 inches wide; if narrow material is used, two breadths must be joined together. First the prepared lining is put on the dress stand and fastened down the front. Take the center of one breadth of the polonaise material and pin it to the back of the dress stand at the neck, and at the waist. Make three plaits on each side of the pin at the neck, bringing the plaits a little way down the shoulder seam, but leaving a plain space of 3 inches between the arm and the edge of the plait. Carry the plaits down to the waist, where they must be considerably narrower, but at the same time, deep enough to give fullness to the drapery.

Now measure on the left side of this breadth 27 inches down from the shoulder seam near the arm. Make three plaits on this side of the back drapery. Join them together with a stitch or two, and bring this group of plaits up to the waist underneath the plaits in the center of the back. This forms a large fold or loop about 4 inches long, below the waist. Drape the right side in the same way, but lower down, and bring the plaits up near those first formed. The material must be made to fit smoothly over the shoulders, and at the sides on each side of the plaits. It is cut away at the shoulders, under the arms, and around the armholes, leaving only the necessary turnings.

Measure the center of the second breadth, and pin this to the dress stand in front, in the center of the neck. Carry the material smoothly up to each shoulder, and make the opening on the left side, from the shoulder in a slanted line to a point below the waist. The lining must fasten in the center; but the plastron that is in front covers this fastening, the polonaise itself being invisibly closed in a diagonal line under the plaits. This leaves the plastron free for any kind of decoration, such as a

piece of the skirt material, embroidery, lace, etc. On each side of the plastron, arrange three plaits and bring them down below the waist, making the plaits on the left side cross those on the right. By following this arrangement, you may easily make the opening long enough to allow the polonaise to be slipped over the head. As the plaits approach the waist, they must be made to lie over each other so that they terminate in a point. Drape the skirt of the polonaise on the right side with a series of plaits, beginning just below the waist. Arrange the drapery to cover the edge of the short side piece, and carry the plaits back until they are concealed under the back drapery. Fit the material over the bust and under the arms, and cut it away, leaving only the trimmings, as at the back. On the left side begin by fitting the polonaise in the same way, and where it joins the side piece, make it the same length as this. Then cut away the material until the tunic is like the other side.

Assembling the Polonaise. The polonaise must now be taken off the dress stand. The side seams and shoulder seams are unbasted and then stitched in the usual way, taking in the material as well as the lining. Any pretty sleeve will do; but if the plastron is of the skirt material an under-sleeve of the same, with a draped over-sleeve of the polonaise, is suitable. A bow with long loops and ends of ribbon on the left side of the polonaise, or some special trimming on this side of the skirt, is an improvement. The polonaise can be worn over a plain or kilt skirt of any contrasting material.

Making the Virginia Polonaise. The Virginia polonaise may be made of any light wool or thin material; double width answers better than single. If, however, the material is narrow, the principal join in front must go toward one side. That is, the center of the material must be put to the center of the front of the polonaise. The lining on which the polonaise is draped is cut like that of an ordinary bodice, with fronts, side pieces, side backs, and backs. All of these are cut with a moderately long round basque, basted in place, and fitted. The fronts are joined down the center with very small flat buttons. The darts, and the seams joining the front and side piece, can now be stitched and finished off.

The polonaise fronts are next cut. The right front is wider than the left, as it includes the draperies on each side of the bodice. The front is the full width of the material, 48 inches. It measures about 44 inches in length, a little more being allowed for tall figures, and rather less for short ones. About 18 inches from the top, a part of the skirt 14 inches wide is cut off, reducing the width at the edge and leaving a width of 34 inches. The side piece is included in the front, and the seam under the arm must therefore coincide with that joining the two side pieces of the lining.

The draperies on each side of the front should next be arranged, either on a person or a dress stand. First plait up the left side and fix these fine plaits closely up to the neck. Fold them down, but not too regularly, as far as the waist. Gather the material closely together down to the hip, and pin it in place. Plait the right side in the shoulder, fold the plaits down to the waist, and there gather the material as on the left side. The drapery on each side is the same width, and care must be taken to make both sides exactly alike, and to make the gathers join at the waist.

A plastron is in front, which may be covered with any other material, such as plush, pekin, or lace. An end of the material is left on the left side, and is folded to form a little coquille. The left side of the polonaise is plain over the bodice, but the fullness of the skirt must be allowed from the waist, as the two sides are caught up in the same manner. The drapery is fastened invisibly on the left side, at the shoulder and at the waist. The side backs are short, like those of a bodice, and joined to the back. The front and back of the skirt are then also joined, and the drapery is the next point.

The back is cut from a full width of the material, and the skirt is the same length, 48 inches, slightly sloped up toward the sides. In draping the sides, a few upward-turning plaits are first formed far back on the hips, leaving a sufficient length for the box-plaits on the side, which are taken out of the fronts of the polonaise, and are very easy to arrange. The back is arranged in large plaits, leaving the usual loop in the center, and sewed on outside the bodice. The drapery should be

arranged so that tapes may be dispensed with, and the whole of the drapery should be as far back as possible. A waist belt of faille ribbon is worn with the polonaise.

Remodeling Dresses

A common mistake is to have one good dress and to wear it on all occasions, thinking it must be more economical than making over some old ones. However, a dress worn on all occasions can never give the wearer the fresh and tidy look that all women of taste desire to have.

Preparing the Material. In making over old material, a great part of what you have on hand must be carefully examined. Much time must be devoted to deciding what pieces will be used and where, and just what arrangement will prove most favorable for hiding the deficiencies of the more worn pieces. A certain amount of piecing is almost unavoidable. It must match the grain of the material, or it will pucker and draw past remedy. Try to arrange the old seams so they will be covered by plaits, as trimming requires considerable art and thought. If the seam is to be covered by trimming, it is better, if the nature of the material will allow, to lay the two edges flat and run them together. The best way to piece cloth is to overhand the edges loosely, taking small stitches that will hardly show on the right side when the seam has been dampened and pressed.

Letting Down a Dress. The dress we are gazing on received a good wetting, which although not changing the color has caused it to shrink so as to be far too short. The front gore is tucked, three tucks also heading the plaiting around the entire skirt. These tucks can be ripped out and carefully pressed. All of the marks, however, cannot be removed. Therefore, the front must be covered with rows of mohair braid set close together, and also heading the plaiting around the skirt, which has first been taken off, pressed out, and replaited. The braid will entirely cover the marks and cause the skirt to look fresh. The back drapery should be taken off, carefully pressed, and redraped.

The bodice is worn, defaced, and very shabby. It looks useless, but careful study decides that the deep jacket basque can be cut off into a pointed bodice, leaving such large pieces that they can be joined together to form a vest, trimmed with rows of braid to correspond with the front gore of the skirt. The cuffs and collar can be similarly trimmed. The whole, when completed, will more closely resemble a new dress than one that at first glance only appeared worth throwing aside.

Adding a Vest. Vests are used on all bodices. Some of these are only halfway down from the neck; others go down from the center to the end of the bodice. The handsomest ones are beaded. These can be readily made and the defaced material of an old bodice will answer, as the beads are put so close together that no material shows between. The cuffs and dog-collar are made to correspond with the rest; and if there is no objection to work and trouble, a front panel or side panels added will make an elegant costume. Old bead fringe or trimming can be cut up to do this embroidery.

Vests gathered from the collar to the waist-line are admirably adapted to freshen up a toilette. (See Figure 17.)

Making Panels. Silk and satin merveilleux dresses that require remodeling, look well with the addition of side panels or a front panel of broché material, stripes, or some contrasting material. Narrow front panels are very easily made; the material is gradually sloped toward the top, and laid on the

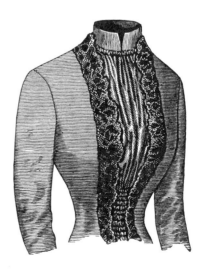

Figure 17. Bodice with shirred vest and wool lace, 1885

267

**Figure 18. Skirt with brocade panel
and velvet revers, 1885**

foundation skirt (see Figure 18). Panels are often simulated by rows of braid, plaitings, ruffles, and rows of lace; they are also very frequently handsomely ornamented with embroidery and passementerie in silks, beads, or appliqués of silk and velvet. If the bodice is too bad to be freshened up by the addition of a vest, collar, and cuffs of the new material, an entire bodice must be made of it.

Adding a Sash. Another easy mode of brightening up a dress is by adding a sash. No matter what the material is, a sash is worn with it; they are used with all kinds of costumes for all occasions. Four to 4 1/2 yards is the necessary length, as they must have long ends and two long loops. With some dresses they are worn exactly at the back, and with others a little to the left side.

Braiding. Old cloth dresses after being carefully ripped up, sponged, and pressed, can be remodeled by being elaborately braided. (See Figure 19.) The braid should not be sewed on flat as in years gone by, but on the side so as to set out.

The front or side panels, vest, or entire jacket, cuffs, and collar are all ornamented. Sometimes the plain foundation skirt is elaborately braided, and in that case only the bodice is decorated.

Making a Tunic. A tunic is a very useful addition to a moderate wardrobe, arranged to be worn over a half-worn princess dress, or any plain skirt and old bodice. Of course, the skirt must be cut off and trimmed with a plaiting or ruffle. This can be done by piecing above and letting the material come down, the piece being hid by the tunic. Double-width material is preferable, but seams can be concealed under the plaits of the bodice if it is necessary to use a narrow material.

Our model is cut in three pieces, and can be worn for day or evening. If for the latter it is cut low in the neck, the old bodice coming above it and finished with a pointed bertha. If for day wear it should be cut lower still and finished with bretelles, carried down to the waist and ending in pointed tabs below it, in place of the bertha. The front of the tunic is cut double in a single piece, which must be 82 inches wide. As no material is made in this width, the center breadth must be folded double, to avoid a seam down the center, and the width must be completed by adding as much as required on each side. To economize in cutting a double-width material, a gore is added on each side of the front gore, which is the full width of the material. This gore is sewed onto the selvage joining the front, two being made to join together; but the back is slightly gored, giving a little additional fullness at the edge. The back also consists of a single piece without a center seam. It is rather over 2 yards wide, and plenty of material must be allowed below the waist to form plaits for the center part of the drapery.

The shoulder seams are now joined, and the tunic should be pinned onto a dress stand or the wearer. The center of the front is pinned in place on the chest and at the waist, and the back is pinned to the figure in the same way. The front is first arranged in four plaits. These are brought close together at the waist, but spread out more on the chest. They can be firmly sewed where the stitches will be covered by the bertha or bretelles on the chest, and by the belt at the waist. Both

Making a Tunic

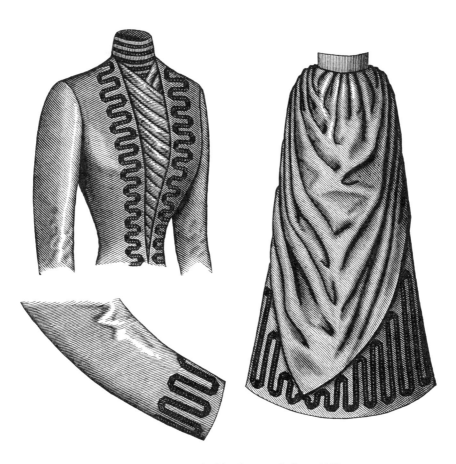

Figure 19. Braided bodice and skirt, 1888

sides of the front are plaited in the same way; or they may be plaited at the waist and gathered at the top. The plaits on one side are made to face those on the other side, all of the plaits being folded toward the center. The same arrangement is followed at the back, which is joined in the center, the tunic being easily slipped over the head and requiring no fastening. There are four plaits on each side of the back, all folded toward the center.

The skirt is mounted in large gathers, and joined to the plaited back. The draping consists of a few plaits high up at the back; this causes the front to fall like a long rounded tablier. There is a box-plait at the side, which is easily arranged. The back may be either puffed at the top, or allowed to fall from the waist in straight folds.

The armhole is very large; in fact it can come down far below the waist if the under bodice will permit of it, the tunic being kept in place by the belt. The trimming consists of three separate pieces, which may be of velvet, plush, or beaded material. The piece to trim the armhole must be cut in an oval, of any stiff material, without a join. It requires fitting on the figure, and must, of course, follow the line of the tunic and the fancy of the wearer. The stiff lining is covered with the velvet or beaded material, neatly sewed to the lining on the inside, and is then fastened on the tunic.

If a bertha is used for trimming, it is also cut from stiff lining. It is pointed in front and back, and narrow on the shoulders. It is covered with velvet or beaded material in the same way as the arm piece. The front part is trimmed with deep bead fringe, and the bertha is joined to the tunic just fitting over the shoulders.

The belt is 3 inches wide and long enough for the ends to cross in front below the waist. It is made of the same stiff material and outside covering of the

other trimmings, the pointed ends being finished with fringe.

We have already mentioned one way in which the tunic may be cut and ornamented with velvet bretelles for wearing with high dresses. In this case the tunic may be brought up higher on the shoulders, and the fronts open with the bretelles in a long point over the under bodice. Another pretty way of cutting the tunic at the neck is to make it in a half-low rounded shape, buttoned on the shoulders or tied up with ribbon bows. The tunic is also sometimes mounted on a yoke of velvet, or some other material.

Making Scarf Draperies. Scarf draperies often take the place of a tunic, especially with young ladies' dresses. A pretty and rather novel style is to make this scarf drapery very full, forming a mass of folds across the front, and to allow it 1/2 yard longer than is required for the scarf only. The end on the right side is closely plaited up under the back drapery; the left side is plaited up in the same way 1/2 yard from the edge. These plaits are fastened down outside the back drapery high up on the tournure. The end that is left falls in a plaited

drapery between the under scarf and back drapery; the plaited end needs a little arrangement to make it fall gracefully.

Combining Materials. Bodices of a different material and color are a boon for half-worn skirts; these are worn for evening as well as for day. Velveteen makes up a nice jacket to wear with old skirts for a street costume. The new brand cord de la reine is very desirable; it somewhat resembles corduroy, but the pile is higher and the material much more pliable. It is also very stylish combined with wool materials as foundation skirts, panels, vests, cuffs, and collars.

Dress sleeves are now being made of a different material from the bodice (see Figure 20). This is a very desirable fashion for a remodeled dress, as the sleeves frequently become defaced before the bodice. The material used for the new sleeves must be also used in some other part of the dress, for the drapery, foundation skirt, or trimming.

In short, if we only will take the trouble, we can dress becomingly in our old clothes made to look like new, and not have but one dress to wear on all occasions.

1884–1888 *Godey's Lady's Book;*
1884–1889 *Delineator*

Figure 20. Bodice with contrasting sleeves and facings, 1887

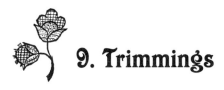

9. Trimmings

First in the list of decorations come the braids—Hercules, Titan, round, soutache, basket, and all of the fancy weaves. They are in all colors, with or without a dash of gold or silver, and may be used in any way that commends itself. On cloth costumes, Grecian designs in soutache are very effective. Dark green, brown, blue, and black materials permit (without demanding) the use of soutache braid contrasting in color, the supposition being that a collar and cuffs, or perhaps a vest, of the same shade will be used. On very dull blue, black or garnet is used; on green, golden brown; on brown, reseda; and on black, white or garnet. On white wool costumes, very wide white braid is arranged in tucks or defined by gold soutache.

Heavy cords are employed for loops on evening costumes, and are elaborately beaded or laced with silver thread. These are all loops, no ends being seen. When ends are desired in looping a drapery, the material is drawn together and tipped with a pendant of some sort. Or else ribbons are arranged and from them swing the fancy ball, acorn, or tassel.

Ribbons are used with great liberality in loops and rosettes. Rosettes do not often contrast with the dress, except when they are to be applied in materials where white and gold braid forms the trimming, when either wide yellow braid or yellow ribbon may form the rosettes. Lacings of narrow ribbon are used to connect panels, etc., and are an improvement on the shoe-string look that braid often imparts. The same ribbon is chosen for lacing peasant bodices. Velvet ribbons are used on skirts to simulate tucks, to outline panels, and to finish tabliers.

June 1885 Delineator

Plomb, jet, rosary, and steel beads are of all shapes and sizes. They are developed in every way possible, and are put on dresses, jackets, wraps, and bonnets. Panels and skirt fronts of jet are very rich,

the nugget-shaped bead being prominent. Bands of passementerie, with beads of any desired kind defining their edges and being set upon them, trim sleeves and vests effectively, and outline panels and Eton jackets. They are in varying widths, and the wider have long pendants of the beads. Entire panels of brown rosary beads look magnificent on a velvet dress. Collars, cuffs, tabliers, and pointed basque fronts outlined with beads are in good form.

December 1885 Delineator

Entire skirts, skirt fronts, skirt revers, bodice lapels, and Figaro sleeves are made completely of passementerie. Beads are usually intermingled with it. There is, among others, a skirt front in a design of fuchsias, executed in pearls and garnets, that is unsurpassed in beauty by anything of the kind produced in the 16th century. All of these pieces are also made in less costly open-work silk embroidery.

February 27, 1886 Harper's Bazar

Cords thick as a finger, as well as the very narrow kind, are obtaining. Entire tabliers are made of thick silk cord woven in fisher's net pattern, and sleeves of the same may be worn. For a house dress the cord alone may form the sleeves, but for street costumes it is only allowable to arrange the cord over a sleeve of the material. Narrower cords, noticeably those in white, gray, and black, are selected for outlining basques, jacket fronts, vests, or any edge that seems to require a finish and yet one that will not be too emphatic.

September 1886 Delineator

On toilettes for the ball-room, the reception, or the street, and on jackets and tea gowns, ribbons are plentifully used. The choice is between grosgrain, moiré, and velvet. The popular edge finishes are picot, button-hole, and tassel outlining. Widths vary from very narrow to the very wide that is used for sashes.

 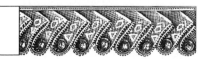

For evening dresses, especially those of tulle, large rosettes of very narrow ribbon with long, loose loops are placed wherever, by the raising of the drapery or any other arrangement, the necessity for a fastening may be suggested. On street costumes long, loose straps of ribbon extend over skirt fronts and side panels, or ribbon about 2 inches wide is arranged in loops and ends. Whenever there are two colors in the dress, the same colors are brought out in the ribbons.

Silk cord is sometimes arranged in the same way as ribbons. A motif made of cords and pendants takes the place of the loops. Jet beads are often used, but when the cord is gray or brown, steel or amber beads take their place. Motifs of jet, steel, plomb, amber, or any of the colored wooden beads are in favor. For plastrons, vests, and epaulettes, the beaded decoration is accurately shaped. For some special arrangements strips of passementerie are bought, and each figure is separately applied as desired. Beaded net is still liked, but basket work of the beads themselves is more popular.

Gold embroideries or passementeries, made of fine gold cord and outlined with small amber beads, are used on bodices and fine cloth wraps. Motifs of them are arranged on each side, on the sleeves, and very often down the back.

April 1887 *Delineator*

Ensembles

A favorite way of combining a figured and a plain material in every part of the dress, is that of putting a single width of figured material down the back and front of the skirt. The sides are of plain material, laid in plaits toward the front. A full breadth of plain material is placed on each side of the figured material at the back. The three back breadths then hang straight and are gathered to the belt. Over them as drapery are two plaited wing-like pieces of plain material, and there are short lambrequin-like draperies on the sides and front. The basque should be of plain material, with a V-shaped piece of figured material inserted (not set on) in the front and back. Figured material is arranged in folds or plaits on the collar and cuffs.

May 9, 1885 *Harper's Bazar*

Buttons of two sizes are provided for each dress. Those for the bodice are flat and about 1/2 inch across, while those for the skirt and jacket repeat the design and are 2 inches across. Wood with metal, and wood with carved pearl, are the buttons for spring wools; the rim, or else the entire foundation, being of wood. Flowers are cut in pearl and set in a frame of carved brown wood; or else the button is of smooth polished wood on which are metal beads or flowers in relief. Sometimes three profiles of helmeted warriors of different metals are grouped together; the metals being bronze, steel, oxidized silver, or dull gilt. A row of eight or ten of these buttons is set down one side, or both sides, or in front of the dress skirt. Smaller buttons are on the bodice lapels, or on the slope beside the vest. Or they are set on a belt, or almost any unexpected place, for ornament merely.

March 6, 1886 *Harper's Bazar*

For sateen dresses, crocheted white laces and Irish point embroidery are used as a wide border at the bottom, or a side band of the skirt, and as a yoke or vest on the bodice. These bordered skirts are always plain and round, not plaited.

August 6, 1887 *Harper's Bazar*

The plain front drapery in Figure 1 is cut in deep points at its lower edge. It is overlaid with a network of braid arranged in pairs, which cross each other in basket fashion so as to enclose diamond-shaped spaces and border the points. The braid terminates some distance from the top. From beneath the lower edge of the drapery, falls a foot trimming laid in clusters of side-plaits alternating with single box-plaits, the arrangement being planned so that a box-plait comes between every two points. The braid-trimmed drapery may cover the front and sides of a skirt, or the front only.

The sleeve shows a similar arrangement. The braid employed is narrower than that used on the drapery, and the points are only outlined. Linen cuffs are usually worn with sleeves thus trimmed.

May 1884 *Delineator*

Figure 1. Braid arrangement for draperies and sleeves

The costume in Figure 2 is shown made up in plain white satin, with white embroidered Brussels net for the drapery, lace edging to match the net, appliqué embroidery, and a satin plaiting. The skirt is composed of three gores and a full back breadth. The gores are fitted smoothly about the hips by darts, and the breadth is gathered on each side of the placket opening. On the gores is arranged a long tablier drapery, which is lifted high on each side by a cluster of five overlapping, upward-turning plaits folded a little below the hip. The side edges are sewed in with the side-back seams, and the top is conformed to the shape of the hips by darts. Both skirt and drapery are sewed to the same belt. Tapes or elastic straps are fastened under the side-back seams and tied together to hold the fullness in place. The bottom of the skirt is cut in long, narrow tabs and underlaid with a satin side-plaiting, over which falls a ruffle of Brussels net edging of almost equal length. A narrower lace ruffle, surmounted by a band of appliqué embroidery, borders the lower edge of the tablier.

The train is long and square. All of the fullness necessary for its disposal is allowed below the curved center back seams and on the front edges below the side-back seams. The fullness is underfolded to form two box-plaits on the outside, with quadruple folds in their inner edges and double folds at their outer edges. These folds are allowed to fall unrestrained for the entire length of the train. The train is lined throughout with satin. It is basted on each side just below the lower corners of the side backs and to the skirt lower down. Its edges are bordered with narrow edging tucked in jabot fashion and falling separate from the skirt below the bastings, thus permitting the train to be lifted over the arm when the wearer is dancing.

The fronts and side backs of the bodice are cut off in basque fashion, with a high curve over the hip and a point at the end of the closing and at the back edge of each side-back part. There are two bust darts in each side of the front. The front is closed with button-holes and buttons, the right side

273

being hemmed and the left underfaced. The neck is cut out square both back and front, and finished with a falling and a standing frill of lace. A spray of flowers is placed on the left side. The sleeves are cut off quite short and curved toward the tops of the arms, each being finished with a lace frill.

September 1884 *Delineator*

Figure 3 illustrates several ways to arrange embroidered chambray edging. The bodice is closed invisibly; and the buttons, which are placed in front of trefoil loops of braid, are merely ornamental. The braid ornaments are developed in white soutache. A band of embroidery, which is curved along its inner edge to decrease in width toward the waist-line, is sewed to the overlapping front edge and turned backward over its own seam. A band of embroidery conceals the high standing collar, being sewed with it to the bodice and turned up.

The sleeve shows narrow soutache braid associated with embroidered edging. The sleeve length is decreased sufficiently to permit of a full ruffle of embroidery at the wrist. On the upper side are three braid ornaments, each of which extends in double lines for a short distance from the outside seam and forms trefoil loops in front of a button.

The narrow skirt front panel is cut from all-over embroidery. Its width is calculated so that when the embroidered edging bordering its sides and lower edge is added, it will extend to the side-front seams and reach from a little below the top to the bottom of the skirt, the space above it being overfaced with plain material. A flounce of deeper embroidery decorates the sides and back of the skirt.

Figure 2. Trained costume

Embroidery in two widths is also requisite to the skirt trimming shown at the bottom of the engraving. The exact breadth of each section of dress material is obtained by experimenting in paper. The depth is regulated by the style of the drapery, which usually overhangs it. A band of wide embroidery borders the lower edge of each section. To one end is sewed a band of the narrower width, the corners of both kinds of embroidery being sloped off where they meet to permit of a neat join. Three side-plaits are laid in a cluster near the untrimmed end, and this end is overlapped by the trimmed end of the next section. This style of trimming is very effective on a skirt that has a deep drapery both front and back.

April 1885 *Delineator*

Figure 3. Trimming for bodice, sleeve, and two skirts

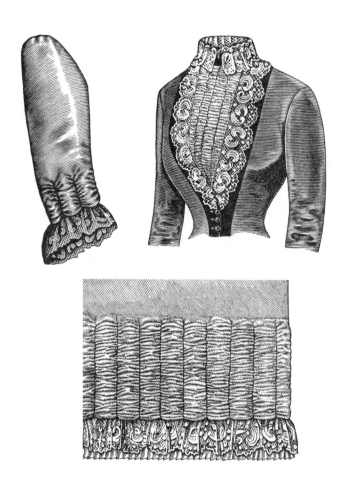

Figure 4. Shirred trimming for bodice, sleeve, and skirt

The shirred trimming in Figure 4 develops well in mull, grenadine, and all kinds of tissues and diaphanous materials. The sleeve shown is cut long enough to permit of shirring it lengthwise, and a full frill of lace is basted inside. A thin lining may be added, or the shirrings may be stayed by fine tapes.

The high collar about the bodice is cut from velvet. A band of velvet starting from each shoulder seam passes down each side of the front. The two bands meet at the closing a little above the waist-line. Above that place, the bodice is overlaid with a mull plastron shirred to form lengthwise puffs on a foundation of thin crinoline or tarlatan. The edges of the plastron are bordered with lace, which is well brought out against the velvet bands on which it rests. The plastron is sewed permanently on one side and attached with pins on the other. A full lace frill sewed inside the collar falls over and conceals it.

Straight breadths are joined to give the dimensions requisite for the skirt puffing. Its depth is determined by the style and arrangement of the drapery. After the shirrings have been made, the lower edge of the puffing is sewed in place over the top of the lace ruffle that overhangs the foot plaiting. The puffing is turned up over its own seam. It is not necessary to provide a foundation for the skirt trimming, as the stiffening of the skirt supplies that.

June 1885 *Delineator*

Figure 5. Decoration for bodice and skirt

The decorations in Figure 5 are especially applicable to striped materials, relieving the long lines that often prove too severe to be becoming. The velvet may be like some color in the striped material; or if the material is plain, the velvet may be a darker shade of the same color or of a distinctly contrasting color. Dresses of cream wool are often trimmed in this way with velvet in bright or dark colors and cream pompons.

The plastron on the bodice is cut from velvet. It tapers to a point just above the waist-line, its top fitting closely about the neck and extending to the shoulder seams. It is sewed permanently on one side and attached with hooks and eyes on the other. Pompons attached by tiny loops of silk cord border it all around, forming a full fringe. The high standing collar is of velvet. Bias bands of velvet are passed about the armholes, their ends being twisted in knots on the shoulders.

The skirt decoration comprises three tablier sections of striped material, which are bordered with bands of velvet lined with crinoline. The lowest tablier overhangs the double rows of knife-plaiting forming the foot trimming. Each is in turn overhung by the one next above it, the top of the upper one being a little below the belt. Each band has a fringe of pompons about its lower edge.

June 1885 *Delineator*

The decorations in Figure 6 show cream mohair braid on dark material. The plaited skirt decoration uses three widths of braid. These are applied before the side-plaits are laid, in the positions represented in the engraving. The widest braid is about 1 1/2 inches wide. It is the same shown on the trimmings for a front gore and a sleeve, the soutache being also represented on the latter; while the third width is a little wider than that represented on the bodice.

On the skirt front, the foot trimming, which passes entirely about the skirt, is applied first. Next in order comes a band of wide braid. Following this is a bias fold about twice the width of the braid, which, after being sewed in place, is turned up over its own seam. This arrangement of braids and folds is continued nearly to the top. Of course, any kind of braid may be used.

The braid used on the bodice is somewhat wider than soutache. It is arranged in the outline of a peasant bodice on the dress bodice. Each strip is turned to form a short loop at the top and frayed slightly at the ends, which extend a trifle below the lower edge. The braid is so neatly applied, and its width so deftly decreased by stretching it at the

Figure 6. Skirt, bodice, and sleeve decorations

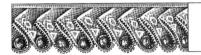

This is a simple but very effective arrangement of velvet, buttons, and simulated button-holes for sleeves and skirt fronts. Figure 8 represents plaid suit material. The velvet is darker than the darkest shade in the plaid.

October 1885 *Delineator*

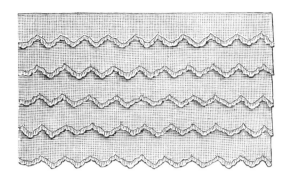

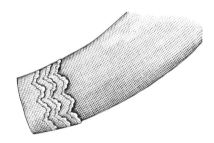

Figure 7. Embroidery for skirt and sleeve

waist-line, that the meeting of the two strips over the bodice closing is not discernible.

In the sleeve decoration, soutache braid is associated with braid about 1 1/2 inches wide. Two bands of the wider braid cross the outside of the sleeve from the inside seam at the wrist, to a point some distance above at the outside seam, their corresponding edges almost meeting. Below the lower band, a graduated scroll design is wrought with soutache.

July 1885 *Delineator*

The embroidery depicted by Figure 7 is known as solid work or mourning embroidery. It is applied on white house and lawn dresses worn by ladies in mourning. The design, which is simple, has none of the open-work characterizing the ordinary kinds. It is woven in strips having several rows of points, and also in strips having only one row of points along the edge.

July 1885 *Delineator*

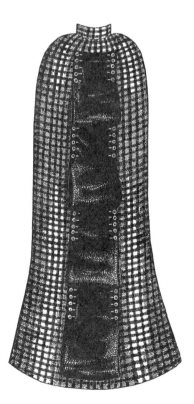

Figure 8. Skirt front and sleeve

 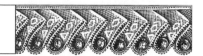

On the sleeve shown by Figure 9, velvet is applied in a broad band a little above the wrist, and tinsel thread is worked in a scroll design above it on the upper side. The skirt trimming comprises a narrow side-plaiting and a wide kilt-plaiting, the latter overhanging the former and having its lower edge bordered with a wide velvet band. On each plait, above the velvet, a scroll design is worked with tinsel thread. Cord or soutache braid may be used instead of tinsel.

November 1885 *Delineator*

In Figure 10, a band of fur is arranged as a border on the front drapery. The latter is lifted high on the left side of the foundation skirt by plaits. It is also raised, but not nearly so high, on the right side by plaits with spaces between them, the trimmed edge presenting a diagonal line between the two sides. Below the drapery, the gores are overhung by a velvet box-plaiting. On the outer folds of the plaits there is a fur border, its application neither

interfering with the laying of the plaits nor adding much to the weight.

On the sleeve, satin is applied as a plaited cuff-facing at the wrist, its outline deepening in a curve toward the outside of the arm. A band of fur surmounts the cuff. Two fur buttons are placed on the upper side of the sleeve.

November 1885 *Delineator*

Figure 9. Fur trimming for skirt front and sleeve

Figure 10. Sleeve and skirt trimming

The trimming illustrated by Figure 11 is braid, but bias bands may take its place with good effect. The skirt has three bands of braid arranged flatly on the lower part of the gores, with spaces equal to their own width between them. The drapery is of contrasting material. One section overlaps the other on the left hip, where it is laid in upward-turning plaits. The overlapping section is also plaited beneath it, and both are draped with plaits at their back edges.

The sleeve has a gathered bias puff of plain material that is graduated widest at the outside of the arm. Above this the braid is placed flatly, and a lace frill is sewed in the wrist.

Any double-breasted basque or jacket may have its closing arranged and its front trimmed as illustrated. Although the fronts overlap in double-breasted fashion, no buttons are added to the overlapping side; and from the neck to the bust hooks and eyes are used. On the bust the overlapping side is faced in Pompadour fashion with plain material and crossed by three bands of braid. On each side, turning from the edges of the facing, is a lapel ornament, which, like the high standing collar, is of plain material. Braid or a bias band may also overlie the collar.

December 1885 *Delineator*

Figure 11. Skirt, bodice, and sleeve trimming

Figure 12. Bodice, sleeve, and skirt trimming

Figure 12 shows three methods of arranging chambrays ornamented with embroidered appliqué edgings of contrasting color. The bodice has facings the same color as the appliqués applied on each side of the closing in a deep, oval outline. These facings are cut in scallops at the outer edges and bound. Beneath the scalloped edges are sewed the inner edges of narrow appliqué embroidery, which is arranged with just enough fullness to present an easy effect. The high standing collar is of the contrasting material. One of the most effective combinations is formed by black appliqués embroidered in white on a stone-colored ground.

The skirt trimming is arranged as a gathered flounce. The top is overhung by the skirt proper, which is cut in scallops and bound with plain chambray. The sleeve trimming is in harmony with the skirt trimming.

May 1886 *Delineator*

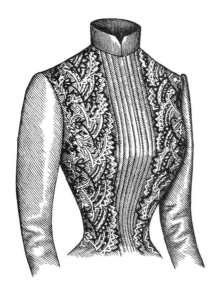 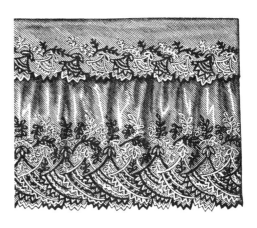

Figure 13. Embroidered bodice and skirt trimming

The trimmings in Figure 13 utilize two widths of edging, consisting of batiste embroidered in a contrasting color. For the bodice, the wider edging is disposed on each side of a tucked vest to suggest a jacket, the embroidery being sewed in with the shoulder, armhole, and under-arm seams. For the skirt, the wider edging is gathered to form a flounce. The narrower edging is turned down over it for a heading or finish.

June 1886 *Delineator*

The bodice in Figure 14 has a shirred plastron vest-facing of contrasting material applied on it. This is sewed on one side, and attached invisibly with hooks and eyes on the other. Overlapping its edge on each side is a band of appliqué galloon, the two bands meeting at the waist-line, where the plastron terminates.

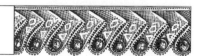
The outside of the sleeve is cut away from the lining in V shape. The space is covered with a shirred section of contrasting material, over which the outside edges are slip-stitched. Following the outline of the lower edges and of the cutaway part is a band of appliqué galloon, which is slanted off along the back edges to reduce its width suitably.

For the skirt, the contrasting material is introduced on the center of the front gore. Its lower edges are shirred, and its top is laid in overlapping plaits that are almost concealed by the overlapping edges of the skirt. Appliqué galloon is applied on the latter. A drapery is arranged on the upper part of the front and side gores. This is shirred up quite short at the center and falls on the right side. On the left side it is only of medium depth, its back edges being lifted by plaits.

September 1886 *Delineator*

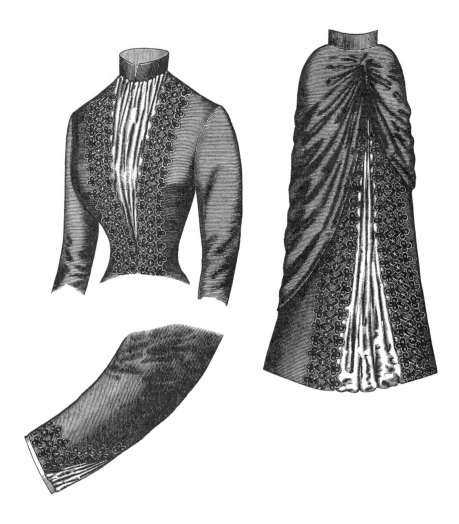

Figure 14. Bodice, sleeve, and skirt trimming

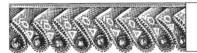

The decorations in Figure 15 are very *recherché* for party dresses. The lace employed is colonial lace, and silk and fine wool are combined in it. It is especially adapted to application on fancy silk and wool materials. It is woven in various widths and is of a cream hue.

The skirt drapery is composed of a single section of material. This is drawn up quite high by gathers at the center of the front, and sewed plainly into the right side-back seam. Passing entirely about the bottom of the skirt is a fine side-plaited foot trimming. Above this, on the front and side gores, is a lace ruffle. Following this ruffle in regular order are six other ruffles, which start from under the overhanging edge of the drapery and end on the left side. Two looped ribbon bows are fastened over the gathered front edge of the drapery.

The sleeve is a little more than elbow length. It is finished with a lace frill, one end of which is carried up the outside, with its selvage at the outside seam. A soft twist of ribbon surmounts the frill, and a bow is basted at the outside of the arm.

September 1886 *Delineator*

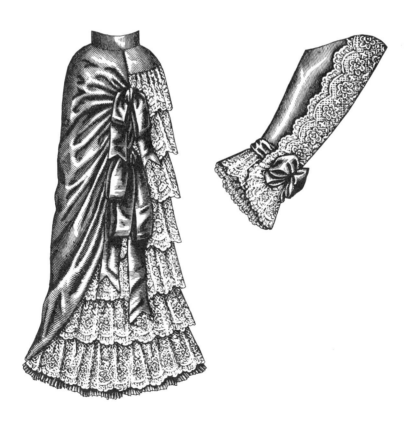

Figure 15. Skirt and sleeve decoration for party dresses

Figure 16. Decoration for bodice, sleeve, and skirt

The bodice in Figure 16 is trimmed as follows. A triangular lapel of contrasting material is sewed to each side of the front along the closing edge, from a little below the neck to the bust. That on the right side has three crosswise strips of medium-wide braid applied on it. The back ends—which are pointed—extend beyond the lapel on the front and are fastened in place under buttons and simulated button-holes. The lapel on the left side is ornamented with much narrower braid arranged in lengthwise lines. For the length of the lapels the closing is invisibly accomplished, while below them buttons and button-holes are used.

At the bottom of the sleeve, narrow braid is arranged in lengthwise lines with scarcely more than 1/4-inch spaces between them all around the sleeve, their lengths growing shorter toward the inside of the arm. Turning upward from the top of this trimming is a cuff-facing of contrasting material. This has three strips of wide braid applied vertically on the upper side, their upper ends being pointed and fastened on the sleeve under buttons and button-holes.

On the skirt, the narrow plaiting that forms the foot trimming passes entirely about the skirt. The drapery on the gores is arranged in the form of a plain tablier, which slightly overhangs the foot trimming. A little to the left of the center is made a perpendicular slash extending about halfway from the lower edge. The edge on the right of the slash is turned back to form a revers. This is faced with contrasting material and trimmed with narrow braid arranged in crosswise lines. The revers is slip-stitched in place along its edges. Extending from beneath it are strips of wide braid pointed at their opposite ends, and fastened over the straight edge of the slash under buttons and simulated button-holes.

November 1886 *Delineator*

Figure 17. Decoration for bodice, sleeve, and skirt

The decoration in Figure 17 is adapted to cloths, handsome suitings, velvets, etc. The bodice shows a band of long-haired fur outside the high standing collar. Frog ornaments of cord cross the closing, which is invisibly made; they gradually shorten toward the waist-line. They are fastened permanently on one side of the bodice and are attached with hooks and eyes on the other. The sleeve decoration consists of a band of the fur about the wrist, and a frog ornament that crosses the sleeve above it at the outside of the arm.

A narrow knife-plaiting forms the foot trimming of the skirt all the way around. On the gores is applied a flat, panel-like drapery, which is folded to form an under box-plait a little to the left of the center. Over the lower part of the plait, three frog ornaments are placed. Overlapping the upper part is a perfectly smooth curtain drapery that extends from the left hip, where it is very short, nearly to the bottom of the skirt on the right side. Its front edge is bordered with fur.

January 1887 *Delineator*

Plain and embroidered silk gauze of a pale salmon shade were chosen for the toilette in Figure 18. The skirt is in the round walking style with steels in the back breadth. It is partly covered with drapery and partly with fine knife-plaitings of the plain gauze. The front drapery presents the effect of two wings of different sizes, lapping on the right side of the front and flaring sharply, the shorter to the right and the deeper to the left. The wings are draped in soft folds by plaits at the back, where they lap, and also in their back edges. The voluminous back drapery is oval in outline, and falls in soft folds that result from two

287

Figure 18. Evening toilette

burnous loops and many plaits at the belt. A long velvet ribbon of a pale olive hue is fastened to the top of the smaller wing. Another is fastened under the deeper wing. Both ribbons are tied in a bow with long notched ends a little below where the wings separate.

The bodice is cut in fancy Pompadour outline quite low in front. The outline is followed with salmon lace insertion and edging nearly to the closing. It is then carried in a curve down each side to the end of the closing, where the trimming is gradually narrowed to nothing. A butterfly bow of olive velvet ribbon is fastened where the lace meets at the top of the closing, and also on the top of the right shoulder. The bodice is deeply pointed at the front and back, and arched short and high over the hips. The sleeves fit smoothly and reach only to the elbows, the lower outline gradually shortening toward the back of the arm. A lace frill edges the ends of the sleeves. Narrower lace is applied in overlapping strips to shape a point at the elbow, the upper strip starting from the seam joining the sleeve to the armhole. Velvet ribbon is carried down each side of the lace strips and bowed over the point.

February 1887 *Delineator*

The decorations in Figure 19 show the effect of pinking on smooth cloth. Pinking irons may be purchased for a small sum, but materials that fray readily should not be pinked.

The bodice has a narrow velvet vest, which is fastened on one side with hooks and eyes and sewed permanently beneath the other. The overlapping edges are pinked, and so is the part of the collar that joins the bodice proper. The vest collar is of velvet and is finished in the usual manner.

The sleeve has a velvet cuff-facing applied on the foundation, with the outside cut in pinked scallops that overlap it. Sometimes a row of scallops underlies the closing of the sleeve.

The skirt has pinked tablier drapery overlapping plain velvet gores. The left side of the tablier is lifted high by the plaits in it, while the right side falls nearly to the bottom of the skirt.

May 1887 *Delineator*

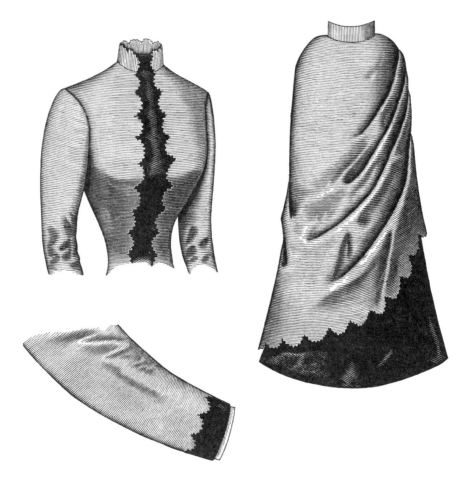

Figure 19. **Pinked decoration for bodice, sleeve, and skirt**

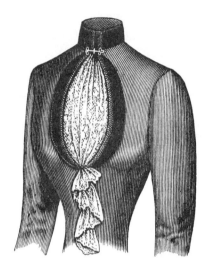 

Figure 20. Decoration for bodice and skirt

The bodice in Figure 20 has a shirt-front effect brought out by the choice of lace net for the little shirred chemisette. The latter is adjusted beneath a plain foundation sewed beneath one side of the front and attached to the other with hooks and eyes. A jabot of lace edging conceals the front closing. Velvet is used for the lapels and the high standing collar. The chemisette may be of surah, crêpe, or other thin material.

The skirt has short pannier draperies bordered with fringe having a netted heading. The plaited drapery that extends from beneath them has velvet facings applied on the outer folds of the plaits at the bottom and on the plain space between them. Heavy lace is sometimes used instead of velvet.

July 1887 *Delineator*

Very often lace net or flouncing is used for the deep drapery on the left side of the skirt. However, in Figure 21 this part and the shorter draperies on the right side are shown made of soft mixed material. The plaiting that falls from beneath them is of plain material. Double frills of lace edging trim the deep drapery, and single frills finish the shorter draperies.

The sleeve has enough of its length deducted to permit of adding double frills of lace. A piece of contrasting material laid in soft, gathered folds trims the upper side.

The front of the bodice has plaited vest ornaments. These terminate near the waist-line. From their edges and the closing edges below turn double frills of lace, which are put on with a little fullness and pass below the collar at the back.

August 1887 *Delineator*

Figure 21. Decoration for bodice, sleeve, and skirt

 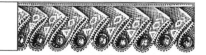

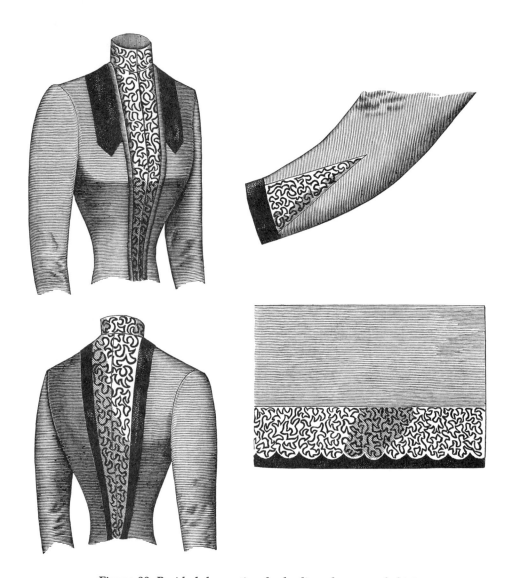

Figure 22. Braided decoration for bodice, sleeve, and skirt

In Figure 22, the front view of the basque shows a narrow vest of white material embroidered with gold braid, and the collar corresponds. The vest is closed down the center with hooks and eyes. The front edges of the fronts overlap it and are hemmed. Back of the hem a forward-turning tuck is made. Along this tuck, from the shoulder to the bust, is applied a velvet strap that is pointed at its lower end.

The back view of the basque shows a V facing of the white material embroidered with gold braid applied down the center of the back. The sides are outlined by a velvet band that tapers toward the waist-line.

The sleeve is decorated at the wrist with a velvet band. Extending from the band on the upper side is a long point of the white material, which is embroidered with braid to correspond to the front and back of the basque.

The skirt is faced for a few inches at the bottom with velvet. Overlapping the top of the band is the scalloped edge of a broad band of white material embroidered with gold braid. For these decorations, soutache in colors to suit the material may be used instead of the gold braid.

September 1887 *Delineator*

292

  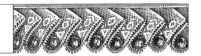

Figure 23. Decoration for evening bodice, sleeve, and skirt

The bodice in Figure 23 is made of faille. It is cut low and square in the neck, both back and front. A vest is simulated with lace and separated into two soft puffs by two velvet cross-straps on each side. A velvet cording is inserted in each forward dart and continued to the neck, outlining the sides of the simulated vest. A standing and a falling frill of lace drawn by a narrow velvet ribbon surmount the vest. The falling frill is continued in a jabot over the shoulders and across the back.

The bodice may be sleeveless, or have fancy puffed sleeves as illustrated at the bottom of the engraving. The puffed sleeve is made of a frill of deep lace sewed into the armhole and gathered a little above the lower edge. It is mounted on a

piece of Brussels net to fall in a soft puff above the frill, and narrow-edged fancy ribbon is arranged as illustrated.

The skirt is made up of plain velvet, faille Française, and lace flouncing. The panel on the front gore is elaborately embroidered in a floral design done with satin-stitch, but the design may be painted if preferred. The panels flare to expose the skirt in a long V on each side. To the left edge of the front panel is joined a long three-cornered revers of faille. In the V on the left side is set a flounce of Fedora lace, which is separated into small soft puffs above a frilled edge by slanted velvet straps. These pass under the front panel and have their opposite ends rounded off and basted

293

onto the left side panel. The V on the right side is covered with several lace ruffles. On this side, the side panel reaches to the belt. From under it passes a short tablier of lace flouncing, which droops over the front and left side panel with the effect of a gracefully arranged scarf. Passing from beneath the tablier, between the two side panels, is a deep lace frill that follows the outline of the tablier and produces the effect of a double drapery.

Any kind of lace may be used. Striped, figured, plaid, or other decorative material may form the front panel or the two side panels. Sometimes one of the panels is richly embroidered with gold or silver braid, alone or in combination with narrow cord or braid of some color in harmony with the material.

November 1887 Delineator

Velvet and silk moiré are associated in the garments shown by Figure 24. For the basque, triple lapels turn back from each side of the closing above the bust. A bow of wide ribbon is basted just below their ends. The front is closed with buttons and

Figure 24. Trimming for bodice, sleeve, and skirt

button-holes. The collar is made to stand high and then roll over deeply, the silk moiré showing on the reversed part.

The sleeves may have beaded epaulette ornaments as shown by the figure of the bodice, and a wrist decoration like the first sleeve, or they may be made up as shown for the second sleeve. The wrist decoration of the first sleeve consists of a pointed cuff of silk moiré that is overlaid at the back of the wrist by a beaded ornament, and a cuff of plaited lisse at the edge. The cuff and sleeve caps require a thin crinoline lining, and sometimes a silk lining is also added. The second sleeve has a turn-up cuff, the top of which is rolled over in a revers and faced with velvet. The cap fits smoothly.

The panel at the center of the skirt front is of silk moiré. The side and back draperies are of velvet. Three large beaded ornaments are placed down each side of the panel, partly resting on the adjoining side draperies.

November 1887 *Delineator*

This evening toilette consists of a basque and a walking-length skirt. Figure 25 shows it developed in black lace net with a pattern of marguerites woven on a striped background, laid over maize-colored surah. The foundation skirt is the standard four-gored shape, which is seen only through the meshes of the net. On the left side of the gores is arranged a plaited panel, the back edge of which is included in the side-back skirt seam. The front drapery owes its many cross-wrinkles to upward-turning plaits in its back edge, and bastings located so that the fullness above them falls over in loops on its hemmed left edge. Its top is also folded in plaits. Its lower edge is basted at intervals to the skirt gores and falls over and conceals the bastings like a sagging pouf. The back drapery falls to the lower edge of the back breadth, the front edges being included in the side-back seams. Near each side edge, the top is arranged in a long burnous loop. These loops, together with gathers across the top and right side, which is folded and brought even with the top, and occasional bastings to the back breadth, produce the shape of the back drapery. The drapery may be of gauze, tissue, or crêpe instead of net.

Figure 25. Evening toilette

The bodice is a pointed basque buttoned at the back; the front is seamless at the center. The bodice is fitted by double bust darts in each side, assisted by side pieces, side backs, and a curved center back seam. The closing is made with button-holes and crocheted buttons. The neck is cut out in low, round style, and the neck and the sleeveless armholes are outlined by a quill-like puffing of net. A bunch of marguerites is fastened on the left shoulder, and larger bunches are set on the left edges of the front drapery.

December 1887 *Delineator*

The costume shown by Figure 26 has a polonaise whose fronts fold back in Directoire revers that reveal the tablier on the skirt. Three materials—velvet, bengaline silk, and novelty silk—are used in its construction.

The polonaise is of bengaline silk. The bodice closes down the center to the tops of the revers with button-holes and buttons. Extending upward diagonally from the left side of the closing are velvet straps, which are graduated to be longest at the bust and shortest at the waist-line, to give a tapering effect. The straps are pointed at their back edges, and a fringe of small beads drops from their lower edges. The pointed epaulettes on the sleeves are outlined with a velvet band, from which a bead fringe also drops. The wrists are decorated with two pointed velvet straps arranged diagonally, their back ends passing respectively into the outside seam and under the wrist edge. A strip of bead fringe decorates the tops of the straps. Below the closing of the polonaise, the front edges are folded over in long revers that are widest at their tops, slope toward the back edges, and taper toward the lower edge. The revers are faced

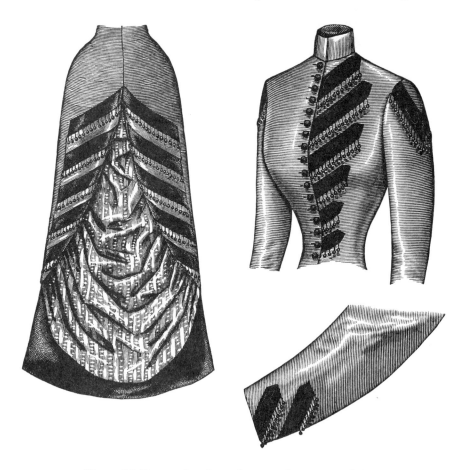

Figure 26. Decoration for polonaise, drapery, and skirt

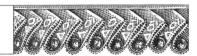
with silk and striped across with velvet bands, from which a bead fringe drops.

The skirt has three dart-fitted gores and a full back breadth. The latter is made bouffant by two steels run in casings formed across it, and tied into curves by tapes sewed at the ends of the casings. The skirt may be made without the steels.

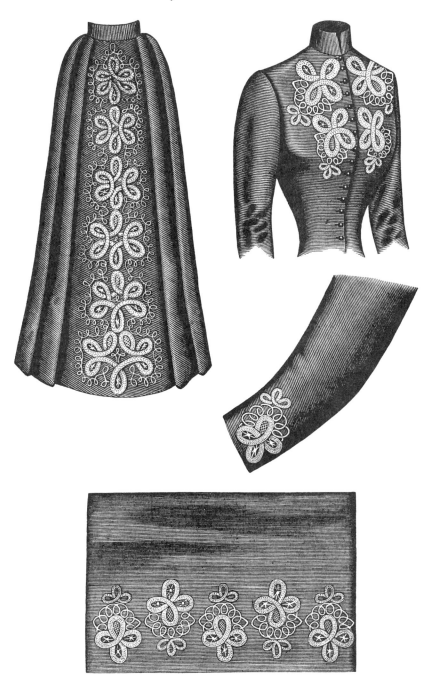

Figure 27. Braid ornaments for skirt, bodice, and sleeve

On the skirt gores is draped an oval tablier of novelty silk, which droops nearly to the edge at the center and curves upward at the sides. Four deep, upward-turning plaits laid diagonally in the sides lift it and form soft folds in the drapery. The back edges are included in the side-back seams of the skirt. A forward-turning plait in the top on each side of the center adjusts the tablier to the belt, to which the tops of the skirt gores and breadth are also joined.

December 1887 *Delineator*

The braid ornaments in Figure 27 may be obtained in colors to match all materials. They are made of wide and narrow braid, the loops formed by the wider braid being filled in with a lace-work of thread. The figure at the bottom shows how they may be applied to the bottom of a plain skirt or flat drapery, the alternating figures being inverted to prevent a too regular effect. The figure on the left shows a panel of braid ornaments laid down the center of the front drapery. This drapery falls even with the edge of the skirt and is laid in three deep kilt-plaits on each side of the decorative panel. The figure of the bodice shows an ornament applied on each side of the closing. The figure of the sleeve shows an ornament applied at the wrist.

December 1887 *Delineator*

Bodices and Jackets

For a jacket of light or heavy cloth, to be worn with a costume, a much-favored decoration is to cut the entire edge in pointed tab shape. The tabs are outlined with broad Titan braid, narrow soutache following the outline on each side of the wide braid. Sometimes the soutache is only on the inner side, and it is then made to form a knot-like loop at each corner.

January 1885 *Delineator*

Five rows of cut jet beads, each as large as a pea, are strung as dog-collars, and attached permanently to black velvet or silk basques. Or else they are mounted on satin and interlined, to be worn with various dresses. Similar rows of Roman pearls make necklets for evening dresses.

November 7, 1885 *Harper's Bazar*

On basques and jackets, tailors outline with braid the curved seams that join the side backs to the center backs. Two lines of braid are laid in a parallel curve on the seam, and finished near the armhole with three curved leaves.

January 23, 1886 *Harper's Bazar*

Dressy jackets are made of smooth cloth, and are elaborately braided with mohair braid that is black, no matter what the color of the cloth may be. This braid stands out in relief, being sewed on the edge instead of resting flat on the garment, and is in vine patterns and in geometrical figures. A braided V-shaped vest, with a similar V at the back reaching to the waist-line, is a very effective arrangement. The high collar and narrow cuffs are also braided, and there may be an inverted V on each of the box-plaits on the tournure.

March 20, 1886 *Harper's Bazar*

Figure 1. Bodice decoration

The style of decoration shown by Figure 1 may be used on either a basque or a polonaise. The front is cut out to form a Pompadour opening of medium width and length. To the sides of the opening are sewed curved lapel ornaments of contrasting material. Fine mull or illusion is folded loosely in surplice fashion inside the opening, but it is so securely fastened that it is not liable to disarrangement. The ends are passed through an opening made on each

side of the closing a little lower down and fastened at the waist-line, where their width is drawn into a very narrow space. This arrangement gives the front a strap-like effect below the Pompadour, and on the strap part is fastened a bow of ribbon matching the lapels in color. A lace frill is sewed to the neck at the back and to the surplice edges of the front. The closing is invisible.

August 1884 *Delineator*

Figure 2 shows a charming method of trimming worsted, silk, or wash materials. The neck is cut out in Pompadour fashion, and the opening is filled in with correspondingly shaped sections of net. These sections are then overlaid with mull frills turning toward the closing. A similar frill is sewed in the neck. Across the lower edge of the opening graduated straps of the dress material are arranged, their narrower ends meeting under a fancy ornament, and their wider ends being fastened at the lower corners of the opening. Turkey red embroidery is arranged to simulate a tapering lapel turning backward from the shoulders to the waist-line, finishing the side edges of the Pompadour opening and concealing the back ends of the straps. Below the Pompadour part, the bodice is closed with button-holes and buttons.

August 1884 *Delineator*

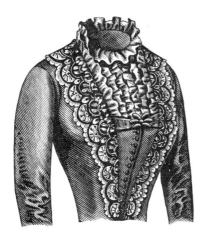

Figure 2. Dressy bodice trimming

The neck is cut out square, and a high box-plaiting of lace is arranged about all its edges (see Figure 3). Following the direction of the lace is a full ruching formed of bias silk strips, pinked on both sides and laid in box-plaits very close together. Several colors may be united. The sleeves are cut in scallops. Each is underlaid with a full frill of lace, which is caught to the shoulder between the curves of the center scallop.

September 1884 *Delineator*

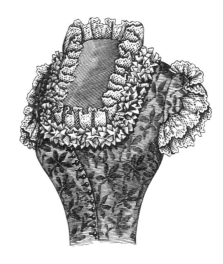

Figure 3. Evening bodice trimming

A pointed opening is made in each side of the front of a round bodice (see Figure 4). On the lining is adjusted the shirred end of a section of silk, surah, etc., which is cut to accord with the opening and extended upward beneath it sufficiently to conceal its own raw edge. The upper edge of the opening is piped and slip-stitched in place. The lower ends of the ornamental parts are gathered, and slipped under the belt worn about the waist. The shirred sections are often of crêpe, China silk, mull, and other soft-textured materials contrasting with the bodice proper. If preferred, however, they may be an exact match.

January 1885 *Delineator*

The bodice shown by Figure 6 is closed invisibly. On the bust is arranged a shirred Pompadour ornament, the edges of which come so neatly together in the center that it appears to be in one piece. Turning backward from it on each side is a narrow lapel ornament of contrasting material, which extends to the shoulder seam. Below the Pompadour a narrow vest-facing, also of the contrasting material, is applied. Three frog ornaments of cord are arranged over the upper part of the vest-facing. They are fastened permanently on one side and hooked on the other. The high standing collar matches the vest-facing and lapel ornaments.

April 1885 *Delineator*

Figure 4. Trimming for round bodice

The trimming in Figure 5 consists of embroidered appliqués sewed on velvet bands, small and large motifs being associated to form a graceful design. The shape of the bands is graduated widest over the bust, and tapered off toward the neck and lower edges of the bodice. The collar is cut from velvet. On the sleeves, the appliqués are sewed to a deep velvet cuff-facing.

February 1885 *Delineator*

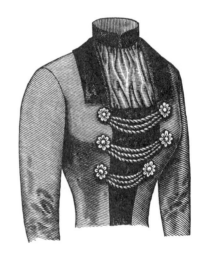

Figure 6. Bodice decoration

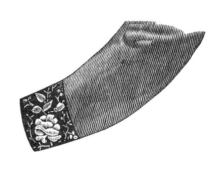

Figure 5. Appliqué trimming for bodice and sleeve

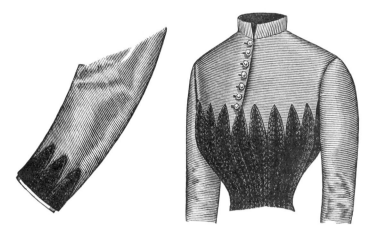

Figure 7. Braid trimming for bodice and sleeve

The arrangement of braid in Figure 7 is very effective on costumes of cloth or plain suiting. Wool or tinsel-and-wool braid is best, as it is soft and yields easily. On the sleeve, each point is composed of a single strip of braid. This is doubled and sewed along the inside to form a point at the top, and the width unnecessary after the point is formed is cut off. The raw edges, of course, are placed next to the sleeve in arranging the ornaments. The outer edges are sewed flatly on the sleeve, and the lower ends are folded underneath the lower edges of the sleeve. Linen cuffs usually form the lingerie.

The pointed braid ornaments are arranged on the bodice by the same method, except that the curve of the waist-line and the expansion of the bust must be considered in shaping the braid. The lower edges may be pointed to accord with the tops, or they may be folded under the lower edge of the bodice. The bodice is closed with button-holes and buttons as far as the top of the decoration, and the rest of the way with hooks and eyes.

May 1885 *Delineator*

Figure 8. Bodice and sleeve trimming

 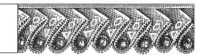

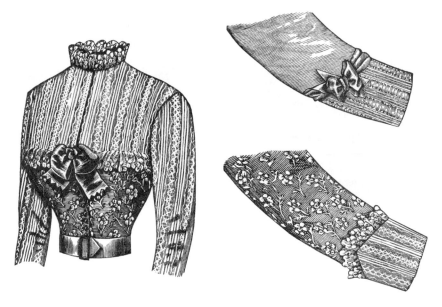

Figure 9. Open-work trimmings for bodice and sleeves

Figure 8 illustrates a tasteful and harmonious arrangement of trimming, although different materials are represented. The folds of satin and plain velvet that compose the sleeve decoration are shaped and arranged as shown. Their ends terminate in the sleeve seams. The upper or satin fold is sewed flatly at its lower edge, the velvet fold being placed a little below it and turned up over its own seam and the seam of the upper one. Three buttons are added in a row on the upper side of the sleeve, in front of the outside seam.

In the decoration of the bodice, satin and plain velvet are united, and the standing collar is cut from velvet. The deep collar ornament, which passes about the neck and flares from the neck, is also of velvet. It broadens toward its ends and overlaps triangular satin ornaments, which in turn overlap a deeper but similar velvet ornament. All of these ornaments extend to the neck and are slip-stitched in place, the longest edges of the velvet ones coming just back of the closing. For their depth the closing is invisible, with buttons and button-holes below. It is advisable to line the decorations with thin crinoline.

May 1885 *Delineator*

The bodice shown by Figure 9 is especially adapted to light-weight wools and fancy cottons. The upper parts of the back and front, and the sleeves, are made of lace tucking. The tucking is joined in yoke shape to the bodice, and the seams are concealed by falling frills of lace. The closing is invisibly performed along the yoke-shaped facings, and with button-holes and buttons below. A standing lace frill conceals the high standing collar. A ribbon belt is fastened about the waist by a buckle. A band of ribbon is placed over the upper button-hole and button. Any kind of open-work may take the place of the lace tucking.

Lace tucking, Hamburg webbing, or any kind of fancy or contrasting material may be used for the cuff-facing on the sleeve represented at the top right of the engraving. The outline of the cuff-facing deepens at the outside of the arm. Across the top is slipped a softly twisted ribbon, the ends of which are knotted in a bow on the center of the upper side.

The cuff decoration applied on the lower part of the sleeve at the bottom right is shown made of lace tucking. However, all kinds of open-work are liked on plain and figured cottons. The cuff decoration is pointed on both the upper and under sides. The upper edge is bordered with lace.

July 1885 *Delineator*

302

 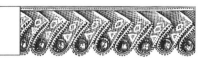

The bodice of any style of evening dress may be cut out and trimmed as shown by Figure 10. Tulle or illusion is festooned alone, or as a veiling over bias twists of satin, about the edges of the neck and carried over the shoulders. On the left shoulder and above the closing of the front, are festooned clusters of fluffy ostrich tips. A passementerie ornament is placed over the basting of the trimming in front and back of the arms. Flowers may take the place of feathers, and lace may finish the neck.

September 1885 *Delineator*

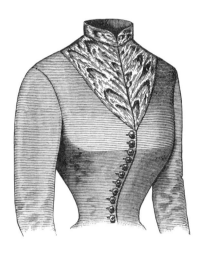

Figure 11. Faced bodice and sleeve

Figure 10. Decoration for evening bodice

The bodice trimming in Figure 11 consists of facings of silk moiré applied on the front and back in the outline of a deep, pointed collar. The high standing collar is also of the silk moiré. The closing is invisible as far as the front facing extends. The silk moiré is applied on the sleeve a little above the lower edge, in the shape of a broad, bias band. Velvet, broad Oriental ribbon, or any kind of material contrasting tastefully with the dress material may be arranged in this way.

September 1885 *Delineator*

Lace is arranged to stand in a full frill outside the collar and carried about the fronts in the outline of a Zouave jacket (see Figure 12). As much fullness is introduced as is necessary to a good effect. A band of passementerie overlies the selvage of the lace. A very stylish contrast is brought out by the application of white lace on black or dark dress materials. Wool laces are fashionable on both silks and wools.

October 1885 *Delineator*

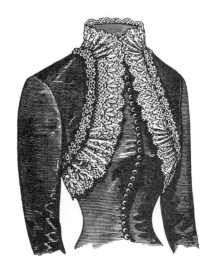

Figure 12. Zouave decoration for bodice

usually in contrast and should always be of a soft material. The shirrings are arranged to come underneath the straps, and the spaces between the straps have a puffed appearance. The neck is completed with a high standing collar.

October 1885 *Delineator*

Figure 14. Bodice decoration

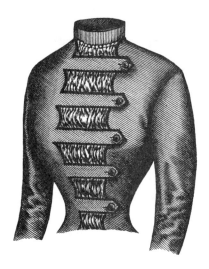

Figure 13. Bodice decorated with straps

For the bodice in Figure 13, extra width must be allowed on the right side of the front to permit of extending the straps beyond the center. The lengths of the straps are decreased toward the waist-line. The edges between the straps are cut in shallow scallops as illustrated, and the strap ends are pointed. Beneath the overlapping side is attached a shirred vest, which is closed invisibly on the opposite side with hooks and eyes. The strap ends are fastened with button-holes and buttons. The vest is

The floral trimming on the front of the bodice in Figure 14 consists of silk-embroidered appliqués in a forget-me-not design. They are applied on a vest-shaped facing of plain velvet. A softly folded surplice ornament of plain satin extends from each shoulder to the corresponding lower edge of the bodice, its width being symmetrically decreased toward the waist-line. A high, standing collar of plain velvet finishes the neck.

November 1885 *Delineator*

Figure 15. Dressy bodice and sleeve trimming

The sleeve in Figure 15 has a broad V-shaped piece cut out of the back below the outside seam. Two full frills, which may be of either black or white lace, fill in the opening. The lower one passes entirely about the lower edge. It is made wide enough to extend to the shortest part of the sleeve by being sewed to a piece of net or footing, which of course is concealed by the overhanging frill. Passementerie showing a solid network of beads borders the lower edges of the sleeve.

The bodice is cut out quite low in heart shape. A full frill of black or white lace is gathered into the neck and cutaway edges, no collar being added. It may be wired to retain it in an upright position about the neck. A piece of illusion gathered across, a short distance from the top, fills in the front to a becoming distance from the neck. A band of passementerie passes about the open edges and down each side of the closing.

December 1885 *Delineator*

The bodice in Figure 16 is cut in a low oval outline in front. Each point of the lace is followed by a fine wire, which is sewed to the under side. When the lace is sewed to the neck of the dress, the wire is bent to hold the lace upright at the back, while it lies nearly flat on the bust. If beaded lace is used, the wire should be heavier than for lighter lace.

January 1886 *Delineator*

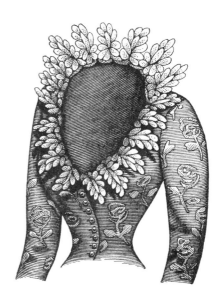

Figure 16. Evening bodice with lace collar

A tucked vest-facing is applied on the bodice lining, and the closing is invisibly performed. (See Figure 17.) The outside fronts are cut away in Zouave jacket outline. Their edges are bordered with velvet bands, which are spread apart on the bust and carried in flat collar outline about the neck below the high standing collar, which is also of velvet. The neck is closed with a fancy clasp.

March 1886 *Delineator*

Figure 17. Zouave bodice decoration

The bodices of dressy summer toilettes of all kinds of thin materials, often have lace or embroidered insertion set into them in lengthwise bands. Lace insertion on mull is represented by Figure 18; pressed Italian lace is much admired. The closing is concealed by a full cascade of lace edging. The neck is finished by a jabot of the same. The sleeves extend only to a little below the elbow and are bordered with lace ruffles, a tied ribbon bow being fastened on the upper side of each.

May 1886 *Delineator*

The decoration in Figure 19 is dressy, but does not involve turning or cutting the dress away as deeply as is necessary for a heart-shaped or a square neck. The fichu may be carried about the

Figure 18. Dressy summer bodice

neck at the back, or it may be in two pieces and its back ends scantily shirred and inserted in the shoulder seams. The front ends are shirred very narrowly so as to bring them to a point at the end of the opening. Both the fichu and the neck edges are bordered with lace, that about the neck being narrower and forming a standing frill. Mull, crêpe, surah, or any contrasting material may be used.

June 1886 *Delineator*

Figure 19. Dressy bodice decoration

 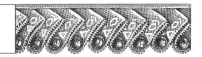

The front of the bodice in Figure 20 is cut out in an oval outline that expands slightly on the bust. The opening is filled in with Fedora lace, which is gathered to the collar and to the lower edges of the opening. A full jabot of lace conceals the collar, and a plaiting of ribbon of a dainty hue finishes the edges of the opening. The edges of the lace decoration fall together and are held in place by pins, which are concealed by the fullness. A vest-facing of contrasting material is applied on the front below the lace decoration. It is closed with button-holes and buttons.

June 1886 *Delineator*

Figure 21. Bodice decoration

Any style of basque or pointed bodice may be turned into a full-dress bodice by cutting out the front and back as illustrated by Figure 22, and shortening the sleeves to suit the fancy. Lace is arranged to border the front and partly fill in the point of the back. The sleeves are also trimmed with lace. Ribbon bows are fastened on the shoulders.

July 1886 *Delineator*

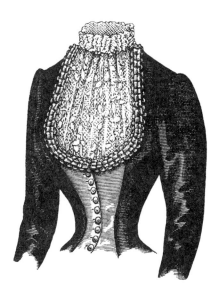

Figure 20. Bodice decoration

The decoration in Figure 21 brings out the idea of a folded chemisette of thin white material, which may be mull, grenadine, India silk, etc. Its folds are arranged to form a point on the bust. On each side three wider folds are laid, with their broadest parts at the top and their outer edges curved so as to produce an oval outline. The edges of the decoration, and also the edges of the collar, are outlined with beaded gimp.

July 1886 *Delineator*

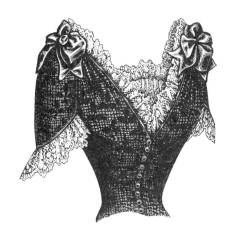

Figure 22. Full-dress bodice

The closing of the basque in Figure 23 is made in the usual manner. The vest, which is of wide lace edging, has its selvage sewed beneath a velvet band applied on the right side. Velvet straps start from beneath this band and cross the vest diagonally, their ends being folded under the free edge of the vest, which is attached to the left side with hooks and eyes. Lace flouncing 1/4 yard wide is not too broad, as the top of the vest must have enough fullness gathered into it to ensure a soft and becoming effect, there being no foundation between the lace and the bodice.

July 1886 *Delineator*

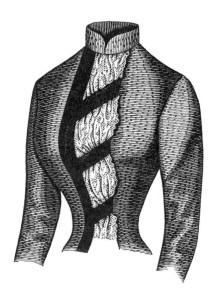

Figure 24. Bodice and sleeve decoration

Figure 23. Bodice decorated with straps

The lace net pictured in Figure 24 is Spanish, and the edging is of the same kind. The front of the bodice is open in a pointed outline from the top of the shoulders to the bust. The opening is bordered with lace edging and filled in with plaited lisse. A ribbon bow is fastened at the end of the opening. A standing frill of white lace edging encircles the neck. This arrangement may be developed in all black, all white, cream, mode, écru, or any color found in laces. The lining is usually of the same color as the lace, although it may contrast if desired.

The sleeve is cut off almost to elbow length. It is finished with a frill of lace edging, which narrows off toward the inside, where a looped bow is fastened. A sleeve lining is optional.

August 1886 *Delineator*

The bodice in Figure 25 is closed invisibly from the neck nearly to the waist-line. Plastron facings of striped material extending to the same depth are applied. Turning back from these facings are velvet lapel ornaments, which extend from the shoulders to the bust and are trimmed with buttons at their back edges. Tapered lapels, also of velvet, overlap the lower ends of the upper lapels and terminate at the end of the facings. Below them the

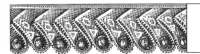 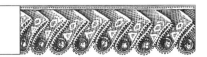

bodice is closed in the usual manner. The lapels may be of the dress material if preferred.

The striped cuff-facing on the sleeve is applied in the same outline on the under as on the upper side. The little revers, which may be of velvet, plush, or any contrasting material, are applied to the upper side only. The wrist is finished with a lace frill.

November 1886 *Delineator*

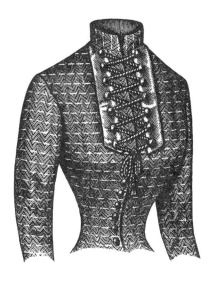

Figure 26. Laced bodice decoration

The bodice in Figure 27 is cut out square both back and front and has no sleeves. About the open edges, white or black lace is sewed along its selvage and is then turned up and basted near the top to hold it in place. It is not, however, drawn so tightly as to detract from the soft, puffy effect produced by turning it up over its seaming. Lace frills are sewed into the armholes.

December 1886 *Delineator*

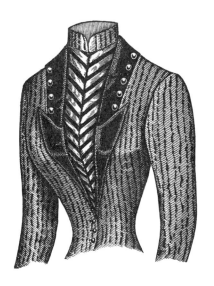

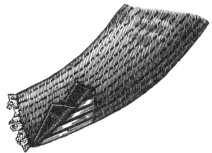

Figure 25. Bodice and sleeve decoration

For the bodice in Figure 26, a narrow, lapel-like ornament of plain material is placed on each side of the front, a little back of the closing between the neck and bust. Along the front edges of these lapels, lacing buttons are sewed. Cord is laced over them, and its ends tipped with tassels and tied between the lowest ones. The bodice is invisibly closed as far as the lacing extends, and below it with buttons and button-holes.

November 1886 *Delineator*

Figure 27. Evening bodice

 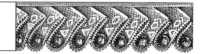

Either a basque or a round bodice may be trimmed as in Figure 28. The standing collar is made of plain dark material. On each side of the front is a little triangular lapel ornament, which starts from a little back of the neck and turns back over its own seam. The girdle-like bodice ornament, which widens with a pointed effect toward its closing edges, is sewed into the under-arm seams, and its front edges are laced. Velvet in high, warm colors or rich dark ones may be associated in this way with both light and dark suit materials.

December 1886 Delineator

Figure 29. Trimming for dress bodice

Any style of dress bodice may be cut out at the neck in the V-shaped outline shown by Figure 30. The facing of beaded net seen on the front may be duplicated on the back. The sleeves are of elbow length and are of the beaded net. Their lower edges, like the neck, are finished with lace frills. Pearl beads are arranged as a finish along the edges of the beaded facings, but beaded gimp may take their place.

January 1887 Delineator

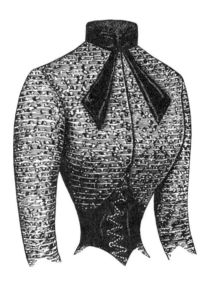

Figure 28. Bodice trimming

Two materials are combined in the construction of the bodice in Figure 29. The sleeves are made of one kind, and the front above the bust is underfaced to correspond and turned back in lapel fashion. The collar, which is of the same contrasting material as the rest of the bodice proper, is sewed to the bodice only at the back. The opening is filled in by a lace chemisette. The chemisette is gathered to show a pretty fullness, and is sewed to a narrow bias band that fastens under and is concealed by the collar.

December 1886 Delineator

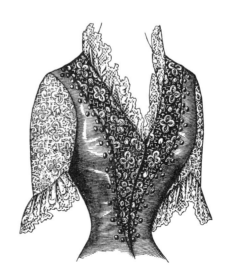

Figure 30. Evening bodice

 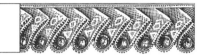

Figure 31 shows a becoming arrangement for feather bands, down, and fancy fur dress trimmings. The bodice fronts are cut out in heart shape. The decoration passes in collar outline across the back and along each side of the opening, narrowing below the bust and extending along the closing to the lower edge.

January 1887 *Delineator*

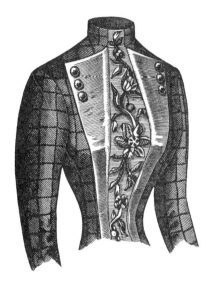

Figure 32. Bodice with embroidery

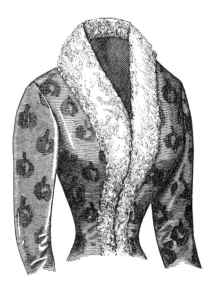

Figure 31. Bodice trimming

Figure 32 shows the use of wrought or ap-pliquéd embroidery for the vest. The design is a lily pattern done in shaded crewels and flosses on a chamois-colored background. The long, tapering lapels are faced with the same light-colored mate-rial. The vest is sewed permanently beneath one of them, while on the other side it is attached invisibly with buttons and button-holes. A separate collar section of the light material is sewed to the vest, and the embroidery is carried to its top. Three large fancy buttons decorate the top of each lapel.

February 1887 *Delineator*

The little puff is of plain wool material the ground shade of the bodice material. (See Figure 33.) It is shirred to a very narrow width at the neck and broadened on the bust, its inner edges falling together over the closing so that it appears to be one piece. Turning back from it on each side

is a lapel of plain velvet. This overlaps the back edge of a shorter lapel made of the same material as the puff. The smaller lapel and the puff may be of the basque material. For a very dressy effect, the puff may be of lace net and the basque may be cut out beneath it.

February 1887 *Delineator*

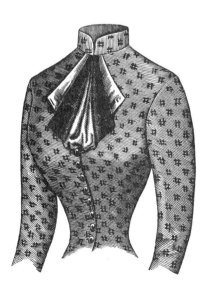

Figure 33. Bodice decoration

Figure 34 shows the back view of an evening bodice. The lacing is merely ornamental, the closing being made invisibly in front, where a vest ornament is arranged. The neck and sleeves are finished with lace frills, and ribbon bows are fastened at the back of the arm. The sleeves may be omitted altogether.

May 1887 *Delineator*

On the bodice, the vest is of velvet and is invisibly closed. Buttons are sewed to the overlapping edges of the fronts, and cord is laced across the vest over these buttons. The standing collar is also of velvet.

September 1887 *Delineator*

Figure 34. Laced evening bodice

The sleeve is separately illustrated at the top of Figure 35. Here the lower part is shown made of silk and the puff of lace net, with lace edging for the wrist finish. A twist of ribbon is brought softly about the lower edge of the puff and bowed at the back of the arm. Another tied about the center gives the puff a double effect. The view of the bodice at the bottom also shows a combination of lace net with silk, surah, or any soft summer material.

August 1887 *Delineator*

The sleeve decoration in Figure 36 consists of a band of velvet ribbon crossing the inside of the wrist. The band is slipped through upright openings made in the upper and under sides of the sleeve, and tied in a bow at the back. A lace frill encircles the wrist.

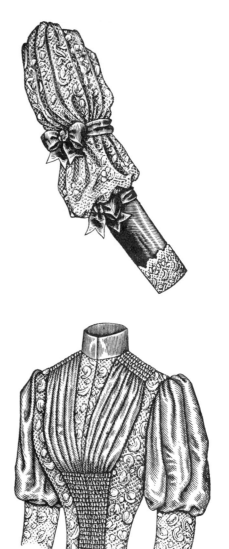

Figure 35. Decorations for bodice and two sleeves

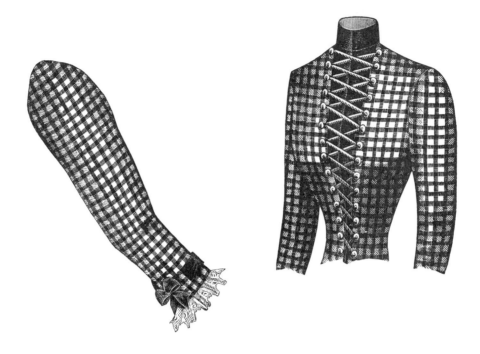

Figure 36. Decoration for bodice and sleeve

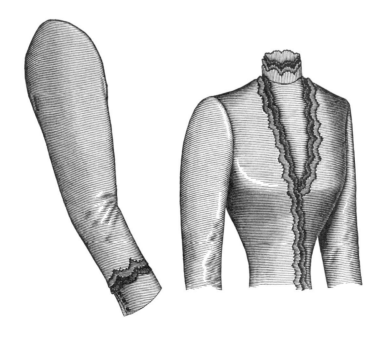

Figure 37. Scalloped decoration for bodice and sleeve

 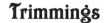 

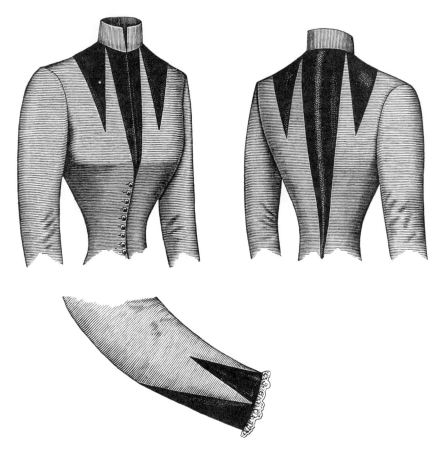

Figure 38. Faced bodice and sleeve

The bodice fronts flare above the bust over a V-shaped vest, and the edges are cut in scallops and pinked. (See Figure 37.) A strip of the material of a darker shade is similarly scalloped and pinked, and applied underneath to extend a little beyond the edges of the basque. From beneath it extends another scalloped and pinked strip of a still darker shade. The upper edge of the collar is trimmed in harmony with the basque. Two or three contrasting colors may be used instead of three shades of one color.

The close-fitting coat sleeve is decorated at the wrist to accord with the basque. From beneath it extends a round cuff, which is left open partway at the back of the wrist and decorated along the opening with a row of buttons.

September 1887 *Delineator*

Perfectly plain bodices of any shape may be given a dressy air by velvet, plush, or silk arranged as in Figure 38. Here the front shows a narrow velvet facing down each side of the closing to below the bust, where the facing ends in a point. The closing is made along the facing with hooks and eyes, and below it with button-holes and crocheted buttons. On each side of the facing is applied a pointed piece of velvet that meets it at the neck and flares sharply, ending just above the bust.

Points to match those on the front are seen on each side of the back. Down the center of the back is a V facing of velvet, which ends just above the waistline and meets the applied points at the neck.

The sleeve has a V facing of velvet that extends from the wrist to the elbow at the back of the arm, and a shorter V facing just in front of the long facing on the upper side of the wrist. The facings meet at the wrist edges and flare decidedly above. The edge is decorated with a lace frill.

October 1887 *Delineator*

The right front of the bodice in Figure 39 overlaps the left in an outline from the center of the figure near the waist-line to the shoulder, and also diagonally below the waist-line. A plaited velvet surplice crosses from the right shoulder to the end of the closing. The soft puffs on the sleeves are of silk; they pass beneath pointed velvet bands. The standing collar is of velvet.

Color combinations are very effective in this style. The overlapping part of the front is frequently faced with white material richly embroidered with metal braids or striped with narrow contrasting ribbons.

December 1887 *Delineator*

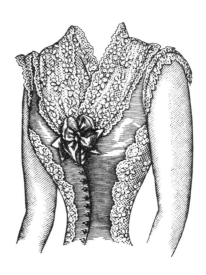

Figure 40. Evening bodice

Sleeves

An easy and stylish way of trimming sleeves is to use 1-inch wide galloon or velvet ribbon instead of cuffs. Begin by sewing it at the end of the sleeve, at its outside seam. Cross it to the inside seam, then take it gradually upward far enough to come back on the front just above the line that is already there. Stop there when halfway across, then finish by turning in the ends in a point.

November 7, 1885 *Harper's Bazar*

Open sleeves reach just below the elbow, fit easily at the top, have but one seam (that inside the arm), and slope open to about 3/8 yard in width at the lower end. The upper half is gathered to the under side about the elbow, giving a diagonal effect when stripes are used. The lining or facing of such sleeves is important, as it shows plainly next to the arm. It is always made of one of the materials of the dress. For instance, a green velvet dinner dress has pointed flowing sleeves without a ruffle, but faced deeply with old rose brocaded satin on which are green velvet leaves. Lace ruffles appear in such sleeves, made of point d'esprit, Alençon, or Valenciennes lace 4 or 5 inches deep. This lace alone covers the upper part of the wrists, where the sleeve is sloped shorter to make a pointed effect below.

October 2, 1886 *Harper's Bazar*

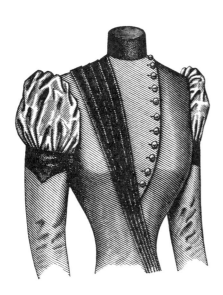

Figure 39. Fancy bodice

Any plain basque may be adapted as shown by Figure 40. The sleeves are omitted, and the neck is cut out in low V shape both back and front. A lace fichu is draped about the neck, its ends being tucked under a rosette bow of glacé ribbon. A band of lace passes forward for a pretty distance on the front from the under-arm seams, and its top is finished with the armholes. Double frills of narrow lace decorate the armholes. Floral epaulettes may be added.

December 1887 *Delineator*

The full sleeve puff extending from below the elbow to the shoulder is usually held in by ribbon, braid, or a band of passementerie. On the cuffs fanciful decorations are in good form. Gold, silver, or Oriental embroidery; coarse lace; or ribbon arranged in stripe fashion may be used.

October 1887 *Delineator*

This sleeve is not shortened, but is cut in a curve toward the outside of the arm at the lower edge. Lace in two widths is added to form a standing and a falling ruffle, as illustrated by Figure 1. The deeper width is used for the standing ruffle, which is caught to the sleeve here and there at its upper edge to hold it in place. A piece of ribbon is arranged in soft folds over the selvages of the two ruffles. Its ends are fastened on the upper side, a little in front of the outside seam, beneath a bow with notched ends.

July 1884 *Delineator*

Figure 2. Sleeve for dressy house toilette

Figure 1. Sleeve trimming

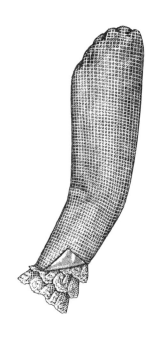

Figure 3. Sleeve trimming

The sleeve in Figure 2 is suitable for a dressy house toilette. It is shortened to about halfway between the wrist and elbow. It is cut in quite a deep curve toward the center of the upper side, and in a shallow curve toward the center of the under side. Double frills of lace are sewed to the lower edge and follow the curved outline, the under one being the deeper and falling a little below the upper one. Surmounting the lace frills is a band of embroidered trimming showing a daisy pattern.

July 1884 *Delineator*

The original pattern for the sleeve in Figure 3 has a lap that is buttoned from the under side over the upper. In this instance the lap is cut off, the outside seam is discontinued a short distance from the lower edge, and the corners are underfaced, turned forward in revers fashion, and basted in place. The opening thus left at the outside of the arm is filled in by a fitted piece of the material. Onto this piece are sewed two full frills of lace. The upper one terminates beneath the reversed parts. The other

 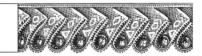
is carried beneath the sleeve with its lower edge extending just below it and overlapping a third frill, which falls entirely below the lower edge. When the sleeve is lined, the lining may be faced between the reversed parts to form a foundation for the upper frills of lace, so that a piece of material does not have to be added.

July 1884 *Delineator*

Any sleeve pattern may be completed like this. The outline to be followed in shaping it is indicated by Figure 4. The edges are bordered with a frill of wide lace set on beneath a ruching of narrower lace. When the ruching is arranged in place, it is sewed along its gathered edges over the seam of the frill. It is then turned up over and back of the seam, and basted in place here and there.

July 1884 *Delineator*

Figure 5. Laced sleeve

The sleeve in Figure 6 is slightly curved at its lower edge toward the outside of the arm, and a lace frill is sewed inside it. A wide band of the material, cut bias, is shirred twice perpendicularly a little in front of the end, about 1 inch being allowed between the shirrings. The band is long enough to extend across the upper side of the sleeve, and each end is shirred once. The end nearer the shirrings first mentioned is drawn up quite short and sewed in with the outside seam. The other end is more scantily shirred so as to leave it much wider, and is included in the inside seam. This trimming is also sewed in place through the double line of shirrings.

August 1884 *Delineator*

Figure 4. Sleeve trimming

For the sleeve in Figure 5, a long, narrow opening in the outline of an inverted V is made a little in front of the outside seam. After its edges are neatly finished, eyelets are worked in them. Through these a fine silk cord, which may be like the sleeve or of a contrasting color, is laced.

July 1884 *Delineator*

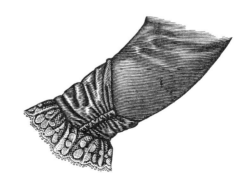

Figure 6. Sleeve decoration

Gilt braid and gilt buttons were selected for decorating the sleeve in Figure 7. Both are very fashionable for trimming flannel, nun's veiling, cashmere, velvet, etc. Worsted braid and covered buttons to match are arranged in the same simple manner on the sleeves of street suits.

August 1884 *Delineator*

Figure 7. Sleeve decoration

For the sleeve in Figure 8, any material contrasting harmoniously with the sleeve may be chosen for the decorative cuff-facing. The lace, which is sewed as a standing frill inside the upper edge, may be of any kind and color in keeping with the general effect. The rosette is of narrow ribbon matching the sleeve itself. The cuff-facing and the lace frill may extend entirely about the sleeve, or only across the upper side.

August 1884 *Delineator*

Figure 8. Sleeve trimming

Two sections of silk or wool material and one of velvet are united in the sleeve trimming in Figure 9. The velvet section is lined with crinoline. One end of it is sewed in with the inside seam, while the other is attached just in front of the outside seam. Each of the silk sections is a triangular piece that is shirred three times on one side. The two are placed with their shirred sides at the outside seam, where they are stitched in place, one directly above the other. The lower edge of the upper one is passed beneath the velvet section, while that of the lower one is carried up under the wrist of the sleeve and sewed on the inside. A frill of lace or lisse completes the sleeve.

August 1884 *Delineator*

Figure 9. Sleeve trimming

For the sleeve in Figure 10, the material is cut in quite a high curve from the outside to the inside of the arm on both the upper and under sides. The lining is left the length the sleeve is to be when finished. On the lining are arranged three rows of plaiting. The lower one extends entirely about the lower edge and falls below it, while the other two terminate beneath the outside. Velvet, silk, or any contrasting material may be used for the ornamental facing. A bow, formed of triple loops and a knot of ribbon matching the sleeve, is fastened at the inner extremity of the facing.

September 1884 *Delineator*

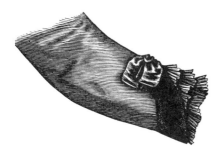

Figure 10. Sleeve trimming

The arrangement in Figure 11 is very pretty for sleeves that are to extend nearly or quite to the wrists. Two lace frills fall from the wrist of the sleeve, the under one being white and considerably deeper than the upper, which is black and may be beaded if desired. Partially overhanging the top of the upper frill is a series of ribbon loops, and concealing the tops of these loops is a band of passementerie. For a less elaborate effect, the ribbon loops may be omitted and the passementerie set close to the upper lace frill.

September 1884 Delineator

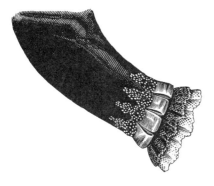

Figure 11. Trimming for dressy sleeve

The sleeve in Figure 12 is cut in a medium curve toward the outside of the arm. To the lower edge is sewed a lace frill, which may be deep or narrow. Falling over the lace on the upper side, is a row of silk pompons suspended by short silk cords. For an all-black sleeve, drop ornaments of jet or silk may take their place. Surmounting the lace is a twist of surah, silk, satin, etc., which likewise extends only along the upper side. It is shirred

into a narrow space at one end and sewed over the outside seam, and into a still narrower space on the other, which is sewed over the inside seam. Both ends are arranged to appear as if they were sewed into the seams.

September 1884 Delineator

Figure 12. Sleeve trimming

Figure 13 shows a sleeve with a double cuff decoration. Two materials, each contrasting with the sleeve, are used. From one is cut a deep, round facing, which encircles the sleeve at the wrist, is piped at its top, and is slip-stitched in place. The other material is used for the demi-facings, which are applied only on the upper side, as shown. A row of buttons along the back edge of the wider one adds to the effect.

December 1884 Delineator

Figure 13. Sleeve trimming

Any sleeve may be enriched by inserting a lace gore of the shape shown by Figure 14. The edges of the gore are piped with satin, silk, etc. The same material is used for underfacing the wrist. The upper side is finished with four buttons placed in a row just in front of the outside seam.

January 1885 Delineator

Figure 14. Sleeve with lace gore

A round cuff-facing is applied to the sleeve in Figure 15. Its ends are left open at the outside of the arm for about half of their depth from the top. The corner of the front end is lined with contrasting silk. It is turned down in a point, and apparently fastened under a button and simulated button-hole. A triangular piece, similarly lined, is slipped beneath the reversed part, turned down over it, and fastened in the same way. In the wrist is sewed a piece of spiral lisse ruching.

January 1885 Delineator

Figure 15. Sleeve trimming

The demi-cuffs illustrated by Figure 16 are each in contrast with the sleeve, although the upper one may be like it if desired. Each is cut from a single piece that is shaped to fit smoothly over the inside seam. The upper one is slip-stitched over the under one, which is both wider and longer and is lined with crinoline. Its edges are slip-stitched to the sleeve. A ribbon is fastened near each end of the smaller demi-cuff, and slipped through a slash made for it in the larger one and beneath its ends. Then the free ends of the ribbon are fastened in a bow at the outside of the sleeve. Such a sleeve decoration permits of lisse ruffs and is not too elaborate for linen cuffs.

January 1885 Delineator

Figure 16. Sleeve trimming

A slash, which extends some distance from the lower edge of the sleeve, is made in the upper side a little in front of the outside seam. (See Figure 17.) A velvet cuff-facing is applied, its ends being finished with the edges of the slash. Eyelets are worked through the ends, and a lace frill is applied about the lower edge of the sleeve and along the slash. Silk cord is then laced through the eyelets from the lower edge toward the top, where its ends are tied, their extremities being neatly finished.

July 1885 Delineator

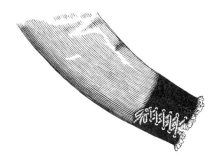

Figure 17. Laced sleeve

The velvet section encircles the sleeve at the wrist and is slanted off on its under side to correspond to the upper side. (See Figure 18.) The other section does not extend beyond the upper side, and its back edge is sewed into the outside seam. Its front edge is overlapped by the adjoining edge of the velvet part, the latter being apparently fastened in place by a row of buttons and simulated button-holes. Both sections are lined with crinoline. Linen cuffs accord well with this sleeve trimming.

September 1885 *Delineator*

Figure 18. Sleeve trimming

Figure 19 shows a method of uniting three materials in the decoration of a sleeve. A medium-wide cuff-facing of velvet encircles the wrist. Extending from the side seams toward the upper side of this facing, are full twists of the sleeve material. The ends are scantily shirred and inserted in the seams, while the opposite ends are shirred very closely and slipped beneath the cuff-facing. A row of silk shell ruching, a band of passementerie, or any decoration admired may border the top of the cuff-facing.

September 1885 *Delineator*

Figure 19. Sleeve trimming

Any sleeve cut off to elbow length and having its lower edge curved concavely may be trimmed as in Figure 20. Lace is applied in a frill to the lower edge. It is carried up the center of the upper side in a double jabot to within a short distance of the top, the width of the jabots gradually decreasing until they end in a point.

November 1885 *Delineator*

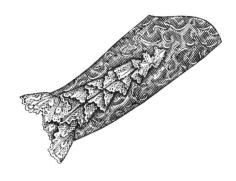

Figure 20. Sleeve trimming

The broad velvet cuff-facing has a circular opening in the upper side. (See Figure 21.) The material is slashed above the opening. The end coming from the inside is pointed and lapped over that coming from the outside under a button and simulated button-hole. The entire cuff is lined with crinoline, and all of the edges are slip-stitched. Lace is worn at the wrist, being sewed in with little full-ness if the pattern is choice.

December 1885 *Delineator*

321

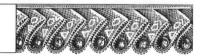

Figure 21. Sleeve trimming

The cuff-facing in Figure 22 is especially suitable for foulard, sateen, and flannel dresses. The shape is easily obtained by experimenting with paper, the under side being of uniform depth all the way across. The cuff-facing is lined with plain material. Two buttons and small simulated button-holes of twist decorate the corner on the upper side. A narrow lace frill is sewed inside the wrist.

May 1886 *Delineator*

Figure 22. Sleeve trimming

The cuff-facing of the sleeve in Figure 23 presents the same outline on the under as on the upper side of the sleeve. The lace frill is carried all about the sleeve as illustrated, bastings being made through it near the top to hold it upright. The buttons that decorate the deeper part of the cuff are added only to the upper side.

June 1886 *Delineator*

Figure 23. Sleeve decoration

For the sleeve in Figure 24, the bias folds are arranged so as to overlap a little more broadly at the outside than at the inside of the arm. This gives them the effect of being graduated. A velvet cuff-like ornament turns from the upper edge, and its shape is the same on the under as on the upper side. The edges are neatly finished, and are held in place by the sewing of the buttons and simulated button-holes.

June 1886 *Delineator*

Figure 24. Sleeve decoration

The sleeves of thin and thick white dresses are often decorated as shown by Figure 25. The sleeve is cut off with a rounded outline toward the outside of the arm. The lower edge is finished with a lace frill, above which a velvet band studded with large cut jet beads is arranged.

July 1886 *Delineator*

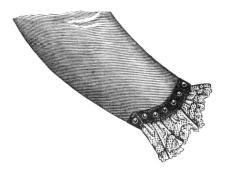

Figure 25. Sleeve decoration for white dresses

Figure 27. Sleeve trimming

A velvet collar and cuffs are often added to the otherwise most severely plain of tailor dresses. This cuff shows an unbroken outline on the under side of the sleeve. Its ends are shaped as shown by Figure 26, the exact shape being obtained by experimenting with a piece of paper. The overlapping end is ornamented with a button and simulated buttonhole. This cuff should be lined with crinoline.

September 1886 *Delineator*

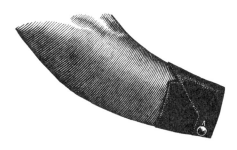

Figure 26. Velvet cuff

A V-shaped piece is cut from the outside part of the sleeve in Figure 27. On the lining is arranged a little plaited fan of contrasting material, over which the sleeve is slip-stitched at its back edge. To the front edge of the opening is sewed a little revers ornament, which is lined with the contrasting material and turned forward to disclose the lining. Sometimes the facings of the revers contrast with the fan, as well as with the sleeve. Linen lingerie, lace, or lisse frills are worn with sleeves trimmed in this way.

September 1886 *Delineator*

The sleeve in Figure 28 is suitable for any style of basque, round bodice, or polonaise. Two materials of any kind seen in any other part of the toilette may be associated, or the sleeve may be in striking contrast to the rest of the toilette. It is shown here in striped material, with the foundation being made of plain material. Only flat decorations at the wrist are suitable, especially lace turned back flatly in cuff fashion.

The foundation is in coat shape and fits the arm closely, but not too tightly. This part is covered to the bend of the elbow by a full section, which is enough wider than the foundation to produce a full, puffed effect. This effect is developed by gathering the top quite closely along the upper side. The puff has its corresponding edges included, along with the foundation, in the seam along the inside of the arm. The lower edge is turned under for a finish and is gathered to the size of the foundation, to which it is sewed, only enough of the fullness being allowed on the under side to give an easy effect. The puff droops over the sewing of the lower edge, and the soft, easy folds in which it rests are rendered permanent by bastings made through them to the foundation. When the sleeve is sewed to a dress, both the outer sleeve and the foundation are included in the join.

January 1887 *Delineator*

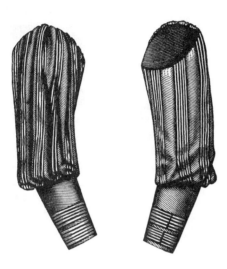

Figure 28. Puffed sleeve

For the sleeve in Figure 29, the cuff outline is the same on the under as on the upper side of the sleeve. However, the lace fan that is sewed beneath the top is arranged on the upper side only. Bastings hold the top of the fan in place. Lisse, lace, or linen lingerie may be worn with sleeves trimmed in this way.

February 1887 *Delineator*

Figure 29. Sleeve trimming

The upper side of the sleeve in Figure 30 is slashed to form four pointed tabs, and the edges are piped with contrasting material. A button-hole is made in each point, and to the back edge is joined a lap, on which buttons are placed. The button-holes are slipped over the buttons. Underneath them is arranged a lace frill, which is carried about the wrist. A finely laid side-plaiting that matches the pipings is arranged to fall over it toward the hand.

February 1887 *Delineator*

Figure 30. Sleeve decoration

The effect of a cuff extending from beneath the sleeve proper is in keeping with the tailor finish of street costumes. (See Figure 31.) The under side of the sleeve is uniform all the way across with the deepest part of the upper side. The reversed front edge of the latter part is faced with velvet matching the darkest shade in the sleeve material. Back of this revers, a rosette bow of ribbon is fastened.

March 1887 *Delineator*

Figure 31. Sleeve decoration for street costume

The sleeve in Figure 32 is shortened a little and curved toward the center of the upper side. Two frills of fine plaiting, one a little deeper than the other, follow the outline. A lace frill extends from beneath the plaitings and forms a jabot just back of the curve, where they appear to terminate.

April 1887 *Delineator*

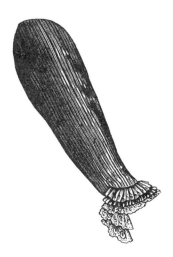

Figure 32. Sleeve trimming

Sleeves of thin dresses are often arranged to present a full effect, although the lining may be in the usual close-fitting coat shape. Figure 33 shows a sleeve of thin material laid in side-plaits, which are basted below the top and also below the elbow. Below the lower bastings, the material is arranged to form a full puff. Both sets of bastings are concealed by the ribbons, which are bowed as represented. Such sleeves usually extend about halfway between the elbow and wrist.

May 1887 *Delineator*

Figure 33. Fancy sleeve for thin dress

Lace net was used for the puff of the sleeve in Figure 34. The lower edge of the puff is stayed by a binding and ornamented with a frill of lace edging. A twist of ribbon is arranged over the join of the frill, a rosette bow being fastened over the outside of the arm.

July 1887 *Delineator*

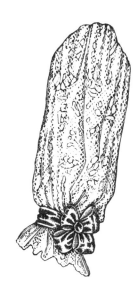

Figure 34. Sleeve decoration

The sleeve in Figure 35 is cut to extend about halfway between the elbow and wrist. To the lower edge is sewed a deep lace frill. This is surmounted by a twist of ribbon and caught up on the upper side, near the inside of the arm, under a ribbon bow.

July 1887 *Delineator*

Figure 35. Sleeve decoration

For the sleeve in Figure 36, point d'esprit net is puffed on a plain coat-shaped foundation of tarlatan or Swiss. The edges of the net meet in the inside seam, and the fullness on the upper side of the arm is upheld by the shirr seam as illustrated. A standing and a falling frill of lace, separated by a folded ribbon that is bowed at the outside of the arm, finish the wrist.

August 1887 *Delineator*

Figure 36. Net sleeve

The sleeve in Figure 37 is suitable for tailor costumes having velvet in combination with plaid, striped, or other fancy dress materials. Two upright slashes are made at the center of the upper side near the wrist and about 1 inch apart, forming straps. About 2 inches above these, two similar slashes are made. Through these slashes are slipped the pointed ends of velvet straps that extend from the inside seam. The velvet straps are the depth of the slashes. A button is placed at the top and bottom of the straps formed by the slashes.

September 1887 *Delineator*

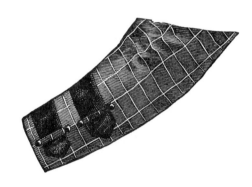

Figure 37. Sleeve decoration for tailor costumes

The upper part of the sleeve in Figure 38 has a long, full puff of India silk that droops below the elbow. It is joined to a long, close-fitting cuff that closes at the back of the arm with hooks and eyes. The puff is bordered halfway between the top and bottom with a fancy piece of rich passementerie that confines it almost closely to the arm. A band of similar passementerie trims the lower edge of the cuff.

September 1887 *Delineator*

Figure 38. Puffed sleeve

The sleeve in Figure 39 is decorated with sections of velvet. These are arranged so that the front edges of the sections nearest the back overlap the corresponding back edges of those in front of them. The sections are shorter at their back than at their front edges, forming a series of saw-tooth points. A row of three buttons decorates the front edge of each point. Silk or any contrasting material may be used instead of velvet.

September 1887 *Delineator*

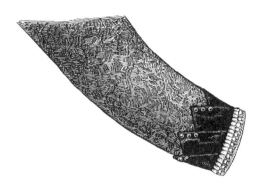

Figure 39. Sleeve decoration

Sleeves of white and delicately colored dresses that are slightly soiled may be covered with any kind of lace as shown by Figure 40. The foundation is a coat sleeve shortened to the elbow. Two lace flounces are laid in fine plaits over the foundation. The upper flounce falls in a frill over the lower flounce. The latter falls in a similar frill at the edge of the sleeve. The plaits are basted to the sleeve, where each flounce is banded by ribbon, which is tied in a bow at the back of the arm.

September 1887 *Delineator*

Figure 40. Lace-covered sleeve

For the sleeve in Figure 41, the sleeve lining or foundation is in the close-fitting coat shape, with a curved inside and outside seam. On this lining is arranged the outside part, which is in one piece. It is laid in plaits that turn backward on the upper side of the arm, and forward on the under side. Just above and a little below the elbow, the plaits are basted to the lining. Between these bastings is arranged a full puff that is deepest at the back of the arm. A downward-turning plait is laid in each front edge of the plaited part about halfway between the bastings. These plaits introduce the desired fullness to achieve the soft, loose effect evident in the puff. The plaits are stayed underneath to retain the folds in place. The plaited part covers the lining except for a few inches at the wrist, where there is a velvet cuff-facing, the top of the facing covering the lower edge of the plaited part.

All kinds of dress materials not too heavy to plait nicely are suitable for this sleeve. The wrist may be trimmed with bands of braid. For evening dresses in sheer materials, the sleeve may combine two materials. Or else the wrist may be striped with moiré or fancy-edged ribbon, or embroidered with gold, silver, or other metal braid or cords.

October 1887 *Delineator*

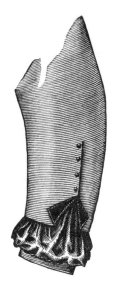

Figure 42. Sleeve decoration

Figure 41. Plaited sleeve

The outside material of the sleeve is cut several inches shorter than the lining, and is deeply slashed a little in front of the outside seam. (See Figure 42.) The lining is faced with the material for a short distance from the edge. Drooping over the top of the facing is a full puff of soft silk that is deepest at the slash, under which it extends for some distance. The edges of the slash are lapped under a row of four buttons, and below the latter are turned over in little three-cornered revers that are faced with velvet. A ruff or a plaited ribbon is added to the wrist edge. Crêpe, China silk, or surah are most effective for the puff, but any preferred materials may be used for the sleeve and facings.

October 1887 *Delineator*

The half-flowing sleeve in Figure 43 is suitable for all kinds of jackets and top coats, and is handsomely lined. It fits closely at the top, where it is trimmed with a long V facing of velvet that gives the effect of a pointed epaulette. At the wrist is a deep cuff-facing of velvet that has flared ends at the inside seam. Any second material used for the garment may be arranged this way on the sleeves. Sometimes the facings are elaborately braided.

October 1887 *Delineator*

Figure 43. Decoration for jacket or coat sleeve

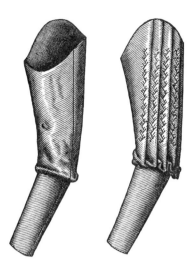

Figure 44. Plaited sleeve

This sleeve is suitable for house and street dresses, and for evening toilettes. Figure 44 shows it in brown cashmere. The foundation is a close-fitting coat sleeve with an inside and an outside seam. It is covered to the elbow with a puff that droops picturesquely, but is not voluminous. The puff is in two parts–a smooth-fitting under part and a plaited upper part–joined by seams corresponding to those of the sleeve. The upper part is laid in four deep backward-turning plaits. The plaits are held in place by a line of fancy stitching done in embroidery silk just where their underfolds come, the stitching ending some distance from the top and bottom of the puff. The lower edge of the upper part of the puff is gathered. This edge of the puff is sewed flatly on the foundation, the puff drooping over the seam and the fullness falling out. Below the puff the sleeve has the appearance of a long, close-fitting cuff and is plainly finished.

Two materials may be united in this sleeve, the softest being used for the puff. The stitching may be omitted if desired. A plain finish may be adopted, or parallel lines of braid or ribbon may be applied.

November 1887 *Delineator*

Any plain coat sleeve may be arranged as shown by Figure 45. The sleeve is shortened with a curve toward the outside of the arm. The outside material is cut away in the outline pictured, the edges being faced with plain silk. The exposed lining is then overfaced with contrasting material. A rosette bow is basted where the curved edges meet at the wrist and elbow. A lace frill finishes the wrist. This decoration is charming for tea gowns made of printed cashmere or Pompadour silk, and house and dancing dresses of all kinds.

December 1887 *Delineator*

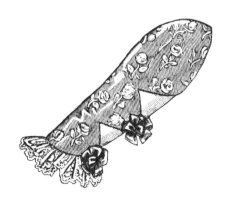

Figure 45. Fancy sleeve

Skirt Fronts and Draperies

The wool guipure laces known as yak laces are seen not merely in trimming widths, but in skirt fronts that are 1/2 or 3/4 yard deep, with a scalloped lower edge and a plain selvage at the top. These are used over fine, sheer wool materials. Sometimes this flat lace front is the color of the dress material, and sometimes in contrast with it.

Another transparent trimming is made of worsted braid of two different widths arranged in very open designs to form wide panels for each side of the skirt, or narrower lengthwise bands to be placed between plaited front gores, or else as a border across the bottom. Smaller pieces are also used to form a vest or plastron, a collar, cuffs, and large square side pockets. Large, showy, open designs are preferred. The braids used are about 1/2 inch wide in the center of the figure, while very narrow soutache outlines the design in many curling and fanciful ways.

March 7, 1885 *Harper's Bazar*

A black lace flounce 10 or 12 inches wide is arranged (without cutting) in a jabot down the left side of the front, is gathered across the bottom in front far back to the right side, and then ascends again to the belt. This trims black silk skirts handsomely, and there should be a series of jet drooping ornaments down the center of the skirt in front.

Another way of using lace is to get 2 yards of the 36-inch-wide lace flouncing that is scalloped on the lower edge. Cut this in two pieces, and gather one at the top of each side gore to hang full. Then catch it up to the center about half its depth with a ribbon rosette, disclosing the silk beneath. The front gore of the skirt should be of the silk in lengthwise plaits.

April 10, 1886 *Harper's Bazar*

French lace shawls are very generally used for tabliers. A costume of black silk or satin is very smart when a shawl is so arranged upon it, especially if the owner thereof is able to arrange a quantity of French lace on the bodice and among the drapery.

July 1886 *Delineator*

On many costumes, sashes are made to form another drapery above that which is already arranged. For this purpose moiré, surah, Roman-striped, and satin ribbons are used, the width being about that of silk. They look very pretty over thin materials. They are not arranged around the waist unless a tablier is desired; in which case the sash needs to be very long and to be cut, for the tablier is regularly draped and securely fastened. If a band is desired, a narrow ribbon does duty, and the sash itself is arranged in long loops and ends over the tournure. On some grenadine dresses, black moiré sashes are made to form half of the back drapery, the other half being of the material.

August 1886 *Delineator*

Ribbons are not only used as trimmings, but to form absolute parts of dresses. Some evening toilettes are composed entirely of ribbons and lace. Those who can wear stripes to advantage, may have over a silk or satin skirt a tablier formed of lace and ribbon. A broad ribbon sash will impart the bouffant effect desired at the back.

July 1887 *Delineator*

Figure 1. Trimmed skirt front

Although very effective and apparently elaborate, the trimmings in Figure 1 are quite simple to arrange. Plain and brocaded materials are united, and fur and cord ornaments contribute to the beauty of the mode. The foot trimming is a narrow knife-plaiting, which is continued entirely about the skirt. The right side gore and the adjoining half of the front gore are overlaid by a plain brocade drapery, which is nearly as deep as the foundation, merely disclosing the foot plaiting. The lower and front edges of this drapery are bordered with fur about 2 1/2 inches wide. From beneath the front edge of the drapery pass knife-plaitings of plain material. These plaitings cover the left half of the front gore and the left side gore nearly to the top, the skirt above the plaitings being smoothly faced with the brocade. Cord ornaments, which may be either purchased ready for application or made up, are applied at intervals across the lengthwise band of fur.

January 1884 *Delineator*

The long drapery represented by Figure 2 is composed of straight breadths sewed together and laid in clusters of four side-plaits, with a broad plain space between every two clusters. The lower edge is turned under for a wide hem. When the drapery is arranged on the skirt, the lower edges fall evenly, the top of the drapery coming some distance from the top of the skirt. The plain spaces are overlaid with wide lace, which is sewed at its selvage beneath the folds of the adjoining plaits and is also basted in place at its scallops.

May 1884 *Delineator*

Figure 2. Skirt front with lace and plaiting

Velvet and silk, silk and wool, or wool and velvet, combine tastefully as shown by Figure 3. The foot trimming is a narrow box-plaiting–always of the darker or heavier material–that is set beneath the lower edge of the skirt. Above this, on the front, is applied a broad, bias fold also of the darker material. Overhanging the fold is a fringe of loops formed of double strips of the lighter material, the edges of each strip being run together to bring the seams on the inside. These loops are in two lengths, the shorter ones being only a little more than half of the length of the longer ones. Their positions alternate regularly. Their tops are concealed by the lower edge of a fold that is overhung by a similar set of loops, the arrangement being repeated until the entire front is covered. The space above the upper row of loops is faced with the darker material.

July 1884 *Delineator*

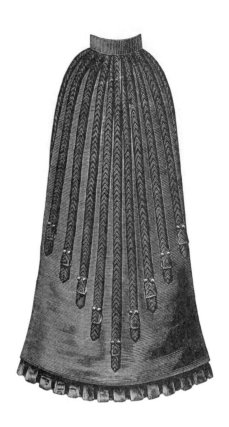

Figure 4. Braid decoration for skirt front

The style of decoration in Figure 4 is adapted to tailor costumes and is especially effective on cloths, camel's hairs, etc. The braid may be from 1 to 2 inches wide, and tiny buttons are added as accessories. The center band of braid is placed directly on the center front of the skirt and extends nearly to the lower edge, its lower end being folded under to form a point and a short loop. Two little buttons apparently hold the loop in place. The other bands of braid are arranged in the same manner on each side of the center one, their lengths being regularly decreased toward the sides and their positions arranged to leave spaces between them. The foot trimming is a narrow box-plaiting set beneath the edge of the skirt.

July 1884 *Delineator*

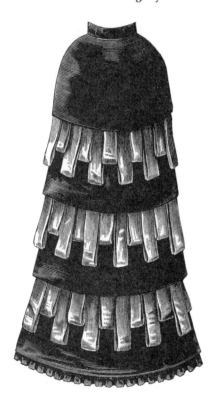

Figure 3. Trimming for skirt front

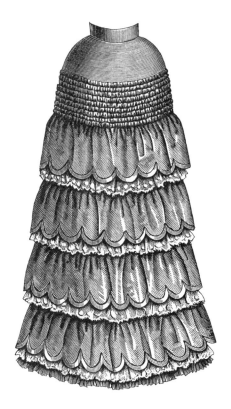

Figure 5. Skirt front trimmed with flounce

Figure 6 shows a flounce of Oriental lace, arranged to fall over a skirt of satin surah trimmed with a knife-plaiting of the same. The flounce goes all the way around the skirt. With this style, a round bodice and a sash worn in baby fashion are much liked. Sometimes the flounce is arranged to extend only to the side-back seams, and the extra length is arranged in pannier fashion about the hips.

August 1884 *Delineator*

Mull, lawn, muslin, thin silks, and all materials that require to be made up with full trimmings in order to look their best, develop beautifully as shown by Figure 5, with lace of any kind for the extraneous trimming. The foot plaiting extends entirely about the skirt, and so may the other trimmings, to any depth suggested by the arrangement of the drapery. The ruffles may be cut bias or straight, as preferred. With the exception of the upper one, they are uniform in width. They are cut in scallops and bound with the material; the lower edge of each ruffle is underlaid with lace. They are each shirred at the upper edge. The upper ruffle is cut about twice the width of the others and shirred at intervals of about 1/2 inch for about half its length from the top, and sewed in place through each line of shirring. When the hip drapery is deep enough to permit of it, the upper ruffle may be cut the same width as the others and shirred but once or twice.

July 1884 *Delineator*

Figure 6. Lace flounce for skirt

Figure 7 shows a skirt front trimmed with two deep flounces of accordion-plaiting. The lower one falls even with the lower edge and is overlapped by the upper one. The upper flounce extends to within a few inches of the belt and is finished at the top with a narrow band.

August 1884 *Delineator*

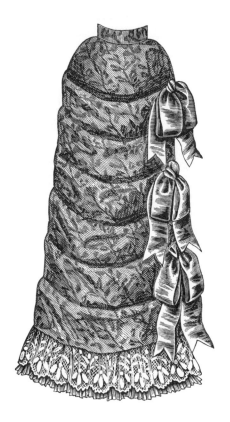

Figure 8. Draped skirt front

Both thick and thin materials drape beautifully as in Figure 8, and the fashion is much admired for skirts that are to have plain or plaited panel side draperies. A section much longer than the skirt front itself is cut out and laid in plaits as illustrated, its side edges being sewed in with the side-front seams. Darts or a couple of plaits may adjust the top. Lace, fringe, embroidery, or any appropriate trimming may border the lower edge. Three graduated ribbon bows, with notched ends, are fastened down the left side. The foot trimming may be a double ruffle, a knife-plaiting, etc.

August 1884 *Delineator*

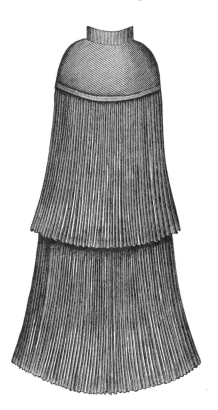

Figure 7. Skirt trimmed with accordion-plaiting

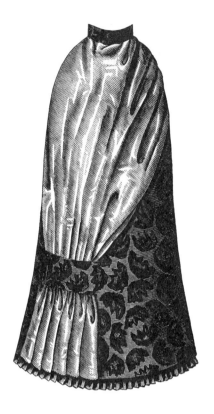

Figure 9. Drapery for skirt front

This trimming for the front and side of a skirt accords with all kinds of rich materials. Figure 10 shows how two materials may be united. The right side-front seam is left open for about two-thirds of its distance from the bottom. To the edges of the opening is sewed a section of plain material about half as wide as a breadth of silk. Its top is gathered into the smallest possible space, and its lower edge is finished with the rest of the skirt. This section is covered with overlapping lace ruffles. The lower ruffle falls over a narrow foot plaiting, which passes entirely about the skirt and is surmounted by a similar plaiting on all of the other parts. This second plaiting overlaps the lower one for nearly its full depth and gives a very full effect. A heavy jetted cord borders the lower edges of the gores above the foot trimming. One band of wide passementerie, or two or three narrower bands, are brought diagonally from high on the left hip to a point low enough on the right to conceal the top of the lace-trimmed part.

December 1884 *Delineator*

A straight breadth forms this drapery. Its top is adjusted on the skirt as illustrated by Figure 9, and its side edges are shirred and sewed into the skirt seams to a little below the hips. Two crosswise slashes are made in the front gore of the skirt, on the right of the center and about a third of the distance from the bottom. The narrow, strap-like division left between the slashes is lined. The drapery is shirred crosswise to draw its fullness into a width corresponding to the slashes, through which it is slipped, the strap concealing the shirring. Below the shirring, the fullness is drawn into side-plaits, which are crossed in their folds and fall even with the skirt. Beneath the latter is set a little foot plaiting. The drapery and skirt may be of the same material, instead of contrasting as shown here. When a contrasting material is used for the drapery, it is usually employed for the foot plaiting as well.

September 1884 *Delineator*

Figure 10. Skirt decoration for rich materials

The trimming in Figure 11 is much admired for dressy dinner and evening toilettes. The narrow side-plaiting bordering the entire lower edge of the skirt is of the dress material. Overhanging it is a deep velvet flounce, which may extend across the back or terminate at the sides. Two broad bands of velvet start from the right side-back seam and pass diagonally downward to a little beyond the center of the front, where each one is turned to form an angle and carried with an upward inclination to the left side-back seam. The upper band commences just below the hip, and the other one considerably lower down. Beneath the lower edge of each band is set a full flounce of cream Fedora lace. Of course, any preferred kind of lace may be selected, and the velvet may be either dark or vivid in color.

February 1885 *Delineator*

Figure 12. Braid decoration for drapery and skirt

Figure 11. Skirt trimming for dressy toilette

A front drapery of the style illustrated by Figure 12 may be easily applied to a round skirt. In doing so without a pattern, enough fullness must be introduced by means of the upward-turning plaits at the sides to produce the gracefully cross-wrinkled effect. On the lower edge is arranged a decoration composed of silk braid and tinsel braid. The latter is very narrow; if desired, soutache may be substituted. Three bands of silk braid follow the outline of the lower edge, spaces about equal to their width being allowed between them. In these spaces the narrow braid is arranged in a fine scroll design.

The bottom of the skirt is finished in tailor fashion to fall over a narrow under plaiting. An arrangement of silk braid simulates pointed straps extending perpendicularly from the lower edge at a uniform depth. One side of each strap is stitched close to the adjoining side of the next one, and each strap encloses a scroll of the tinsel braid.

February 1885 *Delineator*

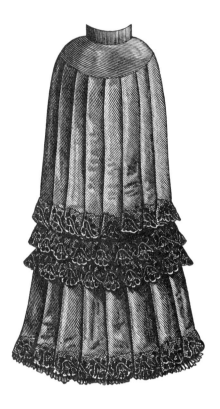

Figure 13. Plaited skirt decoration

The decoration in Figure 13 may be carried about the front and sides of a skirt, or limited to the front. The tiny knife-plaited foot trimming is continued entirely about the lower edge, and the side-plaiting above it is often duplicated on the back. The deeper plaiting is bordered at its lower edge with Spanish lace, and above it on the gores are two ruffles of similar lace. The upper plaiting is also bordered with lace.

April 1885 *Delineator*

These folds are shown developed in brocade on a skirt of plain material. (See Figure 14.) Their shape is easily obtained by experimenting with paper or lining material before cutting the brocade. A side-plaiting of plain satin forms the foot trimming.

May 1885 *Delineator*

Figure 14. Drapery for skirt front

 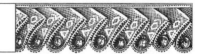

Flowered sateens or cotton crêpes are effectively arranged as in Figure 15 on skirts of plain material, and India foulards and silks associate stylishly with plain satin and velvet. The drapery is laid in shallow upward-turning plaits on the right side-back seam of the skirt, into which it is sewed. It is slanted off forward from the left hip to the lower edge, giving a pointed effect above the bottom of the skirt. Wide lace is arranged in a full jabot down the left side edge and carried in a ruffle across the bottom. The foot trimming for the entire skirt is a narrow side-plaiting set beneath the lower edge. Embroidery, fringe, etc., may take the place of lace.

May 1885 *Delineator*

Figure 16. Skirt front with appliqués

The plaiting that forms the foot trimming for this skirt extends well up under the tabs into which the lower part is cut. (See Figure 16.) The tabs are lined. Velvet with a close, thick pile is the material chosen for the moons and crescents scattered on the front. If the material has a tendency to fray, it is advisable to go over the back of it with a thin coating of mucilage or gum Arabic before cutting it. Unless the shape is stamped by one who thoroughly understands the process, it is best to cut each moon and crescent separately. After being placed in the positions represented, they are outlined with gold or silver tinsel and appliquéd in place. The appliqués may ornament the front and sides, or only the front. The short tablier drapery extends to the side-back seams and is much wrinkled by plaits folded in its sides.

June 1885 *Delineator*

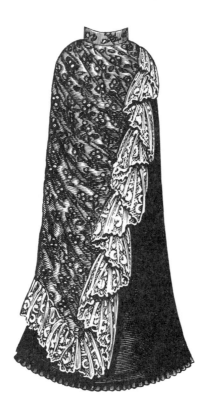

Figure 15. Drapery for skirt front

Figure 17. Skirt with lace drapery

Ladies in mourning will appreciate the suitability of this decoration for the white cotton dresses worn in the house during warm weather. (See Figure 18.) Each flounce is quite deeply hemmed and has two wide tucks above the hem. Threads are drawn, and both hem and tucks are hem-stitched instead of being sewed in the ordinary manner. Such an arrangement is usually carried across the front and side gores, and also across the back breadth, if desired. The upper flounce is omitted if the drapery is very deep.

July 1885 *Delineator*

The effect of this cream Spanish lace drapery over silk or nice wool material is very attractive. (See Figure 17.) The lace flounce that forms the foot trimming for the skirt is protected by an under ruffle of silk, which keeps it from wearing against the boots. The drapery is sewed on one side into the left side-back seam of the skirt, where several shallow, upward-turning plaits are laid in the drapery. Its opposite side is draped very high over the right hip by deeper plaits. The lower edge is bordered with a lace ruffle.

June 1885 *Delineator*

Figure 18. Skirt with drawn-work flounces

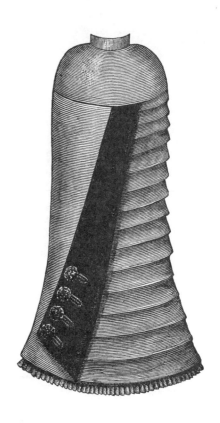

Figure 20. Skirt drapery

Deep flounce embroidery is a favorite trimming for skirts of white and colored cottons. It may be obtained in all widths, and in both white and colored embroideries. Figure 19 shows a favorite arrangement, which may be developed on the front and side gores or carried entirely about the skirt. Of course, the plaiting that forms the foot trimming extends all around the skirt.

July 1885 *Delineator*

The drapery on the right side of the skirt in Figure 20 is applied on the foundation in plain panel form. It overhangs the foot trimming, which is a narrow side-plaiting. Its top is within a short distance of the belt, and its front edge is cut away diagonally with a slight backward inclination. To the front edge is sewed a graduated revers of velvet, on the lower part of which are placed four large buttons and simulated button-holes. Starting from beneath the revers and extending to the side-back seam is a tucked drapery, which is even at its upper and lower edges and has its tucks graduated narrower toward the top.

October 1885 *Delineator*

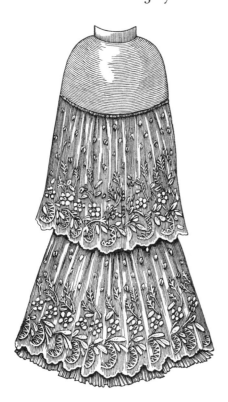

Figure 19. Skirt with embroidered flounces

Figure 21. Skirt front with applied stripes

For the skirt front in Figure 21, the stripes may be of either velvet or plush ribbon. The lowest stripe is wider than the others, which are arranged as represented.

December 1885 *Delineator*

The flounce in Figure 22 consists of a suit material having stripes of a contrasting color or texture, or simulated by the application of plush or velvet ribbon. The stripes are arranged to be crosswise, with breadths joined together if necessary to produce the requisite dimensions. The fullness is but scanty, and the flounce is usually discontinued at the side-back seams. It is gathered and sewed in place at the top, then is turned down over its own seam. The lower edge overhangs a narrow side-plaiting, which forms the foot trimming for the entire skirt.

January 1886 *Delineator*

Figure 22. Striped skirt flounce

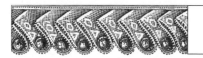 

The side-plaiting that finishes the bottom of this skirt is usually carried all the way around, but it may be terminated at the side-back seams. (See Figure 23.) Five bands of Oriental lace flouncing are arranged to extend from the left side across the side gore and far enough on the front gore to form a diagonal line. In applying the lace, only enough fullness is allowed to produce an easy and graceful effect. The drapery is raised slightly by plaits on the right side. Its front edge is turned back in a revers, the reversed part being faced with contrasting material. A facing of the material crosses the gores above the drapery and upper flounce. Hamburg or chambray embroidery may take the place of the lace.

June 1886 *Delineator*

Figure 24. Trimming for sateen skirt

Figure 24 shows a fashionable trimming for a sateen skirt. A tiny knife-plaiting forms the foot trimming. The lace net fan is laid in three side-plaits, and set between the flat panel draperies on the left side of the center. Extending diagonally from beneath the front edge of the left side panel are three velvet straps with pointed ends, which cross the fan and fasten on the opposite panel under buttons. The overhanging drapery is very slightly draped on the right side, and on the left is lifted high over the hip by overlapping, upward-turning plaits. Its edge is bordered with a lace frill.

July 1886 *Delineator*

Figure 23. Skirt drapery and trimming

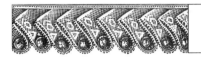 

Figure 25. Skirt drapery and trimming

Figure 25 shows a charming way of combining plain and figured challises, nun's veilings, sateens, etc., and it develops well in both dark and light materials. The foot trimming on the skirt is a narrow knife-plaiting. On the gores it is overhung by a deep side-plaiting, which is of plain material and bordered with lace. The draperies are of figured material and consist of three sections, which cross each other as illustrated. All three are draped by plaits in their back edges, and the lower two have plaits in their front edges. All of them are bordered with lace.

July 1886 *Delineator*

Figure 26 shows a charming arrangement for plain and foulard silks, or plain and figured sateens. The drapery is in tablier shape, with a deep slash on the right side of the center. Plaits in the sides and in the edges of this slash give a soft cross-wrinkled effect, aided by a bunch of ribbon loops and ends fastened at the top of the slash.

The trimming at the bottom of the skirt may go all the way around, or it may be limited to the gores. The foot trimming is a fine knife-plaiting. Overhanging this is a ruffle of pressed Italian lace, from which a heading of narrow lace turns upward. Narrow lace also borders the bottom of the drapery. Of course, any kind of lace may be chosen, and the ribbon may be of velvet, grosgrain, picot-edged moiré, or plain satin.

July 1886 *Delineator*

Figure 26. Skirt drapery and trimming

The drapery in Figure 27 is of very wide Spanish guipure lace flouncing. It is adjusted to the top of the front and side gores, enough fullness being allowed to permit of drawing it up from the center of the lower edge, and also higher up, a knot of ribbon being fastened over each draping. The foot trimming is a narrow knife-plaiting of the dress material. Over this falls a lace flounce, which is overhung by the drapery.

August 1886 *Delineator*

Figure 28. Drapery for kilt skirt

The arrangement of buttons and simulated button-holes in Figure 28 is appropriate for either a kilt skirt or one having a kilted drapery. Sometimes the decorations are arranged on each alternating plait on the front and sides.

September 1886 *Delineator*

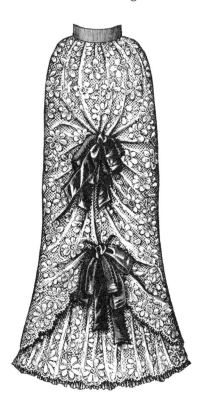

Figure 27. Lace drapery and trimming

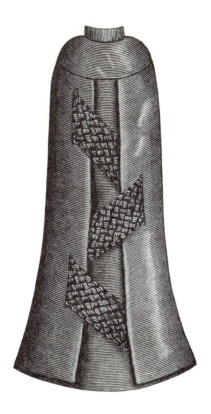

Figure 29. Drapery for tailor skirt

It is wise to experiment with paper before cutting the material, folding the plaits and cutting the lower edge in the curved outline shown by Figure 30. The position of the slashes is then determined. Their edges, and the bottom of the drapery, are underfaced before the plaits are folded in the material. The braid is sewed in place only at the top of the drapery, and its lower ends are frayed out and knotted to form tassel fringe. This drapery may extend from one side of the skirt to the other, or be carried from the right side-back to the left side-front. The tiny foot plaiting that underlies the lower edge of the skirt passes entirely around it.

November 1886 *Delineator*

The panel draperies are sewed into the side-back skirt seams, and their front edges are separated by a space that widens gradually toward the bottom of the skirt. (See Figure 29.) Near the top of the right side panel is a lengthwise slash, and not far from the bottom is another slash. In the other panel, at a point halfway between these two slashes, is still another slash. Through these openings is slipped a band of wide braid, which has its lower end fastened beneath the left side panel.

September 1886 *Delineator*

Figure 30. Skirt drapery with braid

The plaiting visible at the lower edge of the skirt front may be carried entirely around the skirt, or it may be discontinued at the side-back seams. (See Figure 31.) The three sections above it are started on the right side-front seam and carried to the left side-back seam. They are narrowed off toward their left ends. They are cut into pointed tabs, which are lined with silk and interlined with crinoline. A deep lace flounce is set beneath each row of tabs and allowed to fall a little below. The combination of black material and white lace is very fashionable, especially when the material is velvet; but black lace with silk or velvet is equally elegant.

December 1886 *Delineator*

Figure 32. Decoration for tailor skirt

Figure 32 shows a stylish method of decorating either a plaid or a plain skirt. Deep slashes beginning at the lower edge are made at the front and sides. Plaited fans are inserted in these slashes, there being four plaits in each fan and all turning toward the center. A triangular ornament is worked with silk twist at the top of each fan. The bottom of the foundation skirt is bound with leather.

January 1887 *Delineator*

Figure 31. Trimmed skirt front

 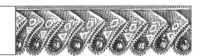

Figure 33. Decoration for tailor skirt

Figure 34 shows a *recherché* mode of disposing bordered dress material to form a front drapery. Plaits are laid in the side edges to produce the cross-wrinkled effect. Halfway between the center and the left side, the drapery is lifted and basted to the skirt, without disturbing the pattern of the embroidery.

May 1887 *Delineator*

Figure 33 shows a fashionable drapery for a tailor skirt, whether the braid is added or not. The plaits in the lower drapery are not very deeply folded, although they are quite broad. They are held in place by tapes basted to them underneath. The braiding pattern is most effective if the braid is not more than 3/8 inch wide, but very narrow soutache is not necessary. The short tablier is lifted high on the left hip by four upward-turning plaits. On the right side it has the same number of plaits folded with spaces between them.

February 1887 *Delineator*

Figure 34. Drapery using bordered material

The braid shown by Figure 35 is soutache, with gold or silver thread woven in herring-bone stitch along its center. The braid may be of the same color as the skirt or a contrasting color. Above the hem of the skirt, it is disposed in band-like fashion and interlaced. The drapery is short and much wrinkled across the front and right hip. On the left side it falls in jabot folds to the bottom, the folds revealing a velvet facing.

October 1887 *Delineator*

Figure 35. Skirt decoration and drapery

Ruffles, Flounces, Etc.

Lace flounces are the only flounces on elaborate grenadine dresses, and when used they are in such numbers that they are more like a combination material than a trimming. Wide lace flounces are arranged in lengthwise curves, only slightly gathered across from the hips on the right down to the bottom on the left side. Still others form lengthwise

panels, and the old fashion remains of gathering them in straight lines across the front and side gores below the drapery.

July 11, 1885 *Harper's Bazar*

Narrow ruffles on summer dresses must be gathered instead of knife-plaited. When made of thick silk or satin they are cut bias, with the hem faced up on the outside. For summer silks, such as striped satins, surahs, or figured India silks, they are made straight, are hemmed, and are quite scant. In the striped surahs the ruffles are cut lengthwise, parallel to the selvage. This has the effect of making the stripes run around the figure, contrary to the way they are used in the bodice, and perhaps the drapery also.

July 31, 1886 *Harper's Bazar*

Among the many elegant trimmings for visiting and dinner toilettes, are shaded feather bands. These bands are from 2 to 3 inches wide. They come in gray, brown, and green, shading from the lightest to the darkest hint of a color, and having a narrow edge or thread of bright red or yellow feathers along the sides.

October 30, 1886 *Harper's Bazar*

Pinked ruches in several shades of one color are in favor for the edges of undraped skirts. Sometimes they are used as plastrons, or for a single side panel.

April 1887 *Delineator*

A fancy exists for placing about the lower edge of the skirt a broad band of embroidery or lace, or gold or silver braid. The embroidery is usually of a very heavy pattern. It may be white or écru in harmony with the material to which it is applied. The gold braid is used chiefly on white, mode, and gray cloths, while silver braid is liked on black and dark green. The braid chosen is a little wider than soutache, and a Grecian design about 3 inches deep is usually traced out. Cotton dresses have embroidery applied in a similar way, and it is selected with a thought of the predominating color.

August 1887 *Delineator*

The trimming in Figure 1 is effective as a heading to other skirt trimmings. Straight strips, which may be from 5 to 9 inches deep, are joined together, and the top and bottom are turned in for a neat finish. Wide box-plaits are then folded with spaces of their own width between them. A band of contrasting material, in this case velvet folded over crinoline, is passed over the plain spaces and through slashes made beneath the folds of the plaits. Instead of having slashes cut in the plaits, the velvet may be cut in short strips, the ends of which can be concealed beneath the folds of the plaits.

January 1884 *Delineator*

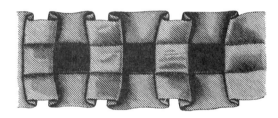

Figure 1. Plaited heading

The mode in Figure 2 is especially appropriate for combinations of plain and figured sateen. The skirt or drapery is cut in long tabs that are straight on one edge and curved on the other. These tabs are bordered with lace and underlaid with a ruffle of contrasting material, which falls a little below them. If for a drapery, the ruffle may be omitted.

May 1884 *Delineator*

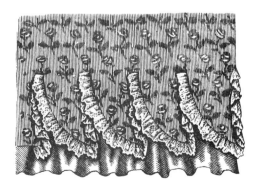

Figure 2. Trimming for skirt or long drapery

The trimming in Figure 3 is effective for lawn, mull, Swiss muslin, silks, satins, and similar materials. The band is made of triangular sections of the material tucked uniformly and joined together as represented. It is edged on both sides with a narrow knife-plaiting of the material, and forms a most decorative heading to a deep knife-plaiting, the latter forming the foot trimming. Laces or embroideries, or ruffles of the material, may be used instead of the plaitings. The tucks may be made in clusters, or in clusters with insertion between them.

June 1884 *Delineator*

Figure 3. Tucked skirt trimming

Skirts of mull, lawn, sateen, summer silks, or any seasonable material may be trimmed as shown by Figure 4. A narrow side-plaiting forms the foot trimming. Overhanging this is a gathered ruffle of medium depth, bordered with narrow lace at its lower edge. The single line of shirring in the top of the ruffle is concealed by a ruffle of wide lace. Above this is another narrow plaiting. This is in turn surmounted by a lace-bordered ruffle overhung by a ruffle of lace. A neat finish is obtained by sewing the topmost lace ruffle in place in such a way that it may be turned down over its own seam.

July 1884 *Delineator*

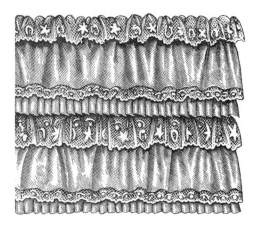

Figure 4. Skirt trimming for summer dress

The decoration in Figure 5 is suitable for skirts of any summer material, and especially those of mull, grenadine, and similar materials. The puff is cut straight and may be from 5 to 11 inches deep. It is shirred and sewed in place at its lower edge. Then it is turned up over its own seam and its top turned in for a finish, four lines of shirring being made about 1/2 inch apart in the upper part. The upper shirring is far enough from the upper edge to leave a ruffled heading. A standing lace frill is adjusted beneath the heading, and the puff is sewed in place through each line of the cluster of shirrings. A lace frill is also sewed beneath the lower edge of the puff, to form a foot trimming. Sometimes a tiny plaiting underlies the lace for protection.

July 1884 *Delineator*

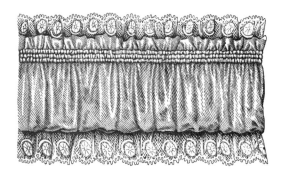

Figure 5. Lace-trimmed puff

For the trimming in Figure 6, the foot plaiting is formed in the usual way, its lower edge being hemmed or a lining added throughout, as preferred. It is deep enough to extend well up beneath the points of the upper decoration. The latter is of plaid material. It is cut in saw-tooth points with spaces between them and then laid in plaits, the points being faced with contrasting material. The diagram shows the shape of the pointed section before the plaits are laid. The Xs and Os indicate the positions of the folds, the Xs being brought over to meet the Os. Those who are not satisfied as to their ability to duplicate this arrangement had best experiment with paper until they are assured.

July 1884 *Delineator*

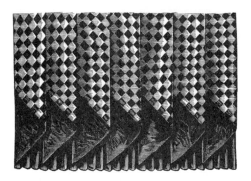

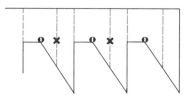

Figure 6. Skirt trimming

For the trimming in Figure 7, the foot plaiting is formed in the usual way, and is deep enough to extend well up beneath the shortest folds of the outer or fancy plaiting. The latter is easily reproduced by first laying in paper a couple of quadruple box-plaits, with narrow spaces between them, and then cutting them into the outlines depicted. Then the folds may be smoothed out and the paper used for shaping the material. This plaiting should always be lined or underfaced at its lower edge, as

its outlines are too curved to permit of hemming. The top is turned in for a finish, and the plaiting is sewed to the skirt far enough from the fold to leave a heading.

July 1884 *Delineator*

Figure 7. Combination plaiting for skirt trimming

Figure 8 shows a simple trimming for the skirt of a walking or traveling costume. It is quite economical, as it requires but little material. Two kinds are united, the plaid material being cut in sections wide enough to form single box-plaits, which may be 4 or 5 inches wide and 10 or 12 inches long. The lower edges are hemmed and the tops turned in. Then the plaits are folded and slip-stitched at regular intervals on a straight section of material. The latter is similarly finished at its top and bottom, and is of equal length with the plaits.

July 1884 *Delineator*

Figure 9 shows a charming decoration for skirts or draperies in thin silks, mulls, etc. A foot trimming is, of course, added to the foundation skirt. Shirrings are made perpendicularly at intervals of 4 or 5 inches in the edges, and are drawn up to form the series of festoons illustrated. A lace ruffle is sewed underneath.

August 1884 *Delineator*

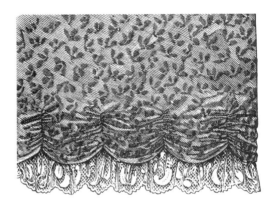

Figure 9. Shirred finish for skirt or drapery

Ruffles arranged as in Figure 10 may be from 5 to 11 inches deep. The lace on the lower edge is turned up flatly to the outside and sewed in place at its lower edge. The lace that forms the heading to the upper ruffle is gathered a little, turned up over its own seam, and caught in place here and there.

September 1884 *Delineator*

Figure 8. Trimming for walking or traveling skirt

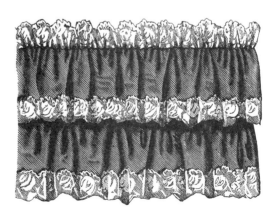

Figure 10. Lace-trimmed ruffles for skirt

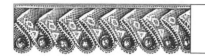 

Figure 11 shows an effective finish for a skirt of velvet and silk, velvet and wool, or one composed of any two materials. The basis is a side-plaiting about 9 inches deep of material contrasting with the dress material. This plaiting is broken into groups of six plaits, each by sections of the skirt material inserted at regular intervals and arranged in double box-plaits. The inserted sections are enough deeper than the others to leave them about 2 inches higher at the top. Half of this excess depth is turned in for a finish, while the remainder forms a heading for the box-plait. The plaiting is adjusted on the foundation or skirt proper.

The outer part is cut in tabs, which taper from a broad oval outline to a point at the lower extremity. A space corresponding in width to the double box-plaits is allowed between every two tabs. The heading of the box-plait is adjusted on this space. The tabs fall over the groups of side-plaits. Of course, the tabs are lined.

December 1884 *Delineator*

Figure 11. Skirt decoration

If the drapery is sufficiently long and has no plaits or gathers near its lower edge, it may be cut in the outline represented by Figure 12 and bordered with bands of contrasting material or wide braid. But when the drapery is short or much wrinkled, the outer part of the skirt is thus finished, the plaiting always being set on the foundation.

The plaiting is composed of sections that are in two widths. After they are joined together with the excess depth at their tops, the lower edge is hemmed. The deeper sections are laid in five side-plaits that overlap each other sufficiently to fall out in full fans. The shallower sections are arranged in groups of six side-plaits. Very often the fans are of contrasting material. When the plaiting is arranged on the skirt, the fans are adjusted to fill the spaces between the tabs, and the side-plaited sections come beneath the tabs. By experimenting with paper, the exact dimensions of the fans and side-plaited sections may be readily obtained.

December 1884 *Delineator*

Figure 12. Decoration for drapery or skirt

A fine knife-plaiting and a side-plaiting are united in the decoration shown by Figure 13. The knife-plaiting is about 7 inches deep, and the side-plaiting 5 inches when finished. The side-plaiting is laid in groups of five overlapping plaits, with narrow spaces between the groups. After being sewed in place so as to overhang the knife-plaiting for about two-thirds of its depth, the topmost plait in each group is caught at its lower corner even with the tops of the folds in the next group, the effect being that of a succession of fans. Sometimes the knife-plaiting is of silk or wool when the fans are of velvet.

December 1884 *Delineator*

box-plaits narrower than those above it. When the plaiting is applied to the skirt, it is sewed through the shirring and invisibly basted beneath the folds of the plaits at the top.

January 1885 *Delineator*

Figure 13. Skirt trimming

The velvet flounce in Figure 14 may be from 7 to 12 inches deep. The Oriental lace, after being sewed to the lower edge of the velvet, is turned up on the outside and caught in place smoothly but invisibly along its top. Four lines of shirring are made in the top of the flounce to form three tiny puffs. Surmounting the puffs is a satin-lined ruffle arranged to form a shell heading.

December 1884 *Delineator*

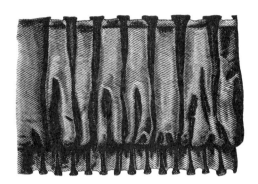

Figure 15. Plaited skirt trimming

The side-plaiting forming a part of this trimming is composed in the usual manner, its depth being regulated to suit the fancy. (See Figure 16.) Each fan is composed of a single section, for which a single breadth of silk is sufficient, the depth being a little less than that of the flounce. The top is laid in plaits, which overlap each other very closely. It is placed even with the top of the flounce, the lower corners being drawn up even with the top and fastened in place to give the fan the open effect illustrated. A bow of the same material as the fans, formed of two conventional loops and ends, is placed over the top of each. A jet buckle is placed between the loops. The fans may be lined or have their lower edges hemmed, as suggested by the material. Silk and velvet, or wool and velvet, develop handsomely in this skirt trimming.

January 1885 *Delineator*

Figure 14. Lace-trimmed flounce

The decoration in Figure 15 is composed of straight breadths of material hemmed at the lower edge and turned in quite deeply at the top for a finish. The top is laid in box-plaits of medium depth, with narrow spaces between them. A little above the lower edge a gathering is made in tuck fashion, the fullness below it being creased into

Figure 16. Skirt trimming

The flounce in Figure 17 is formed of straight or bias breadths joined together and bordered with lace at the lower edge. The top is gathered and is surmounted by a double jabot formed of two narrow, bias ruffles. Each of these is folded along its center, gathered at the edges, and sewed on. It is then basted back and forth as illustrated, the folds of the two ruffles turning in opposite directions. A band of lace is set beneath the upper ruffle to form an upright heading. A narrow knife-plaiting is applied on the skirt for a foot trimming, in addition to protecting the lower lace frill. The jabot ruffles may be lined with a contrasting color instead of being cut double.

January 1885 *Delineator*

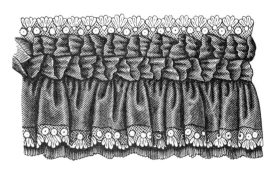

Figure 17. Skirt trimming for evening dress

Three plaitings are united in the decoration shown by Figure 18. The lower one is a narrow box-plaiting about 3 inches deep. The center one, which is 5 inches deep, is laid in double box-plaits, with very narrow spaces between the plaits. The upper one is about the same depth as the lower, and is also folded in double box-plaits. All three are finished with hems at their lower edges. The deepest is arranged to slightly overhang the lower one and is itself surmounted by the one remaining, which is lined with a contrasting color and has the upper fold of each plait drawn down and basted to disclose the lining. Usually the lower plaiting is like the lining of the upper one, and very tasteful contrasts may be developed.

January 1885 *Delineator*

Figure 18. Plaited skirt trimming

An evening dress of nun's veiling or silk and velvet looks very effective trimmed as in Figure 19. The lower two plaitings are formed in the ordinary manner and are each about 3 inches wide when finished. The next one is about 9 inches wide. It is folded in side-plaits at its top and basted in the folds of these plaits about halfway from the lower edge, the fullness below the basting falling out in ruffle fashion. Overhanging this decoration is a succession of velvet points, which are cut on a bias strip. The bias strip is lined with crinoline and hemmed on the lining at all its edges. The pointed decoration may be sewed in place along its upper edge and turned down over its own seam, and is usually overhung by the drapery.

February 1885 *Delineator*

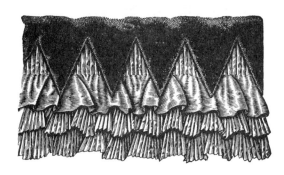

Figure 19. Trimming for evening dress

Silk is the material employed for the plaitings in Figure 20, but any material that may be associated with lace is just as suitable. When the lace is sewed in place, it is run along its selvage and turned down over its own seam, less fullness for a good effect being needed than when it is sewed flatly against the dress.

February 1885 *Delineator*

Figure 20. Dressy skirt trimming

The side-plaiting that forms the foot trimming to the trimming in Figure 21 is usually hemmed. The box-plaiting is hemmed or lined, depending on the material. On each box-plait is placed an appliqué ornament cut from velvet, button-hole stitching or chain-stitching being made all about its edges for a finish. Appliqué trimmings in various designs are very fashionable on silk and wool materials. However, silk, jet, steel, or any other kind of passementerie ornaments may be chosen instead.

April 1885 *Delineator*

Figure 21. Skirt trimming

Lace net and edging are associated with colored silk in the trimming in Figure 22, the latter forming the ruffles that fall under the lace ruffles. The lace net is arranged in puffings. After being gathered at the edges, these are sewed over the ruffles and turned up over their own seams. The top one is finished in any neat manner.

June 1885 *Delineator*

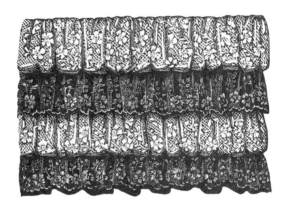

Figure 22. Skirt trimming

Any kind of lace edging and insertion may be applied on skirt plaitings as shown by Figure 23, before the plaits are laid. The material may be cut away from beneath the insertion or not, as preferred. On surah and pale-tinted nun's veilings, the effect is very attractive when the material is left underneath.

July 1885 *Delineator*

Figure 23. Trimming with lace edging and insertion

Skirts of dainty cotton materials or fancy silks are often trimmed with deep, gathered flounces enriched with velvet or satin ribbon as illustrated by Figure 24. On mull and other diaphanous materials, the effect is exquisite when there is a decided or delicate contrast in color. Little fullness is needed in a flounce thus trimmed.

July 1885 *Delineator*

Figure 24. Ribbon-trimmed flounce

The decoration in Figure 25 includes a ruffle or foot trimming of medium-wide lace overhung by a deep flounce, the latter being surmounted by a ruffle of the narrower width. Large crushed roses of a pale pink shade are placed close together in a row on the lower ruffle. Of course, any kind of flower may be chosen.

July 1885 *Delineator*

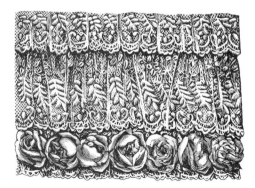

Figure 25. Trimming for evening dress skirt

The lower part of the trimming in Figure 26 consists of a side-plaiting of the dress material. Overhanging it is a flounce of Oriental lace, which is surmounted by a puffing of all-over lace net to match. The flounce is gathered and put on in the usual manner, and is caught up in festoons under appliquéd roses. Each rose has a bud and a spray of foliage attached to it. Any other floral trimming may take the place of the roses.

September 1885 *Delineator*

Figure 26. Trimming for evening dress skirt

The trimming in Figure 27 comprises bias folds of two contrasting materials, one plain and the other brocaded. The folds are of uniform width and lined with crinoline. A brocaded one comes next to the foot plaiting (which is quite narrow and is cut from the plain material), a plain fold surmounts the brocaded one, and so on. As many folds may be arranged in this way as the style of the drapery or the fancy of the wearer calls for, and any two materials may be used.

September 1885 *Delineator*

Figure 27. Skirt trimming with bias folds

356

The side-plaiting at the bottom is very closely laid and extends well up under the outside plaiting and a little below it. (See Figure 28.) Each double box-plait and the plain section adjoining are in one piece. The lower corner of the plain space is underfaced with velvet and turned up on the outside in a revers that is basted in place, disclosing the side-plaiting to quite a depth.

October 1885 *Delineator*

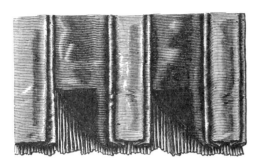

Figure 28. Skirt trimming

Figure 29 shows a kilt-plaiting with a wide band of plaid material applied to plain material. Sometimes several bands of narrow braid are applied just above the plaid material.

October 1885 *Delineator*

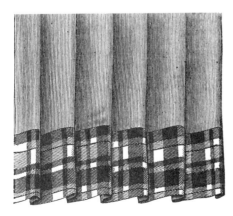

Figure 29. Skirt trimming

The box-plaiting that forms the foot trimming is of velvet, and so are the pear shapes appliquéd on the lower part of the skirt with jet or metal beads, tinsel thread, etc. (See Figure 30.) Very rich effects are produced by velvet in yellow, red, or any rich shade appliquéd on white, black, or other neutral tints. The foot plaiting of course corresponds.

October 1885 *Delineator*

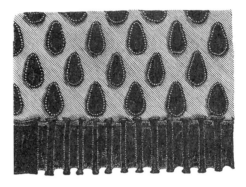

Figure 30. Skirt trimming with appliqués

The plaiting is laid in clusters of four plaits, with a medium-wide space between every two clusters, and is applied on the foundation. (See Figure 31.) The oval tabs are cut on the drapery, or if the latter is too short, on the outer part or on a separate section. The tabs are lined and arranged to fall between the clusters of plaits. Two materials are thus effectively associated, but one may be used if preferred.

November 1885 *Delineator*

Figure 31. Drapery trimming

Dresses of rich material that it is desirable to wear several seasons without re-making often have their skirts trimmed as in Figure 32. The depth of the plaiting usually depends on the style of the drapery and the height of the wearer. Nine inches is a medium very well liked, although 12 inches is sometimes preferred. The lower edge is hemmed, and the top is turned in quite deeply for a heading. Triple box-plaits are then formed with narrow spaces between them. The trimming is sewed to the skirt as far from the top as the depth of the turned-in part permits, bastings being made through the folds of the plaits to give the heading the cascade effect.

November 1885 *Delineator*

Figure 32. Plaited skirt trimming

The material that is cut in broad curves may be the drapery–if it is deep enough–or the outer part of the skirt. (See Figure 33.) The knife-plaiting that borders the curved edges is turned in at the top for a finish and hemmed narrowly at the lower edge. The side-plaiting, which it overhangs, is laid in broad folds and is deep enough to extend well up beneath the curves. This trimming may be carried all about the lower part of the skirt. Or it may be confined to the front and side gores, only the wider plaiting extending across the back. Two materials may be used if desired.

December 1885 *Delineator*

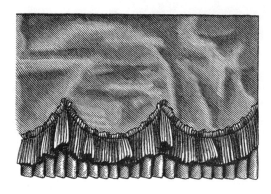

Figure 33. Skirt trimming

For the trimming in Figure 34, the brocaded material is laid in side-plaits with broad spaces between them. On each space a piece of plain material folded in a cluster of six narrower side-plaits is arranged, with the edge of the last plait in the cluster beneath the wider plait, where it is invisibly sewed. The underfold of the front plait is also slip-stitched in place. A bias piece of the plain material is applied in the form of a knot on each cluster of narrow plaits, a little less than half of the distance from the bottom.

December 1885 *Delineator*

Figure 34. Plaited skirt trimming

 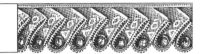

The kilt-plaits are very broad, and their depth accords with the drapery of the skirt or the fancy of the wearer. (See Figure 35.) On each plait is applied a revers ornament of velvet, which extends about two-thirds of the depth of the plait. The broadest end is even with the lower edge of the plait, and the straight edge of the revers is beneath the fold of the plait next to it. Each velvet section is lined with crinoline, and all of the edges are slip-stitched in place.

December 1885 *Delineator*

Figure 36. Skirt trimming

The flounce in Figure 37 is laid in double box-plaits, with broad spaces between them. A deep triangular piece is cut from the lower part of each space. A facing of contrasting material, which is lined with crinoline, is applied beneath the opening. The edges of the opening are slip-stitched to the facing. When white or light materials are made up, the applied pieces may be of velvet in high relief.

March 1886 *Delineator*

Figure 35. Skirt trimming

Velvet and plush, velvet and silk, or either of these materials and wool, develop well as shown by Figure 36. The dimensions of the plaited and plain velvet sections are determined by experimenting with paper. The seams are concealed by the folds of the plaits, one plait in each cluster being folded in the corresponding velvet section. The saw-tooth points that overhang the velvet sections may be cut on the bottom of the drapery, or on a separate section arranged beneath the drapery. At the top of each cluster of plaits is placed a passementerie ornament, which may be of steel, jet, or any color of beads, or of silk cord.

January 1886 *Delineator*

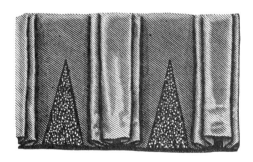

Figure 37. Skirt flounce

The decoration in Figure 38 is appropriate for any summer material. The flounces are of Fedora lace, and the lower one overhangs a knife-plaited foot trimming. Narrow picot-edged ribbon was chosen for the loops and ends, which are fastened in full clusters at intervals.

May 1886 *Delineator*

Figure 38. Skirt trimming for summer dress

For the trimming in Figure 39, the foot trimming is a finely laid knife-plaiting overhung by a wide lace flounce. The outer decoration is deep enough to partially overhang the lace. It is lined with contrasting material and laid in broad double box-plaits with spaces between, the lining being displayed by turning up the lower edge of each plait even with the top and basting it in place.

June 1886 *Delineator*

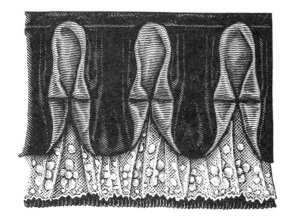

Figure 39. Dressy skirt trimming

The side-plaiting that forms the basis for the trimming in Figure 40 is finely folded and may be of any depth desired. It is attached to the skirt far enough from its top to form its own heading. On it at intervals are placed fancy plaited ornaments. These

are each formed of a single section of contrasting material that is straight across the top and at the sides, and is cut off diagonally from the sides to form a point at the center of the lower edge. This shape is easily obtained by experimenting with paper. When folded in a double box-plait underneath so that the folds turn toward the center on the outside, the effect is the same as shown by the engraving. Each ornament is placed on the side-plaiting with the tops even, and is basted far enough from its own upper edge to allow the latter to fall over as illustrated. The plaited ornaments are prevented from flying about too loosely by being invisibly basted to the skirt.

June 1886 *Delineator*

Figure 40. Skirt trimming

The trimming in Figure 41 consists of straight breadths joined together and laid in wide box-plaits with broad spaces between them. The top is turned in broadly for a heading. Each plait is narrowed some distance from the top by a scanty crosswise shirring. Other shirrings are made perpendicularly underneath the folds to produce the festooned effect between the plaits. When the material is very soft this latter effect may be made along the under folds; but if the material is heavy or thick it is necessary to slash the heading along the under folds before they are made. A double heading is formed by a band of lace set upright beneath the top of the plaiting.

June 1886 *Delineator*

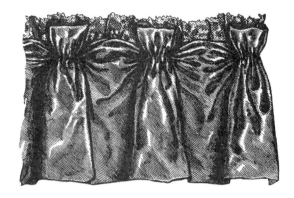

Figure 41. Skirt trimming

Any kind of lace having a heavy pattern may be applied on side-plaiting as shown by Figure 42, with good effect.

July 1886 *Delineator*

Figure 42. Skirt trimming

The trimming in Figure 43 consists of a box-plaiting, which is gathered through its center to throw the fullness of its folds into the round outlines illustrated. The gathering is concealed by a band of passementerie. The plaiting may be of any width admired. It should be folded under sufficiently on each side to ensure a neat finish.

July 1886 *Delineator*

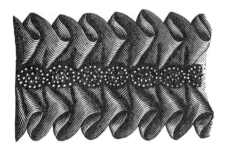

Figure 43. Skirt trimming

The plaiting, and the buttons that trim it, are arranged as shown by Figure 44. The depth of the plaiting may vary to suit the fancy, and the buttons may give way to rosary or glass beads.

August 1886 *Delineator*

Figure 44. Skirt trimming

The broad bands that overlie the plaiting are of velvet ribbon. (See Figure 45.) The lower band is applied to cross the plain spaces and all of the folds of the plaits, while the upper band crosses only the outer folds and the spaces.

September 1886 *Delineator*

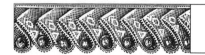

Figure 45. Skirt trimming

Two kinds of plaiting are associated in the trimming in Figure 46. The velvet squares are lined with crinoline and are slip-stitched in place. The velvet may be black, garnet, golden brown, or any color that harmonizes with neutral tints; or it may be the same color as the dress material.

September 1886 *Delineator*

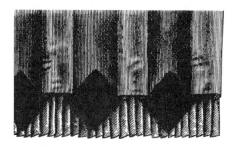

Figure 46. Skirt trimming

Each strip of velvet decorating the plaiting is cut long enough to extend almost to the lower edge after the end is folded in two short loops, and is sewed in place along both sides. (See Figure 47.) Moiré ribbon is often arranged in this way on light dress materials for evening wear.

November 1886 *Delineator*

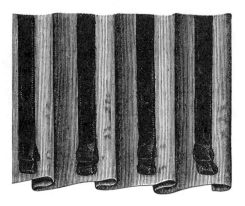

Figure 47. Skirt trimming

On evening dresses, the trimming in Figure 48 may take the place of a front drapery if sufficiently wide lace flouncing is employed. Flounces of medium width enriched in this way make handsome trimmings. The lace is gathered rather full at its top. Near its lower edge, three rows of satin ribbon about 1 or 1 1/2 inches wide are run through slashes made in it in festoon outline. Ribbon rosettes are placed over the angles formed by the two upper rows.

November 1886 *Delineator*

Figure 48. Trimming for evening dress skirt

The trimming in Figure 49 may be developed in plush, velvet, or moiré-striped silk or wool material. Along each side of the plain stripe, a slash extending some distance from the lower edge is made. The ends of the plain stripes are then pointed and underfaced with contrasting material of any harmonizing shade or texture. They are then turned up, and basted in place through their points. The spaces thus left are filled in by clusters of box-plaits of the contrasting material, there being four box-plaits in each cluster.

November 1886 *Delineator*

Figure 49. Skirt trimming

The foundation of the trimming in Figure 50 is a box-plaiting, with broad spaces between the plaits. The spaces are deeply faced with striped material. Above the facings the edges of the plaits are ornamented with buttons, which apparently hold these edges in place. Striped materials showing intermixtures of plush or velvet with wool in monotone or in relief, are readily obtained in colors matching all kinds of plain suit materials, and a small quantity presents a very effective appearance.

January 1887 *Delineator*

Figure 50. Skirt trimming

The trimming in Figure 51 is suitable for the skirt of a street toilette. The space between the rows of buttons may be from 8 to 12 inches. When the width is decided on, slashes extending 6 to 9 inches from the lower edge are made, and to their edges are sewed little plaited fans of the skirt material. A shallow plait is folded above each slash, which takes up as much of the width as has been used for seams in sewing in the fans. On each plait, a row of wool buttons in ball shape is placed. The fans should be well pressed.

The depth of this decoration depends on the style of the drapery above it. Sometimes a single fan and a row of buttons is carried as far up the skirt as is revealed by the drapery, this arrangement being very effective on each side.

January 1887 *Delineator*

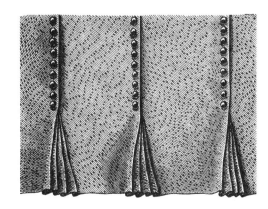

Figure 51. Trimming for skirt of street toilette

Figure 52 shows a deep, box-plaited flounce with broad spaces between the plaits. On each space is adjusted a straight section of the material that is gathered sufficiently at its edges to present a draped effect, its seam being concealed by the folds of the plaits. Sometimes the draped parts are in contrast to the plaits.

February 1887 Delineator

Figure 52. Skirt trimming

The lace flouncing in Figure 53 is gathered with only enough fullness to give an easy effect (more would tend to obscure the pattern). It is placed far enough from the bottom of the skirt to display a narrow foot plaiting. At intervals along its top, ribbons are arranged in four graduated loops, the lowest loop in each cluster falling considerably below the center of the flounce. The effect is gay or stately, according to the colors chosen.

February 1887 Delineator

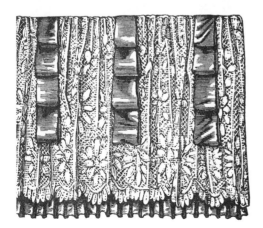

Figure 53. Skirt flounce

The outlines for the plaiting are obtained by folding a piece of paper in ordinary side-plaits with rather wide spaces between them, and then curving the spaces as shown by Figure 54. The straight edges are finished. The curved edges are ornamented with velvet facings, which extend to the folds of the plaits.

February 1887 Delineator

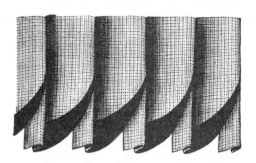

Figure 54. Skirt trimming

Both materials are mounted on a thin crinoline foundation, which is cut the depth the trimming is to be when done. (See Figure 55.) The exact outline of the upper one is obtained by making a slash beneath each plait, and turning the lower edge up underneath as illustrated. Of course, a little material would be saved by cutting each strip into the proper shape before it is applied to the crinoline. However, a much greater amount of labor is involved, and if the material is apt to fray the result may not be as good.

March 1887 Delineator

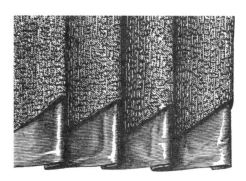

Figure 55. Skirt trimming

The skirt trimming in Figure 56 should extend up under the drapery. The box-plaits are very broad and arranged about their width apart. Between the plaits is a drapery-like disposal of the material. This is formed of a separate section, which is shaped in a deep point at the lower edge and laid in two plaits that turn inward and touch at the top, the pointed outline causing the folds to form a jabot effect at the sides. The point is underfaced with the material, the underfacing showing in the jabot folds. These sections, or the underfacing only, may be made of a contrasting material.

April 1887 *Delineator*

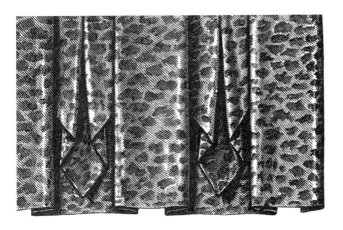

Figure 56. Skirt trimming

Cloths and flannels are most suitable for the style of plaiting in Figure 57, as the edges do not fray easily. The plaiting is pinked at both edges. The lower edge shows a larger scallop than the upper edge, and is shaped to be slightly shorter at the center of the plaits. The plaits are of medium width, with narrow spaces between them. The trimming is stitched on the skirt so as to form a narrow heading.

April 1887 *Delineator*

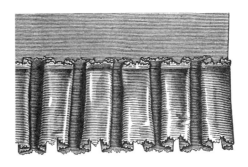

Figure 57. Pinked skirt trimming

The decoration in Figure 58 is formed of straight strips of the material. The lower three strips are each about a quarter of the depth of the upper row. All of the lower edges are piped or bound with braid, velvet, or contrasting dress material. A line of stitching is made about 1 inch from the lower edges. The plaitings are arranged with one overhanging the top of the one below it, the deepest plaiting coming at the top. Two materials may be associated in this decoration, but the effect is quite as good when one material is used throughout, except for the pipings.

May 1887 *Delineator*

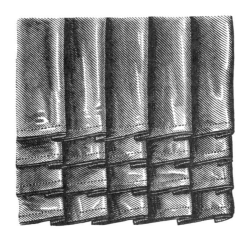

Figure 58. Skirt decoration

For the trimming in Figure 59, it is best to calculate the depth the plaiting is to be when finished and allow two-thirds of this for the deeper part, the remainder being equally divided between the two narrower sections. Each section is bound or piped with braid, velvet, etc., at its lower edge. Then the sections are lapped and stitched flatly before the plaits are laid. Mixed and striped materials arranged in this way have plain pipings.

May 1887 *Delineator*

Figure 60. Skirt trimming

For the trimming in Figure 61, the plaits are arranged in groups of three. The top and bottom of the plaiting are frayed–the bottom more deeply than the top–to form a fringe finish. The material is cut straight if it is firm enough to look well when frayed straight. Otherwise it is cut on the bias, even though the fraying cannot be as deep.

July 1887 *Delineator*

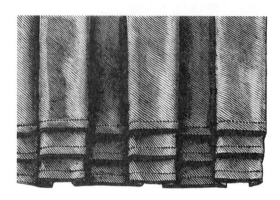

Figure 59. Skirt trimming

For the trimming in Figure 60, before the plaits are laid, their spaces are measured off. Each is ornamented with two strips of wide braid, the ends of which fold under one side of the plait and form points under buttons on the other. The braid may match the dress material or contrast with it. Braid buttons harmonize best with the decoration. On dresses of light material ribbon is often used instead of braid, and the buttons are omitted.

May 1887 *Delineator*

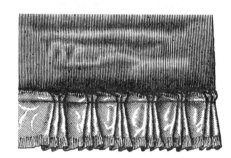

Figure 61. Plaited skirt trimming

366

10. Accessories

It very frequently happens, if you are careful, that there are many little alterations and changes in the toilette that you can carry out yourself, and that not only prove more economical but more satisfactory than if left to a professional dressmaker. For example, the addition of lace ornaments, or other means of lightening a somber toilette for evening or theatre wear.

If the bodice is pointed, three rows of lace or embroidery, sewed together and ending in a point, form a very pretty plastron, which may be fastened onto the dress by a tab or buckle, a jeweled clasp, or a ribbon rosette. A lace fichu crossed on the chest, and with the ends passed under the waist belt, looks well on a short-waisted bodice. Exceedingly pretty fichus are made of all kinds of light materials, such as tulle, plain or beaded gauze, or crêpe, plaited and trimmed with lace. Ladies who go to many evening entertainments are usually well provided with these little accessories, which give an entirely different appearance to the dress, as they ornament the parts most seen, the skirt being usually far less conspicuous than the bodice.

August 1885 *Godey's Lady's Book*

Collars, Jabots, Fichus, Chemisettes, Etc.

High dog-collars of velvet on which is laid crocheted lace, are made to wear with various dresses. They are fastened by hooks and eyes, are stiffly interlined, and are ornamented by a small bow of velvet ribbon on the left side. Red, black, brown, or blue velvet collars are worn with black, white, or colored dresses.

September 19, 1885 *Harper's Bazar*

There are dog-collars of different styles. One has a band of small sparkling jets, with here and there a brown rosary bead. The swinging pendants that reach far down on the bodice have rosary beads and small jet beads strung alternately. This can only be worn with a brown or black dress. Another has its broad band closely covered with tiny plomb beads, while the shape is outlined with nuggets of bright jet, medallion fashion, at intervals in the midst of small beads. These dog-collars are sold in sizes, and they are finished with a satin lining. A Pompadour of cream pearl beads is an artistic addition to a silk or satin dress. Girdles are covered with beads to match.

December 1885 *Delineator*

For a handkerchief vest, either on a round bodice or one that has jacket fronts, two kerchiefs are needed. White is preferred, but any faint shade may be used. Each kerchief is plaited at the top, fastened just at the throat, and then allowed to flare. At the bust the kerchiefs are crossed, and the ends are concealed under a belt or a pointed girdle of ribbon or velvet.

October 1887 *Delineator*

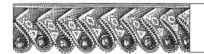  

Figure 1. Lace and net jabot

The arrangement of this vest on the bodice is shown by Figure 2. Its making is equally simple. A broad strip of figured net–Oriental is generally used–is gathered at the top and sewed to a piece of stiff net as a foundation. It is then made to fall over as desired, and is caught underneath to the foundation. A knot of scarlet ribbon gives a pretty finish, although a bouquet or pompon of ribbon cut in cock's-comb fashion might be used.

July 1884 *Delineator*

A narrow ribbon, tied around the neck in the ordinary manner, is supposed to be the foundation for the jabot in Figure 1; but it is entirely separate. The jabot is made of a straight strip of figured net, cut in a point at each end and finished with a frill of Oriental lace. A narrow strip of stiff net is at the top where the material is gathered and sewed on, the end being then turned over to form an ornament. Near the waist-line the net is drawn in to form a puff and sewed to a foundation, and then the point falls full. This is pretty in plain or tinted mull, and is good for hiding a slightly shabby bodice.

May 1884 *Delineator*

Figure 2. Net vest

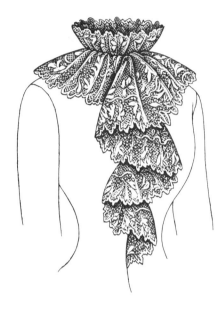

Figure 4. Cascade of lace

Figure 3 shows a method of arranging a slightly puffed lace gilet. The width depends on the figure of the wearer, a slight one being able to wear a much fuller gilet. The neck is shirred at the top and fastened to the neck of the bodice. It is then allowed to fall gracefully in a Molière puff, and is turned under and held in place by an ornamental pin at the waist-line. Clasps or ribbon straps may be used if preferred to the pin.

August 1884 *Delineator*

The standing frill is of Spanish lace, gathered rather fully and stiffened by a fine wire so that it keeps its position. (See Figure 4.) The falling frill is deep. After following the outline of the neck, it descends in a cascade that is made to grow narrower until it disappears at the waist-line. Any lace soft enough to fall in folds may be arranged in this way, but the silky laces are most popular.

September 1884 *Delineator*

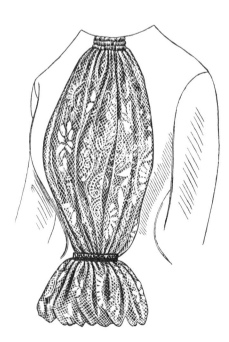

Figure 3. Lace gilet

Figure 5. Arrangement for lace scarf

This method of disposing a very long scarf will find many admirers among those who possess them, but grow tired of one adjustment. (See Figure 5.) It is best to have a strip of stiff muslin on which to arrange the scarf securely. The scarf is drawn together in the center, and fastened at the top with a bow of yellow satin ribbon. Then at regular intervals it is drawn in and tied down with ribbons. At the lower edge, the full frill of lace falls in the easiest way. A black scarf may be arranged in this way, with yellow, scarlet, or pale blue ribbons.

December 1884 *Delineator*

The long jabot in Figure 6 produces a gilet effect. It is made of rose silk mull and white Spanish lace. The plaits of mull are laid on a long foundation. A full cascade of lace outlining the shape, and extending to the top again, is the finish. The stitches on the lace are hidden under a small fan-like jabot of the lace that is placed just at the top and caught by a knot, which appears to stay the entire decoration. Lavender, blue, cream, yellow, or white mull may be substituted for the Spanish lace.

January 1885 *Delineator*

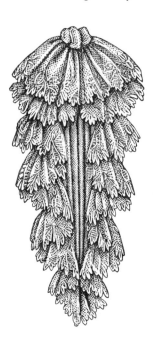

Figure 6. Lace and mull jabot

The jabot in Figure 7 is made of Oriental net and lace to match. The net is laid in full folds, and is caught closely at the top and bottom. A cascade of the lace is then placed on one side as illustrated and made to form a fan at the top, where it flares. At the lower edge is a cluster of ribbon ends and loops, clear yellow in color and of glossy satin. Developed in black Spanish net and lace and with black velvet ribbons, this jabot is very useful to anyone who prefers wearing a great deal of black. Jet tassels may be substituted for the ribbon loops.

April 1885 *Delineator*

Figure 8. Pouf vest

Very broad, soft ribbon of the pistache shade is used for the decoration in Figure 8. The lace is a fine Pompadour. A full frill of lace is around the neck, supported by a white wire skillfully run through it. The broad ribbon is drawn closely to the neck, and then allowed to flare and fall over in a pouf. It is drawn in and a slightly smaller pouf is arranged, the poufs decreasing in size until the fourth and last is achieved. A lace frill is below that, and lace is placed so that it falls in a cascade on one side. A narrow ribbon encircles the neck, and is tied in loops and ends on one side. Crimson, yellow, or any other color in vogue may be used for the ribbon instead of pistache.

April 1885 *Delineator*

Figure 7. Lace and ribbon jabot

371

The plastron in Figure 10 is of dark gray velvet. The decoration consists of silver braid arranged in straps across it and coiled in clover-leaf designs at the ends. The braid is in straight bands around the high collar, inside of which is a linen collar. In black and gold, blue and silver, or white and gold, such a vest is extremely pretty.

June 1885 *Delineator*

Figure 9. Étamine and lace jabot

The jabot in Figure 9 is so long that it really becomes a vest. On a straight foundation of net are laid three folds of écru étamine. These are caught at the top, drawn in with a narrow yellow satin ribbon at the waist, and then allowed to flare. The lower edge and one entire side is trimmed with fine Oriental lace, that on the side being full enough to be drawn in cascades. At the top the lace forms a flared bow, which is caught in the center by a loop of étamine. From under this bow, on the side where there is no lace, fall loops and ends of the yellow satin ribbon.

June 1885 *Delineator*

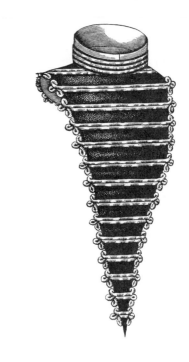

Figure 10. Velvet and braid plastron

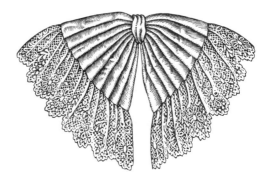

Figure 11. Mull and lace jabot

 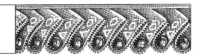

Pale blue mull was used for the jabot in Figure 11. The strip is first finished at each end with a deep frill of white lace. It is then plaited as illustrated, and a knot of the mull catches it just in the center. The jabot is fastened to the dress by a safety pin at the back.

July 1885 *Delineator*

Figure 12. Lace and crêpe gilet

Rose crêpe laid on the foundation in close folds forms the gilet in Figure 12. A full frill of Oriental lace outlines the entire decoration on each side. At the waist, the jabot is formed of the same kind of lace, interspersed with loops of ribbon of a deeper rose than that of the crêpe. Any color preferred may be substituted for rose.

September 1885 *Delineator*

The collar in Figure 13 is to be worn with a bodice that is open at the neck. On a foundation of white net cut the proper shape, is laid fold after fold of cream mull. Above this is a standing frill of white lace. Below, outlining the shape, is a similar frill. The upper frill is held in place by means of a wire run through it. There is a bunch of roses where the collar meets on the bodice; but any desired flower, or ribbon loops, may be substituted. Indeed the wearer may have both, and so effect a change when fancied.

September 1885 *Delineator*

Figure 13. Mull and lace collar

The bow in Figure 14 is shown made of fine blue mull, although white may be used if preferred. The ends are finished with cascades of Oriental lace, but any other lace may be used. This bow may be worn with a rolling collar of white lawn.

October 1885 *Delineator*

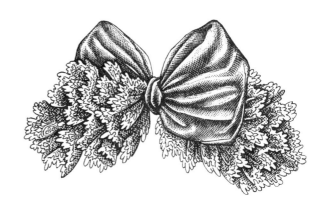

Figure 14. Lace and mull bow

373

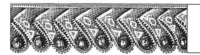 

The chemisette in Figure 15 is shown made of cream étamine having small roses stamped on it. The folds are laid to fit the figure and with some thought as to the shape of the bodices most worn. They are then mounted on a plain thin muslin chemisette. A lace pin may be used to fasten the folds across the breast. Plain white, écru, or any other shade of étamine may be used if preferred.

October 1885 *Delineator*

Figure 15. Étamine chemisette

For ladies who cannot wear a low evening bodice, the little cape in Figure 16 is to be commended. It is cut out of white lace net and edged with a lace frill. It is then gathered to fit the neck, and a lace fraise is arranged above the gathering. The opening of the cape is on one side. It is uplifted on the shoulders and fastened under a large cluster of roses, or a ribbon bow if preferred. A black lace cape may have a cockade bow of black satin ribbon; or if colors are worn, a bow of orange satin ribbon.

November 1885 *Delineator*

Figure 16. Lace cape

Figure 17. Lace collar and jabot

The collar in Figure 17 is formed of a deep frill of cream Oriental lace, made on a properly fitted band of net and then turned over. It flares slightly in front and shows the long, double jabot of lace, which extends to the waist. If a rolling collar is not becoming, a fraise may be substituted.

November 1885 *Delineator*

Figure 19. Lace collar and jabot

For the jabot in Figure 18, the lace is mounted on a strip of white net. One side is gathered plainly and allowed to fall as it will. The other is laid in a fuller frill and then drawn into cascades, a fan effect being achieved at the top. In this instance Fedora lace is used; but any lace, saving one with a very heavy pattern, is suitable. A black lace jabot is very useful if the wearer has many simply made black bodices, as it will do much toward giving a very plain bodice an elaborate air.

November 1885 *Delineator*

A strip of net is cut the proper shape, and the two frills that form this collar are arranged on it. (See Figure 19.) One is allowed to fall below the edge, while the other, which is sewed on the inner side, turns over on the right side. The lace shown is deep Egyptian, but Pompadour, Oriental, Valenciennes, or Spanish lace may be used. It extends far down on each side, forming a jabot as illustrated. On the other side, where the collar part simply joins the jabot, a bow of cresson velvet ribbon is placed. The wearer may have several sets of differently colored bows to wear with the collar.

December 1885 *Delineator*

Figure 18. Lace jabot

The plastron in Figure 20 fits a dress that is cut in Pompadour fashion and fastens at the back. The foundation is of white net cut the proper shape and fitted so that it is smooth over the shoulders and about the neck. The large section is cut out after the lace net has been drawn over it, and is sewed at the lower and upper edges. The neck is finished with a double ruching of soft lisse. A string of beads worn close around the neck below the ruching is pretty, or a narrow ribbon of a becoming color may be drawn around and tied in a bow slightly to one side. The plastron may be made of black lace net, and a velvet or ribbon dog-collar substituted for the ruche.

March 1886 *Delineator*

Figure 21. Ruching for neck and wrists

The ruching in Figure 22 consists of three frills. The upper one is of white lisse and shows a shell-like outline. The center row is a double plaiting having a white silk finish at the top and threads of scarlet chenille (or some other color) thrown over it in long stitches. The lower row is like the first one. If the ruching is basted too full into the sleeves, the effect is undesirable.

March 1886 *Delineator*

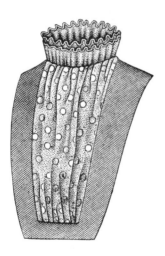

Figure 20. Lace plastron

Figure 22. Ruching for neck and sleeves

The ruching in Figure 21 is formed of alternate loops of scarlet and white ribbon; but black and white, blue and white, or brown and white may be used. The contrast is maintained in the upper and lower rows. The binding is brought well together, but the loops should not be sewed together; and if it can be avoided, must not overlap each other at the join. The fastening in front of the neck is concealed under a many-looped bow of scarlet and white ribbons.

March 1886 *Delineator*

Figure 23. Lace and mull jabot

The jabot in Figure 23 is made of a combination of Valenciennes lace and mull. A fine side-plaiting of the lace is around the neck. It is quite high, fits closely, and is finished with a narrow band of cream ribbon. A strip of mull has a single lace frill on one side and a double frill on the other. The mull is gathered and fastened to the lace plaiting to form the gilet. It is then allowed to flare nearly to the waist-line, where the double frill is drawn over and caught so that a cascade of lace terminates the gilet. There is a cluster of deep crimson ribbon loops on one side, where the lace is fastened, but this may be replaced by a cluster of natural or artificial flowers.

March 1886 *Delineator*

In Figure 24, Oriental lace not too heavy in design was used for the neck ruche, which is closely plaited and presents a very full effect. The jabot is of Oriental lace with a more positive design. It consists of two full frills sewed on a net foundation, the outer frill being much fuller. At the top, in the center, and quite near the edge, are clusters of very narrow blue ribbons having a fancy edge.

May 1886 *Delineator*

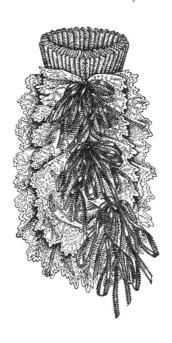

Figure 24. Lace jabot

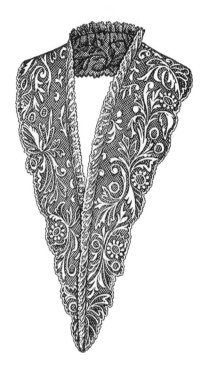

Imitation Valenciennes lace and net was used for the lace vest in Figure 26. The collar is formed of a piece of the lace sewed to a band of white net that fits the neck and is then turned over. For the vest, stiff net is cut the necessary shape, the lace is laid in side-plaits, then it is arranged on the net as illustrated. The vest is outlined by cascades of Valenciennes lace. At the sharp point of the V, just below the waist-line, is an arrangement of ribbon loops and ends. Here the ribbon is bright scarlet; but yellow, blue, lilac, or rose may be used.

June 1886 *Delineator*

Figure 25. Lace fichu

The fichu in Figure 25 is especially pretty worn with a white dress, as the bodice may be turned in from the neck to produce a V neck. Pompadour lace in a heavy pattern is used, the piece being wide enough to permit of the necessary width at the shoulders and allow the narrowing toward the ends. The inner side is finished with an edging of very narrow Pompadour lace, which is gathered quite full. In black lace this fichu may be worn with black costumes.

May 1886 *Delineator*

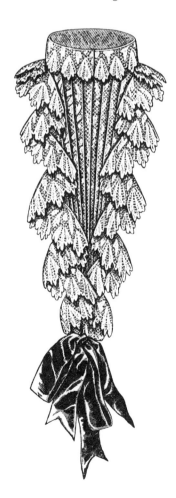

Figure 26. Lace vest

The finest écru étamine forms the chemisette in Figure 27, yellow pearl beads adding to its beauty. The desired shape is first cut. Then the étamine is laid in folds turning to the center and placed on it, a decided V being outlined by the small pearl beads placed close together. The collar is cut in points, and each point is tipped with a bead. White lisse or any of the pale-tinted mulls may be used instead of the étamine. If mull is selected the collar must be of some other material, or give place to a close and not very deep ruche of lace, etc.

July 1886 *Delineator*

Figure 28. Mull and lace plastron

The plastron in Figure 28 is really fan shaped. It is made of rose mull and trimmed with Spanish lace. The mull is plaited as illustrated. On one side the lace that edges it is caught in cascade fashion, while on the other it falls in a regular frill. A many-looped bow of cherry satin ribbon is at the waist-line and conceals the end of the fan. Around the neck is a fraise of the lace made very full and coming up quite high.

July 1886 *Delineator*

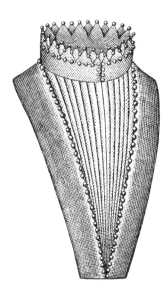

Figure 27. Étamine chemisette

Two very high plaitings of lisse form the collar worn above the vest in Figure 30. Both appear to be firmly fastened together, but in reality the collar is only held by safety pins, and the ruching may be changed without any trouble. The vest is made of a long tissue scarf gathered at the top and securely sewed to a strip of net. It is then allowed to fall in Molière folds, is again gathered in at the waist-line, and the end is drawn around to a curve and hidden under a bow of scarlet ribbon. A bow of scarlet ribbon is also at the neck. Crêpe, piece net, silk, mull, or any light material may be developed in this way.

September 1886 *Delineator*

Figure 29. Lace gilet

The gilet in Figure 29 is a pretty adjunct to an evening toilette. A scarf of white Spanish lace the desired length is fastened to the strip of net that constitutes the foundation. The scarf is gathered at the top, where it is quite broad. A little lower down it is gathered again and drawn in closer, while near the edge it is drawn in still narrower and then allowed to flare. At each of the two lower gathers, a strap of black velvet ribbon comes over it and is caught in the center by a small gold buckle. A high ruche of Spanish lace plaited to fit the neck, and a velvet dog-collar with its gold buckle just in front, finish the neck.

August 1886 *Delineator*

Figure 30. Molière vest

The collar in Figure 31 is of black satin thickly studded with cut jet beads. It is lined with black silk, fits the neck closely, and is fastened on one side. Attached to the collar is a bead plastron, the main part of which is in fisher's net pattern, while the edges are outlined with a fringe. A collar of gray satin with steel beads is pretty, and so is one made of white pearl beads; the latter intended for evening wear with a white dress.

September 1886 *Delineator*

Figure 31. Bead collar and plastron

The plastron in Figure 32 will hide imperfections in a black bodice that is wearing out before its skirt. Spanish piece lace is arranged on a carefully cut foundation of stiff net. Outlining this is a full frill of Spanish lace that makes the plastron seem much larger. The join is hidden by long lapels of black velvet. The high collar is of the same velvet.

November 1886 *Delineator*

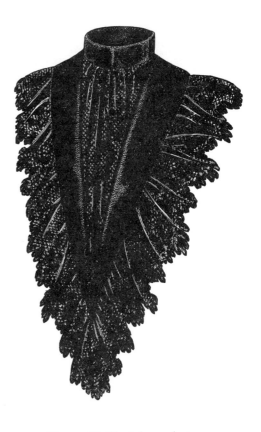

Figure 32. Black lace plastron

The high collar is overlaid with a band of embroidery, while the chemisette has narrow bands of plain linen alternating with bands of embroidery. (See Figure 33.) A narrow lawn tie is arranged about the neck, but it may give place to a fancy scarf pin.

December 1886 *Delineator*

Figure 33. Embroidered chemisette

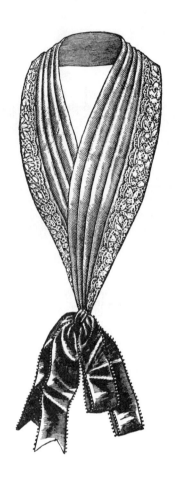

Spanish lace and Nile green moiré ribbon with a picot edge were used in making the jabot in Figure 35. The lace is laid in fanciful twists and turns on one side. The band that encircles the neck is a piece of ribbon folded over, and looped as illustrated, finishing as loops and ends at the waist-line.

January 1887 *Delineator*

Figure 34. Crêpe and lace fichu

The foundation of the fichu in Figure 34 is of net, and on it pale yellow crêpe is laid in regular folds. Pompadour lace, slightly yellow in hue, is placed over the outer edge on the fichu itself. The knot of ribbon at the waist is of yellow moiré with a picot edge. If preferred, the bodice may be turned in and the neck exposed.

January 1887 *Delineator*

Figure 35. Ribbon and lace jabot

 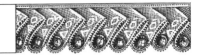

Figure 36. Silk collar and plastron

The collar and plastron in Figure 36 are arranged on a foundation of stiff net. A large, soft, silk handkerchief is used, and the desired shape is obtained without cutting. This example is pale blue. To hide the fastening, as well as for ornament, a cluster of pale yellow buds is fastened on one side. Crêpe squares are also made up in this way.

March 1887 *Delineator*

The high, military collar of the gilet in Figure 37 is of golden brown velvet outlined with golden brown pearl beads. On the center of the gilet foundation is a strip of velvet, with pearl beads arranged in button fashion. On each side, cream Spanish lace is laid in folds. At the sharp point at the waist is a cluster of golden brown ribbon loops and ends, which appear to be carelessly knotted. This gilet may be made in black and white, or mauve and cream.

April 1887 *Delineator*

Figure 37. Velvet and lace gilet

This scarf of Spanish lace is drawn about the neck, the bodice being cut out or turned in, and the short ends knotted in sailor fashion. (See Figure 38.) A cluster of pale blue forget-me-nots is placed close to the knot. If a black scarf is used, a bunch of gold wheat may take their place, or ribbon loops of some dainty shade.

May 1887 *Delineator*

Figure 38. Lace scarf

The chemisette in Figure 39 is a dainty adjunct to a plain bodice and is admirably adapted to some of the cotton dresses worn in the evening. The vest and high collar (which fastens at the back) are made of embroidered muslin laid in plaits. The vest is overlaid with white lace, which is terminated in a jabot below it. The stiff tie is of dark red ribbon.

June 1887 *Delineator*

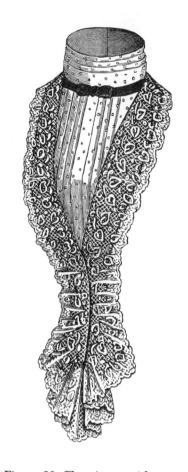

Figure 39. Chemisette with vest

The white chemisette and cuff in Figure 40 are for wear with cotton street costumes. The chemisette is arranged to convey the effect of a shirt front. The high collar is of plain linen, except for the embroidery just in front. The embroidery is dark brown; but blue, red, mode, gray, and black embroidery are also popular.

June 1887 *Delineator*

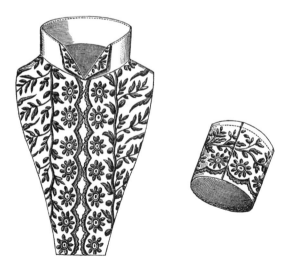

Figure 40. Embroidered chemisette and cuff

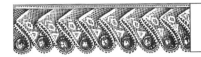 

The chemisette in Figure 41 is of light blue crêpe de Chine and is gathered to the size of the foundation. The high collar fastens at the back and is of amber passementerie, the band being lined with pale blue silk. Strips of the passementerie with pendants overlay the chemisette. Below the waist-line is fastened a ribbon bow of pale blue grosgrain. The passementerie may be in jet, steel, iridescent, or pearl beads. The color of the crêpe de Chine and ribbon may harmonize with the costume. A combination of jet passementerie and white surah or crêpe is adapted to many garments.

September 1887 *Delineator*

Figure 42. Sailor collar with passementerie

Figure 41. Crêpe de Chine chemisette

The front view of the collar in Figure 42 shows it made of silk covered with jet passementerie, and decorated with a fringe of jet pendants. The back view shows the collar made of black velvet on a black net foundation. It is outlined with jet passementerie and finished with a black lace frill. The front, which is cut out in surplice fashion, permits of turning in the bodice and exposing the neck. This collar may be made of silk, satin, crêpe de Chine, silk mull, point d'esprit, or dotted mull.

September 1887 *Delineator*

The beads are of finely cut jet, those in the center being very large and giving a jewel effect, surrounded as they are by innumerable small beads. (See Figure 43.) The edges have a clover-leaf finish in beads. The collar fastens near the back, where the closing cannot be seen. The cuff does not extend under the sleeve, so that it will stand much wear. Steel and amber beads are also smart. Some women take the beads from old dresses. A piece of canvas is cut the required shape, covered with velvet or silk on the side to be beaded, and after the beads are sewed on finished with a thin silk lining.

October 1887 *Delineator*

Figure 43. Jet collar and cuff

The military collar of the decoration in Figure 44 is studded with finely cut jet beads brought out by bands of silk braid arranged at intervals on it. From the lower edge comes a narrow fringe tipped with long jet beads. From under this starts a network of jet in fisher's net pattern that achieves a Vandyke outline and is finished by a long fringe of beads with large pointed jets on each end. This collar is also smart in steel beads.

November 1887 *Delineator*

Figure 44. Jet collar

 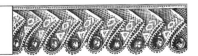

In the center of the plastron a dainty little chemisette is arranged with lace frills. (See Figure 45.) On each side, starting from the shoulders, is a cascade of lace that unites at the waist-line and falls in single jabot fashion below. Over the lace on each side is a lapel of deep brown velvet, and below that and slightly overlapping it is one of brown-and-gold striped velvet. High up on the left shoulder is a cluster of yellow tips. These colors will be found very adaptable, although the plastron should accord with the dress or dresses.

November 1887 *Delineator*

Figure 46. Ribbon collar and lace jabot

The ribbon used for the collar in Figure 46 is a faint heliotrope. It is arranged with the edge folded under to fit the neck. The fastening on one side is concealed by a many-looped bow that shows the fancy edge of the ribbon. Deep Valenciennes lace is plaited in jabot fashion and mounted on a strip of white net, after which it is securely attached to the ribbon collar so that it comes just in front.

November 1887 *Delineator*

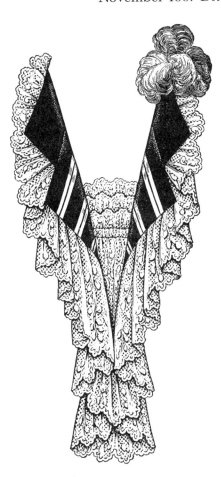

Figure 45. Plastron for evening wear

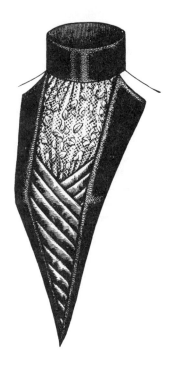

Figure 47. Lace and velvet gilet

Cream Spanish net and golden brown velvet and silk are united in this gilet. (See Figure 47.) The collar is a high straight one of velvet. From it comes the Spanish net, which is slightly gathered at the top and bottom. It extends half of the depth of the bodice, then folds of golden brown surah are arranged below and reach to the sharp point. The shape is outlined by brown velvet lapels, which are broad at the top and gradually narrowed.

December 1887 *Delineator*

The gilet in Figure 48 is of blue and green plaid silk, with an occasional gold thread running through it. The foundation is made of stiffened white net cut the proper shape, and the silk is put on over it. Its decided V shape is outlined with a dark green velvet binding. At the point is a cluster of green velvet ribbon loops and ends. The high collar, which fastens on one side, is of silk, with a velvet band applied to it.

December 1887 *Delineator*

Figure 48. Plaid silk gilet

Hats and Bonnets

A capote of the dress material makes a pretty and economical head-gear. Cloth, silk, or even cashmere is suitable for this purpose. The first thing to do is to line your hat. If the color is light, use any thin material–such as mull, India linen, etc.–that is convenient. If the bonnet is dark, and you have no silk of the same color, take an old silk, such as the covering of a worn-out umbrella. This lining must be put in with great care. Cut a straight piece that will fit in the crown, or sew two pieces together to get the required size. Join the ends. Hem one edge, and gather with a draw-string. Sew the other edge on the wrong side into the crown, so that when turned on the right side the gathered edge will fall inward. Draw the latter close enough to fit the crown, but don't have your lining wide enough to fill it. Remember to take as few stitches as possible.

Facings are harder to manage, and require practice, particularly plain velvet ones, which must be perfectly smooth. If you buy new velvet, get enough to cut a piece that will exactly cover the brim. A facing may, however, be pieced together neatly and look well. Silk facings are usually shirred on. The same remarks apply to crowns. It takes from 1 to 1 1/4 yards of velvet to make an entire bonnet. For bands or folds, the material should be cut bias; for covering the whole bonnet, it should be straight. If you cover the crown with any material other than velvet, it should be shirred or plaited. Thin materials always look better shirred.

Straw and felt hats are easily furnished. They may either be faced or bound with velvet. In the latter case, put the binding on very carefully. Cut the strip the required width and length, sew the wrong side on the upper part of the brim, and join the ends very neatly. Turn over, and slip-stitch on the inner part of the brim, turning in the edge. If you want a narrow binding, sew the wrong side close to the edge. A facing is put on in the same way, except that it is sewed so close to the edge that it does not show on the upper brim.

The same hat or bonnet can be altered into a variety of shapes. For instance, straw or felt hats with broad brims may have these turned up, first on one side, then the other, now in front, now at the back, whichever shape is most in accordance with the prevailing fashion. A straw hat that is not new should always be wired. A hat or bonnet frame may be cut, pressed, and twisted into any number of shapes until it becomes limp, when it must be discarded.

May 1889 *Peterson's Magazine*

The hat in Figure 1 looks well with decidedly pronounced tailor costumes. The crown is of smooth black beaver. The brim is of black velvet laid in side-plaits, which are drawn slightly to one side. Just in front is massed a full cluster of black and gray ostrich tips, while three gilded quills stand out conspicuously.

January 1885 *Delineator*

Figure 1. Hat for tailor costumes

The hat in Figure 2 is of dark blue felt. On it is arranged a large silk kerchief of a glowing crimson. The plumes arranged on the side and coming from the midst of the kerchief are dark blue. A plaid kerchief gives a pretty effect. It may be blue and scarlet, blue and green, blue and écru, or a Scotch plaid showing many shades.

February 1885 *Delineator*

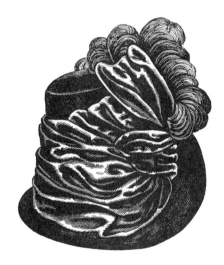

Figure 2. Felt cavalier hat

The crown of the granny bonnet in Figure 3 is first covered with pale rose silk, and then overlaid with cream wool net. The brim is covered on the outer side with frills of a wool lace of a deeper shade than the net, while the underfacing is of the rose silk. On the left side is placed a bow of rose satin ribbon, which is the only added decoration. The ties of rose ribbon are quite long and may be arranged to suit the face, or omitted altogether.

June 1885 *Delineator*

Figure 4. Leghorn hat

The evening bonnet in Figure 5 is of very fine felt so finished that no binding or facing is necessary. It is decorated with several full white plumes, which are shorter than usual and yet are longer than tips. They are arranged artistically in front, and their beginning on one side is hidden under a fancy bow of cresson velvet ribbon. The ties of cresson velvet ribbon complete the other trimming by being laid in fine folds across the back, the folds flaring on each side. The ends are caught by fancy silver pins. If desired, another color may be used instead of cresson; crimson, mordoré, brown, navy, and Lincoln being fashionable.

October 1885 *Delineator*

Figure 3. Lace granny bonnet

The leghorn hat in Figure 4 is especially admired for carriage wear. A band of dark green velvet and yellow ribbon is around the crown, the two materials being joined as pictured by loops of gold cord and straw buttons. Placed on one side, but coming toward the front, is a cluster of green velvet ribbon loops. On the side from which they start, and reaching far up on the crown, are pale yellow and dark green feathers, the green shading from light to very dark tints.

September 1885 *Delineator*

Figure 5. Evening bonnet

The walking hat in Figure 6 is intended to be worn over the face, but fits the head comfortably. It has a rolling brim. It is made of dark blue straw, and the brim is underfaced with dark blue velvet. The scarf is of blue velvet laid in many narrow folds, as illustrated. After encircling the crown, it is fastened in an artistic knot on one side. Stuck just in front, but coming well on the crown, are three long orange quills, the ends of which show from under the scarf. Some small gold pins appear to fasten them in place. Gold or silver quills may be used instead of orange.

October 1885 *Delineator*

Figure 7. Felt bonnet

Leather bonnets need but little decoration, because as much of the skin as possible is displayed. (See Figure 8.) This bonnet is trimmed with a many-looped bow of crimson velvet ribbon placed just in front. Matching strings are fastened on each side and allowed to flare, being looped under the chin. Dark brown, green, navy, and garnet are very desirable colors for trimming alligator bonnets, as they bring out the cuir shade to best advantage.

December 1885 *Delineator*

Figure 6. Walking hat

The bonnet in Figure 7 is of dark brown felt, although from the front it looks as if it were of velvet. The crown is hidden under a velvet puff that extends over the brim in front. The entire brim is then smoothly underfaced with velvet and overlaid with twine lace, which is caught so that the pattern shows well from under the uplifted peak. A row of golden brown feather tips starting from the top extends down one side, the last resting on the edge of the brim. The ties are of velvet ribbon laid in a fold on each side coming over the brim, and arranged in a bow like a bridle under the chin. The ends are pinned up with small gold pins, which are at once decorative and useful.

November 1885 *Delineator*

Figure 8. Alligator skin bonnet

The hat in Figure 9—which is worn well forward—is of fine black straw. The top of the crown is decorated with a piece of gold embroidery, while a deep band of embroidery is around the crown. The rolling brim is smoothly faced with black velvet. Slightly to one side, but near the front, is a many-looped bow of black velvet ribbon with tiny gold spangles on the edges. A cluster of yellow and black feathers is on the other side. This hat may be developed in steel and black, or silver and black; and then the decorations may be gray and black, or all gray.

March 1886 *Delineator*

Figure 10. Straw hat

Figure 9. Straw hat

The hat in Figure 10 is of natural-colored straw. The brim is narrow on one side and at the front, but on the other side it rolls up quite high against the conical crown. A full cascade of Oriental lace extends around the crown and is massed against it in front. Some pale yellow tips are under the uplifted brim and come over the crown, resting against the lace, so that from the front the crown seems almost entirely composed of lace and feathers. Any shade of feathers may be substituted, but white, écru, or yellow are most effective.

May 1886 *Delineator*

The hat in Figure 11 is made of fancy braid of a deep crimson color. The brim is much broader in front than at the back, where the greater part of the trimming is arranged. A full cascade of Oriental lace is laid around the lower part of the crown and falls on the brim. On one side, very near the back and turning toward it, is a cluster of cream ostrich tips. Still farther back are long loops of crimson moiré ribbon arranged as illustrated. A crêpe scarf may be substituted for the lace; and a bunch of flowers, blossoms, etc., may take the place of the feathers.

June 1886 *Delineator*

Figure 11. Straw hat

The crown of this bonnet is of black Spanish lace laid over white silk. (See Figure 12.) The brim, which is tolerably broad, is of fine black braid outlined with jet beads. In front are loops of black grosgrain and a rich cluster of flowers consisting of white chrysanthemums, white roses, and maidenhair ferns. The ties are of black ribbon and start from among the flowers, come down each side, and are caught in the usual way. A bridle of black lace may be substituted for them.

July 1886 *Delineator*

Figure 13. Straw bonnet

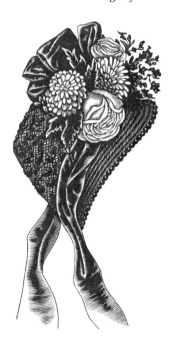

Figure 12. Straw and lace bonnet

The bonnet in Figure 13 is of gray fancy straw, with a coronet brim of gray beads. All of the trimming is massed in front. It consists of loops of gray velvet ribbon mingled with other loops of pale green satin having on it brocaded figures in crimson. A few half-ripe cherries stand out from among the loops. Ties of the gray velvet ribbon start from among the loops, are brought down on each side, fastened, and then allowed to flare, after which they are tied under the chin.

July 1886 *Delineator*

The brim of the hat in Figure 14 rolls far up on one side near the front, so that the black velvet underfacing shows very plainly. From the back, about the crown, is a black lace scarf that forms a fan near the front. Gaily figured écru satin ribbon peeps from its folds, then shows itself in long loops on one side. The écru tips just in front are drawn down so as to seem like bunches of fluffiness. Roses, dahlias, or any large flower may take the place of the tips.

July 1886 *Delineator*

Figure 14. Straw hat

The hat in Figure 15 is decidedly suggestive of a poke bonnet. It is of yellow straw. The broad brim is underfaced with dark green velvet, and a short distance from the edge it is outlined with small yellow pearl beads. Green grosgrain ribbon encircles the crown and is arranged in a four-looped bow just in front. At the back a band of it is drawn to one side of the crown, and terminates in a series of loops just where a cascade of Spanish lace begins. The latter comes down the crown close to the front.

July 1886 *Delineator*

Figure 16. Straw hat

The hat in Figure 17 is worn well on the back of the head. It is of fancy straw of a bright crimson color. The slightly curved brim is so finished that neither binding nor facing is required. A band of crimson velvet is about the crown, and on one side, very near the front, is a high cluster of ribbon loops. Standing out from among them is an écru pompon somewhat after the shaving-brush style. The ribbon is of crimson satin, half of it being brocaded in leaves and flowers.

July 1886 *Delineator*

Figure 15. Straw hat

The high crown is of dark blue satin straw, while the outer part of the brim is of a deep straw color. (See Figure 16.) Neither binding nor facing is required. Around the crown is a narrow scarf of dark blue velvet that terminates under a jaunty little bow on one side. A cluster of white daises stands up high on the crown. Full loops of velvet are drawn up against it and caught by a fancy silver pin, one end of the velvet extending over the brim. Yellow roses may take the place of the daisies, and blue crêpe may be substituted for the velvet.

July 1886 *Delineator*

Figure 17. Straw hat

This medium-sized, gray straw hat is finished in such a way that neither binding nor facing is required. (See Figure 18.) Around the crown is a band of gray ribbon thickly studded in a regular pattern by cut jet and steel beads. In front, slightly to one side, are high loops of gray grenadine ribbon. Coming out from their midst is an ornament formed of sparkling jet beads. Such a hat is in good taste with an all-black, all-gray, or gray-and-black toilette. The ribbon may be of black grosgrain.

August 1886 Delineator

Figure 19. Straw hat

The bonnet in Figure 20 is of dark green velvet smoothly applied to the frame. Over the brim is laid a double row of autumn leaves, which in their golden brown tints contrast artistically with the green. A cluster of leaves and nuts stands up in front, the same golden brown tints prevailing. On one side is a cluster of brown ribbon loops caught in such a way that the stems of the leaves come through their knot. Folds of ribbon are laid down each side, and after being caught, flare at the edge to form the ties and are looped in the usual way.

November 1886 Delineator

Figure 18. Straw hat

This hat is of black fancy straw, the broad brim being faced with rich black velvet that shows to advantage where the brim is rolled on one side. (See Figure 19.) An enormous bow of ladder loops is just in front. It is formed of two kinds of ribbon arranged in alternation, one black and the other cream with a picot edge. The ribbons are of the same width and quality.

September 1886 Delineator

Figure 20. Velvet bonnet

Figure 21. Felt hat

The hat in Figure 22 is of gray felt. The brim is underfaced with dark green velvet. The entire crown is hidden under a covering of green and gray brocaded velvet. At the bottom of the crown is a string of felt beads that hides the seam. On one side are loops of narrow ribbon and three full green tips, each being drawn forward and fastened in place. Cloth or any kind of suit material may be substituted for the velvet.

February 1887 *Delineator*

The high crown of the hat in Figure 21 is of dark brown felt, and the irregular brim is faced with a light tan shade. Around the bottom of the crown is a string of large brown felt beads, the most pronounced trimming being arranged at the side where the brim is raised. Here, against the crown, is a cluster of loops of fancy ribbon that shows brown and tan. Several tips in the same colors are placed back of the loops, and extend over the crown and far back on each side.

January 1887 *Delineator*

Figure 22. Felt hat

The hat in Figure 23 is especially suitable for seaside wear. It has a high crown and a brim that turns up on one side. The straw is a natural light color. The facing, which only shows where the brim is uplifted, is of black velvet plainly applied. A scarf of black and gold net is drawn about the crown high up in front, and stands some distance above the brim. Against this are arranged pale yellow roses and a large bunch of foliage and wild flowers.

May 1887 *Delineator*

Figure 24. Straw hat

The shape of the hat in Figure 25 suggests a large sailor hat, and the edge of the brim curls. The straw is two shades of brown and fancifully plaited to produce an open-work effect. In front are massed several short, full feathers in dark brown and écru.

July 1887 *Delineator*

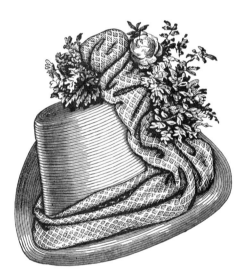

Figure 23. Gainsborough hat

The hat in Figure 24 is of fine Leghorn straw of a medium shade. It has a narrow back, high crown, and slightly rolling brim. Where the brim curves, there is a narrow outlining of dark brown velvet about 1 inch wide. A brown silk scarf is drawn about the crown, and long, full loops of it are arranged in front and reach far up above the crown. Against these loops rest golden brown wallflowers wrought out in velvet, with their leaves in the natural hue; and some grass and small blossoms stand upright in aigrette fashion.

May 1887 *Delineator*

Figure 25. Straw hat

The hat in Figure 26 is of deep écru straw, finished with a double braid about the edge. It is turned up at the back, where it is caught by draped loops of red silk. Bending far forward on the crown are clusters of deep brown cat-tails. The scarf extends a little over the brim at the side, but the effect of a decoration at the back is maintained. Olive silk and short brown tips make a smart contrast.

July 1887 *Delineator*

Figure 26. Straw hat

The hat in Figure 28 is of black Neapolitan straw braid. The rolling brim is much higher in front than at the back. It is finished in such a way that neither binding nor facing is required. The ribbon used for trimming is a delicate yellow grosgrain with a picot edge, and the two rows that encircle the crown are interlaced on each side as illustrated. Just in front is a jaunty ribbon bow, and beside it are two ostrich tips and an aigrette, all of the yellow shade.

September 1887 *Delineator*

The hat in Figure 27 is to be worn well over the face. It is of gray Neapolitan, and its narrow brim rolls on each side and displays the smooth facing of heliotrope velvet. A gauze ribbon having stripes in two shades of heliotrope is about the crown. The decoration, which consists of a large, full fan of heliotrope velvet lined with a lighter shade of satin, is placed against the crown so as to reach above it and allow the lining to be seen. Full clusters of heliotrope stand up against this fan, and some ribbon loops are at the base.

August 1887 *Delineator*

Figure 28. Round hat

The hat at the center of Figure 29 is a large gray felt, the brim of which droops slightly on one side, and is raised on the other side and at the back. The facing is of dark green velvet smoothly applied. The trimming consists of a double fan of green plaid velvet just in front, and a scarf of it that extends over the crown and holds down the brim at the back in strap fashion.

Figure 27. Straw hat

The walking hat on the left is of zinc felt, and its rolled brim is faced with dark zinc velvet. On one side, against and coming over the brim, are three ostrich tips of different shades of zinc.

The bonnet on the right is shown in heliotrope velvet plainly applied, while the brim shows two rows of large, cut jet beads in heliotrope color. In front is an elaborate arrangement of heliotrope grosgrain ribbon with a picot edge, three different shades being used. This bonnet may be developed in any color, but care must be taken in regard to the shades in the ribbon loops, violent contrasts not being in good taste.

October 1887 *Delineator*

Figure 29. Three hats

The dusting cap in Figure 30 is drafted with scale 32. It may be made of any material.

1887 National Garment Cutter Instruction Book

Figure 30. Dusting cap

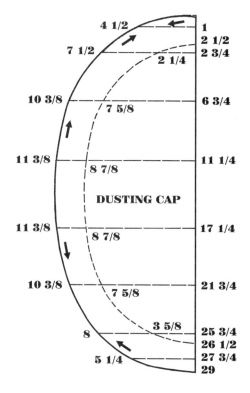

In Figure 31 the article is made up as a dusting cap, in soft cambric with a ribbon bow. It is formed from a single section of material, of an oval shape. A narrow bias strip of the material is run on the under side to form a casing, some distance from the margin. An elastic cord is run through the casing, drawing the cap up to the size of the head and giving the outer edge a ruffled effect. A ribbon bow is placed on the center of the front.

Lawns, prints, muslins, or any light-weight wash materials may be used for dusting caps. Pongee silk and scrim are much liked, and when selected, the edge of the cap is often worked with bright colors in a simple embroidery stitch. A narrow hem is also a neat finish. Oiled silk is the material used for bathing caps, and a tiny hem or a braid binding is the most desirable edge finish. A dusting cap requires 3/4 yard of material 22 inches wide. A bathing cap requires 3/4 yard of oiled silk 25 inches wide.

July 1884 *Delineator*

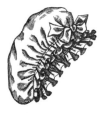

Figure 31. Dusting or bathing cap

Other Accessories

Striped parasols of brilliant red velvet alternating with silk are stylish for carriage use. The stripes extend around the circle. Écru parasols rival those of bright red, and are seen in stripes, or with figures of velvet or plush on écru surah grounds. Green velvet-striped parasols are also new. Black and white satin-striped parasols are carried with black toilettes and with colors as well. Thin India silks are also laid in lengthwise plaits from the center to the edges, and form the thick bulky parasol now preferred. Lace parasols in fluted or accordion-plaits are elegant in white, black, écru, or red lace. Economical women put a gathered net cover over

 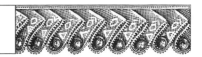

plain parasols. French piece lace, point d'esprit, and marquise laces are favored for this purpose.

June 19, 1886 *Harper's Bazar*

Girdles of ropes of beads, of links of passementerie, or finally of fur, especially sealskin, are imported to rival those of silver. Those made of jet beads, massed in a thick coil with long tassels at the end, are worn with black dresses. Others of colored beads match the color of the dress. The cord passementerie girdles are in loops and links of silk cord without beads. The seal fur girdles are a soft roll about 2 inches in diameter, nearly 3 yards long, and finished at the ends with balls of sealskin pendant from passementerie loops. They cross the back of the waist-line, droop down toward the front, and are fastened low on the left hip.

September 10, 1887 *Harper's Bazar*

The center handkerchief in Figure 1 is ornamented with a deep hem-stitched border. Above this border are squares of hem-stitching alternating with clusters of dark purple pansies, each corner being also ornamented with the pansies. Another has its hem-stitched border decorated with a Grecian pattern in black. A third has simply two black borders, one at the upper and the other at the lower edge of the deep hem. The checker-board effect in black and white is shown in different ways on the other two.

January 1884 *Delineator*

Figure 1. Five mourning handkerchiefs

The bag in Figure 2 is shaped from pasteboard. Two sections of the shape of the larger parts are cut and covered on the outside with velvet or plush, and on the inside with silk, satin, or some other contrasting material. On the lower portion of one part is arranged a piece of pasteboard curved at the top as pictured, and covered smoothly with the contrasting material. This part forms the front of the bag. It is embroidered or hand painted in some pretty design. The exact size of the daisy sprays in this example is pictured on the right of the engraving. The initial letters or monogram of the owner are embroidered just above the design on one side.

The parts are then joined together by a puff of the contrasting material. The seaming of the puff, and also the top of the bag, are decorated with a band of silk cord arranged in clusters of loops in the upper corners. The suspending ties or handle are of wide ribbon bowed artistically, but they may be of cord if preferred.

April 1884 *Delineator*

Figure 2. Hand-bag with daisy sprays

The handkerchief on the left of Figure 3 is of white linen lawn, with an edge finish of cardinal. The polka-dots are white, as are the daisies, but the vine leaves are of cardinal. The handkerchief on the right is of fine linen lawn of a faint blue shade. It has a scalloped edge and a border formed of white polka-dots.

July 1884 *Delineator*

 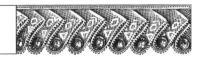

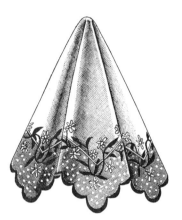

Figure 3. Two fancy handkerchiefs

The parasol on the left of Figure 4 is of white silk and appliquéd with embroidered silk roses and their foliage. At the top is a rosette of pink satin ribbon, and the edge is finished with a full frill of white Spanish lace. The lining is pale pink, and the handle is of natural wood quaintly twisted.

The parasol on the right is of pale yellow silk and covered with black silk lace net, with edging to correspond. The handle is finished with a crystal ball, and on the stick is a bow, with long ends, of black satin ribbon. Yellow ribbon may take the place of black.

May 1886 *Delineator*

Figure 4. Two decorated parasols

The handkerchief at the top of Figure 5 is of fine lawn, with a turreted border daintily hem-stitched and outlined on both sides of the hem with fine scallops. On the extreme edge is a narrow frill of Valenciennes lace. Above the border, at regular intervals, rosebuds are embroidered in bright scarlet.

The handkerchief on the left is of white cambric. On this is set a pale blue border finished with deep scallops in white. From under this border falls a full frill of lace. Above the border are blue polka-dots embroidered in clusters.

The handkerchief on the right is of fine cambric. Above its hem-stitched border is a pale pink band, also hem-stitched. For contrast there is another white border. Sprays of brown and pink wild flowers are embroidered at regular intervals above the hem-stitching, the design seeming almost to be etched.

June 1886 *Delineator*

Figure 5. Three embroidered handkerchiefs

The garters on the left of Figure 6 are made of fine French silk elastic and have an end finish of deep crimson satin. The figures are embroidered in colors, and the flesh tints are exactly copied. The clasp and eyelets are of gilt. The satin part is softly padded.

The garters on the right are made of white silk elastic, the padded part being covered with pale blue silk. A row of small birds is embroidered in warm brown shades. The clasp and eyelets are of gilt.

December 1886 *Delineator*

Figure 6. Two fancy garters

The bag in Figure 7 is most useful as a receptacle for a ball of knitting wool or silk. It is formed of a straight piece of silk lined with a contrasting color, folded double crosswise, and joined at the sides. Two deep slashes are made from the top down for several inches in the front of the bag, the slashes starting from the same point in the edge and diverging in V shape. The point or V thus formed is turned over on the outside, and the rest of the way around the bag is shirred in on ribbon in a line with the top of the revers. The corners above the latter are plaited and caught down back of the revers, displaying the lining. The revers is elaborated by embroidered floral sprays and a row of imitation old coins about the edges. The lower edge of the bag is plaited in along the fold. It is finished with loops and ends of cord tipped with large plush pompons.

The coins may be replaced by gilded acorns or tiny pine cones, plush or silk balls, or any preferred style of drop ornaments.

July 1887 *Delineator*

Figure 7. Knitting bag

 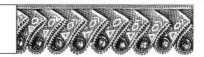

Any kind of wide ribbon may be used for the chatelaine in Figure 8. It is made into a bow with five loops, and two long ends depending from it. Scissors are fastened to one end, and a small cushion for needles and pins to the other. This cushion is shaped like a tomato, and is formed of sections of scarlet or yellow cloth and then stuffed. Any preferred shape may be adopted for the cushion, but it should be small and carefully made. The bow of the chatelaine is fastened to the dress with a safety pin.

September 1887 *Delineator*

Figure 8. Ribbon chatelaine

The pompon in Figure 9 is made of tips in two shades of pink, with the leaf of a flower showing in their midst. Standing high up in aigrette fashion is a cluster of pale pink blossoms mounted on long, wire-like stems. This ornament should be fastened slightly to one side of the hair, which is, of course, arranged very high. In blue, Nile, yellow, or mauve, this pompon is very handsome.

November 1887 *Delineator*

Figure 9. Pompon for the hair

Muffs of fanciful shape and elaborate effect are carried with visiting, driving, and church toilettes. The muff in Figure 10 is shown in velvet, lined with silk of the same shade. The outside and lining are shaped alike and are each in one piece, which has two of its edges seamed along the top of the muff. The side edges of the parts are seamed together. For more than 2 inches in from these seams, the parts are sewed together to form a casing. Into this casing is run an elastic cord that draws the muff in, leaving an opening on each side just wide enough for the hands to pass in. The edges are thus thrown into frills, which are caught over and basted to the muff at the cross-seam. In front of each basting a plait, turning toward the center, is formed at the same time in the lining and outside. This arrangement narrows the muff considerably at the top, and gives the bottom a rounded effect.

Across the front of the muff is cut an opening that extends nearly to the casings. To the edges of the opening is joined a pocket, which is all in one

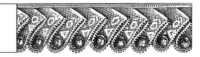

piece and falls in between the lining and outside. It is shaped by a seam extending from the top down each side and ending in dart fashion at the bottom. The pocket opening is concealed by a full jabot of lace that trims the lower edge. Over the left end of the opening is placed a full rosette bow of ribbon. A lace frill underlies the ruffled sides of the muff and extends beyond the openings. Between the lining and the outside are placed layers of cotton batting to give roundness to the shape and make the muff suitably warm.

These muffs frequently match special suits. A bunch of tips, a bird, or a ribbon bow nestled in a soft arrangement of lace make effective trimmings. For general wear, Astrakhan, plush, silk, velvet, or cloth may be used. The sides may be left untrimmed, and a large ribbon bow may cover the pocket opening, or the latter may be left visible. This muff requires 5/8 yard of material 20 inches wide for the outside, and the same amount for the inside.

December 1887 *Delineator*

Figure 10. Muff

Figure 11. Kitchen apron

When drafting the kitchen apron in Figure 11, use the scale corresponding to the bust measure. The apron is in six pieces: Front, back, shoulder strap, belt, pocket, and strap. The binding should be held tight, to prevent enlarging the neck. This garment requires 4 1/2 yards of material 24 inches wide.

1887 *National Garment Cutter Instruction Book*

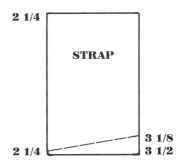

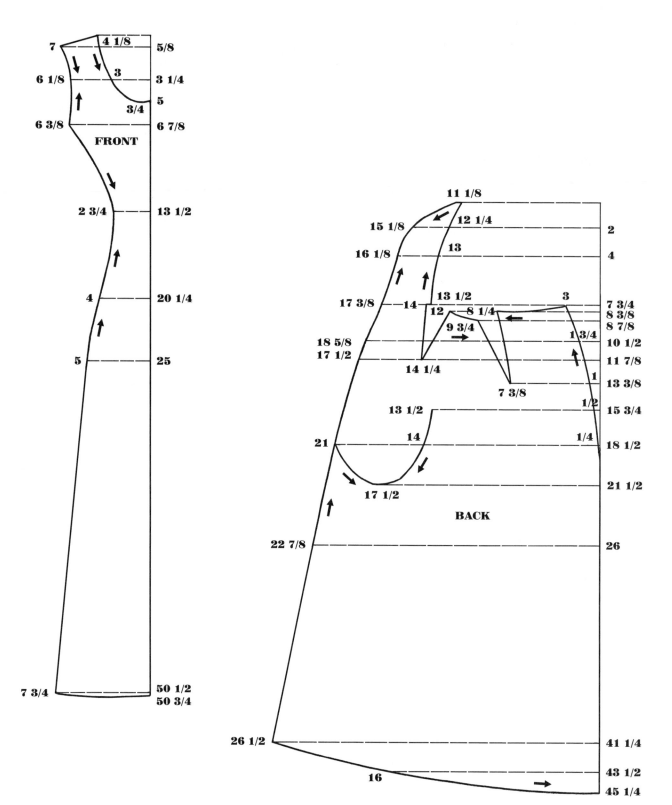

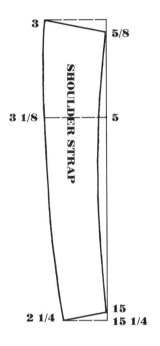

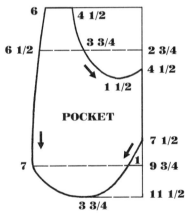

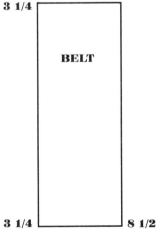

The use of the garment in Figure 12 is not limited to the kitchen, as it is just as much admired for a painting or modeling apron. The apron represented is made of plain cambric, with bands of striped cambric for trimming. The front is cut on a fold at the center, and is fitted by side-front seams that curve over the bust. Its top is cut rather low, but high enough to protect the dress, the shoulder edges being short and joining narrow back extensions that reach to the waist-line. The side-front sections are widened below the waist-line to form the back skirt. Their bias edges are turned under for hems, each side being fitted over the hip by two darts and sewed to a belt section. The ends of the belt sections are broadly lapped and are closed at the back with button-holes and buttons. The edges below them are also united by a single button-hole and button. Beneath the back sections, a little below the shoulder seams, is arranged a wide strap, which is fastened in place at each end with two button-holes and buttons, one end being also permanently sewed. The ends of the back sections are basted beneath the belt sections.

All of the edges of the apron—except the back and lower edges, which are widely hemmed—are bordered with braid or narrow bias bands of material. On the sides are placed ample, prettily shaped pockets. These are also bordered at all edges except their front edges with braid or narrow bias bands of material. The pockets are sewed at their front edges into the side seams and stitched flatly at their remaining edges.

Many ladies prefer white material for aprons of this kind; however, gingham, percale, and other printed materials are just as suitable. For a lady of medium size, this apron requires 4 1/4 yards of material 36 inches wide.

July 1885 *Delineator*

Figure 12. Kitchen, painting, or modeling apron

A. Apportioning Scales and Scroll

The National Garment Cutter system includes 45 scales, 44 of which are provided here. If you require a larger size, use the scale that corresponds to half that size and mark off twice as many units for each measure. For example, if you need a 46 scale, use scale 23; and where the diagram says to mark off 10 units, mark off 20. If you are drafting garments for dolls and need a smaller scale than is provided, use the scale that corresponds to twice the desired size and mark off half as many units. Before drafting, it is best to photocopy the pattern, determine the new measures with a pocket calculator, and write them on the pattern.

Only 10 units have been provided for each scale, as on the originals (plus a little extra length to facilitate pasting). These scales are too short to draw some pattern lines, and the page size did not allow them to be lengthened. In fact, most scales had to be divided in half. (And scale 45 was too long to fit on a page even when divided in half.) However, a scale long enough to draw any line can be created by photocopying.

First figure out which scale(s) you need to enlarge the desired pattern (see Chapter 1). Then find the longest line to be drawn with each scale. The number of units the line requires is indicated on the end farthest from the base-line. You need to lengthen the scale to at least that many units.

The scales read top to bottom for vertical lines and right to left for horizontal ones, due to the placement of the pattern base-lines. If a scale was not divided into halves, copy it as many times as required. Cut out the copies. Lay the first segment of the scale vertically on the table with the identifying tab at the top. On the second segment, fold under (or cut off) the tab at the heavy line under the label. Align this line with the line indicating the "10" unit on the first segment, covering the "1" of the "10." Tape or paste in place. Use a pen to rewrite the covered "1," or change it to "2" to indicate 20 units. Paste any additional segments in the same way.

If the scale was divided, make one copy of each half. Paste the 6–10 segment to the 1–5 segment. Copy and paste this 10-unit scale as described above.

The scales may then be pasted to cardboard or inexpensive yardsticks, cut out (if cardboard), and used for drafting. Or they may be used for measurement only, and lines drawn with a yardstick.

The National Garment Cutter scroll had to be divided into three sections to accommodate the book pages. The sections are laid out vertically in the order of assembly. Photocopy the relevant pages, and carefully cut out each section. Fold under the tab of the top section at the dashed line marked "A." Align this with line "A" on the center section, and tape or paste the sections together. Likewise attach the bottom of the center section to the bottom section, at the dashed line marked "B." Then paste the entire scroll onto light-weight cardboard, let it dry, and carefully cut out the scroll. You may find an X-Acto knife helpful.

Note: In 1998, Lavolta Press published *The Voice of Fashion: 79 Turn-of-the-Century Patterns with Instructions and Fashion Plates*. That book contains patterns from 1900 through 1906 issues of *The Voice of Fashion*. They are designed to be drafted with William H. Goldsberry's Diamond Cutting System. At the time no National Garment Cutter scales were available for examination, but the introduction theorized that the National Garment Cutter and the Diamond Cutting System were one and the same. The patent descriptions agree, the method of use is identical, and a few patterns were repeated in publications for both systems with no change in their measures.

When some National Garment Cutter scales became available, it became apparent that the two systems are slightly different. The National Garment Cutter and the Diamond Cutting System each have a base scale, where 1 unit equals 1 inch. All of the other scales are calculated from that base. In 1895, the firm, at that time Goldsberry & Doran, changed their scales so that the unit corresponding to 1 inch was assigned to the 30 scale instead of the 29, which required small changes to all of the other scales. They also redesigned the visual appearance of the scales, began to use the new units for the patterns in *The Voice of Fashion,* and announced that their patterns now required the Diamond Cutting System.

All of this may have convinced prospective customers that the system had somehow been technically improved or updated. Existing National Garment Cutter customers who continued to use their old scales, would have discovered that the patterns in their new issues of *The Voice of Fashion* did not fit as well. This may have persuaded customers to upgrade to the Diamond Cutting System.

Frances Grimble

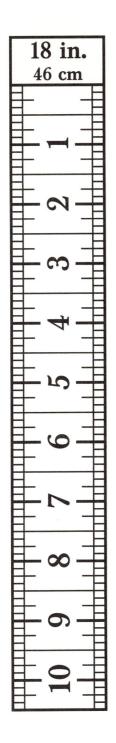

18 in.
46 cm

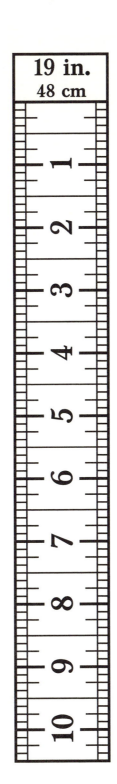

19 in.
48 cm

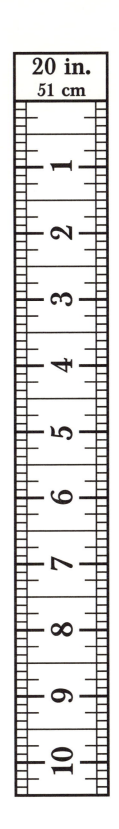

20 in.
51 cm

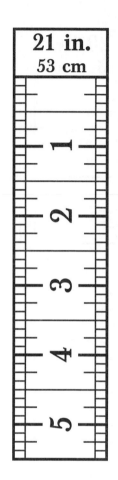

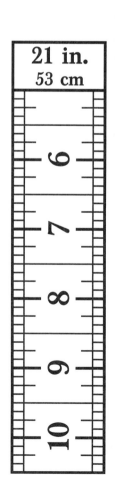

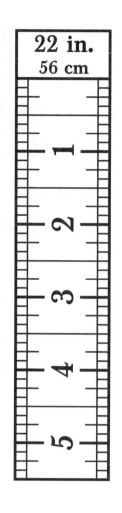

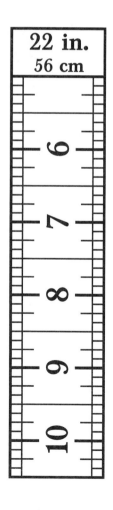

Apportioning Scales

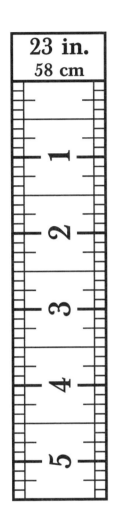

23 in.
58 cm

1 2 3 4 5

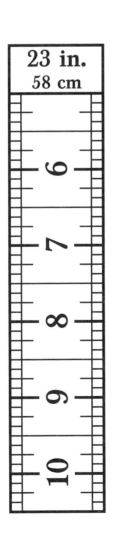

23 in.
58 cm

6 7 8 9 10

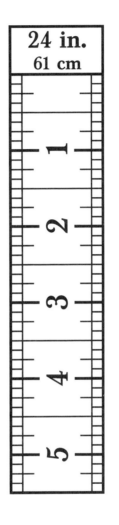

24 in.
61 cm

1 2 3 4 5

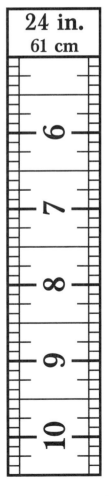

24 in.
61 cm

6 7 8 9 10

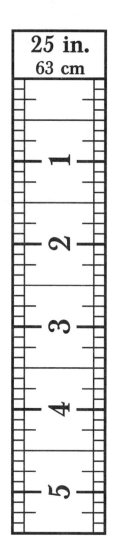

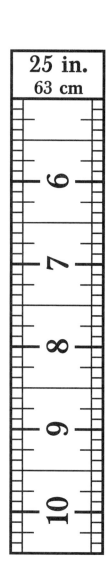

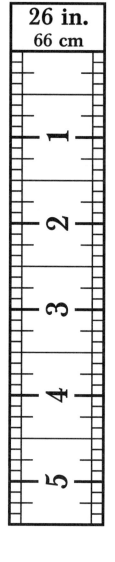

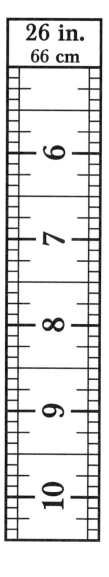

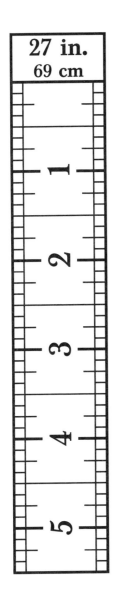

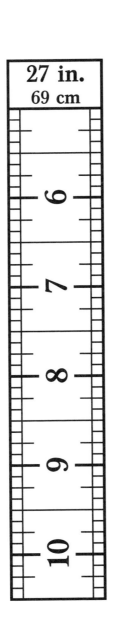

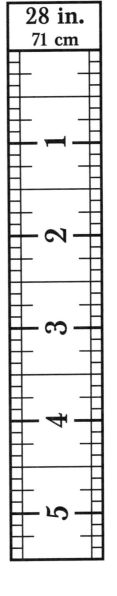

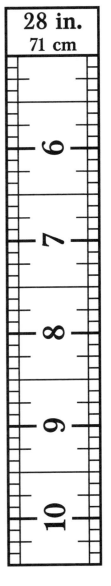

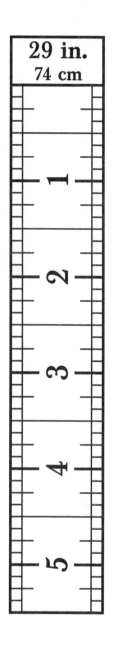

29 in.
74 cm

1
2
3
4
5

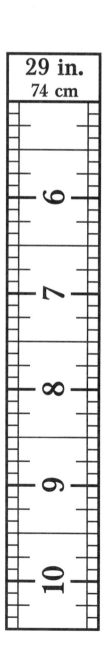

29 in.
74 cm

6
7
8
9
10

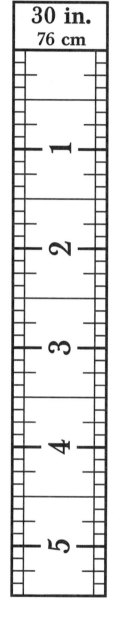

30 in.
76 cm

1
2
3
4
5

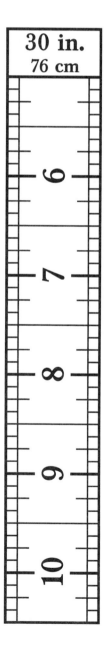

30 in.
76 cm

6
7
8
9
10

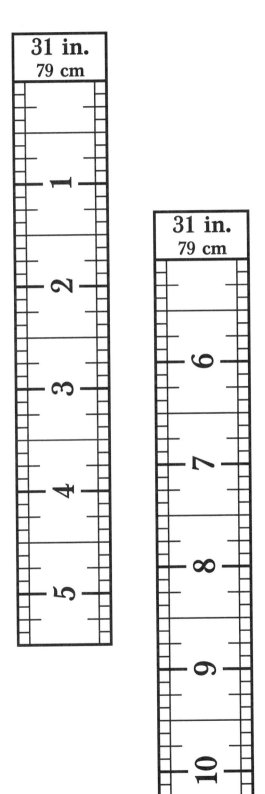

31 in.
79 cm

1
2
3
4
5

31 in.
79 cm

6
7
8
9
10

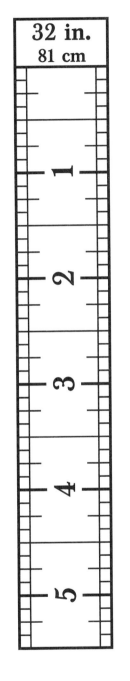

32 in.
81 cm

1
2
3
4
5

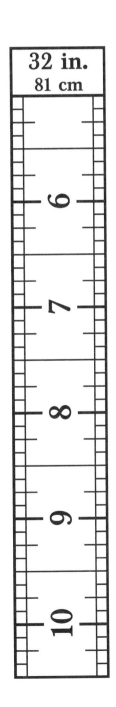

32 in.
81 cm

6
7
8
9
10

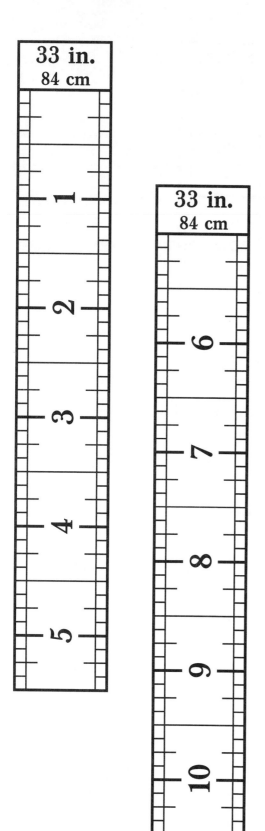

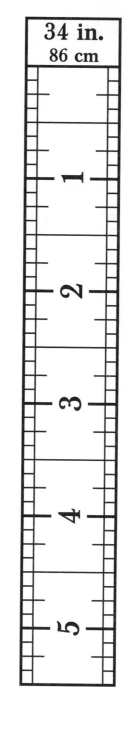

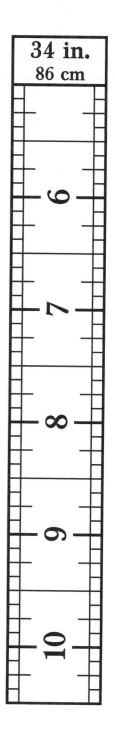

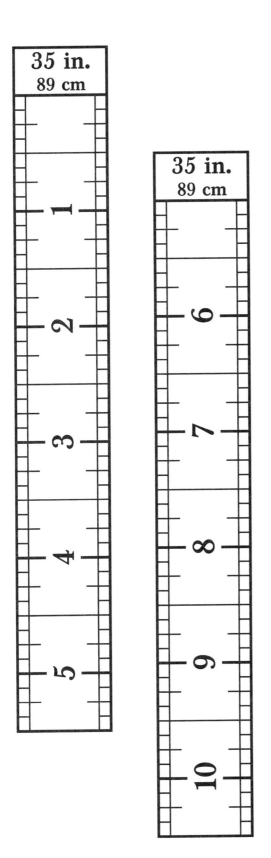

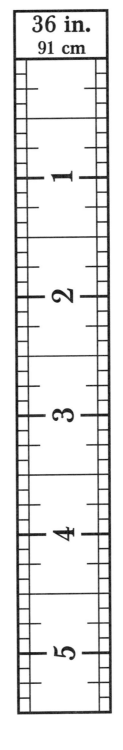

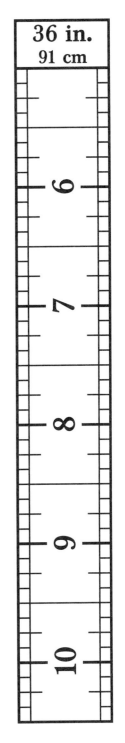

Apportioning Scales

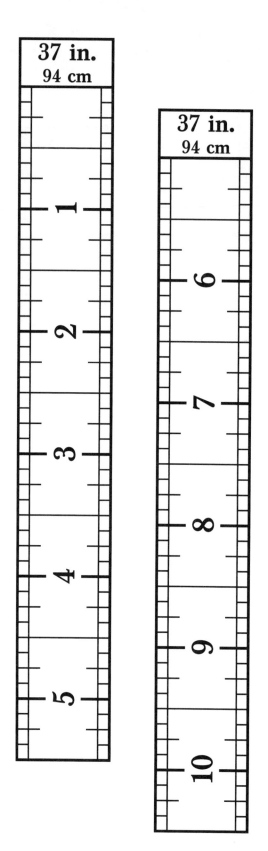

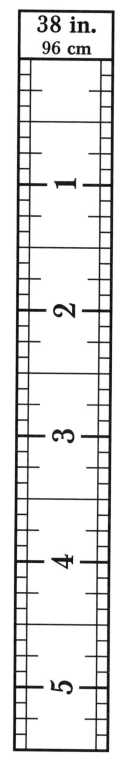

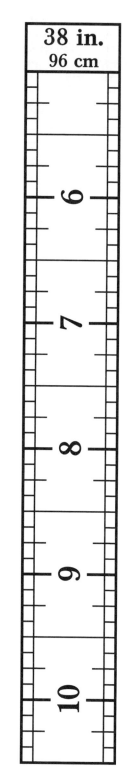

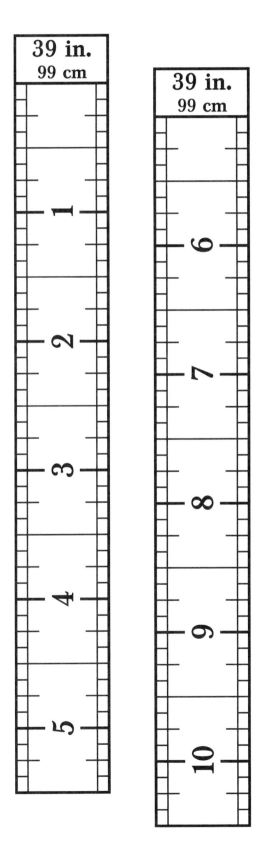

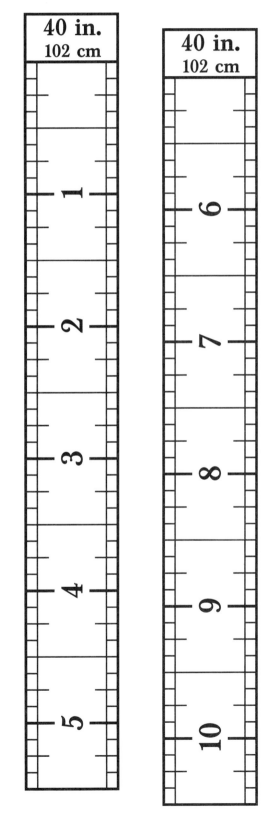

39 in.
99 cm

39 in.
99 cm

40 in.
102 cm

40 in.
102 cm

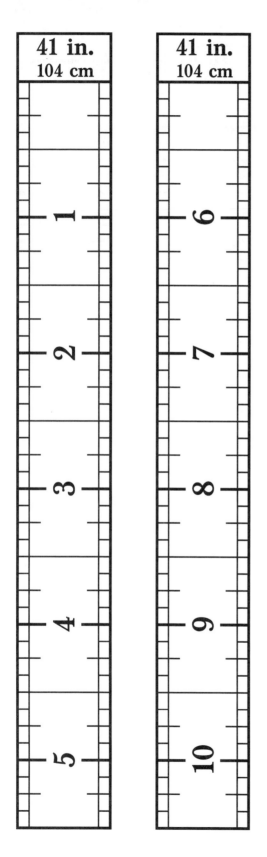

41 in. 104 cm	41 in. 104 cm
1	6
2	7
3	8
4	9
5	10

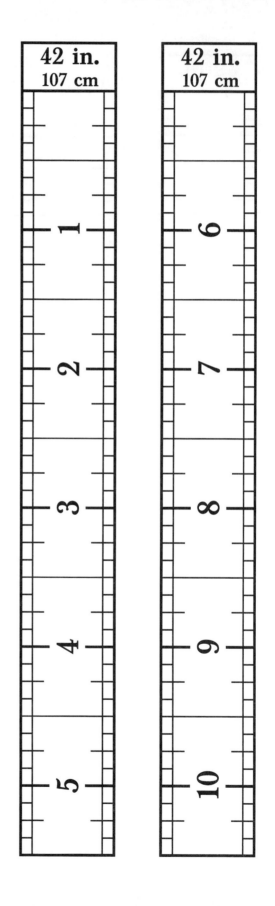

42 in. 107 cm	42 in. 107 cm
1	6
2	7
3	8
4	9
5	10

Apportioning Scales

43 in. 112 cm	43 in. 112 cm	44 in. 114 cm	44 in. 114 cm
1	6	1	6
2	7	2	7
3	8	3	8
4	9	4	9
5	10	5	10

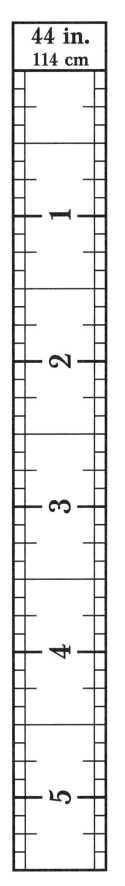

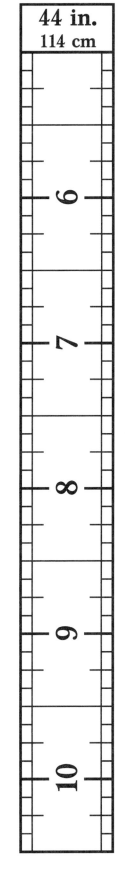

Scroll

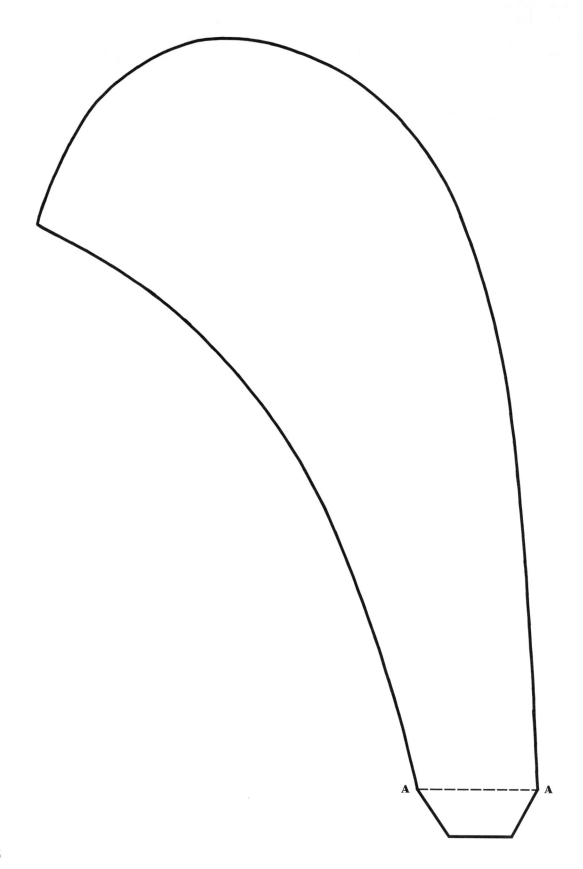

A ------- A

426

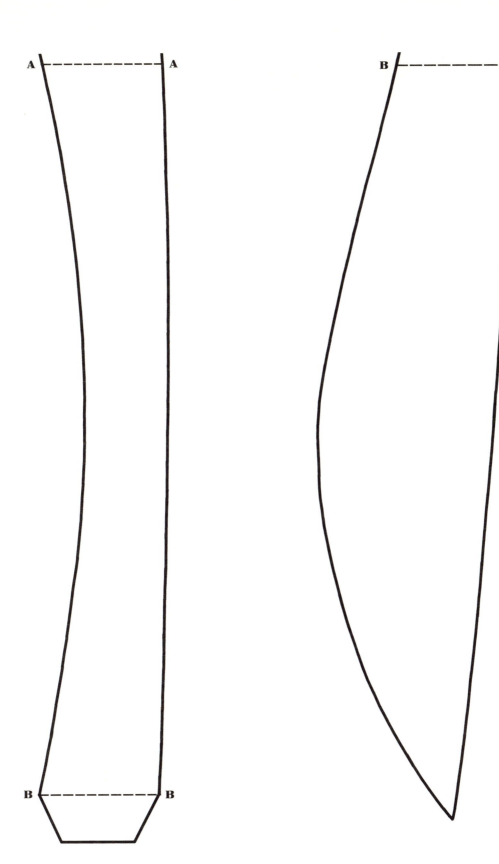

427

B. Metric Conversion Table

Although apportioning scale units are independent of the English and metric systems, many sewing instructions in this book use the English system, which is still common in the United States.

This table is provided for the convenience of readers who reside in other countries. Numbers running to several decimal places and (most) fractions under 1/16 inch have been rounded for easy use.

English Measurement	Metric Equivalent	Metric Measurement	English Equivalent
1/8 in.	3.2 mm	1 mm	1/32 in.
1/4 in.	6.4 mm	2 mm	1/16 in.
3/8 in.	9.5 mm	3 mm	1/8 in.
1/2 in.	1.3 cm	4 mm	5/32 in.
5/8 in.	1.6 cm	5 mm	7/32 in.
3/4 in.	1.9 cm	6 mm	1/4 in.
7/8 in.	2.2 cm	7 mm	9/32 in.
1 in.	2.5 cm	8 mm	5/16 in.
1 1/4 in.	3.2 cm	9 mm	11/32 in.
1 1/2 in.	3.8 cm	10 mm (1 cm)	13/32 in.
1 3/4 in.	4.4 cm	2 cm	3/4 in.
2 in.	5.1 cm	3 cm	1 3/16 in.
2 1/4 in.	5.7 cm	4 cm	1 9/16 in.
2 1/2 in.	6.4 cm	5 cm	2 in.
2 3/4 in.	7.0 cm	6 cm	2 3/8 in.
3 in.	7.6 cm	7 cm	2 3/4 in.
3 1/4 in.	8.3 cm	8 cm	3 1/8 in.
3 1/2 in.	8.9 cm	9 cm	3 1/2 in.
3 3/4 in.	9.5 cm	10 cm	3 15/16 in.
4 in.	10.2 cm	15 cm	5 7/8 in.
4 1/2 in.	11.4 cm	20 cm	7 7/8 in.
5 in.	12.7 cm	25 cm	9 13/16 in.
5 1/2 in.	14.0 cm	30 cm	11 13/16 in.

Metric Conversion Table

English Measurement	Metric Equivalent	Metric Measurement	English Equivalent
6 in.	15.2 cm	35 cm	13 3/4 in.
6 1/2 in.	16.5 cm	40 cm	15 3/4 in.
7 in.	17.8 cm	45 cm	17 11/16 in.
7 1/2 in.	19.1 cm	50 cm	19 11/16 in.
8 in.	20.3 cm	55 cm	21 5/8 in.
8 1/2 in.	21.6 cm	60 cm	23 5/8 in.
9 in. (1/4 yd.)	22.9 cm	65 cm	25 9/16 in.
9 1/2 in.	24.1 cm	70 cm	27 9/16 in.
10 in.	25.4 cm	75 cm	29 1/2 in.
10 1/2 in.	26.7 cm	80 cm	31 1/2 in.
11 in.	27.9 cm	85 cm	33 7/16 in.
11 1/2 in.	29.2 cm	90 cm	35 7/16 in.
12 in. (1 ft.)	30.5 cm	95 cm	37 3/8 in.
1/2 yd. (18 in.)	45.7 cm	100 cm (1 m)	39 3/8 in.
3/4 yd. (27 in.)	68.6 cm	1.25 m	1 yd. 13 3/16 in.
1 yd. (36 in.)	91.4 cm	1.50 m	1 yd. 23 1/16 in.
1 1/4 yd.	1.14 m	1.75 m	1 yd. 32 7/8 in.
1 1/2 yd.	1.37 m	2.00 m	2 yd. 6 3/4 in.
1 3/4 yd.	1.60 m	2.50 m	2 yd. 26 7/16 in.
2 yd.	1.83 m	3.00 m	3 yd. 10 1/8 in.
2 1/2 yd.	2.29 m	3.50 m	3 yd. 29 13/16 in.
3 yd.	2.74 m	4.00 m	4 yd. 13 1/2 in.
3 1/2 yd.	3.20 m	4.50 m	4 yd. 33 3/16 in.
4 yd.	3.66 m	5.00 m	5 yd. 16 7/8 in.
4 1/2 yd.	4.11 m	5.50 m	6 yd. 9/16 in.
5 yd.	4.57 m	6.00 m	6 yd. 20 1/4 in.
5 1/2 yd.	5.03 m	6.50 m	7 yd. 3 7/8 in.
6 yd.	5.49 m	7.00 m	7 yd. 23 9/16 in.
6 1/2 yd.	5.94 m	7.50 m	8 yd. 7 1/4 in.
7 yd.	6.40 m	8.00 m	8 yd. 26 15/16 in.
7 1/2 yd.	6.86 m	8.50 m	9 yd. 10 5/8 in.
8 yd.	7.32 m	9.00 m	9 yd. 30 5/16 in.

C. Glossary

Definitions of fashion and textile terms change over time. The information used to write these was drawn from late 19th-century sources wherever possible.

Absinthe: A light green with a bluish cast.

Accordion-plaiting: One plait laid on another by machinery, steamed and dried so as to retain this position.

Aigrette: An upright tuft of feathers, or an ornament of similar shape, used to decorate a head-dress, hat, or bonnet.

Albatross cloth: A soft, untwilled, wool dress material.

Alençon lace: A needle lace with a thick cordonnet, or outer edge, around each design, which renders the lace firm, durable, and heavy.

All-over: Embroidered or lace material in which the design or pattern extends over the entire surface.

Alpaca: Made from the wool of the llama, mixed with silk or cotton, producing a thin and durable material. What are mostly sold as alpacas now are really a fine make of Orleans cloth, which is a mixture of wool and cotton, dyed in all colors.

Ammonière: Probably a container for smelling salts.

Angel sleeve: A long sleeve flowing from the shoulder, with an open wrist.

Apple green: A light green with some yellow.

Appliqué: Lace, embroidery, or material that is sewed onto another material. The appliqué may be a piece, or a design of leaves, figures, etc.

Arabesque: A scroll effect or design, which may be made with cords, stitching, or applied pieces outlined.

Arab trimming: Possibly Arabian embroidery, or a machine-woven imitation. Arabian embroidery has elaborate geometrical designs in bright colors. It sometimes includes gold and silver thread.

Armure: A silk material, which may be plain, striped, ribbed, or with a small design. Sometimes armure is made of wool and silk.

Arrow-head: One of several kinds of triangular patterns worked in rather coarse silk or twist, to ornament and reinforce the tops of plaits, etc.

Astrakhan braid: Astrakhan braid has a rough surface somewhat similar to Astrakhan. It is made in all of the leading colors and in various widths.

Astrakhan cloth: A silk or worsted material with a long and closely curled pile.

Astrakhan fur: The pelts from young lambs reared in Astrakhan, dyed black.

Balayeuse: The frilling of material or lace that lines the extreme edge of a dress skirt to keep the train clean.

Barège: A kind of gauze, composed of silk and wool, or of wool only. Cheap kinds are made with a cotton warp.

Basket weave: A style of weaving that produces a pattern resembling the plaited work of a basket.

Basque: The end of a jacket or bodice falling below the waist, or a close-fitting bodice that extends below the waist.

Batiste: A fine linen or cotton muslin made in various colors. It is used for dresses, dress linings, and trimmings.

Batting: Raw cotton or wool prepared in thick, but lightly matted, lapped sheets.

Bayadère stripes: Stripes that run from selvage to selvage, giving a round appearance.

Beading: A woven or lace edging with openings through which to run a ribbon.

Bedford cord: A particular style of weave consisting of heavy ribs running lengthwise of the material.

Bell sleeve: A full sleeve that flares at the lower edge.

Belt: The waistband for a bodice, skirt, or over-skirt, or else a separate belt worn outside the garment.

Bengaline: A corded silk of India make, slight in texture, and manufactured in all colors. Or else a French material made of silk and wool, similar to poplin, but with more silk in its composition and a much larger cord.

Biarritz cloth: An all-wool dress material, with a flat rep or cord.

Billiard cloth: A thick, stout material, made of fine merino spun on the wool principle and felted in the finishing.

Bison cloth: A substantial wool material.

Blouse: A loose-fitting dress bodice.

Border: Any trimming put on an edge or above it, and used as a finish to a garment.

Button stand: An allowance or addition to the left front of a garment, for sewing on buttons.

Bouclé: A wool material whose surface is raised in little tufts at regular intervals or in patterns; a rough material.

Bourette: A material on which rough threads or knots appear as straight or broken stripes.

Brandenburg: A military ornament of braid and loops with which a jacket or bodice is fastened, or appears to be fastened.

Breadth: The full width of the material, or else the straight piece forming the back of a skirt.

Bretelles: Ornamental shoulder straps.

Breton lace: An embroidered net. It may be worked in colored silks or floss, and the foundation made of colored net. Or it may be fabricated of Brussels net and cream lace thread.

Brilliantine: A dress material composed of mohair or goat's wool. Brilliantines are silky looking, durable, light, and to be had in all colors.

Broadcloth: The stoutest and best kind of wool cloth. It has a slightly napped face and a twilled back.

Brocade: A material, woven of any fiber, with a pattern of raised figures.

Broché: Any style of weaving ornamented with threads that form a pattern on the surface in imitation of stitching.

Brussels net: A linen or silk net sold by the yard for evening dresses and other articles of wear.

Buckram: A coarse linen or cotton material, stiffened with glue. It is used as an interlining and for making bonnet shapes. It is made in both white and black.

Bullion fringe: A heavy, twisted cord fringe, having intermixed fine gold or silver threads.

Butterfly bow: A bow with the loop and end on each side spread apart like butterfly wings.

Byron collar: A turn-down collar, the fronts of which are not creased, but broadly and softly rolled.

Calico: A cotton material, which varies from coarse material to the finest muslin, and from the richest printed chintz to plain white.

Cambric: A beautiful and delicate linen material. There is also a cheap cotton cambric manufactured for dress linings.

Camel's hair cloth: This material is thick, warm, light, and has a fine gloss. It is unshaved, and the long hairs are of a paler color than the close substance of the cloth. Camel's hair is often mixed with wool or cotton.

Canton flannel: A cotton material napped heavily on one side, used chiefly for under-garments.

Canvas: A plain-woven cotton or linen, used for tailoring.

Canvas cloth: A plain, open-weave wool material, or else a plain-woven cotton made of hard-spun thread.

Capote: A small, close-fitting bonnet.

Capuchin: A small hood, which may be attached to or separate from a cape, jacket, etc.

Cardinal: A deep rich red, somewhat less vivid than scarlet.

Carriage wear: Garments suitable for public display when driving about in a carriage.

Cascade: A fall of lace; usually used for a lace that is made to flow, with zig-zag bends, like a river.

Cashmere: A soft, twilled material, made of the wool of the Thibet goat, mixed with

431

Glossary

sheep's wool. Other varieties are made entirely of sheep's wool, or of Angora rabbit fur.

Cashmere colors: A mixture of the colors used in cashmere shawls.

Challis: An extremely light-weight dress material of cotton and wool, woven without twill; soft and free from dressing.

Chambray: A plain-woven gingham, of one color and without any pattern. It is made of extra-fine cotton thread and stiffly sized with starch.

Chamois leather: The skin of the Alpine goat of that name.

Changeable, or shot: A material may be made to change in color according to the different positions in which it is viewed. This is effected by using a weft of a different color than the warp.

Chantilly lace: A delicate bobbin lace made in both silk and cotton, and in both black and cream.

Chemisette: An article used for covering the neck, made of some light material such as lace or cambric, usually worn under a low-cut bodice.

Chenille: A kind of cord used for embroidery and decorative purposes. The name means "caterpillar" in French, and denotes the hairy appearance of the material. Chenille is made of silk, of silk and wool, and of wool only.

Cheviot cloth: A rough cloth, twilled, and coarser than homespun.

China silks: A term applied to the plain silks woven in China, on a primitive hand loom. The warp and weft are identical in size and color, producing a natural luster. Some of the threads being heavier than others, a somewhat irregular surface is produced.

Choker collar: A close, straight, standing collar.

Chou: A large, soft, cabbage-shaped rosette, made of ribbon, material, or lace.

Chuddah: A light camel's hair material.

Claret: A dark, purplish red.

Cloakings: Heavy materials used for making cloaks.

Cloth: A wool material of several descriptions. Also a generic term applied equally to linen and cotton.

Cloth of gold: A material woven entirely or partly of gold-colored threads.

Coatings: Materials used to make coats.

Coat sleeve: A two-piece sleeve that comprises an under-arm and an upper piece. Used for dresses and other garments as well as coats.

Coquille: Material arranged in a shell-like design.

Corded silk: A silk with a rib or cord forming the predominating characteristic of the material.

Corduroy: A heavy, durable, cotton material. It is woven with a twill foundation and a pile surface, and is corded or ribbed on the surface. There is a very superior kind made especially for ladies' jackets and for the trimmings of warm cloth dresses, which has a very broad rib and a high pile, and is soft and pliable.

Corkscrew cloth: A warp-faced material, woven in fancied resemblance to a corkscrew. The best grades have a French thread worsted warp, while the weft may be of cotton or wool.

Crêpe: A thin, semi-transparent material made of silk or cotton, finely crinkled or crisped, either irregularly or in long parallel ridges. It is made in black, white, and colors. Mourning or "hard" crêpes are woven of hand-spun silk thread in its natural condition.

Cresson: A medium yellowish green.

Crinoline: A stiff material woven of horsehair and linen, or of cotton. It is used as a cheap material for stiffening ladies' dresses, linings, and the like, after the manner of buckram.

Crocheted button: A button mold covered with fine tight crochet.

Crow's foot: A three-pointed silk embroidery stitch, often put at the tops of plaits and the like for ornament and reinforcement.

Cuff-facing: An outside facing at the wrist of a sleeve, in contrasting material, that imitates a simple or fancy cuff.

Darned net: A lace with designs worked on a net ground with a needle handled as if in darning. It may be worked with fine lace thread, with

432

colored purse silks, or with floss and filoselles, upon white, colored, or black net.

Delaine: A plain-woven, muslin-like dress material, made of wool, cotton, or mixed materials.

Demi-train: A short train.

Diagonal material: A worsted twilled so that the diagonal ridges are somewhat prominent and noticeable.

Directoire styles: Imitations of the styles of the French Directory, from 1795 to 1799.

Dog-collar: A wide necklace worn about the throat.

Dolman: A style of ladies' wrap, in various lengths, and characterized by a hanging piece over the arm instead of a sleeve.

Dotted: A material ornamented with small dots.

Dove gray: A pinkish gray.

Down: The fine, soft covering of fowls under the feathers. The eider duck yields most of the down of commerce.

Drab: A dull brownish gray.

Drap d'été: A fine worsted material for summer wear.

Drawn-work: A kind of ornamental work done by cutting out, pulling out, or drawing to one side some threads of the material, while leaving others, or by drawing all into a new form, to produce fancy patterns.

Drilling: A stout twilled material of either cotton or linen, used for bodice linings, pockets, etc. Found in all colors.

Écru: Having the color of unbleached silk or linen, hence by extension any similar shade. Much lace is sold of this color, a hue that may be more accurately described as café au lait.

Egyptian lace: A knotted lace, often beaded.

Eider-down flannel: A thick, soft material with a knitted foundation and a surface of heavy wool, which is brushed to a thick, heavy nap. Available in many colors, and in fancy squares and stripes.

Epaulette: A shoulder ornament or trimming.

Étamine: A coarse wool or cotton bunting or canvas, with fluffy threads, and more or less transparent. It is used as a dress material,

and is usually intended to be worn over a contrasting color.

Eton jacket: A short jacket with lapels.

Faille: A soft, ribbed dress silk distinguished by a prominent grain or cord extending from selvage to selvage. It has a slight gloss.

Faille Française: A silk faille made in France. It is similar to grosgrain, but softer and brighter.

Farmer's satin: A glossy material in satin weave, with a cotton warp and a wool weft. Used for linings.

Fawn: A rather light yellowish brown.

Feather-edged ribbon: Having an ornamental edging composed of picots or tufts.

Fedora lace: An imitation Mechlin lace. Mechlin is a light bobbin lace with a pattern of flowers, buds, etc., outlined by a fine but very distinct thread or cord.

Festoon outline: An outline with open loops or curves.

Fichu: A small covering of silk, muslin, lace, or tulle, for the neck or shoulders.

Figured material: A material ornamented with woven, printed, or another kind of patterns or designs.

Finger: A measure of length, comprising 4 1/2 inches, and much used by needlewomen.

Fisher's net: A coarse, open-mesh material.

Flannel: A loose-woven wool, cotton-and-wool, or silk-and-wool material. The nap may be raised on one or both sides. It may be white, colored, striped, or checked.

Flannelette: A soft, loose-woven cotton material, with a short nap raised on both sides, which gives the appearance of flannel. It may be white, self-colored, or woven in stripes or checks.

Fleur de pêche: A delicate violet-gray.

Floss silk: A soft, fluffy, untwisted embroidery silk.

Fly: A strip of material sewed under the edge of a dress or coat, at the button side of the opening, extending sufficiently far beyond it to underline the buttonholes at their extreme ends. The fly thus conceals the clothing under the dress or coat.

433

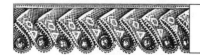 

Foot trimming: A short plaited or gathered ruffle sewed at the bottom of a skirt, to hold it out and to ornament it.

Foulard: A soft, thin, washable dress silk, woven without twill. It is usually printed in colors on black or white grounds. An imitation is also made of cotton, with a medium-soft finish, printed with mingled patterns.

Foulé: A general term applied to twilled materials with a rough face, the material being given considerable shrinking to increase the roughness.

Fraise: A ruff or frill.

French cambric: A very fine, silky, linen or cotton cambric.

French fell seam: What is now called a French seam.

French gray: A light greenish gray.

French lace: A rich and expensive lace. The foundation is of plain cotton illusion. The design, which is often very elaborate, is formed by chain-stitching in coarse cotton thread.

Frisé velvet: A velvet with a looped pile.

Frog: An ornament made of braid in a fancy pattern, which has a loop that fastens on the opposite button or olive. A pair of these ornaments is always used for each fastening.

Gainsborough hat: A large, plumed hat.

Galloon: Originally worsted lace, especially a close-woven lace like ribbon or tape for binding. In modern use a trimming similar to the above, of wool, silk, cotton, tinsel, or a combination of any of these.

Garnet: A subdued, yet warm shade of dark red.

Gauging: A series of close parallel lines of running stitches, which are all drawn up to make the material between them set full by gatherings.

Gauze: A very thin, transparent material made of silk, silk and cotton, silk and linen, or linen. It is either plain, or brocaded in patterns with silk.

Genoese point lace: A rather heavy guipure lace, usually made by the yard.

Gilet: A vest front for a bodice, often a removable accessory.

Gimp: An open-work trimming. It is made of silk, worsted, or cotton twist, having a cord or a wire running through it. The strands are plaited or twisted to form a pattern.

Gingham: A checked or striped material made of cotton or linen, the threads dyed in the yarn.

Girdle: A sash, cord, or belt worn around the waist.

Glacé: A shiny surface applied to silk materials and ribbons.

Gobelin blue: A subdued grayish blue.

Greek plait: A box-plait with about 2 inches of the outside cut away at the hem, and the under sides of the fold sloped to the point where they touch.

Grenadine: A dress material woven in small square meshes or open-work of coarse threads, very transparent. It is manufactured of cotton, silk, wool, and their intermixtures. It is made both plain and figured.

Grosgrain: A firm, close-woven, finely corded or grained dress silk, finished with but a slight luster.

Guimpe: A chemisette worn with a low or square-necked dress.

Guipure lace: This name is applied to all laces having large patterns and coarse, open grounds not filled with delicate work.

Gum Arabic: A water-soluble gum used for glue and to finish textiles.

Hair-line stripes: A color and weave effect in which fine lines, one or two threads wide, occur lengthwise or crosswise in the material.

Half-low neck: A neck-line below the throat, but higher than a full décolletage.

Hamburg: A cotton embroidery worked on cambric, used as an edging or trimming.

Heliotrope: A dull purple-brown.

Hem-stitching: An ornamental edging in linen and cotton materials, produced by drawing out a few threads parallel to the hem, and catching together in smaller groups those running the other way.

Henrietta cloth: A material woven entirely of wool, or with a silk warp and a worsted weft. It has

a twilled face and a plain back, and is like cashmere dress material in all other respects, except for being more lustrous.

Henri Quartre: Imitations of styles worn during the reign of Henry IV of France, from 1589 to 1610.

Hercules braid: A thick, corded, worsted braid, available in widths from 1/2 inch to 4 inches.

Herring-bone stitch: A kind of cross-stitch worked backwards, from left to right. It is often used to secure the raw edges of seams made in flannel.

Hollow: To cut in a concave shape.

Horsehair cloth: A loose, open material, woven with a herring-bone twill. The warp is composed of unbleached cotton, and the weft of horsehair. It is used for stiffening garments.

House-maid skirt: A full, round skirt made of straight breadths of material.

Hunter green: A dark yellowish green.

Illusion: A thin and very transparent silk tulle.

India lawn: A clear, white lawn, woven of very fine cotton threads.

India silks: India silks are classified as cultivated and wild. Among the cultivated are imported corah, mysore, nagpore, and rumchunder; and from the wild, tussah. The kincobs are satins decorated with designs in gold flowers and are employed for ladies' skirts. The mushroos have a silk surface and a cotton back, and are decorated with loom-embroidered flowers.

Insertion: Strips of lace, or embroidered muslin or cambric, with straight edges.

Invisible green: A dark bluish green.

Invisible stripes: Possibly stripes in two similar shades of one color.

Irish lawn: Pure linen lawn.

Irish linen: Irish linen is superior to that manufactured elsewhere in the evenness of the threads, the softness of the texture, and the gloss of the surface.

Irish point embroidery: A cutwork embroidery.

Japan silks: There are three kinds of dress silks, which vary in weight, and all of which may be had in a variety of light and dark colors.

These are the double warp grosgrain; the damassé Japanese, which has a rather small floral design closely covering the ground; and the plain silks.

Jardinière: Of many colors, resembling a flower garden.

Jersey: A close-fitting upper garment made of elastic wool or silk material.

Jet beads: Lustrous black glass beads.

Jetted lace: Black machine lace beaded with jet beads.

Kilt-plaiting: Flat single plaits placed closely side by side, so that the double edge of the plait on the upper side lies half over the preceding plait on the inside.

Lace net: A machine-made mesh.

Ladder-stitch: A cross-bar stitch in embroidery.

Lady's cloth: A class of fine, wide flannels slightly napped, used for ladies' light wraps and dresses.

Lapboard: A board held in the lap as a substitute for a table.

Lawn: A thin, open cambric, slightly sized with pure starch.

Leghorn straw: The straw of a kind of wheat grown in Tuscany, which is plaited and used for hats and bonnets.

Lincoln green: A medium olive green.

Lisse: A sheer, delicate, gauzy material, made of either silk or cotton. It is used for ladies' neckwear and ruchings. When crimped it is called crêpe lisse.

Lustring: A glossy silk material, neither figured nor corded.

Maltese lace: A heavy guipure bobbin lace, with simple geometrical patterns.

Marabou feathers: These are procured from a species of stork. They may be had white, gray, or dyed. They are employed as plumes for head-dresses and bonnets, and as trimmings for dresses, fans, and muffs.

Marguerite: Daisy.

Marquise lace: A black lace with the patterns bordered by a cord.

Marseilles: A stiff, corded cotton material.

Mastic: A light olive brown.

Matelassé: A silk or wool material with a raised figured or flowered design, having a quilted appearance. Those of silk are made in white and in colors, and are much used for opera cloaks.

Medici lace: A simple, rather heavy bobbin lace, similar to torchon, but with one scalloped edge.

Melton: A stout, smooth cloth used for ladies' coats. The nap is sheared close to the surface and is finished without pressing or glossing.

Merino: A thin wool twilled material.

Military collar: A narrow standing collar.

Milliner's fold: A strip of velvet, silk, or the like, folded near both edges, and then again so as to bring one of the original folds above the other.

Mode: A light brown.

Mohair: A material with a cotton or silk warp and a mohair weft. It is strong and defies dust, which makes it especially suitable for traveling. It is often printed with attractive floral designs.

Mohair braid: A black or colored braid, available in various widths.

Moiré: A wavy undulating effect produced on the surface of materials by wetting, crumpling, and great pressure.

Molière: Imitations of the styles of the time of Molière, from 1622 to 1673.

Mordoré: A mixture of crimson with a little brown.

Moss green: A medium yellow green.

Mother Hubbard: A wrapper or night-gown with a long, full skirt falling from a yoke.

Mucilage: An aqueous solution of gum or of substances allied to it, used as an adhesive.

Mull: An extremely soft, thin, and transparent muslin.

Muslin: A thin, plain-woven cotton material, bleached or unbleached. The fancy kinds include Arni muslin, an extremely fine muslin; book muslin, a thin, starchy muslin used for lining cheap dresses; corded muslin, with a thick cord; coteline muslin, a hair-line cord muslin printed in all patterns and colors; Decca muslin, a fine thin variety; figured muslin, with machine-woven figures imitating tamboured muslin; and tamboured muslin.

Nainsook: A fine, soft, bleached muslin, woven in small damasked checks and stripes, and used as a summer dress material.

Neapolitan straw: Horsehair.

Net: An open material of cotton, linen, hemp, silk, or another material, tied and woven with a mesh of any size. Cotton net is employed for stiff linings and foundations.

Nile green: A yellowish green.

Nun's veiling: A wide, untwilled wool dress material, very soft, fine, and thin. It is dyed black, white, and in colors.

Oatmeal cloth: A cotton, linen, or wool material having a corrugated face. Oatmeal cloths are thick, soft, and pliant, and may be had in all colors.

Oiled silk: Silk made waterproof by saturation in oil. It is semi-transparent. It is much used in dressmaking to prevent perspiration from passing through, at the under-arms of garments and as bonnet linings.

Old pink: A pinkish light brown.

Ombré: Shaded with various colors or different shades of the same color.

Open-work: A term used in embroidery, lacemaking, crochet, and fancy work of every other kind. It means that the work is made with interstices between several portions of close work, or of cut and open material.

Organdy: A fine, white cotton material, woven plain, cross-barred, striped, and printed with figures.

Organ-pipe plaiting: Large, rounded plaits.

Oriental embroidery: All of the various kinds of embroidery produced in the East. Characterized by bold designs and costly materials.

Oriental lace: Machine embroidery on machine net with coarse, soft thread.

Ostrich tip: The tip of an ostrich feather.

Ottoman silk: A fine, soft, undressed silk material, woven in large cords, extending from selvage to selvage.

Panel: A piece of different material or color placed vertically on a dress skirt as an ornament, usually in front or on the side.

Pannier drapery: An over-skirt draped or looped at the sides.

Passementerie: Heavy embroidery or lace edgings and trimmings, especially those made of gimp and braid, or covered with beads, colored silk, metals, etc.

Pea green: A light yellowish green.

Pearl button: A button made of mother-of-pearl.

Peasant bodice: A low-necked bodice worn with a chemisette, and which laces or appears to lace in front.

Peau de soie: A silk dress material woven like grosgrain, but with very fine, close ribs.

Pekin: A trimming material, made in alternate stripes of satin and velvet, which vary in width from 1/2 to 2 inches.

Percale: A very closely and firmly woven cotton material. It is printed in fancy patterns on white and colored grounds.

Picot: A small loop used as an ornamental edging on ribbons and laces.

Pinking: A mode of decorating material by means of a sharp stamping instrument called a pinking iron. The edge of the material is cut in points, scallops, or other designs.

Piping: A bias fold, or corded bias fold, put on the edge of a band or garment as a finish.

Piqué: A washable cotton material, woven with a small pattern in relief, usually a lozenge, cord, or rib. It is usually rather stiff and thick. It may be white, or printed with small delicate patterns.

Pistache: A yellowish green.

Placket: The opening left in a skirt to allow the garment to be put on and off the person.

Plastron: A trimming for a dress front, of a different material.

Plomb: Lead gray.

Plush: A shaggy, hairy silk or cotton material. It is sometimes made of camel's or goat's hair. The pile is softer and longer than that of velvet, and resembles fur.

Point de Gene: A machine imitation of Genoese needle lace.

Point de Paris: A simple, narrow bobbin lace or machine imitation. Those made on the Levers machine have simple designs of flower heads or animals outlined with thick cordonnets.

Point d'esprit lace: Net or tulle with embroidered or woven dots.

Polonaise: An over-dress, worn either straight or looped up.

Pompadour lace: Lace in Pompadour colors; that is, a mixture of pink and blue, and sometimes other pastels.

Pompadour neck: A low, more or less square neckline.

Pompon: A fluffy ball of silk or wool, used for trimming.

Pongee: A thin, soft, washable silk material, woven from the natural, undyed raw silk.

Poplin: A kind of rep made of silk and wool or worsted, having a fine cord on the surface. It is produced brocaded, moiré, and plain.

Postilion: An extension of the back pieces of a basque or jacket, or extra tabs set on at the back.

Princess: A long, close-fitting dress with no waist seam.

Radzimir: A rich dress silk, in the weaving of which a weft thread is dropped at regular intervals, usually 1/16 to 1/4 inch apart. This produces a crosswise sunken line on both sides of the material. Between the sunken lines the weave is fine and close.

Redingote: A coat-dress worn over a skirt.

Renaissance lace: A heavy tape lace, also known as Battenberg. A popular kind of fancy work.

Rep: A material with thick crosswise cords, of silk, silk and wool, or wool only.

Reseda: A grayish to dark grayish green.

Revers: A part of the garment reversed, or turned back, such as a cuff, or a corner of a basque. May show a lining of a contrasting color or material.

Revers-facing: An applied facing, in contrasting material, that imitates a revers.

Rhadames: A twilled material of all silk or part cotton, of strong texture and with a bright satin finish.

Roman stripes: Vivid horizontal stripes in different widths.

Rope shirring: A tuck is made in the material, a cord is threaded through it, and the material is drawn to position with the cord.

Rosary beads: Wooden beads, either carved and varnished of a natural color, or black and unvarnished. They are also to be had to match all shades in the material.

Rosette: A collection of bows of narrow ribbon, arranged to form a circle, and attached to a circular foundation of stiff, coarse muslin or buckram.

Round bodice: A bodice that is of even length all around, and usually ends at the waist or a little below it. It may be either full or close-fitting.

Royal armure: The weave of this silk material imitates medieval fish-scale armor, the surface edge always forming a small diamond or other angled figure. It is heavier than ordinary dress silk.

Royale: A plain-colored, ribbed dress silk, in which the ribs are not regular, but run into each other.

Ruching: A plaiting or shirring of net, lace, ribbon, or other light material into bands, which are worn in the necks and wrists of garments and used for trimmings.

Running: A line of running stitches, or of machine stitches.

Russet: A reddish brown.

Russian embroidery: Embroidery in simple and formal patterns, especially on wash materials.

Russian green: A rich dark green.

Sailor collar: A collar that is deep and square at the back, and has square ends in front.

Salmon: A pinkish yellow.

Sandalwood: A light yellowish brown.

Sappho pink: A light purplish red.

Sateen: A twilled cotton material of satin make, glossy, thick, and strong. It is employed for corsets, dresses, and boots. It may be procured in black and white, various colors, and figured in many color combinations.

Satin: A silk twill, very glossy on the face, and dull on the back. Some satins are figured and brocaded.

Satin merveilleux: A twilled satin material, of an exceedingly soft and pliable character, and having but little gloss.

Scarf: A band or strip of material.

Scrim: A soft and loose-woven cotton material, often of a fancy, lacey weave.

Seal plush: A heavy material with a pile of tussah silk, made in imitation of sealskin fur. It is dyed brown or golden color. It is designed for mantles, jackets, hats, and trimmings.

Seed pearl passementerie: Passementerie beaded with small mother-of-pearl or imitation pearl beads.

Seersucker: A washable cotton material, woven in stripes, usually blue and white or brown and white.

Serge: A loose-woven, very durable twilled material. It may be had in either silk or wool. Wool serge may be rough on one or both sides of the material, or smooth on both sides. Serge is dyed in every color, besides being sold in white and black.

Serpent: A pale bluish green.

Shell ruching: A trimming gathered and fulled in a shell-like design.

Shirring: Two or more lines of gathers having a space between.

Sicilienne: A fine poplin, made of silk and wool, and especially used for mantles.

Side-plaiting: Single plaits with the crease not pressed all the way down.

Silesia: A fine-twilled cotton, highly dressed and calendered, used for linings. It is piece dyed in all conceivable solid colors, and sometimes printed, although usually the patterns are woven.

Silk muslin: A thin and gauzy silk, either plain, printed in small patterns in color, or ornamented with raised woven figures.

Skirt braids: These are made of alpaca and mohair. They are cut into lengths of sufficient quantity for a dress, and tied up for sale in knots.

Skirtings: Materials used for skirts.

Slide: A tongueless buckle or ring used as a fastener.

Smocking: Accordion-plaiting caught together alternately in rows, making an elastic material.

Soutache braid: A very narrow silk braid, available in several widths, and having an open-work center. It is produced in many colors, and employed for embroidery and the braiding of dresses, mantles, etc.

Spanish flounce: A deep flounce that is graduated in depth.

Spanish guipure lace: A heavy lace with thick silk designs and cordonnets.

Spanish lace: Any lace made in Spain, or in imitation of a lace made in Spain. Includes a kind of darned net.

Split straw: Plaits of wheat or rye straws that were split before plaiting.

Sprig: An ornament or pattern in the form of a sprig, spray, or leaf.

Sprung out: Widened or flared.

Steel: A dark bluish gray.

Steels: Thin strips of steel or whalebone used to support a skirt or bone a corset.

Stud: A removable button, which is passed through eyelet holes.

Suède: A brownish tan color.

Suitings: Materials used for suits, or complete costumes.

Surah: A soft, fine-twilled silk or silk-and-wool mixture, employed for dresses.

Surplice effect: A bodice that overlaps diagonally in front.

Swiss embroidery: A kind of needle-work in white cotton on fine white linen or muslin. Often made by machine.

Swiss girdle: A belt or belt effect that is pointed at the top and bottom in front, and sometimes also the back.

Swiss muslin: A thin, transparent material, woven rather open, with simple patterns of dots, stripes, or sprigs.

Tabac: Tobacco brown.

Tablier: Part of a dress resembling an apron.

Taffeta: A thin, glossy silk, of a wavy luster. It is to be had in all colors, some plain, others striped, checked, or flowered.

Tamise: A fine, plain-woven wool dress material, the warp and weft of which are of the same size and woven in equal proportions.

Tam o'shanter: A cap with a headband and a large, flat crown.

Tape: A narrow, stout strip of woven cotton or linen, used for innumerable purposes.

Tarlatan: A thin, gauze-like cotton material, much stiffened, so open as to be transparent, and often of a rather coarse quality.

Tassel fringe: A fringe composed of separate bundles of threads or cords tied to a braiding or gimp.

Tennis flannel: A soft, loose-woven cotton flannelette, finished with a slight nap.

Tennis stripes: A light, twilled wool dress material with narrow colored stripes.

Terra-cotta: Reddish orange.

Thibet cloth: A material made of wool with a very slight nap and a rough, unfinished appearance. Or else one made of goat's hair, with a shaggy appearance.

Thread lace: Made of linen as distinguished from cotton and silk.

Tinsel: An ornamental material or cord overlaid with glittering metallic sparkles or threads.

Tissue: Any light, gauzy material, such as is used for veils.

Toilette: A dress or costume.

Toque: A small bonnet with a round, close-fitting crown and no brim.

Torchon lace: A simple bobbin lace with geometrical patterns. Much of it is made by machinery. It is especially suitable for trimming undergarments.

Tournure: The bustle, or the fullness at the back created by the combination of the bustle, the pad and steels in the skirt, and the drapery.

Tricot: A knitted weave, often found in flannel and other wool materials.

Tucking: A fine, white cotton material of lawn, muslin, or cambric, with rows of tucks stitched across, either close together over the entire surface, or in clusters.

Tuck shirring: The tucks are basted, then gathered through both layers of material.

Tulle: A fine silk net, used for bonnets, veils, and dress trimmings. It may be had in black and white, and every color. Sometimes it is ornamented with dots.

Turkey red: A brilliant red.

Turkish cloth: Terry cloth.

Tussah: A raw silk without any cord or woven pattern, although some are stamped or printed. It is very suitable for summer costumes, and will bear washing.

Tweed: A twilled wool material. It is soft, flexible, and durable.

Twill: A weave of any fiber, where the weft threads pass over two and under one, or over three or more warp threads. Many different patterns or surfaces may be produced by changing the order of passing the weft.

Valenciennes lace: A narrow, cotton or linen lace, often machine made.

Vandykes: A series of pointed shapes cut out as a decorative border or trimming.

Velvet: A close-woven silk that has a very thick, short pile or nap on the right side. Inferior kinds are made with a cotton back.

Velveteen: Cotton velvet.

Venetian red: A dark, dull red.

Vest: A simulated vest, applied under the edges of the main part of the bodice. The latter are cut too narrow to meet, so as to expose the vest. The vest may be permanently attached, or be a changeable accessory.

Vest-facing: Contrasting material applied to the outside of a bodice to imitate a vest front.

Vestings: Materials used to make vests.

Victoria lawn: A semi-transparent muslin, to be had in black and white. It is used for skirt linings, for petticoats worn under clear muslin dresses, and for frills.

Wadding: Carded cotton wool. It is available bleached, unbleached, slate colored, and black, cut into sheets of various sizes. It is placed between the outer material and the lining of any garment.

Wash materials: All washable dress materials.

Waterfall drapery: A back drapery that hangs straight down, instead of being puffed or looped.

Watteau plait: An arrangement of the back of a woman's dress in which broad plaits or folds, or more commonly a separate piece imitating them, hang from the neck to the bottom of the skirt without interruption.

Webbing: Heavy, stout tape of various widths, and materials used for purposes where strength is desired.

Worsted: The yarn prepared from the best long-staple wools, well combed and hard twisted. Any of many materials woven from such yarns.

Yak lace: A coarse bobbin lace, made of wool, that imitates Maltese lace. Yak lace may be successfully imitated in crochet.

Zephyr gingham: An extremely soft and pliable kind, woven of fine threads, frequently in small checks or plaids.

Zephyr prints: These are delicate materials, resembling cotton batiste, designed for summer wear, and produced in pale but fast colors.

Zouave: A short open jacket with a rounded front, or a trimming in the outline of a Zouave jacket.

D. References

The bibliography lists (mostly antique) sources for the original patterns, fashion plates, and text. The "further reading" section lists modern and re-printed sources that will help you use the patterns in this book. These include books containing photographs of 1880s garments, books on altering pattern styles, and books on Victorian needle-work.

Selected Bibliography

Butterick Publishing Co. *The Delineator,* Vols. 19–20. London and New York: Butterick Publishing Co., 1882.

Butterick Publishing Co. *The Delineator,* Vols. 21–22. London and New York: Butterick Publishing Co., 1883.

Butterick Publishing Co. *The Delineator,* Vols. 23–24. London and New York: Butterick Publishing Co., 1884.

Butterick Publishing Co. *The Delineator,* Vols. 25–26. London and New York: Butterick Publishing Co., 1885.

Butterick Publishing Co. *The Delineator,* Vols. 27–28. London and New York: Butterick Publishing Co., 1886.

Butterick Publishing Co. *The Delineator,* Vols. 29–30. London and New York: Butterick Publishing Co., 1887.

Butterick Publishing Co. *The Delineator,* Vols. 31–32. London and New York: Butterick Publishing Co., 1888.

Butterick Publishing Co. *The Delineator,* Vols. 33–34. London and New York: Butterick Publishing Co., 1889.

Charles J. Peterson. *Peterson's Magazine,* Vols. 95–96. Philadelphia: Charles J. Peterson, 1889.

Goldsberry, Doran & Nelson. *The National Garment Cutter.* Chicago: Goldsberry, Doran & Nelson, 1885.

Goldsberry, Doran & Nelson. *The National Garment Cutter.* Chicago: Goldsberry, Doran & Nelson, 1886.

Goldsberry, Doran & Nelson. *The National Garment Cutter Instruction Book.* Chicago: Goldsberry, Doran & Nelson, 1887.

Goldsberry, Doran & Nelson. *The Voice of Fashion.* Chicago: Goldsberry, Doran & Nelson, Spring and Summer 1886.

Goldsberry, Doran & Nelson. *The Voice of Fashion.* Chicago: Goldsberry, Doran & Nelson, Winter 1886.

Grimble, Frances. *The Voice of Fashion: 79 Turn-of-the-Century Patterns with Instructions and Fashion Plates.* San Francisco: Lavolta Press, 1998.

Harper & Bros. *Harper's Bazar,* Vol. 18. New York: Harper & Bros., 1885.

Harper & Bros. *Harper's Bazar,* Vol. 19. New York: Harper & Bros., 1886.

Harper & Bros. *Harper's Bazar,* Vol. 20. New York: Harper & Bros., 1887.

J. H. Haulenbeck & Co. *Godey's Lady's Book,* Vols. 110–111. Philadelphia: J. M. Haulenbeck & Co., 1885.

References

Further Reading

Armstrong, Helen Joseph. *Patternmaking for Fashion Design*. New York: HarperCollins Publishers, 1995.

Caulfeild, S. F. A. and Blanche C. Saward. *Encyclopedia of Victorian Needlework*. New York: Dover Publications, 1972.

de Dillmont, Thérèse. *The Complete Encyclopedia of Needlework*. Philadelphia: Running Press, 2002.

Johnston, Lucy. *Nineteenth-Century Fashion in Detail*. London: V & A Publications, 2005.

Kidwell, Claudia. *Cutting a Fashionable Fit: Dressmaker's Drafting Systems in the United States*. Washington: Smithsonian Institution Press, 1979.

Kopp, Ernestine, Vittorina Rolfo, and Beatrice Zelin. *Designing Apparel Through the Flat Pattern*. New York: Fairchild Publications, 1971.

Kopp, Ernestine, Vittorina Rolfo, and Beatrice Zelin. *New Fashion Areas for Designing Apparel Through the Flat Pattern*. New York: Fairchild Publications, 1972.

Kyoto Costume Institute. *Fashion: A History from the 18th to the 20th Century*. Köln: Taschen, 2002.

Musée de la Mode et du Costume–Palais Galliera. *Femmes fin de siécle 1885–1895*. Paris: Paris-Musées, 1990.

Olian, JoAnne, ed. *Full-Color Victorian Fashions 1870–1893*. Mineola: Dover Publications, 1999.

Severa, Joan L. *Dressed for the Photographer: Ordinary Americans and Fashion, 1840–1900*. Kent: Kent State University Press, 1995.

Index

This index provides a different method of locating patterns, illustrations, and descriptions than the table of contents. Because the patterns for the main parts of ensembles–bodices, polonaises, draperies, and skirts–can be exchanged to achieve the desired style, they are indexed separately, in addition to the complete ensembles. If exactly the same pattern (such as one for a foundation skirt) is given with several different ensembles, only the first instance of it is indexed separately. Smaller sections, such as sleeves, are also interchangeable but are not indexed separately. Because some ensembles and accessories have the same name, different references apply to different ones, even if the page number is the same.

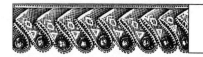 

Index

Books by Lavolta Press

After a Fashion: How to Reproduce, Restore, and Wear Vintage Styles, by Frances Grimble. Covers medieval through Art Deco styles for women and men. Guides readers through each stage of a reproduction project and advises them on all aspects of collecting vintage clothes. 356 pages, 147 illustrations.

The Lady's Stratagem: A Repository of 1820s Directions for the Toilet, Mantua-Making, Stay-Making, Millinery & Etiquette, by Frances Grimble. Contains six French manuals with instructions for dressmaking, corset making, millinery, needlework, hygiene, and etiquette, now available in English for the first time, plus considerable supplementary information from English and American sources. 755 pages, 134 illustrations.

Reconstruction Era Fashions: 350 Sewing, Needlework, and Millinery Patterns 1867–1868, by Frances Grimble. Women's fashion plates, patterns, and instructions from the first 14 months of *Harper's Bazar.* Includes articles on needlework techniques and fashion trends. 529 pages, 609 illustrations.

Fashions of the Gilded Age, Volume 1: Undergarments, Bodices, Skirts, Overskirts, Polonaises, and Day Dresses 1877–1882, by Frances Grimble. Women's sewing patterns from a German manual made available in English for the first time, plus fashion plates, sewing patterns, and needlework patterns from *Harper's Bazar* and other sources. Includes apportioning scales for a German drafting system. 469 pages, 160 patterns, 200 illustrations.

Fashions of the Gilded Age, Volume 2: Evening, Bridal, Sports, Outerwear, Accessories, and Dressmaking 1877–1882, by Frances Grimble. Women's sewing patterns from a German manual made available in English for the first time, plus fashion plates, sewing patterns, and needlework patterns from *Harper's Bazar* and other sources. Includes apportioning scales from a German drafting system and an 87-page dressmaking manual. 541 pages, 184 patterns, 598 illustrations.

Bustle Fashions 1885–1887: 41 Patterns with Fashion Plates and Suggestions for Adaptation, by Frances Grimble. A complete wardrobe of women's sewing patterns, with illustrations and detailed descriptions for variations that can be produced by flat pattern alteration. The patterns were selected from *The Voice of Fashion* magazine and National Garment Cutter pattern books. Includes apportioning scales for the National Garment Cutter system, a manual on 1885–1889 dressmaking, and instructions for trimmings and accessories. 446 pages, 438 illustrations.

Directoire Revival Fashions 1888–1889: 57 Patterns with Fashion Plates and Suggestions for Adaptation, by Frances Grimble. A complete wardrobe of women's sewing patterns, with illustrations and detailed descriptions for variations that can be produced by flat pattern alteration. The patterns were selected from *The Voice of Fashion* magazine and National Garment Cutter pattern books. Includes apportioning scales for the National Garment Cutter system, and instructions for trimmings and accessories. 563 pages, 286 illustrations.

The Voice of Fashion: 79 Turn-of-the-Century Patterns with Instructions and Fashion Plates, by Frances Grimble. Women's sewing patterns for all occasions from 1900 through 1906, selected from *The Voice of Fashion* magazine. Includes apportioning scales for the Diamond Cutting System. 463 pages, 95 illustrations.

The Edwardian Modiste: 85 Authentic Patterns with Instructions, Fashion Plates, and Period Sewing Techniques, by Frances Grimble. Women's sewing patterns for all occasions from 1905 through 1909. The patterns were selected from the *American Garment Cutter Instruction and Diagram Book* and *The American Modiste.* Includes chapters of a 1907 dressmaking manual and apportioning scales for the American System of Cutting. 430 pages, 112 illustrations.

Our books can be purchased in brick-and-mortar and online bookstores, or ordered directly from Lavolta Press. See www.lavoltapress.com for more information.